BRASS ROOTS
A hundred years of brass bands and their music
(1836–1936)

Brass Roots

A hundred years of brass bands and their music (1836–1936)

Roy Newsome

LONDON AND NEW YORK

First published 1998 by Ashgate Publishing

Reissued 2018 by Routledge
2 Park Square, Milton Park, Abingdon, Oxon, OX14 4RN
52 Vanderbilt Avenue, New York, NY 10017

Routledge is an imprint of the Taylor & Francis Group, an informa business

Copyright © Roy Newsome, 1998

All rights reserved. No part of this book may be reprinted or reproduced or utilised in any form or by any electronic, mechanical, or other means, now known or hereafter invented, including photocopying and recording, or in any information storage or retrieval system, without permission in writing from the publishers.

Notice:
Product or corporate names may be trademarks or registered trademarks, and are used only for identification and explanation without intent to infringe.

Publisher's Note
The publisher has gone to great lengths to ensure the quality of this reprint but points out that some imperfections in the original copies may be apparent.

Disclaimer
The publisher has made every effort to trace copyright holders and welcomes correspondence from those they have been unable to contact.

A Library of Congress record exists under LC control number:

ISBN 13: 978-0-367-13639-0 (hbk)
ISBN 13: 978-0-367-13640-6 (pbk)
ISBN 13: 978-0-429-02767-3 (ebk)

Typeset in Sabon by Photoprint, Torquay, Devon

Contents

List of plates		vii
Preface and Acknowledgements		viii
Introduction		1
1	Music in nineteenth-century Britain	7
2	Wind instruments and the growth of the amateur band	23
3	Contests from 1860; the 'Great Triumvirate'; J H Iles	38
4	Unpublished nineteenth-century brass band music and the development of instrumentation	70
5	Published brass band music in the nineteenth century	93
6	Into the twentieth century – the National Brass Band Championships	116
7	Principal arranger/composers and their music	135
8	Popular band music in the twentieth century	162
9	A new type of test piece – the original work	178
10	Retrospect	212
Appendix 1	Opera	216
Appendix 2	Band formation	220
Appendix 3	Black Dyke part-books	221
Appendix 4	Music from Crystal Palace 1860–1863	223
Appendix 5	John Gladney's arrangements	225

Appendix 6	Alexander Owen's arrangements and compositions	227
Appendix 7	Henry Round scores at Besses	229
Appendix 8	Wright & Round successful test pieces	231
Appendix 9	Original works – 1913–1936	233
Glossary of terms		235
Bibliography		239
Index of names and subjects		245
Index of titles of music referred to in the text		254

List of Plates

(between pages 134 and 135)

1. The Distin family
2. Four great figures from the 1880s
3. Front cover of the *Amateur Band Teacher's Guide*
4. Victoria Hall, Queensbury
5. What the composers thought about Black Dyke
6. Edwin Swift booklet
7. The One Thousand Guinea Trophy
8. Black Dyke – Canada and USA tour brochure, 1906
9. Repertoire for Black Dyke's 1906 tour
10. Wingates Temperance Band, 1906
11. Fodens Motor Works Band *circa* 1910
12. Publicity material for Besses' second world tour (1909–1911)
13. Advertisement from the 1924 Crystal Palace programme
14. Front cover of a Besses programme
15. Enticing the public to 'go by train' (1936)
16. Close-up of the Crystal Palace medal

Preface and Acknowledgements

My intention when setting out to research material for this book was to concentrate on twentieth-century brass band music, with perhaps a lengthy introduction outlining the growth of bands and the development of their repertoire during the nineteenth century. However, the deeper I dug, the more it seemed that much needed to be said about what might be called the 'formative years', and gradually the emphasis changed, so that the major part of the book is, in fact, devoted to nineteenth-century bands and their music. It also quickly became evident that, far from being an isolated phenomenon in the field of popular music as is commonly presumed, virtually everything played by brass bands – be it arranged or specially composed – had its roots in the mainstreams of both classical and popular music. Influences from opera, the theatre, song and dance have always been recognized, but to the best of my knowledge have not, until now, been systematically discussed alongside the development of band music.

I had always intended to select 100 years as the basic study period, but it was quite some time before the years 1836 to 1936 emerged as sensible starting and finishing points. 1836 was the year in which the first published music for brass band appeared; it was also around this time that the term 'brass band' became accepted as applying to a regular ensemble.

1936 makes an appropriate break-off point for a number of reasons. First, it was the last year in which the National Brass Band Championships were held at the Crystal Palace – destroyed later that same year by fire, and it was the last of the 'golden' years during which that illustrious group of British composers – Holst, Elgar, Ireland, Howells and Bliss – composed their famous test pieces. It was, in fact, the year of Bliss's *Kenilworth*, the last original work to be written for the National Brass Band Championships until after the war. 1936 saw also the end of an era, with the deaths of Thomas Keighley, who had pioneered the introduction of the original work at the Belle Vue contests (see Chapter 9) and William Rimmer, and the last major contest success of William Halliwell (both discussed in detail in Chapter 6).

My primary research areas have been the collection of early copies of *Brass Band News*, located at University College Salford, and music in various band libraries. I have also spent some time in the offices of the publishers Wright & Round in Gloucester, Boosey & Hawkes in London and R Smith & Company in Aylesbury. The office of *British Bandsman* in Beaconsfield, where past copies of the magazine are located, has also been a useful source of reference.

A further invaluable source has been Jack L Scott's PhD thesis, *The Evolution of the Brass Band and its Repertoire in Northern England*, completed at the University of Sheffield in 1970. I well remember Mr Scott visiting Black Dyke Mills Band whilst I was its Resident Conductor. He examined the older music in the band's library, and together we discovered Enderby Jackson's 'Yorkshire Waltzes' (1856), hidden away in some hand-written part books (to be discussed in Chapter 4), only one of which displayed the actual title. Mr Scott's thesis has revealed a great deal of early information, and I acknowledge a substantial debt to it in the preparation of this present book.

The band historian, Raymond Ainscoe of Kirkby Lonsdale had, until recently, a valuable collection of books, scores, old posters and programmes. He very kindly allowed me to consult these, especially the 1860s Crystal Palace music. I am most grateful to Mr Ainscoe and even though the collection is now dispersed, I refer to it throughout the book as the 'Ainscoe Collection'.

Other sources have been band libraries and the standard books on brass band history, particularly those by Arthur Taylor, Violet and Geoffrey Brand and Trevor Herbert, but especially the one to which all of us, I am sure, have made considerable reference, *The Brass Band Movement* by J F Russell and J H Elliott, published by Dent in 1936.

There are now many 'histories' of individual bands – several written to commemorate a centenary or some other anniversary. Early examples such as those about Stalybridge, Besses o' th' Barn, Bacup Old, Irwell Springs and St Hilda's bands contain a wealth of information about the exploits of the respective bands in bygone years; most later ones are largely anecdotal, but often reveal significant facts about the origins of the particular band. Collectively, these 'histories' have contributed much to my book, as have a number of the *Brass Band Annuals*, published around the turn of the century by F Richardson.

Local History Libraries have proved useful for following up specific events, and details of otherwise forgotten bands. Visits to those in Bolton, Bradford, Bury, Halifax, Huddersfield, Leeds, Manchester and Stalybridge have proved especially useful, and the treasures kept in the Henry Watson Library in Manchester have also revealed much information. The archives of Black Dyke

x *Preface and Acknowledgements*

and Besses o' th' Barn bands have been sources of much information and I am most grateful to these bands for granting me virtually free access.

Almost all the music examples appearing in the book come from the publications of R Smith & Co. Music Sales now owns the copyright for these works, and I am grateful to this company for allowing me to use the extracts.

Many people have influenced the course of the book, but I am especially indebted to two of them. These are Dr Derek Scott of the University of Salford and Rachel Lynch of Ashgate.

Brass Roots does not claim to be based significantly on original research from primary sources, but rather a compendium of information from a wide range of sources – both primary and secondary – many of which are not readily accessible. It is also based on the experiences of well over 50 years as a member of what is affectionately known as 'the brass band movement', with more than half of that time having been spent amongst the leading bands, and as a personal friend of all the leading brass band personalities of the time.

Sifting and collating the facts has been a fascinating experience and though the title *Brass Roots* is by no means original, I hope it will be seen as appropriate.

Note: During the nineteenth century the spelling *Dike* is generally found in references to Black Dyke Mills Band, but from around the turn of the century both *Dike* and *Dyke* are to be found. According to Scott (*Evolution*, footnote on page 69), Harold Foster, a director of the company, requested in 1912 that henceforth the spelling *Dyke* should be used. For the sake of consistency this spelling is used throughout this book, except where original material is quoted.

There is also a difficulty with the name *Flugel Horn*. It comes from the German *flügelhorn*; though still commonly referred to by bandsman as the *flugel horn* or, more often, simply the *flugel*, throughout this book we use what is the more common professional English name of *flugelhorn*.

RN

Introduction

Brass bands in Britain have their origins in the village bands of the early nineteenth century. Their instrumentation included clarinets, ophicleides and serpents, along with valveless trumpets and horns and, later, keyed bugles. Not until the arrival of the valve, and the development of cornets and saxhorns, did the all-brass combination materialize. It first appeared during the early 1830s and by 1836 was on the increase, a fact borne out with the arrival of the first published brass band music.

In *Brass Roots* the origins and development of brass bands and their music during the hundred years from 1836 is examined in detail. Whilst much of the book sets out to show the roots of brass band music and how it developed, it looks first at the roots of the bands themselves, and also at the social climate of Britain as they emerged.

Military bands and the emergence of town and village bands

> *The existence of the military band led to the formation of amateur bands and from the 1830s the starting point of the people's brass bands.*[1]

Wars have often acted as a spur to bands and military music, and the years of the French Revolution – ending in 1815 with the Battle of Waterloo – were no exception. In France in particular, with demands for parades, rallies and festivals, bands were in great demand, resulting in the emergence of that country as the world's leader in the field of band music of the period. Their normal military band comprised four each of the oboe, clarinet, horn and bassoon, though some bands were bigger than this.

Public band concerts first started in Germany during the late eighteenth century,[2] but by the end of the century were established in virtually all European capitals. With the international rivalry this created, bands grew in size; whereas they had formerly been financed by regimental officers, many of the bigger and better bands were now funded by the state.

In England, however, the army had been enlarged mainly through a voluntary militia system and had little effect on bands. The chief function of what bands there were was to provide music for training sessions and parades, and occasionally as an added attraction to special local events or celebrations.

Up to 1815 bands seem to have been nameless, their presence at functions reported with phrases such as 'bands of music were in attendance'. There was probably little organization and a minimum of rehearsal by the bands which were, in effect, collections of players. After 1815 there were fewer of these groups[3] and, along with the demise of church bands, local musicians began to regroup, resulting in the emergence of town and village bands. These early bands still rarely took on a name, but were referred to by that of their leader, for example Peter Wharton's Reed Band (forerunner of Black Dyke), and Clegg's Reed Band (forerunner of Besses o' th' Barn).

The Agricultural and Industrial Revolutions had far-reaching effects on the poorer people of Britain. The change from manual labour to the use of machines, the enclosure system and the introduction of farming machinery pushed society headlong into the age of industrialization and into the employer–employee relationship of the mills and factories. Due to the Napoleonic wars and a series of poor harvests corn prices rose swiftly up to 1815, from when they fell due to the import of cheap foreign corn. High prices were good for farmers but resulted in hardships for the workers, whilst the low prices put many farmers out of business, resulting in unemployment and starvation for more farm labourers, many of whom moved into towns, where there was a better chance of obtaining work. Many mill workers lived in badly-built back-to-back houses in narrow streets, in overcrowded and unsanitary conditions. Water was polluted by waste both from the mills and from the people, and disease flourished. Children were overworked and undernourished, and infant mortality was high.

Reaction to these conditions included machine-breaking by such groups as the Luddites, and demonstrations – some of which ended in bloodshed, like that held in St Peter's Fields, Manchester – known as the Peterloo Massacre. The demand for electoral reform increased and bands were regularly linked with the Reform Movement, where they were needed to lead processions of demonstrators and add to the clamour. Amateur bands fulfilled a similar role for the people's protest marches as that provided by military bands for the establishment, yet to diametrically opposed ends.

Despite this, Scott offers evidence which suggests that during the first two decades of the nineteenth century membership of amateur bands was not restricted to any one social class. However, towards the end of the second decade a more fully delineated class system emerged, and it was those who earned their living by manual work, in particular iron founders, wool and cotton mill hands, leather workers and colliers – members of the artisan class – who became bandsmen.

A few of the more liberally-minded factory owners saw benefits in encouraging music-making amongst workers – not necessarily, as has often been suggested, with ulterior motives in mind. True, it was a diversion from activities such as protest meetings, but it also added to the quality of life of communities to have a band or a choir in its midst. At the same time, if encouraged by the 'master', it contributed to good industrial relations.

Early bands and their instruments

In 1818 the brothers Clegg (John, Joseph and James), cotton manufacturers, formed a band in the village of Besses o' th' Barn, some eight miles north of Manchester.[4] It boasted 12 players, with John Clegg on the keyed bugle.[5] In 1820 another firm of cotton manufacturers, George and Joseph Strutt of Belper, near Derby, formed both a band and a choir, engaging a musician from Derby itself to teach the members to play or sing.[6] At around the same time the London Lead Company encouraged the formation of a band in the village of Nenthead (or Nent Head) in Cumberland, giving £5 per annum in cash, and providing a small rehearsal room.[7] These are just a few of many examples of bands sponsored by local companies during the period.

Arthur Taylor in *Brass Bands* cites various contenders for the title of oldest amateur band in Britain. Stalybridge celebrated its centenary in 1914 and was certainly one of the earliest bands, though there is evidence that in Derbyshire the New Mills Old Band was formed in 1812, and there is a claim that Coxlodge and Hazelrigg Band was founded in 1808, in County Durham.[8] Taylor also suggests that there were a number of other bands in existence by the end of the second decade of the nineteenth century. Peter Wharton's, formed in 1816 (later, Black Dyke) and Clegg's Reed Band of 1818 (to become Besses o' th' Barn) are just two of the more famous ones.

Nor were they confined to northern counties; there are references in Russell & Elliott to several bands in the Winterborne Valley in Dorset, including one in Winterborne St Martin which, as early as 1820, was made up of four clarinets, an oboe and a bass viol[9] (in reality, a church band). They reveal that also in 1820 the village of Piddletown [Puddletown?] in Dorset had a church band comprising a flute, two clarinets, a bassoon and two bass viols,[10] that it 'had previously also had a serpent', and referring to Thomas Hardy's novel *Far from the Madding Crowd*, suggest that the Weatherbury Band existed in the early 1830s. This, in the words of the novelist, produced

> a hideous clang of music from a drum, tambourine, clarionet, serpent, hautboy, tenor-viol, and double bass – the only remaining relics of the true and original Weatherbury band – venerable wormeaten instruments, which had celebrated in

their own persons the victories of Marlborough, under the fingers of the forefathers of those who played them now.[11]

Further north we find the Yorkshire-based Bramley Band. On its formation, in 1828, it boasted four clarinets, a [keyed] bugle and two trumpets, two French horns, a serpent, two trombones and a drum.[12]

As mentioned earlier, the chief instruments in the standard late eighteenth-century military band were the oboe, clarinet, French horn and bassoon, but trumpets and serpents were also used in most early amateur bands, along with keyed bugles and bass horns. The oboe, being a particularly difficult instrument to master, seems not to have been used; the bassoon also presented problems for beginners and did not feature often.

The keyed bugle was invented in 1810 by Yorkshire-born Joseph Haliday,[13] a militia bandsman serving in Dublin. It became an essential feature of early bands, being the main alternative to the clarinet as a treble melody instrument. Despite the advantages of the later cornet, keyed bugles remained popular band instruments until the early 1840s. This was probably because they were cheaper and there was already a large number of them in circulation. Different playing techniques were required for the two instruments, acting as a deterrent to amateur players who were familiar with the bugle. The piccolo was also occasionally found, its shrill sound lending itself to open-air performance, and providing a super-octave melody line.

The trombone, dating from the fifteenth century, though used in early military bands, had fallen out of favour and had not been used very much in English military bands during the eighteenth century.[14] It was, nevertheless, used in most amateur bands during the early nineteenth century.

Another ancient instrument found in early bands was the serpent – really the bass member of the cornett family, used by the Waits and in church bands. Some bands preferred the bass horn, which worked on the same principle as the serpent, whilst in shape resembling the ophicleide. Both instruments were superseded by the ophicleide, which became an almost indispensable band instrument during the middle years of the century, prior to its demise on the emergence of the euphonium and bombardon during the early 1850s. There grew up a generation of quite famous exponents of the ophicleide, the best-known being Samuel Hughes[15] and Alfred James Phasey.[16]

Most bands of this early period had between 10 and 12 players. Clegg's Reed Band of 1818 comprised three clarinets, a piccolo, a keyed bugle, a trumpet, two French horns, a trombone and two bass horns plus a bass drum.[17] With a choice of clarinet or keyed bugle as the treble melody instrument, with the added colour and brightness of the piccolo, and with two bass horns to provide the foundation, here would be a better than average range of sounds for a band of the time.

The advent of the all-brass band

There were many examples of conversion to all brass during the 1830s. Reputedly, the first British all-brass band was at Blaina, in Gwent, South Wales.[18] This band is thought to have converted in 1832, following the purchase of some cornopeans from the Dutch instrument maker Embach. ('Cornopean' is an early name for the cornet and will, along with other instruments, be discussed in detail in Chapter 3.)

The first known English all-brass band was formed in York in 1833 by Daniel Hardman and James Walker. Hardman is described as the last of the York Waits and Walker as a trumpet player who also played the cornopean. Hardman's job was to produce a band, when needed, for civic functions. This unusually large all-brass band had 24 members, playing cornopeans, French horns, trumpets, trombones and ophicleides.[19] A year later another brass band was formed in York by two brothers called Bean, and over the next few years others appeared in different parts of the country.

From about 1836 the term 'brass band' became accepted as applying to a recognizable type of ensemble, and the first published brass band music appeared. It was, however, to be some time before the brass band became the principal form of amateur wind band in Britain, but during the 1850s, by which time the valve had become established, there was a range of reliable instruments. First, the instruments were relatively cheap and certainly more durable; they were not affected by the weather and were therefore well-suited to the outdoor playing required of bands; the three-valve system was easy to learn, lent itself to the rough hands of working men, and the identical fingering of the instruments meant that players could change from one to another with relative ease. Moreover, as Scott points out, 'the exciting, bold and masculine sound . . . appealed to the working class man'.[20] These advantages ultimately combined and led to the popularity of the all-brass band over the mixed brass and reed band.

Notes

1 Farmer, 1912, p. 108.
2 Goldman, 1946, p. 33.
3 Scott, 1970, p. 108.
4 Besses o' th' Barn is a small town situated on the main Manchester to Bury road, and also on the Metro line (formerly the railway line) which joins the two conurbations. Both the town and the band are commonly known as 'Besses' – and will be referred to as such throughout this book.
5 Hampson, 1893, p. 9.
6 Gardiner, 1838, p. 512 and *Harmonicon*, Vol. 1 p. 72.
7 Raistrick, 1938, p. 71.
8 Taylor, 1979, pp. 12–13; see also Perrins, 1984, pp. 18–19.

9 Russell & Elliott, 1936, p. 13.
10 Ibid, p. 14. NB Stringed instruments were often mixed with wind instruments in church bands, brass melody-playing instruments still being rare, and possibly thought of as inappropriate for church use.
11 Hardy, 1993 edition, p. 422.
12 Hesling White, 1906, p. 5.
13 In different accounts he is referred to as Halliday or Haliday, and Joseph, James or John. According to Dudgeon, 1993, note 7 p. 40, Joseph Haliday is correct.
14 Trevor Herbert (1991, p. 10), says that the trombone was obsolete in England by the end of the seventeenth century. It had been a regular member of instrumental groups in earlier times and the main reason for its decline, Herbert maintains, was changing tastes in art music which, at the time, favoured 'homogeneous sonorities of the type produced by balanced string and wind groups'. With the development of the horn in the eighteenth century the trombone declined for a time, and it was left to the military band to rediscover it later in the century. But whereas in its consort days the trombone had been played quietly, an entirely different and louder style of playing was now demanded.
15 Hughes was amongst the elite of ophicleide players, and was appointed ophicleide professor at Kneller Hall in 1859 and at Guildhall School of Music in 1880.
16 Phasey, born 19 January 1834, became quite a versatile musician. According to *British Bandsman* of October and December 1888, in addition to playing with the Coldstream Guards and his work at Kneller Hall, he also played in the Crystal Palace Band, Her Majesty's Band, and for the Philharmonic Society. He played ophicleide, bass trombone and euphonium and appeared as soloist in the Jullien promenade concerts, as well as in duets with both Koenig and Levy. He conducted a number of bands and regularly adjudicated at brass band contests.
17 Hampson, 1893, pp. 9–10.
18 Russell & Elliott, 1936, p. 46.
19 Ibid, pp. 46–47.
20 *Evolution of the brass band*, p. 124.

1 Music in nineteenth-century Britain

The period 1800 to 1850 was one of the most productive periods in Western musical history and saw the transition from Classical to Romantic styles. Beethoven, 30 at the turn of the century, was approaching the height of his creative powers. The first eight of his symphonies appeared between 1800 and 1812 and the ninth, having occupied his mind for a decade, was premièred in 1824. Weber, a key figure in German opera, was 14 years old when the nineteenth century began but as he lived only 26 years more, his whole output belongs to its first quarter. Rossini was born in 1792, but most of his music was written by 1829, the year of *William Tell*.

The works of Schubert, Mendelssohn and Chopin belong to this period, as do most of Schumann's. 1813 saw the births of Verdi and Wagner; Wagner's *Flying Dutchman* appeared in 1841 and *Rienzi* in 1842, around the same time as Verdi's first major success, *Nabucco*. Two more important Wagner music dramas belong to the period – *Tannhäuser* (1845) and *Lohengrin* (1850). Meanwhile, in Russia Glinka (1804–1857) produced *A Life for the Czar* in 1836 and *Russlan and Ludmilla* six years later.

Other composers of the time include Cherubini (1760–1842), Boieldieu (1775–1834), Auber (1782–1871), Spohr (1784–1859), Meyerbeer (1791–1864), Donizetti (1797–1848), Bellini (1801–1835), Lortzing (1801–1851), Nicolai (1810–1849) and Flotow (1812–1883). Music by all these composers found its way into the repertoire of brass bands – some of it almost immediately. Operatic music was used frequently and successfully, reflecting popular taste of the period.

Paving the way for music in the second half of the century, Gounod was born in 1818, Offenbach a year later. Johann Strauss I (remembered chiefly for the march *Radetsky*) lived from 1804 to 1849, whilst his more famous son was born in 1825. Brahms came into the world in 1833, Bizet in 1838,

Mussorgsky in 1839, Tchaikovsky in 1840, Grieg in 1843 and Rimsky-Korsakov in 1844. With the exception of Tchaikovsky, and to some extent Bizet, the music of this later group has played a less significant role in brass band repertoire. The work of the earlier composers had firmly established itself, but that of later nineteenth-century composers was often less easy to adapt. Added to this was the growth in demand for music specially composed for brass band.

Music in England

What a wealth of talented composers there was, and not an Englishman amongst them! Although he died in 1759, Handel was still at the forefront of English music well into the nineteenth century. German-born, he had lived in England for 45 years and had become a naturalized Englishman. Virtually all his performed vocal music was set to English texts (not always with success) and he had taken over Purcell's mantle as England's leading composer. Though initially a writer of opera, his greatest gifts to English music were his oratorios, stimulating the growth of the English choral tradition. Symbolic of this was the establishment, probably in 1715, of the Three Choirs Festival, held triennially in Gloucester, Worcester and Hereford. Here Handel's music received frequent performances. In 1857 the Sacred Harmonic Society (founded by a group of enthusiasts in 1832) established the Handel Festivals at the Crystal Palace. This building proved eminently suitable both structurally and acoustically for large-scale musical events and was to become the scene for huge choral festivals and band contests.

There were, of course, some British composers, for example William Crotch (1775–1847). He became the first Professor of Music at Oxford and the first Principal of the Royal Academy of Music, and yet his 'masterpiece', the oratorio *Palestine*, has been long forgotten. Another composer, Henry Bishop (1786–1855), composed no less than 57 operas, but is remembered chiefly for his ballads, a few of which found their way into brass band repertoire. A little later came the Irish composer Michael William Balfe (1808–1876), whose opera *The Bohemian Girl* (1843) enjoyed substantial popularity. Another Irish-born composer, William Vincent Wallace (1812–1865) had some success with his operas *Maritana* (1845) and *Lurline* (1847), both of which provided material for arrangers of nineteenth-century band music, along with some of the music of Balfe. None of these are classed in the first rank of composers, though they gave much pleasure to many people. Nevertheless, the latter part of the century saw significant developments in British music, particularly in education, with the appearance of George Grove (1820–1900) of *Grove's Dictionary* fame and first Director of the Royal College of Music; composer Arthur Sullivan (1842–1900) and those remarkably successful teachers, Hubert Parry (1848–1918) and Charles Villiers Stanford (1852–1924).

In the field of publishing, the house of Novello was founded in 1811. Publishing standard editions of the classics, particularly choral music, Novello helped foster the English nineteenth-century choral tradition and produced most of the English Victorian oratorios and cantatas. Another important institution, founded in 1822, was the Royal Academy of Music, which supplied the nation with generations of first-rate musical performers, and also produced many fine teachers, in the early years often styled 'professor of music'. These developments in publishing and education led to increased opportunities for musical performance both at professional and amateur level, with a corresponding increase in the manufacture of musical instruments and in the organization of concerts and concert-going.

Another face of publishing was musical journalism. *Musical Times* was first published in 1844 by Novello. A number of other musical magazines followed, but brass bands had to wait until October 1881 before they had their own specialist paper. This was the monthly *Brass Band News*, published by Wright & Round in Liverpool and first edited by Enoch Round. Circulation figures were not disclosed initially, but the paper rapidly became popular, and in 1890 claimed that sales had increased from 5000 to 25000 between the first edition and the end of 1889.[1] It gave much publicity to contests – especially those using Wright & Round publications as test pieces. Issues consisted of letters and news items, reports from different parts of the country and educational features; there were advertisements for miscellaneous items ranging from mouthpieces and uniforms to valve oil, storm lamps for the bandroom, and for instruments and music, with specimen cornet parts for some of the company's latest published pieces included in most editions. 'Professional cards' advertising the skills of conductors and adjudicators were also featured.

The second specialist brass band paper, *British Bandsman*, was founded by Sam Cope in 1887 (see page 154 for more details about Cope's contribution to bands) and had a number of different titles during its early years. Still enjoying success as 'the only weekly for bandsmen', it is now located in Beaconsfield, but was formerly based in London. *The Cornet* was another monthly, published by F Richardson & Co of Sibsey, Lincolnshire; founded in 1896, it survived until the 1940s.

Music of the people

Recent research has emphasized that musical life in nineteenth-century Britain was more vibrant than hitherto believed. Some of the more interesting developments in English music during the nineteenth century were in popular music and also in attempts at making music popular. One of the most fertile areas of performance in the middle of the century was that of street music. Street musicians, primarily out to make money, also played a big part in popularizing music of the times, or that of a few years earlier. Their repertoire, very similar to that of brass bands in later years, included marches, dances and hymn tunes, as well as operatic songs and overtures, and extracts from oratorio. By the 1850s there were between 1250 and 1500 street musicians in London alone[2] – comprising German bands and English bands, hurdy-gurdies, fiddlers and bell ringers, Irish and Scottish pipers, concertinas, barrel organs and even harps. Many street musicians also performed in public houses – anticipating the music hall. The disc musical box, with its interchangeable discs, was invented in 1886. This instrument also found its way into public houses and hotels under a variety of brand names such as 'Symphonium' and 'Polyphon'.[3] Popular tunes of the day, as well as extracts from opera could be heard on these machines, which had a sound not unlike that of the barrel organ.

The success of street music resulted in a growing demand for more organized popular music; by 1860 there were some 250 music halls in London and at least 300 in the provinces. At first they were simply small rooms with a stage at one end, where people could eat, drink and be entertained. Within a decade or so more comfortable theatres appeared, complete with well-equipped stages, orchestra pits and galleries. Towards the end of the century halls in the major cities became big business, with the appearance of more elaborate theatres – Empires, Hippodromes and Alhambras. Here auditoriums were more comfortable and audiences could enjoy leading artists, touring troupes and twice-nightly shows.

Popular musical theatre adopted a variety of forms, starting with Burlesque in the 1830s. This was an entertainment with songs and spoken dialogue – comical, topical, satirical and often poking fun at opera. Pantomime, ballet and revue were also successful genres, but it was musical comedy, appearing in the 1890s, which exercised the greatest influence on brass bands. Along with Viennese and French operettas and those of Gilbert and Sullivan, musical comedy was to provide medleys of tunes which, though never replacing operatic selections on the contest platform, removed them permanently from most concert programmes. In the theatre, musical comedy relied more on the spoken word to carry its story forward than did operetta, but in both genres, the music was light-hearted and easy on the ear.

The first musical comedy was *A Gaiety Girl* (1893), with music by Sidney Jones.[4] This was so successful that it was taken on a world tour – along with its musical director, Granville Bantock – who many years later took a great interest in brass bands. However, the only nineteenth-century musical comedy to find a lasting place in brass band programmes was the same composer's 1896 production, *The Geisha*. Its popularity with bands reflected its enormous success in the theatre. Other successes included *A Runaway Girl* (1898), which contained Lionel Monckton's still popular 'Soldiers in the park' – perhaps better known as 'Oh, listen to the band'. By the end of the century British musical comedy was well established, not only throughout the English-speaking world, but also in Europe.

The ballroom dance

The development of ballroom dancing dramatically affected the course of nineteenth-century popular music and was, in turn, reflected in the repertoire of bands – frequently called upon to play dance music. In the main, such music was imported from Vienna and Paris; dances which enjoyed the greatest vogue during the early part of the century were the waltz, the polka and the quadrille, with the galop also proving popular when it came to London in 1829.[5]

The waltz, by far the most popular nineteenth-century ballroom dance, was first established in Vienna through the work of Michael Pamer (1782–1827). Both Josef Lanner and Johann Strauss the elder played in Pamer's orchestra and through them and the younger Strauss the Viennese waltz attained stylistic perfection. It came to England via France in about 1812 and retained its popularity for over a hundred years. Johann Strauss II (1825–1899) wrote almost 500 dances, many of them waltzes, including perhaps the most famous waltz ever written, 'The Blue Danube'. Although eminently suitable for dancing to, the Strauss waltzes were composed as concert pieces, often with an elaborate introduction – not in waltz time. Emile Waldteufel (1837–1915) gave the French waltz its own particular character, replacing the Viennese 'lilt' with a more deliberate and even rhythm. A Hungarian bandmaster, Josef Gung'l (1810–1879), wrote a number of waltzes which became very popular, whilst Archibald Joyce (1873–1963), composing some 60 – the most popular being his '*Songe d'automne*' – was for a time known as the English 'waltz king'.[6] Other English composers of the waltz include Sidney Baynes ('Destiny') and Charles Ancliffe ('Nights of gladness'). Though the transcription of the waltzes of these and other famous writers seems not to have begun until the twentieth century, literally hundreds of original waltzes by rank and file writers appeared during the early period of band music. Less sophisticated and making fewer demands on the players, these nevertheless filled a need in band repertoire, both for dancing and listening.

The polka and the quadrille also became popular with bands; the 2/4 rhythm, short phrases and characteristic tempo of the polka led to its use as a lively cornet solo, often calling for triple-tonguing, a technique developed quite early in the history of cornet playing. In the pre-brass band era a quadrille band was often advertised as one of the attractions in a village

12 *Brass Roots*

festival or a day's festivities, such as the one which took place at Burton Constable in 1845 (see pages 28–29). These bands were probably simply a collection of local musicians, or possibly members of a visiting circus band, assembled to provide music for the dance. The Frenchman Philippe Musard (1792–1859) was the most successful mainstream quadrille writer, though many were also written by Viennese composers; most brass band quadrilles were written by brass band specialists.

Concerts

As the century progressed concerts took on increasing significance. Concert promotion was undertaken by some of the leading publishers, enabling them to promote their own music and injecting the concerts with a commercial purpose in addition to their role as musical and social occasions. In keeping with the music they published, Novello concentrated on oratorio concerts and Boosey on ballads, whilst Chappell promoted a series of 'Monday popular concerts'.

Concert halls appeared in major provincial cities during the 1850s, providing venues for concerts and organ recitals, with cheap tickets for the working classes. Additionally, many spa towns and seaside resorts built pavilions and employed orchestras and soloists during the tourist season. These appeared in such places as Bath, Bournemouth, Brighton, Eastbourne, Harrogate, Margate, Scarborough and Torquay. The most famous of the resort orchestras was that founded in Bournemouth by Dan Godfrey.[7] Starting as a military band, it was later changed to a spa orchestra and ultimately became the Bournemouth Symphony Orchestra. Many resorts also built bandstands, engaging military bands and the more successful brass bands to play two or three concerts per day – sometimes for a whole week.

Promenade concerts

Concerts mounted in these pavilions and bandstands were greatly influenced by what became known as promenade concerts. These originated in Paris and aimed to entertain those people who did not patronize opera houses or the more serious concerts, at a price they could afford. They catered for the masses of Parisians who frequented the boulevards and gardens, but who also perhaps, on occasion, went to the theatre. The Summer concerts (*concerts d' été*) were held in the open air while the Winter concerts (*concerts d'hiver*) took place indoors.

The first series of London promenade concerts was in the Coliseum, Regent's Park, in January 1838, with a second series later in the year. It was organized by Philippe Musard who had run successful promenade concerts in Paris since 1833. The initial London series, like that in Paris, was organized 'for the performance of overtures, quadrilles, waltzes and galops, so arranged as to offer a promenade between acts.'[8] An essential feature was the performance of solos, especially on the *cornet-à-pistons* and the ophicleide, each of which was still something of a novelty at the time. A selection from a well-known opera, with vocal parts played by soloists on wind instruments also became common; a later series (1838) included a duet from Bellini's *Norma*, featuring two cornopeans. Musard's quadrilles – though written primarily for the ballroom – featured prominently in his concerts which, in London, were held in theatres during both summer and winter, as there was no suitable accommodation in London's gardens at that time.

By the end of the 1840s Musard's place in London had been taken by the more flamboyant Monsieur Jullien, who made his London debut with a series of *concerts d'été* at Drury Lane. Like Musard and Strauss he was primarily a conductor of dance music and, along with Strauss, was one of the first conductors to attract an audience by his own skills and showmanship. He was to hold centre stage in the promenade concerts in England until 1859, and though several others took up the challenge later, not until the arrival of Henry Wood in 1895 was the long-term future of the 'proms' assured.

Louis Jullien (1812–1860)

Louis Jullien was the son of a French bandmaster. His ridiculously long full name[9] is quoted in several books; he was named after every member of his father's band, because they all wanted to be Godfather to the child, and Jullien (Sr) did not wish to upset any of them by inviting only one or two. Much of the following information is taken from *Life of Jullien*, a fascinating biography by Adam Carse.

During his first 10 years in England Jullien directed 15 series of promenade concerts in various London theatres, four summer seasons in the Surrey Zoological Gardens and even tried his hand, unsuccessfully, at staging grand opera. He undertook provincial tours at least once a year, and it must have been during one of these that Enderby Jackson saw him (see pages 29–30) and ultimately followed him in his quest of bringing music to the people.

It was soon apparent that no other conductor in England could, through his own personal magnetism and dynamism, attract such large audiences. Jullien also took on numerous engagements at private balls and social functions, at some of which he was assisted by his star cornet player, Hermann Koenig, apparently also a competent violinist and a composer. Showmanship was Jullien's principal hallmark; when conducting Beethoven he would don white gloves and use a jewelled baton, and to heighten the effects in the

'Storm' movement of the 'Pastoral' Symphony, dried peas were rattled in a tin box!

In 1843 Jullien returned to Paris where he was thrown into prison for an earlier debt.[10] However, he soon talked his way out and was back in London for a winter season at the English Opera House. Here, 'The *Pastoral* symphony and *Der Freischütz* overture hobnobbed with quadrilles, waltzes and galops by Musard, Strauss and Jullien; gaiety, colour and enjoyment prevailed; all for one shilling or half a crown, according to taste and state of one's purse.'[11]

1844 saw the first of three successive years of winter proms at Covent Garden. These featured the 'Post Horn Galop' for the first time (composed and played by Koenig), and in one of his concerts introduced the Distin family, playing their new saxhorns (see pages 27–28). The following year was also eventful, with two provincial tours, a 'Grand Evening Concert' at Covent Garden with an orchestra of 500, a number of fancy dress balls and two 'Concerts Monstre' in the Surrey Gardens. Here a covered platform was erected to accommodate 300 instrumentalists, and each concert attracted an audience of around 12 000. There were many classical pieces in the programme, including 'Suona la tromba', from Bellini's *I Puritani*, performed on 20 cornets, 20 trumpets, 20 trombones, 20 ophicleides and 20 serpents. A second concert was held on a similarly grand scale later in the Summer – the orchestra sporting the largest bass drum ever seen, as well as a contrabass which took 'two sturdy players' to manipulate. Nevertheless, amongst all the gimmicks, audiences were being exposed to more serious music, and as they came to appreciate its language, they were fed gradually increasing dosages. Thus, the 1864 Covent Garden series included Beethoven and Mozart festivals, along with performances of Haydn's *Creation* and Rossini's *Stabat Mater*.

1851 was the year of the Great Industrial Exhibition for which Jullien produced another of his 'spectaculars', the 'Great Exhibition quadrille', performed nightly by an orchestra and four military bands totalling 207 performers.

In the following year Jullien set out on a project of self-destruction as an operatic composer. His *Pietro il grande*, staged at Covent Garden, was a miserable failure, and reputedly cost him £16 000. But before the end of the year it was 'business as usual', with more promenade concerts, featuring most of the familiar soloists, but with the cornet now also played by Jean Baptiste Arban (1825–1889), author of the 'brass player's Bible', the *Method for Cornet*. For the next few years Arban and Koenig were often to be found side by side in Jullien's orchestra.

In 1853 Jullien drew up plans for an American tour, and at a testimonial concert in July at Drury Lane a full house gathered to bid farewell to the 'Napoleon of promenade concerts'. On 3 August he sailed from Liverpool, along with his wife, his agent and some close friends, plus no less than 11 tons of baggage – bound for New York. His publicity machine had obviously preceded him, because the *New York Evening Mirror* of 9 August announced the arrival of the 'distinguished knight of the baton'.[12] Transported to his hotel in a new carriage drawn by four bay horses, he must have looked like a nineteenth-century Liberace! Jullien took 27 of his key players to America, including Koenig and a trombonist named W Winterbottom, a member of a famous family of military band musicians.[13] The orchestra was augmented to 100 members by adding local players from New York. After almost a year away from England the party arrived back in Liverpool on 28 June 1854 and Jullien was soon into another season of promenade concerts.

In May 1856 he toured the northern counties with a 50-piece wind band including five saxophones, ten saxhorns,[14] two ophicleides and a pair of kettledrums. There were also eight basses – possibly a mixture of circular basses and bombardons. Jullien regarded this as a 'model band' and intended to persuade the authorities that all bands of the British Army should be reformed according to his scheme.

In 1858 he began planning a world tour, and Carse cites this as possible evidence of approaching mental instability.[15] The concerts were advertised as 'M Jullien's Farewell and *Concerts d'Adieu* before his departure on a Universal Musical Tour through every city and capital of Europe, America, Australia, the Colonies and civilised towns of Asia and Africa . . .' There were several Jullien pieces in the programme, including his new 'Hymn of universal harmony', inspired by the prospect of taking the civilizing influence of good music to all nations and peoples. The world tour never took place and, in fact, this year proved to be Jullien's last in London.

For 1860 Jullien planned the performance of a series of oratorios, but it was not to be, as his mind finally gave way. It is said that he attempted suicide, and that he even tried to commit a murder. Tragically he ended his days in a French lunatic asylum, still in only his 48th year.[16]

Jullien had been a great showman and had brought immeasurable pleasure to innumerable people. His presentations, though sometimes extravagant and often bizarre, attracted large and diverse audiences and so gave him the opportunity to bring serious music to the ears of the common people.

It is difficult to quantify Jullien's influence on the brass band. At least three members of his orchestra contributed to the development of bands and band music – John Gladney, William (or John) Winterbottom and Charles Godfrey (Jr). Some of Jullien's compositions were played by early bands and Koenig's 'Posthorn Galop' was beloved of generations of cornet soloists. Jullien's impact on a young man called Enderby Jackson was profound (see page 30), and Jackson's contribution to the brass band will be discussed later.

After Jullien's departure from the scene the promenade concerts, lacking a conductor with his appeal, lost much of their popularity, though a brief revival occurred in 1865 when Luigi Arditi (of 'Il bacio' fame) conducted a four-week season with a huge orchestra which included 12 horns, six trumpets, six trombones, two euphoniums and two bombardons. Arditi, primarily an operatic conductor, took only the first half of each concert, the dance music of the second half being conducted by Dan Godfrey. By this time, Wagner's music was becoming well-known in England, and 'Wagner Nights' became popular. In some of these Arditi combined his orchestra with the band of the Coldstream Guards in selections from *Tannhäuser*, *Lohengrin* and *The Flying Dutchman*. During the early 1870s Jules Rivière[17] injected further life into the flagging concerts, whilst other conductors tried in vain to make their marks.

Though the promenade concerts regained a little of their former popularity with Arditi and Rivière, after Jullien's demise they had a chequered existence and again, in the 1890s, were on the verge of collapse. They were saved from this by the man whose lasting tribute is undoubtedly the series of 'Proms' which have been held from 1895 to this day, first in the Queen's Hall[18] and more latterly in the Royal Albert Hall. His name – Henry J Wood (1896–1944).

Opera and other vocal music

Amongst all this 'music of the people', opera also reached great heights of popularity. The British composers Balfe, Macfarren (1813–1887) and Vincent Wallace all made their marks – reflected in brass band repertoire, as did Julius Benedict (1804–1885), a German composer who settled in England. One of the more popular English operas of the time was Balfe's *Bohemian Girl*. Its overture and the aria 'I dreamt that I dwelt in marble halls' were standard brass band repertoire for several decades. Dominant, however, was Italian opera which enjoyed great success in early Victorian England.

There were a number of touring opera companies from as early as the 1840s. They appealed to the popular audience, and many musicians who were to become well-known in the fields of choral music and brass bands regularly attended. The most popular productions were *The Bohemian Girl* (Balfe), *The Lily of Killarney* (Benedict) and *Il Trovatore* (Verdi) – all of which provided musical material for bands in the form of selections of 'highlights'. These selections were by no means sacred to the brass band, however, as they could be heard in the street, the music hall and the home; they were played by pianists, found their way into orchestral concerts and were sung by choirs. But their lasting effect was felt nowhere as much as in the brass band, where they maintained their popularity until well into the twentieth century.

The 1890s saw the formation of many amateur operatic societies, together with the popularization of the operettas of Gilbert and Sullivan. Sir Arthur Sullivan, arguably England's leading composer in the late nineteenth century, exerted considerable influence on the course of band music – albeit unwittingly. Volumes have been written about Sullivan, his music, and his partnership with W S Gilbert, so there is no need to go into detail here, beyond recalling that several selections and one or two overtures were part of the staple diet of bands for several decades in the twentieth century – some even earlier; Sullivan's ballad 'The lost chord' became a best-selling cornet solo as well as a best-selling song, and brass bands still enjoy playing his hymn, 'Onward, Christian soldiers'. Sullivan also helped found the National Brass Band Championships at the Crystal Palace, where three selections of *Gems from Sullivan's Operas*, arranged by James Ord Hume, served as test pieces in the early years of that series of contests (see pages 118–123).

Operatic selections formed a substantial part of contest repertoire. Several were played in contests within a year or two of the first performances of the actual operas. Appendix 1 gives a list of operas, selections from which were used in brass band contests during the nineteenth century. Operas are shown country by country, and whilst the list is by no means exhaustive, it gives an indication of the wide range of pieces that were employed. As will be seen, many selections were from quite obscure works.

Germany

In Germany the foundations had been laid by Gluck and built on by Mozart. In the nineteenth century Beethoven's *Fidelio* (1806–1814) was the first important German opera. This did not appear in brass band repertoire for quite some time but selections from the operas of others did, including several by Wagner. Despite being regarded as a revolutionary, he became quite a favourite, the intensity and emotion of his music appealing to nineteenth-century bandsmen and their listeners. Weber and the now little-known Lortzing were also popular with the selectors.

Italy

In Italy Rossini was the key operatic figure at the turn of the nineteenth century. Bellini and Donizetti were important, but just as Wagner towered above other German operatic composers, so Verdi rose above his Italian counterparts, being almost as conventional as Wagner was innovative. Rossini, Bellini, Donizetti and Verdi were all beloved of arrangers of brass band selections. In a few cases a transcription of the overture was preferred to a selection and in some both became popular. In Italian opera melody was the dominant force; the characteristics of the brass band instruments, especially the cornet and euphonium with their intensely lyrical qualities, and the styles of playing developed by leading soloists were able to exploit this, hence the large number of Italian operas in the list.

France

In France there were two schools of opera – 'grand opera' (to be seen at the Paris Opéra) and 'opéra-comique'. Grand opera was generally based on historical subjects, with the complete text set to music. In comic opera there was spoken dialogue, and the music tended to be more Romantic in character. Meyerbeer, though of German origin, is regarded as the founder of grand opera, whilst Gounod was the leading exponent of comic opera. Both are well represented in the lists of operatic selections. Again, melody was all-important, whilst the grandeur of many of the choruses was exploited in full band passages.

Britain

British opera has already been referred to and, despite its lack of depth, selections from a significant number appeared in the lists. Selections from some of the light operas of Gilbert and Sullivan (*The Gondoliers*, *H M S Pinafore*, *Mikado* and *The Pirates of Penzance* in particular) were also published, but these were used in concerts rather than contests.

A few operas from Russia complete the list.

The operatic selection was the main focus for the majority of test pieces during the second half of the nineteenth century. A common alternative was the composer selection, but even then, much of the material came from operas.

Leaving opera and looking at vocal music in general, one of the most important steps in the development of amateur singing was the emergence of Tonic Sol-fa. Yorkshire-born John Curwen (1816–1880) and the Worcester-born John Pyke Hullah (1812–1884) were two of the most important of a number of people who contributed to the popularization of sight-singing. Their influence spread not only to choir conductors, but also to many band trainers of the late nineteenth and early twentieth centuries.[19]

Singing classes became popular and the standard of musical performance in churches and chapels had improved considerably from the days of the church band. From the late 1850s more organs were installed in churches and there was an improvement in the quality of organ playing. Symbolic of this was the founding of the Royal College of Organists in 1864. As church and chapel choirs improved, their more enthusiastic members formed secular choral societies and, later in the century, competitive choirs.

Brass band music was influenced to a significant degree by church music. Religious festivals held in the open air often called on the services of the local band to accompany the singing. Probably stemming from this, the playing of hymn tunes in concert programmes became extremely common. Much early repertoire had a religious slant with, quite apart from arrangements of sacred music, many short pieces written as anthems, and numerous marches labelled 'sacred'.

Musical evenings in the home became a normal part of Victorian life; fiddles and flutes at first provided the backing for singing, though the piano took over later. The American organ, similar to the harmonium, and the concertina also became popular in mid-century.[20] For bandsmen, the weekly or twice-weekly rehearsal took the place of these musical evenings.

Blackface minstrelsy, originating in America, also found an audience in Britain. The performers were generally caucasians wearing black make-up, and there was a strong element of parody in their performances. Some of the early brass band music reflects this kind of entertainment, particularly in barn dances, which were played by bands around the turn of the century. Titles which would not find favour today included 'The happy coon', 'The darkie's wedding' and even 'Jolly niggers'.

Country folk songs and songs from the music hall were typical of working class musical evenings, but the genre which was to have the greatest effect on band music was the drawing-room ballad, 'much favoured by the middle-class Victorians who possessed pianos and liked to entertain themselves at home with amateur music-making'.[21] These ballads were often of a romantic or sentimental nature. They flourished chiefly in England throughout the nineteenth century and well into the twentieth; many of them were first heard at the Boosey ballad concerts. Though often composed with orchestral accompaniment, it was in the drawing room, with piano accompaniment, that ballads achieved their greatest popularity. Here they were sung and played by amateur musicians, were a social rather than intellectual pursuit, and of necessity were technically undemanding, both for singer and accompanist.

A reason for the popularity of the ballad itself is that, in the language of the day, it was considered to be more 'serious', 'refined' and even 'improving' than songs from the music hall. Many ballads were played by brass bands, and amongst early examples are two by Sir Henry Bishop – 'Home, sweet home' and 'My pretty Jane'. Both were played regularly on the cornet as 'slow melodies' and the latter was popularized complete with variations (the *air varie*). Balfe's 'Killarney' also became a popular cornet solo. Even earlier than those by Bishop and Balfe, are two by Thomas Moore (1779–1852). He was an Irish composer, and his two best-known songs – 'Believe me if all those endearing young charms' (1808) and 'The last rose of summer' (1813) – have both been popular with brass soloists, though it must have been well over half a century before they were first scored for brass band. Two well-known songs dating from 1877 are Frederic Clay's 'I'll sing thee songs of Araby' and Sullivan's 'The lost chord'. This much-maligned song had to wait until 1902 for its cornet solo version, which then became almost as popular as the original. Another ballad from the 1870s which was to enhance brass band repertoire was 'Silver threads amongst the gold', by Hart Peace Danks, whilst the 'hit' from the 1880s, as far as cornet soloists were concerned, was 'Love's old sweet song', by the Irish composer James Molloy. There is quite a clutch of songs from the 1890s, including 'Passing by' (Edward Purcell), an early Wilfrid Sanderson song, 'Drake goes west', Ethelbert Nevin's best-seller 'The rosary' and Liddle's setting of 'Abide with me', popularized by Clara Butt. There were also several by Stephen Adams, including 'The star of Bethlehem', and one of the most popular of all ballads, 'The holy city'. Stephen Adams was the pen-name of Michael Maybrick; he was a composer and singer, generally singing under his real name but writing under his pseudonym. Not surprisingly, Maybrick frequently sang Adams! The words of both these songs, and of many others were by Frederic E Weatherly (1848–1929).[22] Many ballads did not reach the brass band until after 1900. But nevertheless, they represent an important branch of popular music from the Victorian era.

Another popular vocal form was the glee. This was a kind of part-song for three, four or five male voices. Though not many were written after about 1830, the glee club became an important institution – for both musical and social reasons. Of the many glees which found their way into the bandroom, 'Hail smiling morn' by Reginald Spofforth (1770–1827) is easily the most well-known. Glees were sung unaccompanied, and a particular feature was the high counter-tenor or alto voice – commonly known as 'falsetto'. The glee was melodious, rhythmical, and appropriate to solo voices – a kind of vocal chamber music. When, later in the century, the brass quartet, comprising two cornets, tenor horn and euphonium became popular, the glee repertoire provided a ready source.

Brass band and choral society

With all this musical activity and the opportunities it offered it was inevitable that, as the century progressed, a more musically literate population would emerge. Ironically, the years of the 'Great Depression' (1876–1896) brought about a wave of prosperity which contributed to a rise in musical standards and interests. There was only a slight increase in wages, but with a 40 per cent decrease in prices, the net value of the wage packet increased to the tune of something like 66 per cent.[23] Additionally, industrialization brought with it increased leisure time.

One of the manifestations of this social and economic change was the growth of the two greatest British amateur musical traditions, the brass band and the choral society – the most significant and lasting features of nineteenth-century amateur music-making. By the end of the century there were literally thousands of each in Britain. As will be shown, brass bands had developed from the village band – made up of a few members playing an *ad hoc* collection of instruments into a unified ensemble with over 20 players using a standardized instrumentation, and with a large repertoire – some of its music borrowed but much of it specially written.

Brass bands and choral societies had much in common: an overlap in repertoire and audience, many joint performance opportunities, strong family ties within their member-organizations, and each having some input from the middle classes at the organizational level. However, there was a broader geographical base in choral societies and, certainly up until about 1850, there was a preponderance of the more 'respectable' classes amongst the membership, which ranged from the skilled working class to the upper middle classes. Choirs turned to competition much later than brass bands, and in general their attitudes towards it were rather different, summed up in the words of Sir Henry Leslie of Oswestry who, in 1880, said that musical competition was 'fundamentally a vehicle for musical education, and not an excuse for prize-hunting and self-glorification.'[24] For brass bands, it has to be said that prize-winning has been taken more seriously than the educational aspect, and yet contesting has been educational, contributing enormously to the playing skills and musical understanding of bands.

A significant difference between bands and choral societies has been the strong links between the choral society and the orchestra, strengthened through the performance of oratorios. This, in turn, attracted compositions from mainstream composers much earlier than did brass bands, with a consequent greater recognition by the musical hierarchy, helping to foster the perception of the brass band as isolated from the rest of the musical world. Socially this may have been true, but the music played by brass bands early in their history was very much a reflection of the music of the times.

Notes

1 *Brass Band News*, January 1990, p. 3.
2 Russell, 1987, p. 64.
3 Temperley, 1981, p. 79 and Pearsall, 1973, pp. 192–194.
4 Sidney Jones (1861–1946) was the eldest son of J Sidney Jones (1838–1906). Both were bandmasters of the 5th Dragoon Guards and both made brass band arrangements. Prior to his success with musical comedy in London, Jones (Jr) had played in a number of 'resort' orchestras and toured England and Australia, conducting light opera. (Information from Gammond, 1991, p. 304.)
5 Temperley, 1981, p. 112.
6 Gammond, 1991, p. 307.
7 The Godfreys were a famous family of band musicians – including two named Dan and three named Charles. The first Charles (1790–1863) was bandmaster of the Coldstream Guards from 1825 until his death. Three of his sons – Dan,

Adolphus Frederick (Fred) and Charles also took up careers as military bandmasters. Dan Godfrey (1831–1903) was bandmaster of the Grenadier Guards for 40 years before forming his own band and Fred (1837–1882) succeeded his father as bandmaster of the Coldstreams. Charles (Jr) (1839–1919), after study at the Royal Academy of Music, played with Jullien's orchestra, but is remembered chiefly as bandmaster of the Royal Horse Guards (1868–1904) and for his work as an arranger of test pieces and adjudicator at brass band contests. This Charles had a son, also Charles, who worked with various military bands and orchestras, and another son, Arthur, who worked mainly in the theatre. The most famous member of the family was the other Dan (1868–1939) – son of Dan and grandson of the first Charles. He is commonly referred to as Sir Dan Godfrey (Jr). He was never in the army, though he conducted military bands, as well as opera. He is chiefly remembered for his work at Bournemouth. (Information from Gammond, 1991, pp. 228–229.)

8   From *Musical World* 5 January 1838, quoted in Carse, 1951, p. 4.
9   The full name is: Louis Georges Maurice Adolph Roch Albert Abel Antonio Alexandre Noé Jean Lucien Daniel Eugène Joseph-le-brun Joseph-Barème Thomas Thomas Thomas-Thomas Pierre Arbon Pierre-Maurel Barthélemi Artus Alphonse Bertrand Dieudonné Emanuel Josué Vincent Luc Michel Jules-de-la-Plane Jules-Bazin Julio César Jullien.
10 Carse, 1951, p. 46.
11 Ibid., p. 47.
12 Ibid., p. 74.
13 Gammond lists six members of the Winterbottom family, including John (1817–1897), described as a well-known bassoon player who started his playing career with the Jullien orchestra, and William (1822–1889), a trombonist in the Life Guards, who became bandmaster of a number of military bands before returning to the Life Guards as bandmaster. He was a prolific arranger of band music and must surely be the one who toured the USA with Jullien.
14 Carse, 1951, p. 89 gives the following list of saxhorns: one each in high B♭ and high E♭, and two each in B♭, E♭ (tenor), B♭ (baritone) and E♭ (bass).
15 Carse, 1951, p. 93.
16 Ibid., p. 97.
17 Jules Rivière (1819–1900) was a French conductor who settled in England in 1857. He is discussed further in his role as an arranger/composer, in Chapter 7, p. 143.
18 Opened in 1893 and destroyed during an air raid in 1941.
19 The writer recalls playing under the baton of a band trainer called Noel Thorpe, who always sang his musical illustrations (no matter how quick) in Tonic Sol-fa.
20 Most so-called harmoniums in Britain were actually American organs.
21 Gammond, 1991, p. 35.
22 Weatherly wrote the lyrics to some 1500 songs, including those by Adams, as well as 'Danny boy' ('The Londonderry air') and 'Roses of Picardy' (Haydn Wood).
23 Russell, 1987, p. 12.
24 Ibid., p. 41.

2 Wind instruments and the growth of the amateur band

It is not within the scope of this book to give a detailed account of the development of band instruments as there are already several books which do this more than adequately.[1] It will, however, be useful as a prelude to the consideration of music played by bands later in the nineteenth century, to examine the major changes which they underwent during its middle years.

The treble melody instruments

In the early years of the century the flute and the clarinet were the chief melody instruments in bands. Because of its incisive tone the clarinet dominated, and in some bands – despite the shift to all brass – it held its place throughout the century. The quaint justification for its inclusion was that, despite being a reed instrument, models used in amateur bands were generally made of brass. The first challenge to the clarinet's position came with the keyed bugle (sometimes called the Kent bugle). The keyed trumpet had been in use on the continent for some years (Haydn's *Trumpet Concerto* was written for such an instrument) but the keyed bugle was more successful and had many good exponents, some of whom were reluctant to concede that the later cornet was a superior instrument.[2] The keyed bugle was a huge step forward for the brass family because it was able to play all the notes of the chromatic scale rather than simply those of the harmonic series, as was the case with the early trumpet. Crooks could be used to lengthen the trumpet's tube and lower its harmonic series (see the Glossary), but at no one time were more than half a dozen or so notes available on the 'natural' trumpet, and though used by many early bands, it played no lasting role. The slide trumpet had a wider range of notes but was difficult to play, and it is unlikely that many (if any) amateur bandsmen would be able to handle it with any degree of competence.

The keyed bugle player produced notes in between those of the harmonic series by controlling keys which opened and closed holes at certain points on the instrument. The advantage of this was, to some extent, counteracted by the resultant tonal weaknesses and intonation problems. What was needed was a mechanism which would instantaneously add to or subtract from the length of tubing in order to change the pitch of the harmonic series. This mechanism emerged in the shape of the valve, invented around 1814 and incorporated initially in the design of horns and trumpets. When depressed, the valve directs air through the instrument via a different route, changing the distance it has to travel and therefore, the series of notes playable. Various types of valve were tried, along with varying numbers, but from about 1832 the three-valve system became standard and, along with the Périnet valve, developed in 1839 by the Parisian instrument maker Etienne François Périnet, resulted in the production of a range of instruments not vastly different from those in use today. The valve was to revolutionize brass instruments, and was almost entirely responsible for the development of the all-brass band.

The most significant change in band instrumentation was the arrival of the cornet, which was to become the equivalent of the violin in the orchestra and the clarinet in the military band. It first appeared *circa* 1828. The bore was more conical than that of the trumpet and narrower than that of the keyed bugle, making its sound brighter than that of the latter but more mellow than that of the former. Technically it was very agile and this, coupled with its natural warmth and lyricism, made it attractive to many players, particularly in France and Britain. Developed from the posthorn, it was known in France as the '*cornet-à-pistons*' and in Britain, for a time, as the 'cornopean'. Early in its history it was produced in two versions – one pitched in D♭ and the other in A♭. During the 1850s and 1860s these were superseded by E♭ and B♭ instruments, the E♭ becoming the soprano cornet of the present-day brass band, and the B♭ becoming the principal melody instrument. Nine B♭ cornets are to be found in today's standard contesting band. The cornet is also used in the military band[3] and occasionally in the orchestra.[4]

During the 1840s the keyed bugle was gradually replaced by the cornet, though the bugle's characteristic colour lived on in the flugelhorn, its natural successor. But it was some time before the flugel came into regular use as a band instrument in this country and, as will be seen, it has had something of a chequered career.

Other instruments of early bands

In early bands, horns, like trumpets, were of the 'natural' type – that is, without valves, but players carried sets of crooks which enabled them to change the instrument's pitch. However, changing crooks took time, and could rarely be done during the short pieces which bands played. The modern French horn, with its system of rotary valves, has become indispensable both in the orchestra and the military band, but it survived for only a short time in the amateur brass band. Because of the length of its tubing it requires a different lip technique from other brass instruments, and was seldom used in amateur bands after 1860, by which time it was being superseded by the tenor saxhorn (see page 81–82).

The trombone, which originated in the fifteenth century, has been a regular member of amateur bands almost from their beginnings. From the mid-1840s many bands made use of the valve trombone, on which valves replaced the slide. Working on the same principle as other valved instruments, this could be played by any competent valve-instrumentalist.[5] However, it was tonally inferior to the slide trombone and was unable to keep pace with later developments. The alto trombone was used in some early bands, but alongside the G bass trombone was found to be lacking in power, and so two tenors and one bass became standard.

One of the most important developments of the 1840s and 1850s was the introduction of lower brasses. The euphonium, first appearing in about 1843, made by the German instrument maker Sommer, was to succeed the ophicleide. In Germany it was known as the euphon*on* but in Britain it appears always to have been called the euphon*ium*. Alfred James Phasey, the ophicleide soloist of the Coldstream Guards and one-time professor at Kneller Hall, was a key figure in its development in England (see note 16, page 6). In 1848 he began playing a valve instrument of the sax bass type but suggested certain improvements, including widening the bore. As a result of these improvements, one biographer claimed that Phasey 'was practically the inventor of the euphonium', even suggesting that the instrument should be called the 'Phaseyaphone'.[6] In fact, a similar instrument had been available for about five years. Further, Phasey's model was pitched in C and quickly gave way to one pitched in B♭. This is the euphonium in common use today, and which is often referred to as 'the cello of the band'.

The term 'bombardon' was first applied to a Viennese-made 12-keyed ophicleide, but was then adopted by the Prussian instrument maker Carl Wilhelm Moritz for some of his tubas. It became traditional to refer to the instrument as a tuba in the orchestra, but as a bombardon in the band.[7] However, despite this instrument's qualities and availability, the ophicleide – which had been in general use in bands since about 1840 – remained the most common bass instrument for several more years. When eventually the bombardon became more widely accepted, the ophicleide remained in many bands as a tenor instrument, supplementing or even displacing the bass saxhorn which, after 1850, gave way to the euphonium. Bombardons were pitched in E♭, a fifth lower than the euphonium or bass saxhorn, exactly as is the modern E♭ bass. Cerveny of Bohemia is generally credited with having first invented the larger contrabass – in both BB♭ and CC – around 1845. It arrived in England during the early 1850s, but it was several years before it found its way into amateur bands.

The circular bass – convenient for marching – originated in Russia, appeared in Vienna in 1849 and in England two years later. Its German name was 'helicon' and, conveniently, it had the same valve scheme as the bombardon. However, possibly due to its higher cost it did not survive for long in brass bands.[8] (Another possible reason for its non-acceptance is pointed out by Algernon Rose, who suggests that they 'were difficult to stow away in railway carriages'!)[9]

Saxhorns, the work of Adolphe Sax (1814–1894), brought about the most important development in brass instruments after the arrival of the cornet. There was a large range of sizes, the more commonly-used ones being the soprano in E♭ (superseded by the soprano cornet), the (contr)alto in B♭, with the same range as, but less successful than, the cornet, the E♭ tenor saxhorn, which became known simply as the tenor horn, and baritone and bass saxhorns in B♭. The latter was superseded by the euphonium, whilst the smaller bore B♭ baritone saxhorn became known simply as the 'baritone' – the name it still holds – to the bewilderment of non-band people, who invariably ask 'baritone what?' Saxhorns used the same valve system as the cornet.

Adolphe Sax and the Distins

Adolphe Sax was born on 6 November 1814. The son of Charles, a successful musical instrument maker, he was the first of 11 children, and within a year or so the family moved from the small Belgian town of Dinant to Brussels, where Charles set up a business, making mainly serpents and flutes.[10] At the age of 14 Adolphe Sax became a music student, concentrating on singing and playing the flute. Later he took up the clarinet, and it was through this that he came to join his father in the workshop, carrying out several improvements to this instrument. He also worked on the bass clarinet, but his most important projects, begun *circa* 1840, were his development of the instruments which became known as saxhorns and saxophones. In 1839 he spent some time in Paris where he encountered many famous musicians, including Berlioz and Meyerbeer, but he was compelled to return home to share in the family grief as no less than eight of his brothers and sisters died. He had tasted life in Paris, however, and in 1842 moved there permanently.[11]

Several factors affected his decision to live in Paris, one of the most important being a visit he received from Lieutenant-General Compte de Rumigny, an influential French military officer. Concern was being expressed in Paris that, due to the work of the instrument maker Wilhelm Wieprecht, German instruments and German military bands had become superior to their

French counterparts. De Rumigny encouraged Sax to move to Paris, in order to help raise the standard and reputation of French military bands.

Having moved, Sax patented his new instruments in 1843, but faced years of acrimony from his competitors for naming and patenting them as *sax*horns. They claimed he had not actually invented a new instrument, but had simply improved existing ones. In fact, it seems it was not Sax who first used the term, but some over-enthusiastic friends.[12] Nevertheless, the saxhorn proved to be such an improvement on other valved instruments that it stayed, producing a dramatic effect on the course of music for brass – in particular on the development of the British brass band.

A year later (1844), a British touring musical family, the Distins, whilst visiting Paris, met Sax and adopted his instruments. The head of the family, John Distin, had first come into prominence as a soloist on the keyed bugle in the Grenadier Guards. His wife played the piano, each of the four sons followed in John's footsteps by playing a brass instrument, whilst their young sister was a singer. The first appearance of the family brass quintet was in the Adelphi Theatre, Edinburgh in 1837.[13] John played a slide-trumpet and the sons (aged between 12 and 19) played, respectively, three horns and a trombone. After several British tours the family crossed the Channel and toured in Europe, but they did not impress their audiences there as they had done in Britain. By now their instrumentation consisted of a slide-trumpet, a cornet, a keyed bugle, a French horn and a slide trombone[14] – a somewhat odd assortment of instruments. Fortunately for them they heard Sax playing in a concert, and visited him in his workshop. He not only provided them with a matched set of instruments, but also gave them tuition, enabling them to play to a higher standard.

This, at least, is the account given by Oscar Comettant, Sax's biographer. Henry Distin, writing of the event some years later,[15] suggests that it was Sax who owed a debt of gratitude to the Distins, as it was they who promoted the use of his instruments. The argument is taken even further in an article in *Music Review* (Vol. 6), which discusses the conflicting reports; the Distins even claimed to have rescued Sax from failure by their skilful playing of his horns, whilst Sax insisted that he had saved the Distins' fortune by providing them with better instruments. Whatever the truth of the matter, the saxhorns were an improvement on earlier instruments, capable of better intonation, with a better overall sound quality, and able to blend more satisfactorily with other members of their family.

In 1846 Meyerbeer heard the Distins performing on their new quintet of saxhorns. He was apparently quite moved by their performance and wrote to them, praising 'the noble style of their delivery and their ensemble'.[16] The new instruments were a huge success, and there can be little doubt that the rapid rise in the popularity of the saxhorn was due largely to the later tours by the Distins.

28 *Brass Roots*

Saxhorns first appeared in England during October 1844, when they were played by an ensemble which included Sax himself. On this occasion they were not a success, but they fared better when played by the Distins in a Jullien Promenade Concert two months later, though Jullien's manager refused to allow the use of the name 'saxhorn' because of their earlier failure.[17]

J F Russell points to the year 1845 as 'the approximate beginning of the extraordinarily marked increase in amateur brass bands', noting that 'it was amongst the new bands that the sax instruments were largely found'.[18] A glance at the instruments played at Burton Constable in 1845 (below) indicates how rapidly they were accepted. Superior to other brass instruments available at the time, their effectiveness was confirmed in 1853 when, playing a brand new set of saxhorns, bought from Henry Distin and all with upright bells, Mossley Temperance Band took first prize in the first Belle Vue brass band contest.[19] This was, indeed, the signal for the mass change to all-brass bands, some being newly-formed but many converting from other types of band.

By 1850 Henry Distin was the agent for Sax, but later he began making his own instruments, dropping the name 'sax' and using the term 'tuba'. This led, not surprisingly, to a rift between Sax and Distin, resulting in the appointment of Rudall, Rose and Carte as agents for Sax. In 1868 Distin sold out to Boosey & Co and moved to Philadelphia.

Though the bands of 1860 may not have appeared very much like the bands of today, the above indicates that virtually all present-day instruments were available, albeit in less sophisticated models. Developments in scoring and publishing over the next decade were to marshal these instruments into an ensemble much more closely resembling the modern brass band. These developments will be considered in detail on pages 79–83.

The Burton Constable contest

Undoubtedly the most significant event in band history in the 1840s was a band contest, held as part of a fete taking place at Burton Constable, an estate near Hull – and home of Sir Clifford Constable. There is a full and vivid account of it in *The Brass Band Movement*, with further detail in *Bands*.[20] Instrumentation and music played were as follows:

1. Lord Yarborough's Brocklesby Yeomanry Band (leader: J B Acey)
    4 cornopeans, 2 sax tenors, 3 trombones, 1 sax bass and 2 ophicleides
    Test piece: *A selection of Sir Henry Bishop's Works*
2. Holmes Hull Tannery Brass Band (leader not named)
    1 sax *cornet-à-pistons*, 3 cornopeans, 2 sax tenors, 3 trombones, 1 sax bass and 2 ophicleides
    Test piece: Mozart's *12th Mass*

3. Hull Flax and Cotton Mills Band (leader: James Bean)
    1 sax *cornet-à-pistons* (no further details of instrumentation)
    Test piece: 'Hail, smiling morn'
4. Wold Brass (leader: James Walker – a composite band from Malton and Driffield)
    1 D♭ soprano cornet, 1 sax *cornet-à-pistons*, 2 cornopeans, 2 valved French horns, 3 trombones, 1 ophicleide, 1 valved bass[21] and 1 valved tuba
    Test piece: Extracts from *The Barber of Seville*
5. Patrington Band (leader: James Dalton)
    3 cornopeans, 1 trumpet, 2 trombones, 1 ophicleide and 3 serpents
    Test piece: *A Pot-Pourri of Country Airs*

(Bean, playing *cornet-à-pistons* and Walker, on D♭ soprano cornet were probably the musicians referred to on page 5).

The rules of the contest decreed a maximum of 12 players per band, with no percussion allowed. In the event the adjudicator – a local organist, Richard Hall – could not differentiate between band number two and band number four. Both were recalled to the platform, Holmes Tannery to play a secular piece and Wold Brass a sacred piece. The Hull group played music from Weber's *Der Freischütz* but Wold Brass won the day with its performance of Handel's 'Hallelujah Chorus'.

The trumpet used by Patrington would doubtless be of the 'natural' type, but though early French horns were also usually 'natural', the two used by Wold Brass were early examples of the valved French horn, found in a few early brass bands.[22] Sax tenors and sax basses were evidently already in vogue at the time of the Burton Constable contest, though serpents were still present (Patrington using three). The ophicleide had, however, become the main bass instrument for the time being. The use of the word tuba for the bass instrument in the Wold Brass Band is unusual.

The Burton Constable competition was an indication of the growing popularity of bands by the early 1840s. The reasons were two-fold: there had been great improvements in the manufacture of brass instruments, and with the arrival of the 3-valve system they were undoubtedly easier to learn to play.

Enderby Jackson (1827–1903)

Present at the Burton Constable contest was a young man who was to become one of the first important figures in British brass band history. Enderby Jackson was born in Hull, son of a tallow-candle maker. Amongst the customers of the family business was the Hull Theatre Royal, where the footlights consisted of three long rows of candles. Jackson was educated at Hull Grammar School, but studied music privately with local teachers, learning to play French horn, trumpet, piano and flute, as well as studying harmony and composition. He became a regular visitor to the Theatre, later recalled seeing the great violinist Paganini, and vividly remembered seeing and hearing Jullien and his orchestra. It is not recorded which music he heard played, but he was particularly impressed by some of the members of the orchestra – 'Vivier, with his full chords on the French horn; M Prospère, unrivalled on the ophicleide; with magnificent players always on the trombones . . .'[23] Both Paganini and Jullien had profound effects on Jackson. Hearing Paganini fostered his ambition to become a professional musician himself, but at the Jullien concerts he was struck by the effect which the music and the orchestra had on the audience, creating in him a desire to bring music to the people – precisely what Jullien himself was doing.

To the disgust of his father Jackson eventually turned his back on the candle-making business, deciding to earn a living through music. He went on tour with an opera company but kept himself busy in his spare time arranging and composing for bands. In the towns he visited he made contact with local musicians, giving them copies of his music in the pursuit of his ambition – 'the Propagation of Music amongst the Working Classes'.[24]

At the age of nine Jackson had played trumpet in a band formed in Hull in 1836, but nine years later was playing flute in the quadrille band engaged to entertain the guests at Burton Constable. Here he witnessed the band contest already described and, like the Jullien concerts several years earlier, it had a deep effect on him; in later years he was to organize many band contests himself, providing the stimulus for the improvement of playing standards. During the late 1850s and early 1860s Jackson was to become a dominant figure in the growth of the brass band.

The 1850s

According to Herbert, most of the developments which 'generated a brass band movement' took place during the 1850s,[25] as works bands developed alongside subscription bands. Stalybridge and Besses were well-known examples of subscription bands and Black Dyke Mills Band stood at the head of the list of works-sponsored bands. Black Dyke's original benefactor, John Foster, owned the mills, located in the village of Queenshead (later named Queensbury), situated between Bradford and Halifax. Foster himself was an amateur French horn player and had played in Wharton's reed band in Queenshead (see page 3). When, in 1855, a band in the village was fighting for survival, he took it over, appointing James Galloway as bandmaster and leader, providing rehearsal facilities and jobs for each member of the band. In *Brass Band News* of 1 May 1899 there is a report of a concert by Black Dyke, which also incorporates several historical details, including the fact that 'In 1855 Messrs Foster joined the band to the works, found each member employment, bore the expense of new instruments and uniforms, found a first-class tutor in the person of Mr Samuel Longbottom, of Mixenden, and so put the band well on the way to success.' According to the *Halifax Courier* of 15 September 1855 this band, formed in 1833 as a brass and reed band, and known as the Queenshead Band, had already become all brass before Foster took it over.

Another band supported by a wealthy industrialist was based in South Wales. This was the Cyfarthfa Band, founded in 1838 by Robert Crawshay, master of an ironworks in Merthyr Tydfyl. Again the necessities for survival were provided, including jobs for the bandsmen – an attraction to high quality players and an inducement to young brass players to practice hard in order to achieve a standard that would ensure a job and a position in a works band.

Saltaire Band – like Black Dyke located just outside Bradford – also had considerable financial help, being founded in 1855 and sponsored by the industrialist Titus Salt. It is significant that these three bands took the top places at the first Crystal Palace brass band contest in 1860 (the order being 1st Black Dyke, 2nd Saltaire and 3rd Cyfarthfa).

The idea for a major band contest seems to have been first floated as early as 1851, when three band enthusiasts met, probably by chance, at the Great Industrial Exhibition at the Crystal Palace. They were Enderby Jackson, James A Melling (conductor of a number of bands in the Manchester area) and Tallis Trimnell,[26] an organist and band conductor from Chesterfield. All would be there to view the display of the latest brass instruments. They discussed the progress of amateur bands and laid plans for the 1853 Belle Vue contest, held annually to this day, except for the year 1859 when only three bands entered and the contest was cancelled. After the demise of Belle Vue itself in 1981 the contest, now known as the British Open Brass Band Championship, was held in Manchester's Free Trade Hall until 1996.

Contests from 1853

During the 1850s the development of the railways improved the mobility of bands and their supporters, and railway companies were sometimes persuaded to let bands travel cheaply – even free – to contests. Thus, in 1853 bands were able to travel quite easily to Belle Vue, Manchester, for the first of its brass band contests. The railway companies were well compensated by many of the 16 000 spectators who travelled to hear the eight bands play.[27] The three-year-old Mossley Temperance Saxhorn Band, playing on its new saxhorns, won first prize and added weight to the argument that these were the brass band instruments of the future. The full set of saxhorns played by Mossley was the first known such set to be played in England, and contributed significantly to the spread of the all-brass band.

The rules for the contest decreed that two own choice items must be played by each band and that professional musicians were not allowed to participate, except as conductors. A ballot was held to determine the order in which the bands should play. There were three adjudicators – John Ellwood, John Oakden and a Mr Dowlingate, screened from the bands, all of which combined at the conclusion of the contest in a performance of 'God Save the Queen'. The contest was a tremendous success, despite a number of hiccups such as the late arrival of some trains. The winners, Mossley, arrived too late to play in the order in which they were drawn, but were allowed to play later. Of the Mossley win Clifford Bevan says 'There is little doubt that it won on sheer quality of sound: a matched blend contrasting favourably with the various timbres of keyed bugle, French horn, trumpet and ophicleide common in bands of the time.'[28]

Dewsbury Band won second prize in the contest. Its history dates back at least to 1824, though the 1853 band was apparently an amalgamation of Batley and Dewsbury bands, and comprised three keyed bugles, two cornopeans, three trombones and three ophicleides. Mossley soon slipped out of the limelight, appearing only twice more in the prize lists before disappearing. Though they pioneered the saxhorn as a band instrument, the models they used were quickly improved upon. Their instruments were pitched in A♭ and D♭, but within about a decade it had become statutory to use instruments pitched in B♭ and E♭. Thus, Mossley's success led to its downfall, as it was unable to buy the newer instruments necessary to keep up with developments. Chiefly owing to lack of support from the townspeople, the original Mossley Temperance Band was disbanded in 1868.[29]

Meanwhile, the Belle Vue September contest continued, but with mixed fortunes. The 1854 contest attracted an entry of 14 and an audience of 20 000,[30] and in the following year 15 bands attended. Then came a decline – seven bands in 1856, five in 1857, a slight upturn to eight a year later, but then a low point in 1859, when the contest was cancelled because there were but three entries. A possible explanation for this temporary decline is the growing number of alternative contests. Fortunately the Belle Vue authorities persevered, and the contest became firmly established from 1860 onwards. From 1855 to 1857 the musical requirements were one set test piece and one selection of the bands' own choice. In 1855 the set test was an original overture by James Melling, *Orynthia*, probably the first original test piece. Unfortunately, no known copy exists.

In 1856 and 1857 the set tests were the overture *Stradella* (1844 – Flotow) and a selection from Verdi's *Il Trovatore* (the opera then a mere four years old). 1858 saw a change from opera to oratorio, bands playing two extracts from Haydn's *The Creation* (the trio 'On Thee Each Living Soul Awaits' and the final chorus from Part II of the oratorio, 'Achieved is the Glorious Work'). All were individually scored for the bands by their leaders, because there was still no standard instrumentation, and little published music.

At the 1853 Belle Vue contest the size of band varied from 10 to 18 and in the following year the sizes were about the same. 1855 saw the start of the increase in the average size of bands. Though they still carried between 10 and 18 players, 11 had 16 or more. In the same year the first National Brass Band Contest took place in the Royal Gardens, Leeds. Fourteen bands played and though some were as small as 12, two bands had 16 players, one had 17, two had 18 and one had 20.[31] This contest was held on Whit Monday and Tuesday, 28 and 29 May, as part of the Leeds Temperance Society's Gala, and was the first brass band contest to be called 'National'.

It is not clear just how much Enderby Jackson influenced the early Belle Vue contests. Although not present at the first one, he always maintained that many of the ideas incorporated were his, particularly with regard to obtaining concessions from the railway companies. In his unpublished autobiography he wrote, 'Mr Jennison of Belle Vue Gardens, Manchester, listened to some of his band [the players in his own professional band, presumably], and seized my plan. I now knew the anguish of the inventor who sees his schemes falling into the hands of others.'[32]

Hull 1856

Over the next few years Jackson was the driving force behind many other contests, such as a series which began in his own city of Hull in 1856. The first of these took place in the Zoological Gardens and, like the Belle Vue event of 1853, was a huge success. Jackson had persuaded the railways to offer special reduced fares, with the result that an estimated 14 000 people attended. He maintained that several bands which took part in the contest were specially formed for the event. Of the 21 which had entered, only 12 actually played – each made up of between 12 and 17 players. According to Nield,[33] Black Dyke had 16 players in 1856 for the Hull contest. He lists the instruments as D♭ clarinet, A♭ cornet, A♭ alto tuba (predecessor of the flugelhorn), E♭ and D♭ tenor horns, trumpet, tenor and bass trombones, ophicleide and drums. Nield does not specify the number of players per part, but it would be reasonable to assume that the extra players performed on cornet, alto tuba and ophicleide.

Jackson himself composed the test piece, 'The Yorkshire Waltzes' (to be discussed on page 74). Each band was required to play this, along with another piece of its own choice. A pianoforte arrangement of the waltzes was published in London by J H Jewell,[34] and Jackson visited many towns to explain the music to local teachers, encouraging them to arrange it for their bands. There was a total of 18 guineas in prize money; that would probably have bought two good cornets, which today could cost anything up to £2000. The six adjudicators,[35] a mixture of local musical dignitaries and military bandmasters, declared the following result:

1st	Smith's (Leeds)	Richard Smith
2nd	Black Dyke	Samuel Longbottom
3rd	Batley	(conductor not named)

In addition to the set test piece at the Hull contest, the winners played a 'grand' selection from Verdi's *Attila*. Black Dyke played a selection from *Giulietta e Romeo* by Vaccaj,[36] whilst Batley played 'The Heavens are Telling' from Haydn's *The Creation*. Other pieces played included extracts from *Ernani* (Verdi, 1843), *Nebuchodonosor* [sic] (Verdi, 1841), *Lucia di Lammermoor* (Donizetti, 1835), *Il Pirata* (Bellini, 1827) and the Introduction and Grand March from *La Prophete* [sic] (Meyerbeer, 1849). A *Mass* by Paxton was probably an arrangement of music by Stephen Paxton (1735–1787), an English composer of glees, catches and masses.

Interestingly, three of the bands played pieces which had been composed, rather than arranged, no doubt attempting to emulate Melling's *Orynthia*. One of these, simply listed as 'MS' (manuscript) was by William Hesling, conductor of Buslingthorpe Band. According to the *Leeds Intelligence* of 5 July 1956, however, this piece, by a 'weaver-composer', 'contained many plagiarisms'.[37] There was also an overture, *The Swiss Family* by Wegel and an *Introduction and Polacca* by W Perry.

Richard Smith was undoubtedly the leading brass band trainer of the time, and probably the first of the breed of specialist brass band conductors. He conducted several bands, including three in Leeds. An unplaced Leeds Joppa Band was conducted by him in the 1856 Hull contest, whilst across the Pennines at Belle Vue he had a successful run with both Leeds (Smith's) and the Leeds Railway Foundry Band. With the latter he won first prizes in 1854 and 1855, whilst his Leeds (Smith's) Band were runners up in 1856 and winners in 1857, giving Smith himself the distinction of two top places in 1856 and three wins in four years. He both conducted and played solo cornet, and as conductor of the winning band at Belle Vue in 1854, won the special prize of a new bombardon, presented by a Manchester instrument maker. Smith also wrote brass band music and founded one of the first brass band publishing houses, in 1857 in Hull – the *Champion Brass Band Journal*. He is discussed in detail on pages 108–109).

At other contests organized by Jackson two more of his own compositions appeared. The first, called 'Londesborough Galop', was composed for the second Hull contest of 1857,[38] and a year later he wrote his 'Venetian Waltz' for a contest in Sheffield. Writing of this contest, the *Sheffield Independent* expressed the view that the bands exhibited 'a good deal of skill and proficiency, but that the "Venetian Waltz" was really a difficult piece of music'.[39] Neither of these seem to have survived.

Jackson busied himself with many more contests during 1857–1859 and in addition to those already mentioned he organized events in Lincoln, Bristol, Grantham, Peterborough, Hampton [Northampton?], Leicester, Birmingham, Liverpool, Doncaster, Boston, Darlington, Ipswich, Norwich and Leeds.[40] Several of these were actually set up as contests but others would, more than likely, be part of some other event, in the same way that the 1845 Burton Constable contest had been. Thus, Jackson continued his travels, stimulating the formation of amateur bands, offering new music and the opportunity for bandsmen to visit other towns to attend contests, with the chance of winning cups, presentation batons and new instruments.

The brass band movement was growing, as was the number of contests. Funding obviously varied, and from 1859 a new branch of the brass band movement emerged, with the formation of the Volunteers, through which many bands became, in effect, part-time military bands, though generally retaining their all-brass status. They became attached to military units, receiving financial help as well as the provision of rehearsal facilities and uniforms.

This, then, was the position of brass bands prior to 1860. The number of bands was on the increase but there was still no standardized instrumentation; a certain amount of published music was available but the majority of bands relied on their leader to provide band parts. Bands were now known by their own name, or that of their sponsor, rather than by the name of their leader, as formerly. Though appearances at local functions were still important, contesting seems to have become the prime *raison d'être* for many bands, providing opportunities for travel, meeting other bandsmen, and measuring their own progress against that of rivals. 1860 was to be an important year, as that was the date of the first brass band contest to be held in London. In the years that followed the brass band movement grew rapidly, building on foundations laid during the first half of the century.

Notes

1 See, for example, Baines, 1976, and Bevan, 1978.
2 For an account of a competition between Ned Kendall on keyed bugle and Patrick Gilmore on cornet, in what might be described as 'The last stand of the keyed bugle', see Schwarz, 1957, pp. 31–36.
3 The term 'military band' is used here in its literal sense. Until comparatively recently it implied a mixed group of woodwind and brass – whether attached to the military or not. Civilian forms of this type of combination are nowadays generally referred to either as wind bands or concert bands. Many of them use the trumpet rather than the cornet, although some larger bands use both. The standard British military band still, happily, favours the cornet.

4 In the orchestra, the cornet was first called for by Rossini in the opera *William Tell* (1829), and later by Berlioz in a number of works, notably in the *Symphonie Fantastique* (1830).
5 The valve trombone found itself in the middle of a storm at the Belle Vue September Contest of 1873. Black Dyke's euphonium soloist, Phineas Bower, after playing the euphonium solo in the test piece (Meyerbeer's *Dinorah*), put the instrument down, picked up the valve trombone and proceeded to play the trombone solo. According to a letter from Arthur O Pearce (Black Dyke's Bandmaster from 1912 to 1948), to *Brass Band News* of 1 November 1931, players were checked as they mounted the platform to ensure that each had one instrument only. Bower, in fact, had 'smuggled' a soprano cornet onto the platform inside his coat, carrying his euphonium in the normal manner. Pearce stated that the soprano player took the valve trombone onto the platform and then switched instruments. Immediately it was announced that Black Dyke had won the special prizes for both solos (the prizes were actual instruments), a member of the band collected them on Bower's behalf. However, an objection was lodged and upheld, and Bower requested to return the trombone. Dour Yorkshireman that he was he refused, and ultimately the dealer presented another instrument to the legitimate winner – the trombone soloist of Meltham.
6 Brown and Stratton, 1897, p. 318.
7 Scott, 1970, p. 67.
8 Ibid., pp. 75–76. The ophicleide player of Black Dyke was presented with a Distin circular bass in E♭ when the band won first prize at the 1860 Crystal Palace contest. (*The Times*, 11 July 1860.)
9 *Talks With Bandsmen*, p. 244.
10 Much of the information about Sax is taken from Horwood's *Adolphe Sax 1814–1894, his life and legacy*.
11 Horwood, 1980, p. 23.
12 Ibid., p. 29.
13 According to *British Bandsman* of March 1889, the players were engaged for a one-night stand, but were so successful that they were booked for six weeks.
14 Horwood, 1980, p. 50.
15 See Enderby Jackson, 'Origin and Promotion of Brass Band Contests', in *Musical Opinion* of July, 1896, pp. 673–675.
16 Horwood, 1980, p. 51.
17 Ibid., p. 52 and Carse 1951, p. 52.
18 Russell and Elliott, 1936, p. 56.
19 Ibid., p. 102.
20 Russell and Elliott, 1936, pp. 79–86 and Herbert, 1991, pp. 103–104.
21 Probably a sax bass, similar to the euphonium.
22 Russell and Elliott, 1936, p. 84.
23 Ibid., p. 90.
24 Autobiography, typescript, p. 2.
25 Herbert, 1991, p. 23.
26 Thomas Tallis Trimnell, BMus (Oxon) – Herbert, 1991, pp. 21 and 119 (note 17).
27 Taylor, 1979, p. 39.
28 Article by Bevan in Herbert, 1991, p. 105.
29 Russell and Elliott, 1936, footnote, p. 127.
30 Herbert, 1991, p. 105.
31 *Leeds Times*, 26 May and 2 June 1855, quoted in Scott, 1970, p. 140.

32 *Autobiography*, typescript, p. 3.
33 *Black Dyke Mills Band*, quoted in Scott, 1970, p. 141.
34 See Herbert, 1991, p. 43 for a copy of the front cover.
35 Advertising material in the Ainscoe Collection lists the adjudicators for the 1856 Hull contest as 'Mr Deval, RA Mus, Member of the Royal Conservatoire, Brussels, and Conductor of the Hull Subscription Musical Society, Mr T Hopkinson, Conductor of the Hull Harmonic Society, Mr E Short, Leader of the Operatic and Dramatic Season, Royal Queen's Theatre, Hull, Mr J Brown, Band Master to the Right Honourable Lord Londesborough and Mr J Oakden, late Band Master of the First or Royal Dragoons'. Mr R Bowser, of Hull, was described as the 'Final Referee'.
36 This is the spelling shown in the contest publicity in the Ainscoe Collection. In fact it must be Nicola Vaccai (1790–1848), an Italian composer of opera and sacred music.
37 Quoted in Russell, 1987, p. 260. Hesling must be the one named in *A Short History of Bramley Band*, 1906, as a trumpet player in Bramley Reed Band at the time of the coronation of William IV in 1831.
38 Russell and Elliott, 1936, p. 106.
39 Ibid., p. 107.
40 *Autobiography*, typescript, p. 4.

3 Contests from 1860; the 'Great Triumvirate'; J H Iles

Early Crystal Palace contests

1860, the year of the first Crystal Palace contest, was a major landmark in the history of brass bands. It may also be seen as a turning point in the development of instrumentation, with the start of significant moves towards the format of the modern brass band. Keyed bugles, trumpets and French horns had almost disappeared and in their place were cornets and saxhorns. Ophicleides were still in use, as was the brass clarinet, and three trombones were to be found in many of the larger bands.

The first series of Crystal Palace contests, organized by Enderby Jackson (see pages 29–30), ran for only four years – from 1860 to 1863. The first contest took place on Tuesday and Wednesday, 10 and 11 July 1860. It was an even more spectacular success than the first Belle Vue event of 1853, attracting an estimated crowd of some 29 000 over two days. Day one was set aside for leading bands and day two for the remainder. Apart from those gaining firstt or second prizes on the first day, bands were free to enter on both days and some did – Cyfarthfa gaining third prize on the first day and winning on the second.

Entries totalled 72 and 98 respectively for the two days, though in fact there was a total appearance of only 70 different bands, some playing on both days and others which had entered, finding themselves unable to attend. This was not unusual, as bands often faced such problems as illness, a test piece which proved too difficult, or the inability to raise sufficient funds to cover the cost of travel. It was also likely that holding the contests on working days created problems for many bands.

Following each day's contest a massed band consisting of all the players assembled and played under the baton of Jackson himself.[1] Playing 'Rule Britannia', 'Hallelujah Chorus', Mendelssohn's 'Wedding March', 'The Heavens are Telling' and 'God Save the Queen', they drew the following comment from *The Times*: 'The effect of the combined legions of "blowers" (upwards of 1200 strong) was tremendous. The organ, which accompanied them, and which on less exceptional occasions is apt to drown everything, was scarcely audible in the midst of the brazen tempest.'[2] The spectacle must have been impressive, but the resultant sound does not bear thinking about!

On the first day six preliminary 'knock-out' contests were held, from which 12 bands were selected for the final play-off. The following is a list of prizewinners, together with names of conductors and of test pieces played in the Final:

1st	Black Dyke	Samuel Longbottom	'Gloria' from the *12th Mass* (Mozart)
2nd	Saltaire	Richard Smith	Selection: *Lucrezia Borgia* (Donizetti)
3rd	Cyfarthfa	Mr Livesey	Selection: *The Bondsman* (Balfe)
4th	Darlington	N Hoggatt	'Kyrie & Gloria' – *Mass No. 2* (Haydn)
5th	Dewsbury	J Peel	Selection: *Preciosa* (Weber)

Other test pieces played included selections from *Ernani, Il Trovatore, Nabucco* (Verdi) and *William Tell* (Rossini). The operatic selection was already well to the fore as an own choice test piece.

On the second day Cyfarthfa switched to *Nabucco* and Dewsbury to *Ernani*, picking up first and second prizes respectively, whilst Mr James Bagnall's Ironworks Band (Staffordshire), not in the first day finals, played a 'Scena and Polacca' by Perry,[3] taking third prize. Chesterfield, also unplaced on the first day, took fourth place with a selection from *Lucrezia Borgia*. Meltham Mills, a band which was to feature prominently in brass band history in later years, having gained fifth prize at Belle Vue in 1858, achieved a similar placing on the second day at Crystal Palace in 1860 playing the 'Hallelujah Chorus'. Full reports of the 1860 contest appeared in *The Times, Telegraph* and *Musical World*; all were substantial and largely complimentary. The *Daily Telegraph*, for example, began:

> The first 'Contest of Brass Bands' ever held in the south of England took place yesterday in the Crystal Palace. Unfamiliar as these contests are, even by name, to Londoners, such *concours* are held continually in the northern districts . . . It was a happy thought of the inventor of the scheme to increase the proficiency of the executants and heighten their interest in the most humanising and elevating of all pastimes, by fanning an *esprit de corps*, and sustaining it by the healthy excitement of emulation.

It was customary for bands to pay an entrance fee if they wished to attend a contest, and the rate during the late 1850s and early 1860s seems to have been half a guinea. In return, prizes were offered, and at the 1860 Crystal Palace contest five awards were made on each day, ranging from £40 for the winner on the first day to £5 each for the two fifth prizes; additionally, the winning conductor on both days received a silver cup. The winning band on the first day received a circular contrabass (helicon) valued at 35 guineas, whilst the winner on the second day was presented with 16 bound volumes of Boosey's *Brass Band Journal*, valued at 12 guineas.[4] Both were presented by Boosey and set a pattern for such awards at future events.

A letter from a Frank Gray which appeared in *Brass Band News* of April 1894 revealed some interesting information although, written 34 years after the event, there is doubt about the accuracy of some of the details. At the time of writing, Gray was bandmaster of the Border Rifles Band in Hawick, Scotland, but the letter referred to the second day of the 1860 contest, when he was the leader and conductor of Yeadon Old, one of the bands which participated.[5]

His claim that 40 bands played on the first day and 70 on the second is a fair approximation, but his statement that a pitch fork was given to every bandmaster to enable him to tune his band to the pitch of the great organ is probably three years out. An account in Russell and Elliott[6] gives as a possible reason for the low number of entries for the 1863 contest a rule stating that 'no band will be allowed to compete unless it is tuned to the pitch of the Crystal Palace organ.' Gray then goes on to say that a band of 2000 instrumentalists played at the conclusion of the contest, but this also must be regarded as a trick of memory. Russell and Elliott lists the instruments played by 1390 players (see note 1 at the end of this chapter), though the consensus in the press is that the total was about 1200. However, Gray claims that each band played an own choice selection plus a set of quadrilles composed by Jackson. This may well be true, though it is not mentioned in other contemporary reports (see further comments about this possibility on page 78).

Another interesting anecdote takes up a substantial part of the letter. As already stated, the contest took place on a Tuesday and a Wednesday; as many bands were expected to arrive in the capital on the Monday, Gray says that the Cremorne Gardens Company organized another band contest for that day. However, as Jackson had negotiated with the railway companies for free rail travel to and from London for competing bands, he decreed that any band playing in the Cremorne Gardens contest – or anywhere else on the streets of London for that matter – before the conclusion of the Crystal Palace contest, would be deemed to be abusing the privilege of free travel, would be disqualified from the contest, and would have to pay its own return fares.

Despite this, Bramley Old Band played at Cremorne Gardens. Gray believed they actually won, though he could not confirm this. Bramley then played in the Crystal Palace contest, with some success, since they were amongst the 12 finalists. True to his word, following the final play-off, Jackson announced that Bramley Band was disqualified as a result of having played in the rival contest, and that they were to 'clear off the ground as soon as possible'. According to Gray a lawsuit followed, which Bramley Band lost.

It is interesting to compare the account by Gray with the version in Hesling White's *Short History of the Bramley Band*, which refers to the contest on 10 July as follows:

> After signing articles we received our railway pass. The Cremorne Company sent out a circular for a Contest to be held at their Gardens on the 9th of July, thinking that, as the bands had travelled to London at the Palace Company's expense they would save all that. But the Crystal Palace Company sent out a second circular prohibiting bands going to play anywhere in London before their contest, on pain of losing their pass home. However, the Cremorne Company pressed on us, and sent us a pass, so we had a pass from each Company. They stated that they only wanted six bands, and offered prizes only £5 less than the Crystal Palace Company, for which there were more than fifty bands entered for the first day's contest, and more than 100 for the second day . . .[7]

It would seem that the Cremorne Gardens contest did not actually take place, but that Bramley Band played two pieces for a fee of £5, thereby breaking Jackson's rule. Their performance in the preliminary round of the Crystal Palace contest on the first day earned them a recommendation from adjudicator Charles Godfrey that they qualify for the finals, but according to Hesling White, the Manager of Crystal Palace, Mr Bowley, told them they were disqualified, and therefore they did not play in the finals. However, as a result of their appearance at Cremorne Gardens on the Monday, they were offered a further engagement on the Wednesday, with a fee equivalent in money terms to the second prize at Crystal Palace. This, along with the free rail pass home supplied by the Cremorne Gardens Company, made for a pleasant few days in the capital and, according to Hesling White, all the members of Bramley Band went home with presents for their families and a little money to spare.

A third of the adjudicators at the first Crystal Palace contest were distinguished military bandmasters, and included James Smyth (Royal Artillery), Dan Godfrey (Grenadier Guards), Charles Godfrey Jr (also Grenadier Guards), Charles Godfrey Sr (Coldstream Guards), Carl Boosé (Royal Horse Guards) and Haydn Millars (Rifle Brigade).

Amongst the other adjudicators (18 in total) were Henry Farmer, a composer from Nottingham (not to be confused with the military band historian), George Leng, conductor of the Harmonic Society in Jackson's home town of Hull, and a brother of Koenig, the famous cornet player. Adjudicators would have been chosen by Jackson, who seems to have had absolute power over the running of the contest.

Finance was managed by the Crystal Palace Company, with probably either an agreed fee or a percentage of the profits going to Jackson for his services. With an estimated audience of 7000 paying 2s.6d. each for admission on the first day, 22 000 paying one shilling each on the second,[8] and with 170 bands each paying an entrance fee, the income must have been in excess of £2000 over the two days – a considerable sum for that time.

The 1861 Crystal Palace contest was another two-day affair, taking place on Tuesday 23 and Thursday 25 July,[9] and was again highly successful. However, the euphoria created in 1860 seems not to have been repeated in the later events. Northern bands probably found travelling to London irksome when there was a perfectly good contest in Manchester. Not only that, in 1863, there was the inconvenience of having to tune to the pitch of the organ, already mentioned. (The implication here that there was no standard pitch amongst the reported 1390 players in 1860 beggars belief!) A mere 21 competitors performed in 1863, though 44 had actually entered, and following this Jackson organized no further Crystal Palace contests. Not until 1900 was London to become again a major centre for band contests.

Gradually Jackson lost his enthusiasm for bands and in 1871 sailed to Melbourne as agent to a small concert party,[10] also visiting several other places in Australia and New Zealand. He made contact with bands, but felt that in Australia the climate was not conducive to serious rehearsal and that in New Zealand there were insufficient bands even to contemplate contests.[11] In 1876 he went to America as agent for a musical instrument firm and also became involved with Patrick Gilmore's band's European tour. However, although Jackson had quit the British brass band scene for good, his influence lived on as contesting developed.

Test pieces at Belle Vue

The idea of both a set test piece and an own choice continued at Belle Vue until 1866 (with the exception of 1864 – see page 45), after which bands played only the set test. Between 1860 and 1899 the operatic selection was by far the most popular choice and during these years excerpts from 35 operas were heard. There was also the overture *Zampa* (Hérold – 1860), three composer selections – *Reminiscences of Auber* (1864), *Souvenir de Mozart* (1872) and a *Grand Fantasia from the works of Mendelssohn* (1898), and a selection from Spohr's oratorio, *The Last Judgement* (1879).

Eighteen composers were represented, ranging from Verdi (six selections – including the one set in 1857) and Meyerbeer (five selections) to lesser-known names such as Bemberg (1859–1931, excerpts from whose *Elaine* was played at Belle Vue in 1893) and Pizzi (1864–1940, whose *Gabrielli* was heard there in 1896). Many of the selections were quite contemporary; that from *Il Trovatore*, for example, being played at Belle Vue in 1857, only four years after the opera was first performed, while Meyerbeer's *L'Africaine* was heard in its brass band version a mere 17 months after its première in April, 1865. The Irish composer, Balfe, could have heard excerpts from his 1858 opera *Satanella* within three years of its debut, and his posthumously-produced opera *Il Talismano*, first performed in London in 1874, appeared at Belle Vue in selection form only a year later. A selection from Goring Thomas's *The Golden Web*, another 'posthumous' production, was the set test at Belle Vue in 1894 – just over a year after its first performance in Liverpool, whilst the selection from Engelbert Humperdinck's *Hänsel und Gretel* appeared in 1895, only two years after the first stage performance.

All the Verdi and Gounod selections were played during the lifetime of their composers, as were those based on works by Auber (*Muette di Portici* – 1862 and the '*Reminiscences*' – 1864). Both Meyerbeer and Rossini appeared in the lists within a few years of their deaths but the trend to look back further started in the 1870s, with music by Weber, Spohr, Mercadante, Donizetti and Lortzing. Mozart is the only composer from the Classical era to appear in the post-1860 list ('*Souvenir*' – 1872).

Whilst brass band conductors and leading players are reported to have attended performances of opera it is unlikely that regular opera-goers would, to any significant extent, have heard brass bands performing the selections. Audiences at band functions were made up almost entirely from the working classes and would consist of people the majority of whom would have neither the time, inclination, nor the money to go to the opera. Nevertheless, bands playing the selections brought some of the music of opera into the lives of working-class people and must have converted a few, at least, into opera-goers.

In the early days at Belle Vue, conductors arranged their own selections as the size and instrumentation of the bands was not standardized. Not until 1866 do the records show the name of an official arranger, the first cited simply as 'Grosse'. He was doubtless the Herr Grosse who played clarinet in the Hallé Orchestra and conducted the Droylsden Reed Band.[12] He arranged a selection from Meyerbeer's *L'Africaine* (see also pages 83–84). The first name to appear in a series of Belle Vue arrangements is that of William Winterbottom, the military bandmaster who may have played in Jullien's orchestra (see note 13, Chapter 1). He arranged at least four Belle Vue test pieces (selections from *Der Freischütz* – 1867, *Le Prophète* – 1869, *Ernani* – 1870 and *Il Barbiere* – 1871). James Waterson, another military bandmaster and for a time editor of *British Bandsman*, arranged Meyerbeer's *Robert the Devil* for the 1869 contest (see pages 84–85).

In 1872 and for the next 40 years Lieutenant Charles Godfrey of the Royal Horse Guards (see note 7, Chapter One for further information about the Godfreys) arranged all Belle Vue test pieces, including those for the July contests, introduced in 1886 for bands of a lower standard than that required for the September contest (see page 57). The logic of employing people like Winterbottom and Godfrey as arrangers was that, based in London and working regularly with leading military bands, they were well placed to keep abreast of modern developments and musical fashions. Through choice of music, and in their adjudications, they must have had a considerable influence on the course of band music and styles of playing.

But what about contesting from the point of view of the bands themselves? Histories of some older bands reveal much about the importance to the bands of contests, and though a significant venue, Belle Vue by no means had a monopoly; by the early 1890s there were well over 200 brass band contests held annually in England, Scotland and Wales.

Bacup Old Band

The *History of Bacup Old Band* (compiled by Isaac Leach) makes fascinating reading and paints a vivid picture of contesting and other aspects of banding in the 1860s and 1870s. Bacup is a small town in central Lancashire, some 15 miles north of Manchester and eight south of Burnley. Its first band was formed in 1858 as the Broadclough Band. This became the 4th Lancashire Rifle Volunteers (LRV) a year later, and enlisted the services of George Ellis of Blackburn as tutor. Ellis had, on leaving school, served an apprenticeship as a joiner, but had then become a member of Wombwell's band, touring with the famous menagerie.[13] Later he became the band's leader, but after some years as an itinerant musician settled in Blackburn, becoming tutor of the 4th LRV (Bacup) Band, as well as of several others. His connection with Bacup was a highly fruitful one; over the next few years it was to become one of the most successful of all bands, by 1870 claiming to be the champion band of the country, with 13 consecutive first prizes to its credit. The choice of Ellis as tutor proved to be an inspired one. He was apparently a versatile musician; in 1840 (probably prior to his involvement with Wombwell's) he had formed Blackburn Choral Society, and two years later was hired to train the newly-formed Accrington Band.[14]

Bacup's first contest was at Belle Vue in 1862, where it gained fourth prize, playing the set test *Muette de Portici* (Auber) and for its own choice, a selection from *Lurline* (Wallace). In the following June the band attended what was described as a 'mammoth contest' in Liverpool, with 32 bands – split into four groups – the first two from each going into the final play-off (the same system as that used at Crystal Palace). Bacup qualified but did not secure a prize. Later in 1863 Bacup made its second appearance at Belle Vue, playing a selection from Gounod's *Faust*, and as its own choice, one from Macfarren's *Robin Hood*. Black Dyke and Bacup were recalled to the platform for a play-off, the former having come top in the own choice and the latter top in the set test. The final judgement went to Black Dyke, though the players at Bacup felt hard done by, having come top in the set test piece part of the contest – generally regarded as the more important element. Nevertheless, this was a remarkable achievement for a band not yet five years old.

In 1864 Bacup attended two contests, one at Skipton – part of the Craven Agricultural Show, and the other at Belle Vue. Black Dyke were the winners at Skipton, playing selections from *Semiramide* (Rossini) and *Die Zauberflöte* (Mozart). Bacup earned second place playing *Robin Hood* and *Faust* – indicating that at this contest the requirement was two own-choice pieces. A few days later, however, the Bacup band achieved the first of its four Belle Vue wins. Fourteen bands took part – a larger entry than usual – and the own choice test was dispensed with, all bands simply playing *Reminiscences of Auber*. The *History of the Bacup Old Band* claims that the cornet cadenza 'was the most difficult ever sent out' but that their solo cornet player, John Lord 'came off finely'.[15]

Local support for the band had by now reached boiling point. Two special trains took over 1000 supporters from Bacup itself to Belle Vue,[16] plus an equal number from neighbouring villages. When the band returned, victorious, some time after midnight, it seemed that the whole population of the town was waiting to greet it. Marching triumphantly from the station to its headquarters, it played 'John Brown's Body' and, not surprisingly, 'See, the conquering hero comes'.

The band continued its winning way in 1865, appearing at six contests and crowning the year with its second Belle Vue win, playing selections from *Un ballo in Maschera* (Verdi) as the set piece and *Semiramide* for its own choice. During this period stability was an important feature of the band, with only four changes in personnel over a period of several years. There was also a family connection, common to this day in many brass bands. At Bacup, eight members of the Lord family were connected with the band. One of the elders of this family was also a local choirmaster, and his son, John, won renown as the band's leader.

What is described as 'a dark page in the history of the band' occurred in 1866 when Richard Lord, a tenor horn player, was taken ill a few days before the Belle Vue contest, with the band attempting to secure its third successive win. Band parts were rearranged, but the quality of the performance was obviously affected and Bacup were placed fourth. Early in October the 27-year-old Richard died. As was customary on such occasions the band accompanied the funeral cortège, playing appropriate music including 'The dead march in Saul' (Handel), and another popular favourite at Victorian funerals, 'Vital spark' (Harwood).

Though largely concerned with competitions, the *History of Bacup Old Band* gives some detail of concerts. There is mention, for example, of a concert given in conjunction with Burnley Valley Choral Society, and another for which the Trawden Band came to Bacup to give a joint concert to a large audience in the Co-operative Hall.[17]

The *History of the Bacup Old Band* waxes lyrical about the band's key soloists (on cornet, soprano cornet, tenor horn and euphonium), claiming that they were 'the best set of soloists in any band'.[18] The band also, apparently, had a repertoire of pieces it played without music – all properly harmonized, according to the account. Such pieces as 'Hail, smiling morn', 'Dashing white sergeant', 'Let me like a soldier fall' and others were played to entertain wellwishers who turned out to see the band departing for a contest; at Christmas time the conductor simply announced the name of a carol and the key in which it should be played. Whether all this was an act of memory or of natural musicianship is not clear, but one must assume that the playing reached a higher standard than that of average street-corner busking or, indeed, of other bands of the time (see also the Introduction to Chapter 4).

Between 1867 and 1870, out of 33 contests, the 4th Lancashire Rifle Volunteers (Bacup) Band won 26 first prizes, a joint first-second and six seconds.[19] This indicates that the band was now attending an average of about eight contests per season. The expansion in brass band contests was, therefore, under way from the late 1860s, and very attractive they were to the general public. Between 8000 and 10 000 people were said to have attended a contest in Accrington on Friday, 4 April (probably Good Friday) and a further 8000 went to a contest at Nelson in the following June. Following Bacup's fourth successive win at Skipton during August, a crowd of some 2000 awaited the band's triumphal homecoming.

The 1867 Belle Vue contest proved to be a fiasco, with the winners, Clay Cross, actually being an amalgamation of three bands – Matlock, Chesterfield and the real Clay Cross. This was considered to be morally if not legally reprehensible and caused possibly the biggest crowd uproar at any contest. Winterbottom had arranged a selection from *Der Freischütz* and, together with Alfred Phasey, John Gladney Sr, W Williams and A G Crowe, formed the adjudicator's panel (as always, screened from the bands). Bacup, according to various reports, should have taken first place, but were actually placed second.

Undeterred, they gave a very successful concert in the local Mechanics Institute a few weeks later, hundreds of fans having to be turned away. The programme – hardly lightweight – included pieces with which the band had had success, with selections from *Der Freischütz*, *Maritana*, *The Amber Witch* and two choruses from *Messiah*.

Contests continued, and so did the anecdotes. Bacup arrived at a contest in Todmorden in August 1869 intending to play a selection from *Oberon*. Finding that two of the adjudicators were organists they decided it would be better to play something sacred. Their ploy paid off because, playing two oratorio choruses, Bacup won first prize. There was also a further competition at this event, with various instruments to be competed for by soloists playing pieces of their own choice. Though by no means standard practice, this solo contest was not unique, as several contemporary contest reports indicate. Between 1868 and 1870 the players of Bacup Old won two sopranos, two cornets, two tenor horns, two euphoniums and a flugelhorn. In some cases they were for the best soloist in the contest performance and in others, for winners of actual solo contests.

After such a successful decade it comes as a shock to learn how quickly the Bacup Old Band came to an end. On 8 October 1871 George Ellis died, following an apoplectic fit.[20] He had been the band's tutor since it became the 4th LVR Band in 1859. His last involvement was at the 1871 Belle Vue contest when, for the second time in its history, Bacup was attempting its third successive win (the 'hat-trick') at this illustrious contest. Had they succeeded they would have been the first to achieve the feat. In the event, Black Dyke were victorious – Bacup being placed third. Towards the end of 1871 another of the band's stalwarts, James Lord, also passed away. The customary ritual of the band attending the funerals took place in both cases, the streets lined with onlookers. Some months later a number of local bands assembled to pay tribute to the memory of Ellis, and played the following programme:[21]

United bands:	'Kyrie and Gloria' (Mozart)
Clayton-le-Moors:	'Hallelujah to the Father' (Beethoven)
Ramsbottom Rifles:	*La Favorite* (Verdi)[22]
Blackburn:	'O, Great are the Depths' (Mendelssohn)
United bands:	'Worthy is the Lamb' and 'Amen' (Handel)
Accrington:	*Atilla* (Verdi)
Church:	Chorus from *The Mount of Olives* (Beethoven)
Bacup:	'La Neige' (Auber)
Colne:	*William Tell* (Rossini)
United bands:	'Hallelujah Chorus' (Handel)

The loss of these two personalities sounded the death-knell for the Bacup band; to add to its problems several players left their jobs in local mills and factories and went into business – some as publicans. This put a strain on the band, already heavily committed with concert bookings. In 1870 the band had parted company with the Volunteers because it could not fulfil its commitments.[23] These would probably have involved the band in weekly drill sessions, an annual camp, and various other functions throughout the year. It then assumed the name 'Bacup Old Band', but though successful for a time, Ellis's death proved to be a mortal blow, and the band seems to have gone out of existence following the concert referred to above. This highlights the dependence of amateur bands on a few dominant personalities. If, for any reason, a number of such people are lost within a short space of time, it is difficult for those remaining to maintain the momentum required for continued success.

There can be little doubt that it was the contest which was the stimulus and driving force behind the progress of bands towards the top of the pyramid. For the better bands contesting was a profitable business – more lucrative than presenting concerts. Between 1862 and 1871 the Bacup band (under its two names) earned £1463 from its contest successes. This was probably shared by the players – quite an incentive in the days when not all bandsmen would earn even £1 per week in the mill; the soloists often won new instruments, presented as 'special' prizes by instrument manufacturers, who then advertised their instruments as played by star soloists in famous bands.

Another perspective on the value of prize money is highlighted by Algernon Rose, when he points out that in a period of 13 years Stalybridge Old Band, playing on a set of second-hand instruments bought in 1880 for £160, won some £3000 in cash and special prizes. This, Rose points out, had been a very good investment and was probably partly why the band was able to buy a new set of Besson instruments in May 1893.[24]

Throughout the history of brass bands better players, even though claiming to be amateur, have probably regarded themselves as semi-professional musicians, able to supplement their wages by paid performances. Many came to rely on this to maintain their standard of living. In the process they may often have had to neglect their families, but have justified this by contributing to the family purse. Money earned through playing with a good band has been, therefore, a very real incentive.

Virtually all public playing by bands in the nineteenth century was in the open air – even at major contests. Unlike today, when bands have standard seating arrangements – the equivalent of those of the orchestra – early bands stood in a circle or a square, with the conductor (if there was one) in the middle. Where the square formation was used the principal soloists – cornet, soprano cornet, tenor horn and euphonium at that time – would each occupy one of the corner positions, hence the origin of the term 'corner-men', still applied to the leading players. The 'leader' in early times was the soprano cornet player, but later was generally the solo cornettist, and he would at times conduct, in the absence of a professional conductor. Later he became known as the 'bandmaster', a term borrowed from the military. In many cases the professional conductor (if there was one) also played the principal cornet solos.

Perhaps it should be pointed out that from the 1880s top professional conductors regularly conducted four, five or even six bands in a contest – enhancing somewhat their odds on winning prizes! Partly as a result of this, personalities became significant, and a group of three musicians came to dominate the brass band scene for the final quarter of the nineteenth century – two of them well into the twentieth. Known as 'The Great Triumvirate', they were John Gladney, Edwin Swift and Alexander Owen. Between them they frequently conducted as many as 15 bands in a single contest.[25]

John Gladney (1839–1911)

Gladney was born in Belfast, son of the bandmaster (also John) of the 30th East Lancashire Regiment.[26] Gladney (Sr) adjudicated at the Belle Vue contest in 1867. Young John started playing the flute when he was eight and the violin and various other instruments a year or so later. It was as a clarinettist that he became a professional musician, touring with opera companies, playing clarinet and conducting the Scarborough Spa Band, and playing with the Hallé Orchestra for some 30 years.[27] According to Hampson[28] he was associated with Jullien's orchestra. In all probability – if the assertion is correct – he would have been a member of the 50-strong wind band with which Jullien toured the northern counties in 1856 (see page 15).

During 1871 Gladney conducted a Volunteer band in Burnley, gaining fifth prize at Belle Vue, and around the same time became conductor of Meltham Mills Band. According to one of Meltham's officials, Jack Manchester, whose family connections with the band stretch back to the early days, it had played at a contest adjudicated by Gladney and had been placed last. As a result, he was invited to visit the band to take a rehearsal. Some of the members were so impressed with his teaching that he was offered the conductorship on a regular basis.

From the start of the appointment Gladney and the band contested regularly. As a result of its relationship with Jonas Brook, a firm of cotton thread manufacturers based in Meltham, the band was encouraged to make contesting its main activity, suggesting that perhaps the company saw contesting as a means of self-promotion. The band had been founded in 1843 as a reed band, converting to all-brass a few years later.

It is often thought, not surprisingly, that Meltham Mills is the name of a mill or a factory. In fact, there is a town called Meltham and adjacent to it is the village of Meltham Mills, so-called because of an ancient corn mill called Meltham Mill. There was however, in Meltham, the mill of Jonas Brook & Bros, a world-famous manufacturer of cotton thread, and it gave the band considerable financial assistance. Probably known as 'Meltham Mills' because of this early association, the present-day band is, in fact, known as Meltham and Meltham Mills.

The band had had a number of conductors but had met with little success in contests. But during Gladney's first two years Meltham Mills Band entered 13 contests, winning several prizes including six firsts. In 1873 the ten contests they attended also brought six first prizes, including the band's first Belle Vue win – which carried special prizes of a B♭ bombardon, a trombone and a gold medal, as well as a £30 cash prize. Between Gladney's appointment in 1871 and 1883, Meltham won 72 first prizes and tied four times for joint first place, together with 23 second prizes and a further tie. Meltham Mills Band succeeded Bacup as Britain's premier band during the 1880s, its winnings totalling £3805.[29]

During this time Gladney remodelled the band, and the instrumentation of today's bands owes much to his work. In a letter to *Brass Band News*[30] he wrote, 'When I took up Meltham Mills in 1873,[31] I modelled its instrumentation on the lines of the present contesting band of 24, and all the rest quickly followed the example.' Whilst remodelling the band Gladney also surrounded himself with proficient players, and just as the Lord family had been important to the success of Bacup Old, the pillars at Meltham were members of the Stead family – three brothers and their Uncle James. The brothers – Wright, Richard and Edwin played soprano cornet, solo euphonium and first trombone, whilst James played E♭ bombardon.[32] Meltham's solo cornet player was Alexander Owen, destined to become the third member of the 'Triumvirate'.

Much of Gladney's success may be attributed to his arranging skills. As mentioned previously, from the early days of banding it fell to the leader to arrange music for his band, and this trend continued to the end of the century. At many contests during this period the test piece was 'own choice' and conductors of leading bands designed their arrangements to show off the particular strengths of the band. Amongst Gladney's arrangements are several operatic and composer selections, most of which were made, one suspects, for Meltham. There is also a selection from Gladney's pre-Meltham days of music from Donizetti's *Lucrezia Borgia*, arranged for a contest at Bacup in 1869. In the letter referred to above, Gladney also wrote some interesting comments about this piece:

> When I arranged *Lucrezia Borgia* for the great contest at Bacup in 1869, I wrote a solo for slide trombone and insisted on its being played on a slide, and as I was to judge it could not be shirked; but up to then trombones had never been used as solo instruments.

However, he then casts doubt on the veracity of this statement by adding, 'There was a trombone solo in *Roberto* at Belle Vue in 1868, but it was played by valve instruments.'

Lucrezia Borgia is a less substantial selection than the later ones, and makes fewer demands of players. Though never actually printed it would, theoretically, have been published and made available to bands taking part in the contest. (A more detailed survey of Gladney's scores is given on pages 85–87, and a list of his arrangements is given in Appendix 5.)

Meltham was the first band to win the Belle Vue contest three years in succession. Following this they were barred for two years in accordance with the rules of the contest, during which time Black Dyke achieved its first two wins. After this Meltham's prowess as a contesting band deteriorated. It returned to Belle Vue in 1883 but took second place to Black Dyke, thus completing its hat-trick. Though the maestro continued to conduct Meltham for some years, one by one the more prominent players left. As in the case of Bacup, the demise was quick, although it could not be said to have been brought about by the deaths of older, experienced players. It does, however, lend force to the argument that when key players leave it is difficult to maintain the standard; it also suggests that in their heydays, neither Bacup Old nor Meltham Mills bands had a youth or training policy, and that they gave little thought to their own futures.

Gladney, however, was to remain the most dominant figure at Belle Vue for many more years, as may be seen from the following list of winning bands, all conducted by him:

Year	Piece	Band
1873	*Dinorah* (Meyerbeer)	Meltham
1874	*Il Talismano* (Balfe)	Kingston Mills
1876	*Aida* (Verdi)	**Meltham**
1877	*Jessonda* (Spohr)	**Meltham**
1878	*Romeo e Giulietta* (Gounod)	**Meltham**
1884	*La Gazza Ladra* (Rossini)	Honley
1885	*Nabucco* (Verdi)	**Kingston Mills**
1886	*La Favorite* (Donizetti)	**Kingston Mills**
1887	*L'Etoile du Nord* (Meyerbeer)	**Kingston Mills**
1890	*Euryanthe* (Weber)	Batley Old
1891	*Das Nachtlager von Granada* (Kreutzer)	Black Dyke
1893	*Elaine* (Bemburg)	Kingston Mills
1895	*Hänsel und Gretel* (Humperdinck)	Black Dyke
1896	*Gabrielli* (Pizzi)	Black Dyke
1899	*Aroldo* (Verdi)	Black Dyke
1900	*La Gioconda* (Ponchielli)	Lindley
1901	*Mirella* (Gounod)	Kingston Mills
1902	*L'Ebreo* (Appoloni)	Black Dyke[33]
1903	*Caractacus* (Elgar)	Pemberton Old
1904	*Semiramide* (Rossini)	Black Dyke

Note: Bold type indicates hat-tricks.

For good measure, in addition to his personal six successive Belle Vue wins, in 1902 Gladney led Black Dyke to victory in the new National Brass Band Championships. Founded by John Henry Iles in 1900 at Crystal Palace, the 'Nationals' will be discussed later. Gladney's services were obviously in demand – not only with the famous – and it has been estimated that during his career he was involved with over a hundred different bands.

He had a particularly productive period with the Kingston Mills Band, achieving his second hat-trick at Belle Vue with them in the years 1885–1887.[34] In 1888 he took up another major appointment as professional conductor of Black Dyke. Here also he was surrounded by fine players (including Edwin Stead, his trombonist from Meltham) and benefited from three of the first of what has been described by later members of Black Dyke as the 'royal succession' of cornet soloists – Fred Birkinshaw from 1889, John Paley from 1891 and Ceres Jackson from 1901. He also had good service from his bandmasters. The renowned euphonium player Phineas Bower (see note 5, Chapter Two) was bandmaster when Gladney first moved to Black Dyke, and was succeeded in 1895 by his brother, Harry, who had played cornet with the band since 1881. The Bowers were another great banding family; a third brother, Alfred, also played in the band and Phineas's son, Fred, later played solo trombone. When Fred retired in 1929 there had been a member of the Bower family in Black Dyke for 64 years, and the four of them had given a total of 150 years' service.

Gladney saw Black Dyke through one of the many important periods in its history – a period when concert work took on more significance. In 1906, aged 67, he accompanied the band on a six-month concert tour of Canada and the United States. He retired in the following year and little more was heard of him until his death in 1911.

Gladney's success in contests was never equalled, and as an arranger, though not particularly prolific, he nevertheless helped establish the format of the modern brass band. According to an article in *The Cornet* of 15 October 1896, 'To Mr Gladney alone belongs the honour of introducing solos on the trombone.' He is also credited with introducing the BB♭ bass, and he became known as the 'father of the brass band'.[35]

Edwin Swift (1843–1904)

Swift, the second member of the 'Triumvirate', was the son of a handloom weaver and was born in Linthwaite near Huddersfield, only a few miles from Meltham. He left school at the age of nine and became a 'shuttler'.[36] His elder brother played cornet but it was not long before the younger Swift became the better of the two, and at the age of ten he joined Linthwaite Band. Not only a natural player, he was also a good reader, could transpose at sight, and at the age of only 14 became solo cornet player and conductor. This dual role was quite normal – many conductors played the cornet one-handed, directing the band with their free hand. Swift also took an interest in the wider musical scene and was soon composing and arranging. Later he operated a loom in a local mill, but his mind was more on music than on weaving, busying himself arranging pieces for the band, while frequently leaving the loom to get on with its job. This did wonders for the band's library, but led to many fines for faulty workmanship.[37]

Linthwaite Band became the 34th West Riding of Yorkshire Volunteer Band. As had happened in Bacup, freed from financial problems, the Linthwaite band was now able to become one of the north's premier bands. During the early 1870s Swift gave up playing cornet in order to devote more attention to his conducting and arranging. He had remarkable success with Linthwaite, in 1874 winning ten first prizes in contests, including one at Belle

Vue – beating rivals Meltham Mills under Gladney. But not until 1875, when aged 32, did he leave the mill in order to concentrate wholly on music. He later remarked that he was 'a weaver by trade, and a professional musician by accident'.[38] Swift was now in demand by many bands. Never claiming the adoration accorded to John Gladney, he nevertheless worked with over 30, some of them very highly regarded, including the celebrated Wyke Temperance Band.

As with Gladney, much of Swift's success was due to his skill as an arranger. He supplied his bands with a succession of pieces tailor-made to suit their strengths. He was a great champion of Wagner, introducing much of his music to brass bands during the 1870s, and pitting Linthwaite and his selection from *Tannhäuser* against the might of Meltham, Gladney and *Elijah*. Swift's most successful selection, *Bayreuth*,[39] contained music from several Wagner operas. Despite their success, some adjudicators condemned the Wagner selections as being 'before the age'.[40]

1895 proved to be an especially interesting year for Swift. By now the two leading bands were Black Dyke and Besses, conducted respectively by the other members of the 'Triumvirate' – Gladney and Owen. There had been much speculation in the band press regarding which of these bands was the better and, when both were to take part in a contest in the town of Nelson, the band world was agog to see which would come out top. The results were not as expected, Swift taking first and second places with Wyke and Cornholme bands, whilst Besses were third and Black Dyke fourth. A few days later the 'giants' met again at Kidsgrove, playing the same test piece to a different adjudicator. Here, Swift took first and third places with Wyke and Mossley,[41] whilst Besses were placed second and Black Dyke fourth. Then, on 27 April in a contest at Keighley, when only three bands played, the result was Wyke, Black Dyke and Besses, in that order. At a contest later in the year in Durham, Swift led Linthwaite into first place with a selection from Berlioz's *Faust*, Wyke coming second. Success followed success, and this was in no small measure due to the quality of Swift's arrangements, in particular his *Bayreuth*, Berlioz's *Faust*, Meyerbeer's *L'Etoile du Nord* and the overture William Tell. Further details of Swift and his arrangements are given on pages 87–88.

During his later years Swift did not enjoy good health. He also suffered greatly from the deaths of two sons in 1899 and 1900. Fred, at the time of his death, was a choirmaster and bandmaster in Dumfries, Scotland, but had at one time been bandmaster at Linthwaite. Lawrence, the younger of the two, was an organist and is described in the booklet as 'a musician of great promise'. These losses were a great blow to the already ailing Swift. In 1901 he conducted *Gems from Sullivan's Operas Number 3* at the Crystal Palace contest. This contained the funeral anthem – 'Brother thou art gone before us' (from *Martyr of Antioch*). During the performance, by Wyke Temperance, Swift was overcome by emotion, and when asked from where the inspiration had come, he replied 'Eh, lad, when playing that, I am following my two lads to the grave'.[42] It would be a happy sequel to record that Wyke won the contest, but alas, they were not successful on that occasion.

On 9 February 1904, Edwin Swift died aged 60 from cancer of the kidneys. Despite his humble background and his lack of formal training, he had been a key figure in the brass band world throughout the last quarter of the nineteenth century.

Alexander Owen (1851–1920)

Skill with the pen as well as skill with the baton also applied to the third and last member of 'The Great Triumvirate', Alexander Owen. Little is known of Owen's early years, except that he was brought up in an orphanage in Swinton, near Manchester, and was later apprenticed to a cavalry bandmaster.[43] In 1868, on the recommendation of a Mr Salkeld of Manchester, he joined Stalybridge Old Band. During 1869 this band, like so many others, became attached to the Volunteers. But in 1871 'differences developed within the band' and Owen left, forming the Stalybridge Borough Band.[44] By now he had acquired a reputation as the greatest all-round cornet player of his day. His tone, compass, free production and expression were said to be charming and his stamina described as astounding. He was obviously destined for higher honours than he could achieve in Stalybridge and, in 1875, came under the influence of John Gladney (12 years his senior), joining Meltham Mills.

Owen stayed with this band for five years, contributing to their Belle Vue hat-trick of wins (1876–1878). At the same time as he was playing cornet at Meltham he was also conducting various other bands, and in 1880 was appointed professional conductor of Black Dyke, following its Belle Vue win under Joseph Fawcett the previous year. Owen led this band to further Belle Vue wins in 1880 and 1881, thus completing the hat-trick. As had happened with Meltham, Black Dyke was barred for the two years following its hat-trick, but Owen completed his own personal treble, winning with Clayton-le-Moors Band in 1882. In 1884 he was appointed professional conductor at Besses and for four years he led both that band and Black Dyke. By the time he left the latter, in 1888, he claimed to have directed 45 first-prize winning performances with them. Like Gladney and Swift, Owen conducted many bands, but remained with Besses until his death in 1920. In a diary which the writer saw some years ago, he claimed that between 1881 and 1885 his bands had won 378 first prizes, 84 seconds and 58 thirds.

It was during the 1880s and 1890s that Owen penned most of his contest selections which, as with Gladney and Swift, helped bring victory for him and his bands. The two most successful were *Rossini's Works* and *The Damnation of Faust* (Berlioz). Between November 1884 and August 1891, Besses gave 27 contest performances of the former under his direction, winning no fewer than 20 first prizes. At a contest held in Norland (near Halifax) in July 1887 the rules were so framed that Besses were not allowed to play *Rossini's Works*, as they had won the contest with it in the previous year. Instead, they played Owen's arrangement of *Beethoven's Works*, but still achieved top place as joint winners. Owen was now working on the Berlioz selection, which was given its première at a contest in Barnoldswick on 2 June 1888, where it helped start the run of 19 first prizes which Besses won with it – in 20 contest performances. On two occasions the band played both the Rossini and the Berlioz selections, each time taking first prize. A few other bands also played Owen's selections – especially *Rossini*, and there are instances of Besses being outplayed as, for example, in a contest in Queensbury (the home of Black Dyke) in 1885, in which the Oldham Rifles Band, conducted by Owen and playing *Rossini,* took third place. Besses, with the same piece and the same conductor, finished seventh.

At Hyde in 1891 Owen conducted and played solo cornet with all seven bands in the contest – a rather unique way of guaranteeing personal success. With such a range of commitments, it was small wonder that Owen began to experience health problems. His doctor, however, found a suitable remedy. *Brass Band News* of 1 December 1897 reported, 'The malady from which Mr Owen is suffering is insomnia, in so acute a form that his physician has ordered a long sea voyage and a prolonged rest with change of scene and surroundings.'

Owen took this advice and sailed to Australia – but not before winning the 1897 Belle Vue contest with Mossley Band. Whilst in Australia he visited Albany, Melbourne, Sydney and Adelaide. The cruise helped him to regain his full fitness, and he arrived back in England towards the end of the following March. *Brass Band News* carried the following advertisement: 'Come and give Mr A Owen a welcome – come to hear the marvellous *Valkyrie* selection.' This was apparently his latest arrangement – possibly made during the cruise, and was to be played in a concert in Stockport by Besses.[45]

Owen's musical activities were not confined to brass bands. In his adopted town of Stalybridge he became conductor of the Harmonic Choral Society and also conducted at some of the town's annual singing festivals. Many years later Thomas Keighley stated, 'Alexander Owen I knew personally. I played under him in oratorio and opera.'[46] Apart from his music Owen was very active in his private life. He was installed as Worshipful Master of the Stamford & Warrington lodge of Freemasons, Stalybridge, in October 1884, and in November 1887 was elected to Stalybridge Town Council. Despite his popularity and success, Owen could be something of a martinet and certainly knew how to stand up for his rights. He was not happy about certain aspects of the Belle Vue contest, for example. The 1885 contest featured 31 bands, started at 11 o'clock in the morning, did not end until 9.30 pm, and attracted a crowd of 100 000, though as the contest was held indoors we must assume that the majority of the people did not see the inside of the hall. *Brass Band News* of October 1885 published a letter from Owen complaining about conditions at the contest. To give a flavour of Owen and his times, the letter is here reproduced in full:

BELLE VUE CONTEST, MANCHESTER

To the Editor of the Brass Band News:

Dear Sir, – It is but fair to inform your readers of the many unpleasant features respecting the above. After the awards were announced at this year's contest, I, in company with a party of musicians (numbering at least twenty), had the opportunity of acquainting Messrs Jennison with the complaints that have so long fettered this contest. It has been a source of regret for a long period among the 'competing bands', as well as their supporters, that the remarks of the three judges are not published like other contests. A great drawback, or I may say an injustice, is appointing the same judge [Charles Godfrey] year after year. At this contest, two judges were engaged that judged last year. But the worst evil of all is, in my mind, allowing the contest to take place in the large hall, which being practically void of ventilation, the 'stagnant air' becomes so very noxious, and is at times simply frightful; so much so, that bandsmen have been completely overpowered, and have had to be carried fainting from the scene. May I ask, why not have the contest outside, especially on a fine day? Another matter of complaint is the fact that the arrangement of the test piece seems permanently confined to one musician [Charles Godfrey]. With all due respect I would ask, can no other competent person be found to perform this duty, if only for a change? I must here remark that Mr James Jennison said he thought it very strange these complaints or suggestions had not been mentioned to him before. Now, the only reason I can imagine for this is, that no one has had the courage or manliness to speak out. For my own part, well knowing the difficulties the bands have to play under, I feel surprised that this matter has not been publicly vented earlier, as there has been no lack of dissatisfaction expressed. However, the only request I ask is, that some of your readers will corroborate my statement, and urgently press upon Messrs Jennison to consider the matter for the benefit of all concerned. In conclusion, I anxiously await the opinion of others on this important subject; meanwhile, if nothing can be done to improve this just cause of complaint, I shall, in future, decline to compete with any band. Apologising for trespassing so much on your valuable space, I beg to remain, Sir, yours respectfully,

A. OWEN
September 20th, 1885

There were several replies, taking up various points raised by Owen; some agreed and others disagreed. Many felt that there was an element of sour grapes in Owen's comments, as he had not complained in the years in which his own bands had won (there had been three such years). One correspondent posed a question to Owen himself, asking if he thought it fair that he (Owen) should insist on playing solo cornet with every band he conducted. However, the Belle Vue authorities took note of Owen's criticisms. As a first step they announced that they were to introduce a qualifying contest, 'Open only to Amateur bands that have not won a prize at any of the four last contests held at Belle Vue.'[47] The qualifying contest duly took place, on 10 July 1886, the first of the series of 'Belle Vue July' contests which were to run until 1951. It was restricted to 20 bands and though for obvious reasons leading bands were not present, the top conductors were in evidence – Swift conducting three bands, Gladney two and Owen one. However, the winning band, Glossop Volunteers, was conducted by Thomas German, a member of the Hallé Orchestra.

The principle of running additional contests for lower grade bands was clearly a sound one. On the 25th anniversary of the founding of the July contest (1910), two divisions were introduced – with 20 bands in each – all bands playing the same test piece. The two-division system operated until 1914 after which, due to the war, there were insufficient bands to make this feasible. From 1931 there was a Class 'A' and a Class 'B' in the July contest, in effect for second and third grade bands, though third grade bands had been catered for between 1922 and 1930 in a further series of Belle Vue contests, held each May. Then, from 1931, as well as the two divisions at the July event, there were four more contests held (classes 'A' to 'D') in May. This series, along with the top grade bands playing in September, the two lower grades contests in July, and the remaining four in May continued until the outbreak of the Second World War in 1939, comparing favourably with the multi-sectional festival which had developed at Crystal Palace (see pages 188–123).

Returning to 1886, not only was there a restricted entry for the July contest, there was now also the opportunity to control entries in September, and although 35 bands applied, only 20 were accepted. Further, the hall's ventilation had been improved, so Owen's letter had not gone unnoticed. However, the authorities refused to take the contest outdoors, not wishing so important an event to be left to the mercy of English weather; nor was Godfrey replaced as arranger or adjudicator. This was not enough for Owen and, true to his word, he and his bands boycotted the 1886 September contest. Swift conducted seven of the 20 bands and Gladney five, amongst them the first and second prize winners, Kingston Mills and Heywood Rifles.

In *Brass Band News* of 1 August 1887 there was an appeal to Owen not to boycott Belle Vue again and indeed he attended, with his two rival bands – Black Dyke and Besses, which took second and third prizes respectively. Alexander Owen was to become a legend in his own lifetime and will be discussed again.

Other nineteenth-century contests

Though the Belle Vue contests were now undoubtedly the pace-setters there were, by the 1890s, also literally hundreds of other contests. The majority were held in the North of England where a large number of contesting bands were located. Initially comprising only one class or section, they stimulated the better bands but offered little encouragement to less able ones. Gradually the term 'second class contest' was introduced to describe contests which helped the lesser bands through the use of easier test pieces, though usually with lower prize money. Music publishers encouraged this as there were many more bands in this category, and they could reasonably assume that by catering for these they would sell more music. Contests were still held mainly outdoors, were still often part of a larger event – perhaps a flower show or a temperance demonstration – and continued to attract large crowds. During the 1890s many 'small ads' in the band press were for contests actually run by bands for bands.

Though second class contests were on the increase there were still many outlets for the top bands, both at local level and further afield. Contests were held all over Yorkshire and Lancashire, and those held in Colne, Hawes, Loftus, Middleton, Nelson, Rochdale and Trawden regularly attracted leading bands, as did those in larger centres such as Blackpool, Bradford, Sheffield, Leeds, New Brighton and Liverpool. Scott describes the music of Victorian bands as the 'Reader's Digest' of the day,[48] and goes on to say that band contests were 'inexpensive and *cultural* family entertainment', indicating that local annual band contests had become a good opportunity for a family day out. However, for many of the thousands who attended, the chief attraction would probably be social rather than musical or cultural.

One or two contests call for special mention. 1887 was Silver Jubilee year, and a busy time for bands. A series of contests was organized in Blackpool as a knock-out competition. Called the Jubilee Contest, it comprised a number of preliminary heats held on different weekends, with the finals in July. At this, bands were required to play a specially written piece, the overture *Victory*, composed by Henry Round (see pages 141–142). Despite good advance coverage, reports following the finals were rather low key and not even a list of prizewinners was given. With most of the better-known bands taking part the fact that a complete outsider, Hanley Mission, was overall winner probably provided more embarrassment than satisfaction. It is well to remember, of course, that the object of a band contest is to find the best performance, not necessarily given by the best band. Brass band contest history is littered with examples of 'outsiders' taking away premier awards. In some cases they go on to win other contests and so find themselves becoming the 'favourite'. However, Hanley Mission does not appear to have enjoyed any great subsequent success.

Failures in London

At about the same time as the Blackpool contest, an ill-fated 'Victorian Era' contest was arranged and scheduled to be held at London's Earl's Court. According to *Brass Band News* of June 1897, never previously had a contest been so well advertised, with full-page advertisements in the paper itself and 10 000 circulars distributed. Nine preliminary rounds were organized on a regional basis, starting with one on 28 May for Yorkshire bands only, followed by a further heat on 11 June for bands from Northamptonshire, Lincolnshire, Leicestershire and Bedfordshire. Similar heats for various other regions were also arranged, and the series was to culminate in the 'Grand Final for the Queen's Prize', in October. All preliminaries were to be held on Fridays (which, as a working day, again shows a lack of thought on the part of the organizers), but to make the journey to London more worthwhile another series of contests was arranged, to be held in Wembley Park on the Saturdays of the same weekends, with a different test piece, and open to any band. The test piece for the preliminary rounds of the Victorian Era contest was to be *Souvenir of Richard Wagner*, arranged by J A Kappey,[49] and William Short,[50] of Her Majesty's Private Band, was to act as adjudicator. The highest placed three bands from each heat were to be invited to the finals.

It will be recalled that the railway companies had been persuaded to offer concessions for the early series of contests at Crystal Palace – and indeed for the Belle Vue contests. These often amounted to free travel for bandsmen and cheap day return tickets for supporters. Alas, the railways refused to cooperate with the 1897 events, a factor which was to sound the death-knell for the contest, despite all the hype and publicity. *Brass Band News* of August 1897 announced, 'We regret to say that the Railway Companies have killed the London contests.' In fairness, one has to say that with the demise of the 1860s Crystal Palace contests, the railway companies probably concluded that there was little or nothing to be gained by them if they offered concessions. However, kill the contest they certainly did. Of the mere 13 entries from Yorkshire for the first heat, only seven attended, and this set the pattern. By the time of the issue of *Brass Band News* of July it had become apparent that no Lancashire bands were even preparing for their heat on 23 July. They simply could not afford the 15 shillings per player train fare from Manchester to London (probably the equivalent of four days' wages for most of them) plus, presumably, a further similar amount for the privilege of playing in the finals for bands which qualified. Finally, the September issue of *Brass Band News* announced that the Victorian Era contest had been abandoned.

In 1888 another London contest met with problems. This was organized in connection with an Irish Exhibition and, apparently in an attempt to attract a wide range of bands, there were to be two sections. Only 21 bands entered, though not even these all appeared. The event seems to have been badly mismanaged, with little advance publicity and not even a mention in *Brass Band News* until the issue of October, the publication of which coincided with the first day of the two-day contest. It was announced that the contest would be held in Olympia, and that the 'cracks' would perform on the first day and 'less celebrated prize bands' on the second. The report went on to say that Black Dyke, Oldham Rifles and Besses had declined to compete because the winner was required to play in the Exhibition on the following four days, apparently without fee.

In the November issue the contest was reported with scorn by the paper's own correspondent, though reports from five other newspapers were reported in full, including one from the *Daily Telegraph*. The most comprehensive report appeared in the *Illustrated Sporting and Dramatic News* of 6 October. It began:

> On Monday and Tuesday there was an interesting contest at the Irish Exhibition between various amateur bands from the North of England, where music is cultivated to an extent that entirely negatives the reproach of foreign musicians that 'we are not a musical nation'. The sturdy workmen of the forge and factory, the homely toilers who spend the bulk of their lives amidst fire, smoke, and the eternal din of machinery, yet find time to cultivate the gentle and refining art of music . . . could not fail to awaken the sympathies of the audience.

With the exception of the Limerick National Band from Ireland, all other competitors were from the Midlands or the North of England and, for the record, prizes were awarded as follows:

	1st day	2nd day
1st:	Wyke Old (John Gladney)	Stalybridge Borough (Alexander Owen)
2nd:	Leeds Forge (Edwin Swift)	Rushden Temperance (G F Birkinshaw)
3rd:	Wyke Temperance (Edwin Swift)	Batley Old (B D Jackson)

Perhaps more interesting are the facts recorded about the prelude to and the sequel of the contest. Many of the competitors were visiting London for the first time and, courtesy of the instrument manufacturers F Besson, a 'sumptuous repast' was provided on their arrival in the capital – some 600 participating. According to the report in *Reynolds* of 14 October the bandsmen 'exhibited considerable vocal taste in the singing of the preliminary grace'.[51] Their high spirits at the conclusion of the event are reflected in an extract from the tongue-in-cheek report in *Referee* of 7 October:

> It happened the other evening that I was walking towards King's Cross station . . . I was suddenly struck by the fact that almost every man I passed had a trumpet or a clarinet . . . under his arm . . . Cabs rattled by with trumpets on the roof. Presently railway omnibuses passed me, and all the passengers inside and out had trumpets . . . Following the vast trumpeted crowd I arrived at King's Cross station. It was eleven o' clock, but the platform was a seething mass of men and trumpets . . . The trains were filled long before they were timed to start, and then there commenced a brazen row which I shall remember to the last day that my hearing is left to me. The Nottingham train played 'Cheer, boys, cheer', while the Leeds train played 'Rule,

Britannia', the Cambridge train played 'Auld Lang Syne' and the Manchester train played 'Killaloe' . . . I don't think I shall be able to look at a brass instrument without a shudder for many a long day to come.

With such exuberance and excitement (no doubt aided by the consumption of alcohol by many of them), the bandsmen prepared for their homeward journey late in the evening following the contest. Nevertheless, *Brass Band News* had to report that 'the impression made on the London public was very slight, as the London public was not there'. Maybe it was due to the lack of advertising, but with such a poor reaction from Londoners it was beginning to appear that the capital was no place for a brass band contest.

In the same year, but some 400 miles north, another contest was announced,[52] also taking place over two days as part of the Glasgow Exhibition. For the first day (26 October) 20 bands had entered the 'Scotch Contest' – for Scottish bands only – each required to play Round's selection from *Maritana*. Twenty-eight bands were entered for the 'Open Contest' of the following day. These were mostly from England and included all the more famous bands. The test piece for this event was *Wagner*, also arranged by Round, and the adjudicator for both competitions was Herr Franz Groenings.[53] A report appeared in *Brass Band News* the following month and the lengthy report gave not only an analysis of the test pieces, but also the adjudicator's written remarks to all bands on both days[54] and a verbatim report of his comments to the audience at the conclusion of each day's contest. Galashiels Band won the 'Scotch Contest', whilst the awards for the open class were as follows:

1st prize:	Kingston Mills
2nd prize:	Wyke Temperance
3rd prize:	Besses-o'-th'-Barn
4th prize:	Leeds Forge
5th prize:	Wyke Old
6th prize:	Oldham Rifles

The adjudicator's remarks were full, detailed and in general, criticism was constructive. Despite poor weather both days were hugely successful, and it now seemed that contests held in the North were likely to achieve greater success than those in the South.

This was further confirmed when another London contest was mounted in 1895. It took place in the Agricultural Hall on 15 June, and was billed as 'The Champion Brass Band Contest'. Only 15 bands out of the 28 entries actually played, and again the London banding fraternity gave little support, though the contest seems to have been a musical success, impressing (according to the *Brass Band News* correspondent[55]) the many professional musicians said to be present.

A regular feature of early band contests was the recalling to the stage of a number of bands to play again, thus giving the adjudicator a chance to separate their marks. Despite this there were frequent examples of ties. *Brass Band News* of September 1883 quoted a rather extreme example when, at a contest in Rochdale, adjudicator Charles Godfrey announced three joint winners – Black Dyke, Linthwaite and Boarshurst. This received the approval of neither bands nor supporters, but when questioned about what was seen as a negative result, Godfrey tersely commented that he would have liked to have heard the three bands again but owing to a late start it was too dark by the end of the contest to do this, and so he had decided to share the prize.

Towards the end of the 1890s there was a slight decline in interest in contests, and during 1899 *Brass Band News* featured a number of articles and letters on the subject of contests versus engagements. The paper's line was very much in favour of contests, even accusing non-contesting bands of laziness. One wonders whether the view was generated by musical or commercial considerations. In fact, the reduction of interest in contests was symbolic of the decline in the popularity of brass bands in general, as well as in that of many other kinds of organizations in the second half of the 1890s. A significant factor in the decline was the effect of counter-attractions, for example the growing popularity of musical comedy, and particularly of sport. Bands were victims to these changes in popular taste, many finding it difficult to maintain the dedication required, especially in younger bandsmen. Another factor was that there were now more outlets for band concerts, which some bands were taking very seriously and attracting large crowds. For example, a report in *British Bandsman* of October 1888 gives an account of a Sunday concert in Keighley which attracted a crowd estimated at between 12 000 and 15 000.

Brass bands in concert

Outdoor events were still the most common types of engagement, and amongst the more prestigious bookings were appearances at some of the great exhibitions.[56] Between 1886 and 1893 a number of these took place – in Edinburgh, Manchester, Newcastle and Saltaire. At the exhibitions, bands were often engaged to play for a whole week, and at some a contest was held during the final weekend, attracting good bands and large crowds. The contest at the Edinburgh International Exhibition, which took place on 23 October 1886, was hailed as the 'Championship of Great Britain'. Besses were winners and Black Dyke runners up. Black Dyke had played at the Exhibition for a week during August, playing two programmes per day, and this was said to be the first appearance of a brass band in Edinburgh. The band played a total of 91 different pieces, including seven overtures and 40 fantasias or operatic selections.[57] During the preceding months the same band had also played for a fortnight and two separate weeks in Newcastle, for a week and three separate days in Manchester, and also at Saltaire – quite a commitment for a so-called amateur band.

In an article headed 'Where the Bands Are' in *Brass Band News* of September 1887 it was reported that Black Dyke had fulfilled a week's engagement at the Manchester Exhibition, had played for a week at Saltaire Exhibition, starting on 22 August, and for a further week at the Newcastle Exhibition, a week later.[58] Wyke Temperance were, at the time of publication of the article, playing for a week at the Newcastle Exhibition, whilst Linthwaite were playing in Liverpool, where Wyke were to follow them for a further week. Leeds Forge Band also had week-long engagements at both Saltaire and Newcastle, whilst Oldham Rifles, following a week in camp in Cleethorpes with their Regiment from 27 August, were engaged to play for a week at the Newcastle Exhibition. This was certainly a busy time for these bands.

One perennial topic discussed in the band press over many years, even in the present era, is the fact that bands rarely advertise what music they will play in a particular concert. Opinion usually concludes that it is the band's name which attracts an audience, not what it will play. There are occasional exceptions, and probably one of the earliest examples was in connection with a Black Dyke concert in 1897. The following advertisement appeared in the December issue of *Brass Band News*:

> Albert Hall, Sheffield, William Brown's Concerts
> Saturday December 11th 1897
> Black Dike Prize Band, conductor John Gladney esq
> The finest Brass Band in the World will play the following Concert Programme:
>
> | | |
> |---|---|
> | Overture "*Zampa*" | Herold |
> | Selection "*Patience*" | Sullivan |
> | Selection "*La Africaine*" [sic] | Meyerbeer |
> | Selection "*Pirates of Penzance*" | Sullivan |
> | Selection "*William Tell*" | Rossini |
> | Cornet Solo "*La Neige*" | Hartmann |
> | (Mr J Paley) | |
> | Trombone Solo "*Evening Star*" | Jeffery |
> | (Mr C Jeffery) | |
>
> Commence at 8   Admission 6d and 1/-

From early days Herold's *Zampa* overture seems to have been a favourite with bands, rarely failing to create a good audience response. The *William Tell* selection would almost certainly be Gladney's own arrangement, and the inclusion of two Gilbert & Sullivan selections reflects their popularity.

As there seem to have been no reports about the Sheffield concert it is not possible to say whether or not the above is the complete programme. It is hardly likely to have been played in the order shown, and probably a number of lighter pieces would be included to add variety. In addition, it was customary for soloists to play encores and also for the band to respond with encores – not only at the end of a concert, but at any other point if a particular piece received exceptional applause.

The two soloists at Sheffield were amongst the recognized brass band stars of the day. John Paley was a leading cornet player and also went on to make a name playing the trumpet. In 1892, against the wishes of his father, he had gone to America where he had been introduced to Patrick Gilmore. The famous band leader was very impressed with his playing, and Paley became the youngest member of his band. Following Gilmore's sudden death later in the year Paley returned home, and in 1893 became Black Dyke's cornet soloist.

Charles Jeffery, less well known than Paley, was nevertheless a very experienced bandsman. After having violin lessons from the age of seven, he switched to cornet and played with his local town band (Calverley, near Bradford). Later he played with both Bramley and Saltaire bands and for a time conducted Marriner's Band in Keighley. After a short spell as a baritone player, he took on a 24-week professional engagement in Morecambe playing the euphonium, but on his return to Saltaire took up the trombone, was heard by someone connected with Black Dyke and invited to become a member. Joining Black Dyke at the age of 35, he developed into a fine player, appearing as soloist with orchestras as well as bands.

A report of a concert given by Black Dyke in Birmingham appears in *Brass Band News* of April 1898 and, as it quotes from local newspapers, it gives an insight into the reactions of non-brass band critics of the time. The reports are quoted from the *Birmingham Daily Post*, the *Daily Mail*, and *Daily Gazette*. All are highly complimentary of the band's playing, though the *Post* is critical of the choice of some items, describing the arrangements of excerpts from *Elijah* and Beethoven's C Minor Symphony as sacrilege. 'Corno', the correspondent of *Brass Band News*, not happy with the band playing Gilbert & Sullivan, wrote, rather sanctimoniously, 'the jingling quadrille and the valse rhythms of Sullivan's comic operas do not fill the aching void'. The reporter from the *Mail* painted on a broader canvas:

> The extraordinary increase of brass bands all over the country, and keen competition for supremacy, have given an impetus to this branch of music culture that is almost unparalleled. But it is in the Black Dike and the Besses we find such wonderful perfection, such startling ensemble, and an almost electrifying attack. Only a few months ago we heard the Besses, the great rivals of Black Dike, and, in matters where so much similarity exists, it is difficult to express an opinion without touching upon the delicate ground of comparison. Hearing Black Dike again, especially under such favourable conditions as on Saturday, we were startled by their almost overwhelming tone power, and their unsurpassed mode in producing a graduated crescendo.

These are interesting comments, which also identify the fact that it was the impetus of the competition which pushed the best bands towards perfection. Later in the year, Black Dyke played twice daily for a week on Bridlington

Quay, drawing the following comments from a local unnamed correspondent who, in *Brass Band News*[59] eulogized thus:

> It speaks volumes for the capabilities of a band when it can present Wagner, Beethoven and Spohr, in palatable form to the many people whose knowledge of music is based on the rendering of a typical song by a music hall artiste, or *buskers* on the sands. Yet the *Dike* do this, and do it very successfully, as the nightly crowd round their bandstand testifies. The passionate and irresistible *abandon* of their crescendos, excelling in finished attack and musicianly phrasing, the tender and beautifully sustained pianos and diminuendos cannot but carry conviction to the soul of the rankest Philistine.

Here the writer's emphasis is mainly about the effect of the music on the listeners, returning to the thoughts and ideas of Enderby Jackson almost 50 years earlier. Taking music to the people through concert programmes was now becoming important, though the value of the contest remained in that it helped keep the standard of playing high. It was also apparent that bands which were consistently successful in competitions were, through the resultant publicity, the ones which were offered the more prestigious concert engagements.

John Henry Iles (1871–1951)

On the first Monday in September, 1898, a local holiday, a Bristol-born business man, John Henry Iles, found himself in Manchester with time to spare. This date had, since 1853, been Belle Vue contest day. Enquiring of his hotel porter what he might do to while away the time, he was advised to go to the contest, and as something of an amateur musician himself, decided to go along. Some years later he wrote:

> I regarded the suggestion of attending the Manchester contest as anything but attractive. I was, however, persuaded to go, and then I heard these bands which had been described to me as 'wonderful'. It is not too much to say that I was positively astounded . . . I came away from that contest a completely converted enthusiast for their cause.[60]

On his return to London he took steps to buy the publishing house of R Smith & Co and *British Bandsman*. Later he became president of the London and Home Counties Brass Band Association. Determined to bring the North's finest bands to London he set about trying to revive the Crystal Palace contests. To even attempt such a venture, considering the recent history of contests in the capital, was remarkable. Accounts of how he succeeded, with the support of Sir Arthur Sullivan, are outlined in Chapter 6.

The year 1900 brought both a new century and a new era in the history of brass bands. Though Gladney and Owen were still active, a new generation of players and conductors was in the making but, more important, brass bands now had a new champion in Iles. He was to dominate the scene for almost 50 years, as organizer of the Crystal Palace and Belle Vue contests, as organizer of extensive overseas tours for Besses, and as the instigator of the specially composed brass band test piece. The Crystal Palace contests and specially composed test pieces will be examined later, but first it is necessary to review some of the developments in later nineteenth-century band music, in instruments, instrumentation and scoring.

Notes

1. The band is said to have comprised 144 soprano cornets, 394 cornets, 205 althorns, 100 baritones, 74 tenor trombones, 75 bass trombones, 80 euphoniums, 133 ophicleides, 155 E♭ contrabasses, 2 B♭ contrabasses, 26 side drums, a monster gong and the organ (Russell and Elliott, 1936, pages 114–115). However, in view of the number of withdrawals, there must some doubt as to whether the band was as large as is claimed.
2. *The Times*, Wednesday, 11 July 1860.
3. Possibly George Perry (1793–1862), composer of opera, oratorio and orchestral music, and for a time musical director of the Haymarket Theatre.
4. *The Times*, 12 July 1860.
5. *Brass Band News* of January 1904 (p. 8) announced the retirement of Gray from the post of bandmaster of the Border Rifles Volunteers at Hawick, Scotland. Born at Yeadon, near Leeds, in 1839, he had been a handloom weaver – like his father. At the age of 14 he had joined Yeadon Young Band, playing 2nd cornet, and later 2nd soprano cornet. A year later he became bandmaster of Yeadon Old Band, the band with which he attended the 1860 Crystal Palace contest. Gray became bandmaster of the Border Rifles in December 1860.
6. P. 134.
7. Pp. 20–21.
8. *Musical World*, 14 July 1860.
9. Taylor, 1979, p. 57.
10. According to a letter to me, dated 23 January 1981, from Mrs Pat Hogarth of Scarborough who has undertaken a study of the life of Jackson, this was called 'Enderby Jackson's London Star Company Comique'.
11. The first contest held in New Zealand was in 1880 (Newcomb, 1980, p. 126).
12. See *Brass Band News*, August 1891.
13. Wild beast shows enjoyed immense popularity at fairs; one of the earliest was Wombwell's Menagerie which travelled all over the country. Its founder was George Wombwell (1778–1850) (Lea, 1900, p. 345).
14. Taylor, 1979, p. 25. (Accrington became one of the leading bands during the 1850s, though not under the direction of Ellis.)
15. Leach, 1908, p. 12.
16. According to local census figures, this was almost 10% of the population of Bacup which was 10 935 in 1861. (This figure comes from a census list in Bacup public library.)
17. Leach, 1908, p. 20.

18 In this period of band history the trombone did not perform much solo work. Not until the 1870s did it take its place alongside cornet and euphonium in the trio of 'primary' soloists.
19 Bands did not have to prepare different music for every contest. Many were own choice, so bands could use whatever material they had rehearsed, and even in set test piece contests, promoters chose pieces from the latest brass band journals.
20 Leach, 1908, p. 64
21 Ibid., p. 68.
22 Most likely *La Favorite* by Donizetti
23 Leach, 1908, p. 53.
24 *Talks with Bandsmen*, p. 125. There is no reference to this in the *Stalybridge Old Band* centenary booklet.
25 In the 1885 Belle Vue contest there were 31 entries, of which Gladney conducted four, Swift six and Owen eight. In 1889, of the 18 bands entered, only three were not conducted by one or other of the 'Triumvirate', and Swift conducted four of the six prizewinners. In the years 1880, 1881, 1882, 1884, 1886, 1887, 1888, 1890 and 1894, the three conducted all six prizewinners.
26 Herbert, 1991, p. 11.
27 Ibid., p. 44.
28 P. 27.
29 Massey, 1996, pp. 39–41. Based on the approximate cost of brass instruments then and now, £3805 in 1883 represents a sum approaching £400 000 today.
30 November 1904.
31 Possibly a mistake on Gladney's part; 1871 is the year generally accepted as the date of his appointment at Meltham.
32 The Steads were local musicians and formed the backbone of Meltham Mills Band during its heyday. Richard (1841–1915), the euphonium player, went on to become a leading brass band and choral adjudicator; Edwin, according to *Sketches of Famous Bands* 'stood head and shoulders above the best that England could produce at that time . . .' He was quite obviously a key factor in Gladney's development of the instrumentation of the brass band, particularly with regard to the trombone's development as a solo instrument. Immediately after Meltham's hat-trick of wins at Belle Vue, Edwin Stead joined Black Dyke, achieving a similar feat with them in the years 1879–1881. He thus played in six successive winning performances at Belle Vue – a record which remains unique to this day.
33 At around this time it becomes gradually more common to see the modern spelling of 'Dyke' (see Preface note).
34 Kingston Mills was a band which took its name from a cotton mill in Hyde, Cheshire. Founded in 1855, it was very famous for a time, regularly appearing in the prize lists at Belle Vue between 1875 and 1901, including its hat-trick. According to *The Bandsman's Everything Within*, Hyde British Legion Band was formed in 1946 'from a nucleus of the famous Kingston Mills Band' – but even that band is no longer in existence.
35 Taylor, 1979, p. 74.
36 This probably entailed keeping the shuttles clean and loaded with full bobbins.
37 Biographical details are taken from a booklet, *Life and Career of the late Mr Edwin Swift, a Self-made Musician, Bandmaster and Adjudicator, Trainer of many of the leading Brass Bands in the North of England*. No author is named, but it was published shortly after Swift's death in 1904.
38 *Life and Career of the late Mr Edwin Swift*, p. 7.

39 Bayreuth is the town in Bavaria where Wagner built both his home and the festival theatre, specially planned to house performances of *The Ring* – first performed there in 1876 when Swift was 33 years old.
40 It must be remembered that during his lifetime Wagner was a controversial figure. Amongst other things, he was himself very critical of composers such as Mendelssohn and Meyerbeer, both beloved of the kind of people who populated the brass band world.
41 By now Mossley had a new band, formed in the early 1890s.
42 *Life and Career of the late Mr Edwin Swift*, p. 14.
43 *Stalybridge Old Band* centenary booklet, p. 24.
44 Ibid., p. 26.
45 May 1898.
46 Quoted from *British Bandsman* of 7 December 1929. Keighley was a teacher at the Royal Manchester College of Music and by this time a well-known composer of brass band music and a respected adjudicator. Further details about his compositions/arrangements are given on pp. 191–193).
47 *Brass Band News*, December 1885.
48 *Evolution of the Brass Band*, p. 259.
49 Jacob Adam Kappey (1826–1906) was born at Bingem-on-the-Rhine. He entered the German army in 1844, but some years later, came to England as bandmaster of the 89th Regiment, 2nd Battalion, Princess Victoria's Royal Irish Fusiliers. serving with several other corps before being offered a post with the Royal Marines, Chatham. He was also a composer, and in 1869 was appointed editor of Boosey's *Military & Brass Band Journal*. He wrote a number of brass band test pieces and regularly adjudicated. (Information mainly from Zealey, 1926, p. 32.)
50 According to *Brass Band News* of July 1911, Short was born in Lancashire and brought up in a Liverpool orphanage. No dates are given, but he was a member of the royal band during the reigns of Victoria, Edward VII and George V. He was also described as a 'King's Trumpeter', and he adjudicated at several brass band contests – including Crystal Palace.
51 In the writer's own experience a hearty rendering of 'Be present at our table, Lord . . .' to the tune of the 'Old Hundredth' was a common ritual even in the 1950s whenever the members of a band sat down collectively for a meal.
52 *Brass Band News*, November 1888.
53 Franz Groenings was born near Cologne in 1839. He came to London in 1862, but settled in Middlesbrough as teacher, organist, conductor and band trainer. From 1887 he was musical director for the Brighton West Pier Company, whose band he reorganized. He adjudicated regularly at band and choral contests.
54 This was not unusual. The pages of *Brass Band News* regularly contained adjudicators' notes from contests.
55 July 1895.
56 The Manchester Exhibition, known as the Royal Jubilee Exhibition, featured such things as art, gardens and the latest developments in engineering. It devoted much attention to music, with a resident band as well as appearances by leading brass bands, and the Band of the 2nd Dragoon Guards. (Information from *The Manchester Guardian*, August and September 1887.)
57 There are accounts of Black Dyke in Edinburgh in *Brass Band News* of September 1886 and of the contest in *Brass Band News* of November 1886.
58 *British Bandsman* of 15 September 1887 (the first edition) reported that Black Dyke also played at the Manchester Exhibition in that year. The report says that

they were paid £150 for seven days' attendance – possibly equivalent to £15 000, and way above the likely fee for such an engagement, were one to be offered today.
59 October 1898.
60 Quoted in Russell and Elliott, 1936, p. 172, from an article (undated) in *Guildhall Music Student*.

4 Unpublished nineteenth-century brass band music and the development of instrumentation

Introduction

In their article *From 'Repeat and Twiddle' to 'Precision and Snap': The Musical Revolution of the Mid-Nineteenth Century*[1] Vic and Sheila Gammon give an interesting account of the transition, during the first half of the century, from playing by ear to playing from written parts. They suggest that early bands were made up mainly of members who played by ear, with a minority who actually read music. Those playing by ear would indulge in various forms of elaboration, decoration and variation, adding elements of improvisation and individuality to their performances. The article points out that there were profound changes in the musical style of performances as the balance shifted from being predominantly aural to being based on musical literacy (see also comments about Bacup Old Band on pages 44–48). This chapter takes up the story from a point at which it is assumed all bandsmen could read music – though not necessarily to a high standard. The responsibility for teaching musical literacy would generally lie with the leader, who therefore not only wrote out band parts, but also taught his bandsmen how to read and play them.

But from where did the leaders obtain the music in the first place? We saw (page 30) how Enderby Jackson – on tour with his opera company – visited local musicians and gave them copies of his music. It is inconceivable that he was alone in doing this, and further light is shed on the matter in two articles which appeared in the band press. The first, in *Brass Band News* of December

1883, was part of some editorial comment by an unnamed writer. It stated: 'The bands of Wombwell's Menageries may, without doubt, be classed as the foundation of the good English brass bands.'[2] The significance of this was enlarged upon some years later by James Ord Hume in an article in *British Bandsman* of February, 1899, headed *A Chat about Amateur Bands*. He wrote:

> At one time, within the memory of many thousands of bandsmen, the only way that a village band could obtain any music was when a travelling menagerie would be visiting some large town within easy distance. This was a grand thing for the leader (or bandmaster) of the menagerie band, and also for the members. The leader used to arrange the music and the bandsmen would copy hundreds of band-parts, and needless to say, there was always a ready sale.

This would be especially beneficial to bands whose leaders were unable to produce enough of the necessary music for their bands, and no doubt many of the menagerie band leaders became important figures in the field of the amateur band in later years. At least two are discussed in this book – Richard Smith, the most prominent conductor of the 1850s and founder of the publishing firm of R Smith & Co, and George Ellis, tutor of 4th LRV (Bacup) Band.

Parallel with the transition from 'Twiddle' to 'Precision', the ethos of arranging made a *volte face*. Whereas formerly the business of the arranger had been to produce band parts for the players and instruments at his disposal, gradually it became the arranger who stipulated what instruments he was writing for, taking into account such niceties as balance and colour, and the variety of combinations available within the limits of the instrumentation. The seeds of this process were planted by people like Smith in their manuscript arrangements, and cultivated by music publishers in the mass publication of printed music – at first catering for various sizes of band but gradually settling on a format for the 'standard' band.[3]

According to Enderby Jackson, in 1847 Leeds Temperance Band undertook a 'lengthy engagement' in Scarborough.[4] It is not clear quite what this meant; was it a week's engagement or an afternoon and evening, or simply a one-off concert? It was probably the latter; but what music was played? The likelihood is that it consisted mainly of dances interspersed with short extracts from oratorio and opera. Whatever form it took, it seems to have been successful, as the exercise was repeated in 1848 and again in 1849.

There would be many examples of engagements for bands during the middle years of the century, but it is unlikely that programme details were kept, or that copies of the music played will ever be found. It is, in fact, quite possible that some of the players in bands such as Leeds Temperance had actually been taught to play their parts without having been taught to read music, and that others were still using the technique of playing 'by ear'.

Instruments and instrumental techniques were undoubtedly developing during these years, but scoring as such seems to have been little more than a means to an end. Study of existing parts makes one wonder if full scores were in fact prepared, or whether those parts were extracted direct from piano versions or vocal scores. By and large there was a melody, a bass and a middle accompaniment, with the melody generally at the top. It is likely that early arrangements were transferred to band parts via some sort of rough full score, but few such scores have survived. Nor were they regarded as a necessary aid to performance. This links bands with other branches of music as, during the 1830s and later, it was standard practice for leaders of orchestras to play and lead from a first violin part. Band leaders did the same, from a band part which indicated what they themselves had to play, along with useful cues for entries by other instruments. It would, of course, have been impractical to play from a full score, with the necessity of turning over pages every few bars.

Black Dyke part-books

Amongst the earliest known unpublished collections of brass band pieces is that contained in a set of part-books in the archives of Black Dyke Mills Band.[5] It comprises a series of hand-written parts in hardback manuscript books labelled 'BLACK DIKE MILITARY BRASS BAND'. These were probably in use from the time of the band's establishment in 1855 until around 1860. Eight books have survived, for the following instruments:

Clarinet in D♭	Alto sax horn in A♭
Fugle [sic] horn in E♭	Tenor trombone
Solo cornet in A♭	Ophicleide
Cornet secondo in A♭	Bass drum

The clarinet takes the top part and is, in fact, the precursor of the soprano cornet. The E♭ 'fugle' is scored in the manner of a second soprano, often complementing the clarinet in the same way that cornet secondo complements solo cornet. The trombone and ophicleide books use bass clef throughout, appearing in concert pitch. Even with this limited instrumentation there was scope for players to change to another instrument without having to learn a new technique. It would be a simple matter to transfer from cornet to flugelhorn and only a little more difficult to move from either of these to the saxhorn, or to the trombone which probably had valves. Clarinet and ophicleide would, of course, each require specialist players.

Scott discusses these part books at some length[6] and concludes that cues in the later pieces suggest a gradual increase in the size of the band. He maintains that there should be books for trumpet and bass trombone, the evidence being a number of cues for trumpet, and one instance in which the trombone player is instructed to 'change books with bass trombone'. He suggests that the books were written between 1855 and 1863, the years in which John (or James) Galloway was bandmaster. The writer's theory is that the books were probably completed within two or three years of the founding of Black Dyke in 1855. With 43 pieces in total, even if they appeared at the rate of only one per month, the books would have easily been completed by the end of 1858. The instrumentation of the 1860 band (see page 79) seems to be too far removed from the instrumentation of the books for them to have been of any use by then. Further, the pieces played by the band at the 1860 contest were 'Gloria' from *12th Mass* (Mozart) and a selection from *La Sonnambula* (Bellini). Though there is a *Sonnambula* selection (described as a cavatina) in the books, it appears as Number 9, and it is really not feasible that this could be the version played in 1860. The 'Gloria' does not appear in the books at all, though it could conceivably have been Number 15, which is missing. The one piece which gives a firm clue to the date of the books is Number 17, 'Yorkshire Waltzes', played by Black Dyke at the Hull contest in June 1856 (see pages 33–35). This seems to dispel any possibility of Number 15 having been the 1860 test piece, and suggests that pieces were added at a rate of at least one per month in the early stages.

The books have not remained intact; there are pages missing, for example, from the clarinet book, and piece Number 15, as already mentioned, has been completely removed. Of the 42 remaining pieces, just over half are arrangements of music from the classics. The rest are mainly dances, appropriate to the kind of engagement the band would be called upon to fulfil. Appendix 3 lists the pieces in the order in which they appear in the books.

There are four overtures – *Tancredi, The Magic Flute, The Caliph of Bagdad*, and one unnamed and, so far, unidentified. In addition to the overtures, transcribed faithfully as far as was practical, there are nine named operatic selections. Not all of these are categorized as such, but the pieces headed 'cavatina', 'aria' or even 'grand scena' are quite obviously selections. Donizetti is represented by *Anna Bolena, Lucrezia Borgia, Torquato Tasso* and *Linda di Chamounix*. There are also four Verdi selections – *Il Trovatore* and *La Traviata*, and two different versions of *Attila*. Selections from two of Bellini's best-known operas are also included – *Norma* and *La Sonnambula*. Many of the tunes used in these Italian operas are not well known, though there are some exceptions, including Bellini's 'Mira, O Norma', 'The Miserere' from *Il Trovatore* and, from *La Traviata*, the 'Prelude to Act III' and the famous 'Drinking Song'. From this we may deduce that the operatic selection was well established in the concert repertoire of bands even in the 1850s. This type of piece has been criticized for its lack of structural cohesion. Perhaps it should be pointed out that not only the selection, but also complete operas of this period lacked form – except within their individual numbers, and that it was not until the later operas of Wagner and Verdi that musical structure became an important feature. The playing – by bands – of operatic extracts must have helped to popularize both the extracts themselves and the operas from which they came.

Other pieces in the part books from the more august side of the repertoire include the 'Hallelujah Chorus', 'The Heavens Are Telling' and Mendelssohn's 'Wedding March'. The remainder of the collection is made up mainly of dance music – waltzes, polkas and quadrilles, along with a galop and two unnamed marches.

Of the seven waltzes in the books (four without titles), the most interesting, historically, is the 'Yorkshire Waltzes' of Enderby Jackson, composed for the 1856 Hull contest. Like others in the books and, indeed, the 'classical' waltz structure, it has an introduction (not in waltz time), a number of contrasting waltzes, all basically in binary form, but with the use of the *da capo* occasionally creating a ternary shape, and a finale, referring to earlier material. This piece differs from others in the books mainly in the care with which dynamic markings have been added – in red ink – suggesting that as this was a contest piece, extra thought needed to be given to this aspect of performance. Several of the other waltzes are confined to their home key and its subdominant. 'Yorkshire Waltzes' also visit the dominant. Harmony is basic – predominantly diatonic, with occasional chromaticism in the melody, the use of diminished chords, and a few examples of modulation.

The quadrilles are subject to similar stylistic restrictions. Again, three are unnamed, but the more interesting sets are 'Horton' by Jullien and 'Bonnie Dundee' (a medley of Scottish tunes arranged by F Galloway).[7] This is the only piece in the books with a named arranger, and it is presumably on this evidence that Scott bases his assumption that all the pieces were written out by Galloway. At one point, 'Bonnie Dundee' calls for triple-tonguing by the solo cornet player, and at another there is an imitation of the sound of bagpipes. In referring to earlier material towards the end, the quadrilles follow the example of the waltzes. Each set conforms to the standard pattern of five sections, with a mixture of simple and compound duple rhythms, and making use of binary, ternary and rondo forms.

The only named polkas are 'The Soldier's Polka' – bearing the hallmarks of an early triple-tonguing cornet solo, and 'The Echo's [sic] of Mont Blanc' by Jullien, dating from 1852. This makes use of 'echo' phrases in the coda and, like the other polkas, is in rondo form, staying within the tonic-dominant-subdominant framework of keys. The one galop (unnamed) has but a single key and is a rondo, with plenty of call for double-tonguing (as opposed to the triple-tonguing of the polkas and quadrilles). In the same way that the waltzes have an introduction in a non-waltz rhythm, so this galop (in simple duple time) has an introduction in 3/4 time. The remaining two pieces are unnamed marches – one 'quick' and the other 'grand'. Both are in the typical march and trio form and both written in 'alla breve' time, though the grand march requires four beats to the bar. These part books form an interesting link with music of the brass band in the 1850s. Despite the fact that at least one of the pieces in the books was used as a test piece, the set as a whole must be typical of music played by bands at local functions and in their earliest concerts.

The Cyfarthfa collection

The Black Dyke part-books are amongst the oldest known such books. There is, however, a far more substantial collection of early band pieces, accumulated in a total of 105 part books from the library of the now defunct Cyfarthfa Band of Merthyr Tydfil. Trevor Herbert has written at length both about this band and its music.[8]

Both Cyfarthfa and Black Dyke took part in the 1860 Crystal Palace Contest (see pages 38–39), but there the similarity ends. John Foster, the mill-owner and benefactor of the Yorkshire band, formed his group from the remnants of an existing band, appointing a local musician to tutor the members (see page 31). Crawshay, the master of Cyfarthfa ironworks, on the other hand, started his band from scratch. He regarded it as a private band rather than a works or community band, elements of both of which were present in Black Dyke. Crawshay ensured his band's success by acquiring the best players of the day, including some from London, some from the circus and even a family of professional musicians from Bradford, a mere three miles from Queenshead – home of Black Dyke. He also employed a French musician called D'Artney to arrange the band's music. According to Herbert, information gleaned from two catalogues which accompany the six sets of part books suggests that there were earlier sets, but these are lost. The existing sets were probably started at around the same time as the Black Dyke books, but were added to over a period of some 70 years.

Apart from the obvious difference in sheer quantity, a brief comparison between the Black Dyke and Cyfarthfa books reveals that more players were used in the Cyfarthfa band than at Black Dyke and that, as time went by, a far wider range of pieces was accumulated. Whereas Black Dyke would come to rely heavily on the large quantity of published music which became available, Cyfarthfa appears to have built a complete repertoire in its hand-written part books. As with the Black Dyke books there are, apparently, no full scores. The average number of books per set is 17, and a photograph of the band from about 1855 indicates that the band was 21-strong at that time, with 3 keyed bugles, 4 cornets, 2 tenor horns, 4 trombones, 1 euphonium, 1 ophicleide, 2 bombardons and 2 more unidentified brass instruments, plus bass and side drums.[9]

The books contain more than 350 pieces, over half of which are transcriptions or arrangements of classical music. Around 70 are from opera, including many selections, whilst some 50 may be categorized as 'sacred' – mainly extracts from oratorio. There are also a few transcriptions of piano pieces, songs, glees and an organ fugue, but by far the most remarkable part of the collection is the series of 40 or so orchestral transcriptions. These include overtures and orchestral extracts from opera; there are also complete symphonies – one each by Haydn and Mozart, and three by Beethoven (1st, 2nd and 5th), as well as single movements from some other symphonies. The overtures are mainly the popular ones, but at least two are unusually adventurous – Rossini's *William Tell* (a very early transcription) and Wagner's *Tannhäuser* (dated 1910, but a *tour de force* for a brass band even then). One piece which calls for special mention is the *Tydfil Overture* – composed and arranged for Cyfarthfa by Joseph Parry (1841–1903). He composed oratorios, operas, orchestral works and hymn tunes, the most famous of which is his 'Aberystwyth' (commonly sung to the words 'Jesu, lover of my soul'). Actually born in Merthyr, Parry went on to become Professor of Music at the University of Aberystwyth, and was therefore the first composer of stature to write for brass band.

On the lighter side there are well-known Strauss waltzes and Gilbert and Sullivan selections. These were probably scored during the 1890s, earlier than many of the published versions which were to become popular with bands. Most solos are for cornet, with three by Jules Levy,[10] including his famous 'Whirlwind Polka'. There are no solos for the trombone, and only one for euphonium. Familiar names amongst the composers and arrangers of the lighter pieces include Jullien, Rivière, Dan and Charles Godfrey and John Hartmann. This collection is surely the most remarkable legacy of band music, and thanks to the enthusiasm of Herbert and trumpet virtuoso John Wallace, commercial recordings of some of the pieces in their original scoring and played on period instruments are now available.

Crystal Palace band music

The next collection to be discussed consists of pieces which were written in full score, copies of which were presumably sent to bands so that their leaders could prepare band parts to suit their own needs. In the first of the 1860s Crystal Palace contests, bands played own choice test pieces (see page 39), but unfortunately no copies of these seem to have survived. During the succeeding years there were set tests, all arranged by James Smyth.[11] They comprised selections from *Le Prophète* (Meyerbeer – 1861), *Robert le Diable* (also Meyerbeer – 1862) and *La Forza del Destino* (Verdi – 1863). Copies of the scores of each of these have survived in the Ainscoe Collection, along with items played by the massed band. There are also some sets of band parts, and all appear, pasted in a large book, in the order shown in Appendix 4.

The 1860 massed items[12] are listed in Appendix 4, and at least three were arranged by Jackson. Only one full score of these remains – that of 'God Save the Queen'. The scoring of this is for D♭ soprano, A♭ cornet, A♭ 2nd cornet,* E♭ alto, D♭ alto,* B♭ bary [baritone], tenor and bass trombones, solo bass and bass.* As with the Black Dyke part books, trombone and bass parts are all in bass clef, at concert pitch, with treble clef parts transposed according to the pitch of the instrument.

Most of the band parts for 'Rule Britannia' and 'Wedding March' have survived, and indicate that the instrumentation and scoring was similar to that of 'God Save the Queen'. The melody is given to soprano and 1st cornet and also, at times, to the E♭ alto [saxhorn] – usually sounding at the sub-octave. Bass trombone, solo bass and bass all take the bass line, whilst the remaining parts, all independent, fill in the middle harmonies. The structure of 'God Save the Queen' is worthy of comment, each half being played twice – *pp* first time and *ff* the second. (In many of the scores *f* is indicated by the letters '*for*', *ff* by '*ffor*' and *p* by '*pia*'.) 'The Heavens are Telling', arranged by Tidswell,[13] was performed solely in the 1860 concert. Only the parts remain but they suggest that his scoring was similar to that of Jackson's, except that there is a 'divisi' part for the soprano, and the bass trombone takes on a dual role, alternating between providing a supplementary bass and an addition to the lower harmonies.

Though the 'Hallelujah Chorus' was performed in all four concerts, the version in the collection is dated 1862 and was arranged by Smyth. This is probably a later version than that used in the earlier years, now presumed lost, but probably scored by Jackson. The instrumentation shows a marked step forward from the 1860 scores, with E♭ soprano, B♭ cornet, B♭ 2nd cornet, solo, 1st and 2nd E♭ altos, E♭ corni,* B♭ bary, 2 trombones (probably tenor and bass), solo bass and basso. E♭ and B♭ instruments and the group of three altos give the score a more modern look. The altos were forerunners of what are now called tenor horns and the 'corni' and 'bary' fulfilled similar roles to those of the modern baritone. Study of the scores confirms that the 'solo bass' part is for bass saxhorn, forerunner of the euphonium.

There is little difference between the technical or musical demands of the 1861 and 1862 test pieces. However, the earlier score calls for more individually exposed playing, and even includes a short cadenza for 'alto primo', whereas the only solo passage of any significance in the later one is for solo cornet. The duration of each is around eight minutes, and the scores confirm

---

* = divisi, that is, music for two separate instruments on the one part.

that the change from D♭ and A♭ to E♭ and B♭ instruments took place in 1862.

The 1863 score (*La Forza*) differs slightly from that of 1862 (*Robert*) in that the 'B♭ bary' is now designated 'B♭ alt', and the three trombones (alto, tenor and bass in the 1860 and 1861 scores) have become 1st, 2nd and bass trombone in that for 1863. There is also a stave marked 'Tymp' but this, in fact, calls simply for bass and side drums. *La Forza* is an altogether more comprehensive test and was, historically speaking, very modern, the opera having been premièred in 1862, and not being performed in England for another five years. There is a greater sense of drama in this score than in its predecessors, together with a cadenza, solos in various styles and an accompanied recitative for solo cornet. There are also solos for soprano cornet and solo bass, and a wide range of demands for the ensemble. This approximately 13-minute piece forms an important link with later selections.

Returning to the massed band pieces of 1861, the 'Coronation March' (from *Le Prophète*) was included in the programme. Surprisingly, only one brief passage from this was used in that year's test piece – a selection from the same opera, also arranged by Smyth. The other new piece was called, simply, 'General Jackson's'; it was a schottische which introduced what must have been something of an innovation at the time, singing by the bandsmen. The title may have referred to the contest promoter himself, but the piece is more likely to have been named after the American Civil War general, commonly known as 'Stonewall Jackson'.

Two further massed band pieces in this set are composed by Jackson: his 'Volunteer and Rifle Corps March' (played in 1862 and 1863) and 'Das Musikfest Waltzer' (played in 1863). Both call for E♭ and B♭ instruments but show no scoring or structural innovations. For another piece played by the massed band in 1862, Jackson followed Jullien's example, entering the world of the spectacular; for the performance of Henry Farmer's 'Rifle Galop' a corps of regimental buglers was engaged to play calls and solos, under the direction of Henry Distin.

The only piece not mentioned so far is the 'Grand Prize Quadrille' after which, on the score, appear the words 'Crystal Palace Contest' and Jackson's private address. There is no mention of this piece anywhere, but it is possibly the quadrille referred to by Frank Gray in his letter, quoted on page 40, raising the possibility that it was used as a test piece during the 1860 event.

Jackson had composed other pieces, before the days of the Crystal Palace contests. These included his 'Londesborough Galop' and 'Venetian Waltzes' of 1857 and 1858 respectively. As mentioned previously, no known copies of these exist, which makes the scores in the Ainscoe Collection and the 'Yorkshire Waltzes' in the Black Dyke books especially valuable.

Instrumentation from 1860

Even in 1860 the size and instrumentation of bands still varied, providing on the one hand a hindrance to mass publication of brass band music and on the other a challenge to publishers to create flexible scoring which could be adapted to a range of sizes and formations. The 1860 instrumentation of three of the most well-known bands is as follows:

	Dyke[14]	Besses[15]	Stalybridge[16]
Soprano cornet	1 (E♭)	–	–
Clarinet	1 (E♭)	1 (D♭)	–
Cornet	4 (B♭)	6 (A♭)	8
Flugelhorn	1	–	–
Alto (saxhorn)	1	–	–
Tenor (saxhorn)	1	3	4
Baritone (saxhorn)	1	2	2
French horn	1	–	–
Trombones	2	2	3
Euphonium	1	–	–
Ophicleide	1	1	2
Bombardon (E♭ bass)	2	1	2
Drums	–	2	2
Total	17	18	23

Scott points out that with the retention of both the clarinet and the French horn, and with the introduction of a soprano cornet, flugelhorn and euphonium, Black Dyke's instrumentation provided a variety of instrumental colour not typical of the brass band of any era. Perhaps, as Scott further points out, this was due to the influence of the band's professional conductor, Samuel Longbottom, possibly striving to find a kind of 'brass orchestra'.[17] The band's use of E♭ and B♭ instruments is a little ahead of the date of the general move to these pitches from D♭ and A♭ instruments. The alto saxhorn was probably, to all intents and purposes, a second flugelhorn, and with a similar range. The French horn, however, though also in B♭, would sound an octave lower. The ophicleide, in view of the presence of bombardons, probably doubled the euphonium part. Information is taken from the signatures form for the 1860 Crystal Palace contest, and this explains the absence of drums – not played in contests.

Neither of the other combinations boasts a soprano cornet or a flugelhorn, and both have dispensed with the French horn; neither has a euphonium, and it is reasonable to assume that in these bands, as in Black Dyke, the ophicleide fulfilled a similar function to this instrument. The pitch of Stalybridge's cornets is not recorded, but whichever it was, and despite the absence of a soprano and a euphonium, one must agree with Scott that this formation starts to approach that of the post-World War I contesting band (see Appendix 2).

Moves towards the modern brass band

With one exception (see page 109), not until 1900 were printed full scores available, and even then, at first they were published only for the National Championships. This meant that generally, conductors had to write them out by hand, constructed from band parts. Many such scores have survived in the archives of Besses, most written by Alexander Owen; there are also a few early scores or sets of band parts in the libraries of Black Dyke and Meltham bands, and from all of these it is possible to see some of the work of early arrangers, and to make deductions about the instrumentation of bands as they emerged from the experimental years of the 1860s and early 1870s. The later scores bear a close resemblance to those of today, and it will be useful to consider the layout, section by section, and the respective functions of the instruments.

Cornets

The top stave on the score is for soprano cornet, the 'piccolo' of the band. The second stave down is for solo cornet, and in early scores this seems to have been for one player – the leader (or the conductor) – who played all solo passages as well as some of the tuttis: The non-solo elements were allotted to two other cornet players, written on the third stave down and referred to either as 1st cornet or repiano. Gradually it became standard to show solo cornet and 1st cornet/repiano notation on the second stave down, and for the players themselves, or the conductor, to determine who played what.[18]

The name 'repiano' has been a source of confusion and was probably, in the first instance, a corruption or mis-spelling of the term 'ripieno', meaning supplementary.[19] This name was quite appropriate in early scores, where it really was a supplementary solo cornet. However, its role has changed over the years and many feel it would now be more logical to call it 1st cornet. Whatever its name, it soon commanded its own stave, the third one down, where it has remained. To complete the cornet section, of both the 1870s bands and bands of today, there were 2nd and 3rd cornets, each with their own staves, with one player per part formerly, but with two as the size of the band increased.

Flugelhorns

The flugelhorn appeared occasionally during the 1860s and was, indeed, in the instrumentation of Black Dyke for its 1860 winning performance at

Crystal Palace. However, it was some time before it became a regular feature and in many scores it receives no mention. As the size of bands grew in the 1870s, the inclusion of one or more flugelhorns became common. Nevertheless, as late as August 1888, a correspondent in *Brass Band News*, enquiring why parts were not published for flugelhorn, was told that few non-contesting bands had them.

Several nineteenth-century scores, particularly some of those by Gladney and Owen, called for three flugelhorns. Extra staves were required, shown thus:

Repiano (still on the third stave down)
1st flugel
2nd cornet, 2nd flugel
3rd cornet, 3rd flugel

Second cornet and second flugel shared the same band part, using a single stave when playing the same line and separate staves when playing independently. The same applied to the band part for third cornet and flugel. Shortly after 1900, flugels two and three were dropped;[20] not only did they collectively create intonation problems, they detracted from the brightness of a full cornet section. One was retained, however, because of its potential as a solo instrument. For several years it shared staves with repiano cornet before acquiring its own – either immediately below repiano or, in modern scores, above solo horn, taking on the role of the treble member of the horn section.

Tenor horns

The horn section also underwent some changes before reaching the present-day norm of three tenor horns – generally but rather confusingly designated solo, 1st and 2nd. As has been seen, the French horn was not much used by amateur bands after 1860. The favoured instrument which replaced it, and which took on a similar role to that of the viola in the orchestra, was the tenor saxhorn in E♭. This name also has been the cause of confusion because, relative to other band instruments, it plays in the alto range. In some countries it is known as the alto horn, but in Britain the name tenor persists. I would suggest that the name tenor horn stems from the fact that in the original range of saxhorns the soprano was the high E♭ cornet, the alto was the equivalent of the modern B♭ cornet or flugelhorn, and therefore the next one down, in E♭, became known as the tenor saxhorn. Early scores make use of four horns – two sax tenors in E♭, and two horns in E♭ – possibly French horns. The 1st sax tenor was, in reality, the solo horn, whilst the E♭ horns were almost (but not quite) dispensable. An article about the E♭ saxhorn, in *British Bandsman* of July 1899 gives a clue regarding this stage of development of the horn section:

About 1848 the instrument began to be adopted in military and brass bands, and in time its usefulness became so apparent that it took rank as one of the most necessary instruments in a brass band, and a very desirable one in a military band. In the latter there are generally two saxhorns and two French horns.

The horn quartet persisted even without the French horns, and it was not until after the 1914 war that a trio of horns became universal in the brass band.

Baritones and euphoniums

By the time of these hand-written scores 1st and 2nd baritones were firmly established, each occupying its own stave. In some early scores there is only one stave for euphonium, though it is always marked 'solo', implying that there may have been a second player. A score by Richard Smith shows two separate staves for euphoniums, and though that for second is not fully written out, it seems that it doubles solo euphonium at certain times and B♭ bass at others. Many later nineteenth-century scores show separate parts for the two euphoniums, but in most printed scores, until as late as the 1970s, only one stave is used even though, from time to time, the instruments play separately. Baritones have always appeared immediately below the horns in the score, but the euphonium, for many years situated below the baritones has, in more recent times, been shown immediately above the basses.

Trombones

The trombone was firmly established by the time of the hand-written scores, with two tenors and one G bass trombone – a prominent feature of bands until the late 1960s. The 'G' had a quite distinctive sound and, of course, the famous handle, needed by all but the longest-armed players in order to reach the more extended slide positions.[21] Prior to 1873 bands were free to use slide or valve tenor trombones. Though the valved version was tonally inferior to its cousin, it had the advantage that players of any other valve instrument could play it without having to learn how to manipulate the slide. After 1873 it was outlawed from contests (see the reference to Phineas Bower of Black Dyke in note 5, Chapter 2).

Unlike other instruments so far discussed – all written for in treble clef and transposed relative to the key of the instrument – trombones, though pitched in B♭, were written for in concert pitch. The tenor trombones, formerly written in bass clef, spent some time in tenor clef before eventually settling in the treble – as B♭ transposing instruments. In the scores of some early twentieth-century published pieces, trombones appeared at the very bottom of each page. With the use of tenor and bass clefs they were written as non-transposing instruments – the only ones in the band. Later they were moved to a point in the score immediately above the basses and below the euphonium. Today they are generally located between 2nd baritone and euphonium, the latter appearing immediately above the Basses. In the scores studied trombones are shown on the next three staves below the euphonium.

Basses

By the 1870s serpents and ophicleides had been replaced by basses. At first a B♭ bass saxhorn (forerunner of the euphonium) and one E♭ bass (or bombardon) provided the foundation. It then became standard practice to include two E♭ basses. Later still there were two E♭ basses, one small-bore B♭ model and one BB♭ bass – known for years as the 'Monstre double B'.[22] Meltham and John Gladney are credited with stabilizing the bass section and for a time they had five instruments – including the 'Monstre' BB♭s.[23] However, from about 1875 the normal bass section became two E♭[24] and two BB♭ basses, and it has remained so to this day. Some of the early E♭ bass parts are shown in bass clef, but otherwise all bass parts are transposed and use treble clef.

Many musicians hearing a good brass band for the first time find it bottom-heavy, but for those with the acquired taste, the sonority provided by the basses is one of the chief attractions of the sound. Certainly, all the best bands within living memory have had fine bass sections, though it was some time before this depth of sound was achieved.

Criticism has often been levelled at the brass band for its persistent use of treble clef for its lower brasses which, in other musical spheres, are invariably shown in bass clef at concert pitch. There are very good arguments for both systems; the answer is to print parts in both notations, a practice several publishers now follow.

An early Belle Vue test piece

In Black Dyke's library there is a set of printed band parts for the Belle Vue set test of 1866, post-dating the hand-written part-books by some years. This is a selection from Meyerbeer's opera *L'Africaine* headed 'Journal No 47 – Chappell', and arranged by Herr Grosse (see page 98). The parts are for the following:

Printed	Hand-written
E♭ piccolo piston (or E♭ clarinet)	2nd baritone
1st B♭ solo piston	2nd trombone (tenor clef)
2nd B♭ solo piston	Solo euphonium
1st B♭ piston or flugel	E♭ bass
2nd B♭ piston or flugel	B♭ bass
Corni in E♭ ad lib (3rd tenor)	
1st & 2nd trombones ad lib (bass clef)	
Althorn in B♭ (1st baritone)	
Drums (bass drum & cymbals)	

By implication there must also have been parts for 1st and 2nd horn and probably for 2nd euphonium and bass trombone. 'Piston' is one of the old names for the cornet, and the optional 'corni' part would be for bands which still had a French horn. This instrumentation forms an interesting link between the Crystal Palace scores (pages 76–78) and the two scores discussed next.

Gladney and his contemporaries

Improvements in printing and paper-making, and increased demand led to the advent of cheap, printed music in the 1870s, with the necessity for handwritten music diminishing considerably. Nevertheless, leading conductors such as Gladney continued producing special arrangements for their own bands, showing off strengths and hiding weaknesses. This practice did not meet with universal approval, though there can be little doubt that it contributed enormously to the development and popularity of bands.

The careers of Gladney, Owen and Swift have already been discussed. Though they made some commercial arrangements, their fame – apart from their respective conducting successes – was in the special arrangements they made to exploit the qualities of their bands. Gladney in particular experimented with and standardized the instrumentation, but all three left a legacy of music which, though out of fashion today, formed an important part of the development of brass band music, contributing significantly to its popularity.

The instrumentation of the better bands began to stabilize by the late 1860s and it is interesting to compare two sets of band parts, one almost certainly from 1868 and the other quite definitely from 1869. The first set is in the archive of Meltham and Meltham Mills Band. Headed *Grand Fantasia on Robert le Diable – opera de Meyerbeer*, the arranger is shown as Jas Waterson. The most comprehensive record of the early Belle Vue contests is that which appears in *The Rakeway Brass Band Yearbook 87*.[25] It lists arrangers and adjudicators for most of the early contests, but gives no arranger for 1868. The adjudicators are shown, however, as James Waterson,[26] Sam Hughes and George Carr. Meltham actually competed that year and, conducted by J Bery (prior to Gladney's appointment), won fourth prize. It seems reasonable to assume, therefore, that these parts were the ones used by Meltham at the 1868 Belle Vue contest, an assumption reinforced in the letter from Gladney to *Brass Band News* of November, 1904 (referred to also on page 50), in which he further stated:

> Mr Waterson of the 2nd Life Guards arranged *Roberto* (1868) for the 'Courtois Union Band', a band of professional brass instrument players who all played Courtois instruments.[27] This band was organised by Messrs Chappell and Co. Mr

Jennison [manager of Belle Vue and organiser of the contest] merely adopted this piece.

The parts which have survived are shown in the following table, and added in italics are parts which probably existed but which are now lost. The part marked 'euphonium' on its outer cover has the name 'B♭ bass' on the part itself, suggesting that it was played on a bass saxhorn. The bombardon part contains a cadenza which is not shown on the E♭ bass part, though in other respects the parts are similar. All parts are hand-written except that for 1st cornette [sic]; the fact that this is printed provides evidence that the arrangement was published. It is also the only part which names Waterson as the arranger, though there is no doubt that the hand-written parts belong to the same set.

The *Lucrezia Borgia* selection (Donizetti), discussed on page 86, arranged by John Gladney in 1869, is for a very similar line-up to that used by Waterson – with perhaps one more baritone, and less quaint names for the horns. The two euphonium parts are independent of each other, the option of using flugels with 2nd and 3rd cornets points to future Gladney scores, and the use of treble clef for most of the bass parts seems to suggest that interchanging of players was already occurring. The parts (still intact in the archive of Black Dyke) are as shown in the table, which provides an opportunity to compare the two quite similar instrumentations, and showing a further step towards modern scoring.

Waterson score	Gladney score
E♭ soprano cornet	E♭ soprano cornet
1st cornette in B♭	B♭ solo cornet (leader's copy)
2nd solo cornet	B♭ repiano
B♭ flugelhorn	B♭ flugelhorn
2nd cornet	*2nd cornet* (or flugel)
3rd cornet	*3rd cornet* (or flugel)
E♭ tenore primo	1st E♭ tenor horn
E♭ 2nd sax	2nd E♭ tenor horn
E♭ 3rd sax tenor	3rd E♭ tenor horn
B♭ baritone	1st & 2nd baritones
Tenor trombone primo	1st trombone
2nd tenor trombone	2nd trombone
Bass trombone	Bass trombone
B♭ bass (euphonium)	Solo & 2nd euphoniums
Bombardon E♭	B♭ bass
E♭ bass	Basses (bass clef)
BB♭ bass	BB♭ bass

These two arrangements form an important link in the chain of development, being quite a step forward from the 1866 arrangement by Grosse. Not only do they use more up to date nomenclature, they also call for proper families of instruments within the band.

Scott states that prior to 1873, bands competing at Belle Vue were restricted to a maximum of 19 players. He goes on to say that in that year the maximum was raised to 24.[28] It was to remain at that figure for the next 75 years and of course, percussion was still not used in contests. (There is a slight conflict with this in a letter from Richard Stead, of Meltham, in which he states that, according to an old programme in his possession, in 1874 there was no rule regarding numbers of players, but that most bands carried 22.[29]) This increase in size brought about the possibility of extra solo cornets and/or basses and also, if the conductor wished, increased use of the flugelhorn. Printed music seldom called for a flugel, but it became standard practice for bands to have at least one.

It is difficult to establish with certainty the dates of Gladney's later selections, but it seems likely that they were all scored during his time at Meltham, that is, between 1871 and 1883. He would obviously take some with him to other bands, but with increased demands on his time – travelling and conducting, and also with more published music available, he probably indulged less in the time-consuming occupation of arranging and part-copying after 1880. The most comprehensive set of Gladney scores is in the archive of R Smith & Co, and there are also a few sets of parts, as well as some isolated scores, in various band libraries. A list is given in Appendix 5.

Only the early scores are dated, *Lucrezia Borgia* and *Attila*, both from 1869 and *Il Flauto Magico* from 1870. The dates of the other scores are largely a matter of conjecture, though there seems to be a clue in the clefs used for lower instruments. *Lucrezia* is an exception because, certainly on the parts at Black Dyke, treble clefs were used throughout, except for bass trombone. With the other scores there appears to be a gradual shift from the use of concert pitch bass clef for lower instruments in what are or seem to be the early scores, towards B♭ treble clef in those which apparently came later, with tenor clef used for tenor trombones in what are possibly the scores from the middle years of Gladney's arranging career. There is further evidence to support this theory in Gladney's use of cadenzas for linking the sections. In what I believe are the early scores he rarely resorts to these – with one at most per selection. In what must therefore be the later ones he has written three or, in one case, five. Three flugels seem to have been standard in Gladney's scores, and in at least one he also calls for the use of a second soprano cornet – a ploy often considered in recent years, but not put into practice.

As may be seen in Appendix 5 there were, in addition to the selections, a few transcriptions. A particularly interesting one is a solo for bass trombone – probably the first in the brass band repertoire. Titled 'Aria from Il Flauto Magico' it is, in fact, 'O Isis and Osiris', the famous bass aria from Mozart's opera. What is even more interesting is that the accompaniments are provided entirely by the mellow-toned instruments – horns, baritones, euphoniums and basses. The Gladney selections and transcriptions seem not to have been published, though *Lucrezia* was, in a sense, in that it was supplied to bands taking part in the contest for which it was arranged, in Accrington in 1869. The only printed Gladney piece found is a march 'Le Tourni' (anon.), published in 1886 by Wright & Round.

We turn now from the instrumentation to the content of two Gladney selections. That from Mendelssohn's *Elijah* is in the archive of Black Dyke, though it was scored long before his time there (1888–1907), having been played by Meltham as early as 1876. One of Meltham's 'party' pieces, the full selection would take well over 20 minutes to perform. It contains some of the oratorio's most popular sections, including the air, 'I Am He that Comforteth' and the chorus 'Baal, We Cry to Thee'. The penultimate section is the touching and emotional 'O Rest in the Lord', which leads into the rousing final chorus, 'Thanks Be to God'. The selection thus ends triumphantly, no doubt whipping up the enthusiasm and cheers of the crowd, and quite often earning the approval of adjudicators. The selection is also spiced with sections designed to show off the skills of the soloists, as well as demonstrating the technique and stamina of the full band. The excerpts are substantial though not all complete and, in keeping with other selections, there is no regard for the order in which they appear, nor for their original keys. Mendelssohn's music was rewarding to play and pleasing to listen to; it was emotional rather than intellectual and, to working-class players and listeners, quite soul-stirring.

The other piece, *Beethoven*, is described as a fantasia but is in reality a selection, and is based largely on instrumental music. It begins and ends with the opening and the finale of the overture *Egmont*, and contains extracts from the 2nd, 3rd and 5th Symphonies, along with some instrumental settings of vocal excerpts from the opera *Fidelio*. In the archive of Besses is to be found the rare luxury of both a score and a set of band parts for one of these early pieces, an air and chorus, *Inflamatus* from Stabat Mater (Rossini – 1842). No date is given for the arrangement, but as Gladney conducted Besses from 1879 to 1883 it seems reasonable to assume it dates from this period. It calls for Gladney's usual instrumentation with three flugels and three tenor horns. Having performed the piece with a band the author vouches for the fact that the use of three flugelhorns instead of the usual one has a significant effect on the band's sound, making it unmistakably darker. A parallel would be if half of the 2nd violins in an orchestra were to play their parts on violas.

We move now, briefly, to Gladney's contemporary, Edwin Swift – four years his junior. Not much of Swift's music seems to have survived. The library of the band around which he carved his career, Linthwaite, contains none of his selections, and the other band with which he had much success, Wyke Temperance, no longer exists. There are, however, sets of parts for two selections in Black Dyke's archive, and an arrangement of a glee, 'The Seasons' (Cooke[30]) at Besses. The latter, dating from 1885 calls for the four horns of older scores, but the other two suggest that he generally used only three, along with a single flugel. The selections are from *L'Etoile du Nord* (Meyerbeer) and Swift's *Tour de force* based on Wagner's music, *Bayreuth*, both of which brought Swift considerable contest success. He also arranged selections from some of the lesser-known operas of Donizetti.

At Linthwaite there was an accomplished cornet player called George Raine, totally unknown today, but a key player in Linthwaite's contest successes as well as the winner of many solo prizes. He seems to have had a good upper range, as in solo passages Swift frequently took his cornet line to the D above the stave, a note not used, as far as I have seen, in other band music of the time. This is just one example of exposing the strengths of players. As more band music was being published at the time Swift was writing than when Gladney had made his arrangements there were, presumably, more publishing opportunities. Several Swift pieces were published and these are referred to in the next chapter.

Alexander Owen, it will be recalled, came under the influence of Gladney when he played solo cornet at Meltham, between 1875 and 1879. He was 12 years younger than Gladney, and though unable to compete with his mentor's record of contest successes at the highest level, seems to have taken on his mantle as an arranger. His first selection was an instant success. Variously known as *Rossini's Works*, *Reminiscences of Rossini* or simply *Rossini*, it was arranged in 1882.[31] The score calls for three flugelhorns, lasts some 35 minutes when played in its entirety, and is built mainly on extracts from *William Tell* and *Semiramide*. Containing several solos, it exploits all the band's principals, and has a particularly difficult euphonium part, with a cadenza which calls for top register work as well as pedal notes (see Glossary). It is a tuneful selection, and no doubt it was its musical content – in particular the finale from the *William Tell* overture – which made it more popular than later selections, rather than any outstanding features of scoring. Owen's other highly successful contest piece, specially arranged for Besses, was his selection from *Faust* by Berlioz (see page 55 for details of the band's success with these two selections).

In the year in which he joined Besses (1884) Owen made an arrangement called *Heroic*, based on music by Weber, and including extracts from *Oberon* and *Euryanthe*, as well as other unidentified pieces. An interesting feature of this selection is a genuine timpani part, in his own handwriting, one of the first such parts in brass band music. Weber seems to have been a favourite with Owen (as Wagner was with Swift); he named an 1890 selection after the composer, and in 1898 compiled a selection from the same composer's *Oberon*. Other selections by Owen include *Il Profeta* (Meyerbeer), *Tristan und Isolde* and *Die Walkure* (Wagner) and *Beethoven's Works*.[32] There were also a number of concert items, mainly of a sacred nature.

During the later 1890s, Owen became so incensed at the number of inaccurate versions of his selections being played that he had sets of the more popular ones printed and made publicly available. In *Brass Band News* of January 1898, he announced the publication of a limited edition of six of his selections, on offer at two guineas for a set of 24 parts. Thus, part of what was essentially a collection of private arrangements, intended for use by a limited number of bands, was published. Literally hundreds of these sets were still, at the time of writing, stored in Besses' bandroom. Like Swift, Owen had several pieces published; these are mentioned in the next chapter, and a list of Owen's pieces is given in Appendix 6.

Two outstanding features of the 1890s were undoubtedly the domination of Besses under Owen, aided by his arrangements, and the increasing number of own-choice contests. *Brass Band Annual* of 1900 (published by F Richardson) stated that two-thirds of all contests allowed bands to choose their own test pieces. Nevertheless, many promoters campaigned for the set test, a move which found support amongst music publishers – naturally.

Besses o' th' Barn, its Origin, History, and Achievements was published in 1893. Its author, Joseph N Hampson – a cornet player with Besses – was not happy with the set test contest, arguing that whilst it was acceptable for average bands it did not stretch the better ones. He also inferred that as a result of its introduction the standard of bands was declining and that there were now fewer 'crack' bands.[33] The proprietors of *Brass Band News* were incensed, and in the June issue of 1893 published a damning criticism of Hampson's views. First, they did not agree with his arguments against the set test piece, writing, 'As to the statement that bands are deteriorating in consequence of test pieces [this] is utter twaddle'. The Gladney, Owen and Swift selections, they contended, were fine for bands which could offer £30 per annum for star players on cornet, trombone and euphonium. But, they concluded, 'The sham amateur band is going. Let it go: its room is better than its company!' Mercifully, the 'sham amateur band' did not go. It continued to set the pace for the brass band movement for many more years before giving way to even greater heights of 'shamateurism' in the shape of heavily subsidized works bands, some of which gave considerable financial rewards to their principal players.[34]

Owen continued arranging until well into the twentieth century, but the majority of the later pieces, along with some compositions, were intended for concert performance. The value of Owen's output lay not so much in any advances he made in scoring techniques or instrumentation, but rather, in building on the foundations laid by Gladney, in his high quality arrangements and music-making which he brought to his bands and their audiences.

This chapter has traced the development and stabilization of instrumentation from the early part books of Black Dyke to the sophisticated but largely unpublished scores of Gladney and Owen. Already the music publishing business was expanding rapidly, and it is now necessary to revert to the late 1830s, when the history of such music begins.

Notes

1. Herbert, 1991, Chapter 4.
2. See also note 13, Chapter 3.
3. Composers and arrangers in the twentieth century have not enjoyed such luxury. Due partly to the rules of contesting, but also largely as a result of the tradition of having a regular 'team', with an almost specified membership, bands have stuck tenaciously to the instrumentation evolved in the nineteenth century, and composers have been expected to tailor their musical ideas to the set form of the band.
4. Taylor, 1979, p. 90.
5. All references to Black Dyke will use the modern spelling, apart from those in quoted material.
6. *Evolution of the Brass Band*, pp. 229–237.
7. Probably Frank Galloway, possibly a relative of John (or James), Black Dyke's Bandmaster from 1855 to 1862. Frank conducted a band in the 1857 Hull contest, winning fourth prize with them, and is named as the soprano cornet player of Black Dyke at the 1860 Crystal Palace contest. On the entry form he is described as a warehouseman, and would certainly be employed by John Foster. An added note on the entry form indicates that he died in 1895. (There is some confusion about Frank, James and John Galloway. Recent research leads me to the conclusion that they were all one and the same person.)
8. Some details are given in *Bands*, and see also Herbert (1990), pp. 117–132.
9. Herbert, 1991, p. 14.
10. Levy (1838–1903) was one of the pioneers of the cornet as a solo instrument and, in his own time, one of the most celebrated of cornettists. Born in London, his father refused to let him have a cornet as a boy, but he obtained a mouthpiece on which he practised assiduously. Not until he was 17 years old did he acquire a cornet, bought for 15 shillings from a pawnbroker. Within a year he was playing in the band of the Grenadier Guards. Later he played in theatres, and toured in France, Holland and the USA. Eventually he settled in America, playing in the bands of Gilmore and others, becoming a household name in America and Canada. There are recordings which he made towards the end of his career, in his 60s which, though exhibiting his incredible technique at that time, were said not to be a true reflection of his playing whilst in his prime. Not of a modest nature, Levy is reputed to have said, 'I am the world's greatest cornettist', and styled himself 'King of cornet players'. He was at his zenith during the 1870s and 1880s. (Information from Bridges, 1972, pp. 56–60.)
11. James Smyth (1818–1885) was Bandmaster of the Royal Artillery Band (Woolwich) from 1854 to 1881. He had a distinguished career and considerably enhanced the status of this band, already considered to be one of the leading bands in the British Army. Amongst other things, he increased the band's size from 51 to 71; his brass section comprising 4 cornets, 2 trumpets, 2 E♭ soprano cornets, 2 each E♭ and B♭ flugels, 2 baritones, 4 French horns, 4 trombones, 2 euphoniums and 4 bombardons – a brass band in its own right! (Zealley, 1926, p. 18.)

12 The information about pieces played at Crystal Palace comes mainly from contest programmes in the Ainscoe Collection.
13 There seem to have been a number of Tidswells (or Tidewells) in brass bands. This is probably the one who formerly conducted Wombwell's Band and, during the 1850s, the professional brass band at Belle Vue (see Taylor, 1979, p. 43 – called 'Tidewell' in that account).
14 Crystal Palace entry form 1860 – located in Black Dyke's rehearsal room.
15 Hampson, 1893, p. 15.
16 *Stalybridge Old Band 1814–1914*, p. 20.
17 Samuel Longbottom, of Mixenden near Halifax, Black Dyke's first professional conductor, was an organist and a violinist, accounting for the fact that his favourite band pieces were selections from oratorio. He had a successful time with Black Dyke, conducting it in four major championship wins – Crystal Palace 1860 and Belle Vue 1862, 1863 and 1871, remaining with the band until his death in 1876. This information comes from an article by Black Dyke's euphonium player and Bandmaster, Phineas Bower, in *British Bandsman* of October 1889.
18 Three solo cornet players were standard for a long time. Four is now normal, though some bands carry five, to help share the considerable workload of this part.
19 The term should not be confused with the *ripieno* parts in the Baroque concerto grosso.
20 Scott, 1970, p. 160.
21 The G bass trombone went out of fashion when bands changed to low pitch in the 1960s. The instrument now used has a larger bore than the tenors, and one or two triggers, which facilitate playing in the lower register; though still notated at concert pitch, it is actually a B♭ instrument, like the tenors.
22 The term 'Monstre' seems to have been first used in Gladney's scores to differentiate between the large BB♭ bass and the smaller B♭ bass.
23 See photograph in Taylor, 1979, p. 70.
24 The modern E♭ bass is often referred to as a 'double E'. It is of the same pitch as earlier models, but its bore is now larger, as is that of the 'double B'. Both instruments are often fitted with a fourth valve to extend the range downwards.
25 In the section compiled by Alan Littlemore, pp. 307–319.
26 Waterson had also adjudicated at the 1864 Belle Vue contest. He was to become one of the early editors of *British Bandsman*.
27 Courtois was a well-known Parisian instrument manufacturer.
28 *Evolution of the Brass Band*, p. 155.
29 *Brass Band News*, February, 1905.
30 Thomas Simpson Cooke (1782–1848), Irish singer, instrumentalist and composer.
31 The earliest report I have found of it being played concerns a contest in Mossley on 24 June 1882, when of the four bands conducted by Owen, three played *Rossini*. They were Boarshurst, which won 2nd prize, Oldham Rifles and Trawden. (Information from the July *Brass Band News* of 1882.)
32 The two Wagner selections are currently enjoying something of a revival. having been recorded and performed under the baton of the distinguished conductor, Elgar Howarth.
33 Hampson, 1893, pp. 48–49.
34 It has often been contended that some heavily-subsidized works bands should not be allowed to compete in the same classes as public subscription bands, many of

which often struggle to survive. Other contentious issues have been the use of musicians from full-time service bands, brass instrumental teachers and full time music students. The rules of contesting now accept players from any of these categories and, indeed, fully professional musicians, for example, from major symphony orchestras.

5 Published brass band music in the nineteenth century

Introduction

Of the three largest music publishers in England during the post-war years – Boosey & Hawkes, Chappell and Novello – Boosey (not associated with Hawkes at the time) was the first to include brass band music in its catalogue. Chappell's interest came a little later, that of Hawkes later still, and it was not until the twentieth century that Novello catered for the genre. Over the years many other companies have published such music; three – R Smith & Co, Wright & Round and F Richardson & Co – devoted their catalogues either wholly or largely to music for brass bands, yet none of them were pioneers in the field.

The unstable and irregular instrumentation of early bands was a hindrance to mass publication because there was little point in going to the expense of printing unless the end product was attractive to a significant number of bands. Therefore, early publishers endeavoured to print music in accordance with the most common band instrumentation of the time.

Early publishers

Early printed music probably reached relatively few brass bands, most of which still played from hand-written arrangements. However, Jack L Scott, quoting from *Musical World* of 18 March 1836,[1] points out that as some editions were reissued there must have been a degree of demand. According to Scott, Robert Cocks issued the first published music for brass band in 1836 – 'Eight Popular Airs', arranged by George MacFarlane.[2] R Cocks & Co were leading publishers of wind instrumental music of the period, and during the next four years published no fewer than 50 tutors, a journal for keyed bugle and scales for 16 wind instruments, as well as music for military band. The 'Eight Popular Airs' were arranged for 3 keyed bugles, 2 trumpets, 2 horns, 3 trombones and a serpent. In 1838, Cocks published 'Praeger's Thirteen Melodies', with parts for a similar instrumentation, but with only two keyed bugles. In a later edition, the name 'keyed bugle' was changed to 'cornet'.[3]

In 1837, just a year after the first Cocks band pieces, two further publishing houses introduced brass band music into their catalogues: D'Almaine published a set of songs, dances, marches and tunes from opera arranged by J Parry,[4] described by Scott as the 'first published arrangements of contemporary music for brass band and the first published attempts to provide serious or formal music for brass band'.[5] At the same time, Wessel & Co issued a weekly *Brass Band Journal* of popular airs and selections by contemporary composers.[6] These included pieces of a more substantial nature, for example, an excerpt from Donizetti's opera *L'Elisir d'Amore*, possibly one of the first steps towards the operatic selection, which was to be the principal form of serious band music for many years.[7]

Military band music was also published during the 1830s, but the foundations for Boosey's *Band Journals* were not laid until 1845, when Carl Boosé published a selection from *Ernani*. The name Boosé should not be confused with that of Boosey, despite the similarity and the fact that both were in the music business – even in the same company. Boosé (1815–1868) came to London in 1835 as a clarinettist, having served in the German army; in 1848 he became Bandmaster of the 9th (Queen's) Lancers, and later of the Band of the Scots Guards. He was well noted for his arrangements and his 1845 *Military Band Journal* was one of the earliest such publications in Britain.[8] Within a year Boosé was appointed sole editor for Boosey, who was now publishing the journal.

It was to be a few more years before the company entered the brass band field but the *Musical Directory*[9] gives a list of pieces from the first two series of Boosé's *Brass Band Journal*, dating respectively from 1852 and 1853. Almost all the pieces were marches or dances and no arrangers were named. The only composer identified was Wagner, with an excerpt from *Rienzi*.[10] There seems to be little more information about the early brass band music of Boosey, though a set of its journals was presented as a special prize at the 1860 Crystal Palace contest (see page 40).

Cocks returned to the scene again around 1840 with 'Handley's 24 Airs for Brass Band', along with some cornet solos, and during the early 1860s published further band music, using more modern names for the instruments. Again it was for a band of ten – 3 cornets, 2 E♭ saxhorns, 2 trombones, euphonium, bombardon and drum. In a later edition there were also parts for E♭ soprano cornet and baritone.

Variety in the size and instrumentation of bands continued to test the ingenuity of publishers; by 1857, Henry Distin was publishing music suitable for brass or brass and reed bands with between 10 and 24 instrumentalists, with a recommended limit of 17 for the all-brass combination.[11] For the ten-piece band there were parts for E♭ piccolo cornet (today's soprano cornet), 2 B♭ cornets, 2 B♭ alto tubas (today's flugelhorns), 2 E♭ alto tubas (tenor horns), B♭ baritone tuba (the baritone), B♭ bass tuba (the euphonium) and E♭ contra basso. It is interesting to note that B♭ and E♭ instruments are specified, pre-dating the prescribed changeover at Crystal Palace by five years (see page 77).

For bands with 15 players, in addition to the above, Distin offered parts for E♭ clarinet (brass), E♭ trumpet and an extra cornet, providing quite a range of treble sounds. These were complemented by two E♭ tenor tubas (yet another name for tenor horns) making a total of four horns – two called altos and two called tenors. For the 17-piece band there were parts for an additional trumpet and for a trombone. Rather surprisingly, Distin publications almost ignored the trombone, which appeared only in the larger bands, and then in the singular.[12] The fact that no instrument was referred to as a 'saxhorn' was probably due to the severance of links between Distin and Sax, and the so-called 'tubas' were virtually saxhorns under a different name.

As the 1850s and 1860s progressed and more all-brass bands appeared, other companies became involved in publishing for them. As well as Boosey's *Brass Band Journal*, Richard Smith founded his *Champion Brass Band Journal* in Hull in 1857, and the *Alliance Musicale* (Rivière & Lafleur) was established in 1860. Jules Prudence Rivière (1819–1900) was a Frenchman who had settled in England in 1857. Three years later he went into partnership with fellow countryman René Lafleur, a Paris music publisher, publishing the *Alliance Musicale*, a monthly journal of music for reed or brass band. Distin followed up his early scores with the *Distin's Brass Band Journal*, founded in 1862; Chappell's *Journal for Brass Band* also dates from *circa* 1862.

The amalgamation of Boosey and Hawkes took place in 1930, but the histories of both parts of the business go back much further. Boosey's roots stretch back to 1792, when Thomas Boosey opened a business as a bookseller. Hawkes and Co was founded in 1865 by William Henry Hawkes (1830–1900) in partnership with Jules Rivière – who acted as manager. The Hawkes and Rivière partnership of 1865 began with the founding of *The Musical Progress*, a journal which specialized in military and, some years later, brass band music. In 1876 the company's name was changed to Rivière & Hawkes, and though the partnership was dissolved in 1884 the company retained the same name until 1889 when Oliver, the only son of William Henry, became a partner.[13] Known then as Hawkes & Son, the firm became one of the leading publishers of brass and military band music during the later years of the nineteenth century and the early years of the twentieth, prior to amalgamating with Boosey's.

It was some time before printing of brass band music on a grand scale began. Not even the test pieces for the Crystal Palace contests of the 1860s were printed, and the first printed Belle Vue test did not appear until around 1866. Meanwhile, at a more commercial level, shorter, more functional pieces provided the material for some of the earlier printed music. There are, no doubt, several collections of early published band music but alas, most of them from this era have been destroyed, either as bands have folded, or as enthusiastic librarians have disposed of older music to make space for more recent publications.

Goose Eye band books

My attention was drawn to the 'Goose Eye' band books by Scott's thesis,[14] which induced me to visit Keighley in an attempt to see them. Keighley is located a few miles north west of Bradford, almost in Brontë country and just south of the Yorkshire Dales. The area nurtured numerous bands during the nineteenth century, its most celebrated band being that of W Lister Marriner, which came into prominence when it won first prize on the second day of the 1861 Crystal Palace Contest.[15] But the band which is of most interest here came from two small villages on the outskirts of Keighley, Goose Eye and Newsholme.

A collection of nine band books is located in the museum of Cliffe Castle, Keighley. Unfortunately they do not match up with each other, and they reveal little more than a string of titles. One book is dated 1852, but little if any of the music which has survived is likely to be from such an early date. Some of the books have lost their labels and, in a few cases, their outside covers. Those which have remained more or less intact are labelled Solo cornet, 2nd cornet, 3rd cornet and Euphonium. The book labelled Euphonium actually contains a mixture of parts for euphonium, alt horn in $B\flat$[16] and 1st $B\flat$ baritone. All are printed and seem to cover a period of about 50 years. Most of the earliest group of pieces are arranged by J Sidney Jones (see note 4, Chapter One) and several mention the name Montgomery, for example his 'Whisper of love waltz', and the 'Golden stream varsovania' – both arranged by Jones, and 'The fair lady schottische', by a W H Montgomery.[17] There are also 'Three beautiful glees', including (of course) 'Hail, smiling morn', along with selections from *Martha*, *Masaniello* and *Lucrezia Borgia*, as well as a selection of 'Christy's Minstrels' songs'[18] – all arranged by Jones, and a selection from *Les Huguenots* arranged by W H Hawkes[19] and published by *Musical Times*.

The second cornet book, probably the earliest in the collection, contains 20 short pieces, all in manuscript, and mostly arrangements of glees or hymn tunes. Another book, without designation, contains a similar number of short, hand-written pieces, though the glees of the other book appear to have been replaced by short instrumental pieces, with titles such as 'Moss rose waltz', 'Confidence' and a well-known 'German waltz'.

The third cornet book is the most interesting, though certainly not the oldest. It contains a mixture of hand-written and printed parts. Of those which are hand-written, three bear the name Edward Newton.[20] The printed pieces are interesting because out of a total of 16, ten are by Richard Smith, and some of them could, conceivably, be from one of his early *Champion* journals of 1857. The Smith contributions are mainly marches, but there are also arrangements of some sacred pieces. None of the titles of the R Smith pieces in the books which I saw tally with those listed by Scott.[21] Those which I saw are the quicksteps 'Dear old days', 'Mother kissed me in my dreams', 'The Amazon', 'Darling Josie', 'Christy's gem' and 'The starry night' (all composed by Smith), and his arrangements of the anthems 'Sing unto God', 'Hark the glad sound' and 'Glory to the new born King', and a hymn tune 'Trinity'. There are also two more Edward Newton pieces amongst the published ones. (Smith and Newton are discussed in more detail later in this chapter.)

The book marked Solo cornet is a disappointment. Had it remained intact it would probably have been the most interesting in the collection. Inside the front cover, in manuscript, is 'Silsden quick step'. No composer is named, although Newton would be the most likely candidate. Sadly, the remainder of the original pages of this book are missing, and in their place are vocal copies of glees. Perhaps Goose Eye Band became Goose Eye Glee Club!

A return to Scott's thesis revealed something of a mystery, as he had quite obviously seen a totally different set of part books, apparently more orderly and in better condition. These contained 38 short, light compositions, including five by Richard Smith, and a Grand March by Tidswell (or Tidewell), bandmaster of the Belle Vue Band, one-time conductor of Wombwell's Menagerie (see note 13, Chapter Three), and the arranger of some of the pieces for the massed band concerts at Crystal Palace (see Appendix 4). It would seem, therefore, that there are two separate sets – the one described above, and the other discussed by Scott in his thesis. So far, I have been unable to locate the Scott Goose Eye Books. As a result of his researches, Scott concluded that the Goose Eye Band did not become a contesting band, and that it may be considered typical of the small village band of the period, a view supported by the pieces in the other set described. Early brass band music would be targeted at bands such as the one at Goose Eye, but what about the publication of more substantial pieces? It seems that this lagged behind by a few years.

Belle Vue tests in the 1860s

It is not clear precisely when Belle Vue test pieces were first published. During the early years of the contest each band had its own musical arrangements, a fact confirmed in a letter from Richard Stead (see note 33, Chapter Three), which appeared in *Brass Band News* of November 1904. He wrote:

> My connection with Belle Vue dates from 1858, when the contest was held in the open-air, at the top end of what is now the dancing platform.[22] I remember that year so well because the test-piece was Haydn's 'On Thee each living soul awaits', and 'Achieved is the glorious work'. It was a test for bandmasters as well as bands, for no parts were sent out. The vocal score was sent to each band and the bandmaster had to arrange it himself. The Accrington Band had a famous ophicleide player who played the bass solo. We (Meltham) played it on bass trombone . . . Accrington was the great band of that day.[23]

According to Allan Littlemore,[24] the first time an arranger was named was for the contest of 1866, when Herr Grosse arranged a selection from Meyerbeer's *L'Africaine* (see pages 83–84). This may also have been the first time band parts were provided, a theory strengthened by the fact that 20 bands competed – the largest entry in the history of the contest up to that time.[25] If it is, this could be classed as the first published Belle Vue test piece.

William Winterbottom (note 13, Chapter One) is the next named arranger, providing test pieces for the Belle Vue contests of 1867, 1869, 1870 and 1871. No arranger is given by Littlemore for the 1868 test (*Robert le Diable*), but as was seen on page 84 this was arranged by James Waterson. In 1872 the name Charles Godfrey appears (see note 7, Chapter One for information about the Godfreys). He arranged all Belle Vue test pieces for the next 40 years (see pages 145–146 for a more detailed study of Godfrey's arrangements, and information regarding their printing and distribution).

Into the 1870s

1873 was the twentieth anniversary of the Belle Vue September contest. Referring again to Gladney's letter in the November issue of *Brass Band News* in 1904: he had attended Belle Vue for the first time in 1867 and first conducted there in 1871, when he secured fifth prize for Burnley Band. In the letter he states that at that time there was no fixed instrumentation and that bands generally had between 16 and 20 players, adding:

> Reeds were not debarred until 1873 if I remember right, as in that year the new rules came in force re numbers allowed. Reeds were freely used, so far as I have been told, up to the middle of the 60s, and then began to fall out.

There were many other contests, of course; the expansion was a reflection of the increasing numbers of bands, though it was some years before estimates of the number of these in existence appeared. Opinions vary as to whether the contest was the cause or the effect of the success of amateur bands, but there can be little doubt that it contributed significantly to their popularity. It seems also that bands which were regularly successful in competitions were also in greater demand for other types of engagement – consistent success being perceived as an indication of quality.

With the proliferation of bands and band functions, the need for a ready supply of music and an expanding repertoire was now growing. The increase in the number of publishers who included band music in their catalogues was certainly part of the solution, but whilst many publishers were based in London, the majority of successful amateur bands were in the North and the Midlands. The London-based publishers, though well-placed for keeping abreast of developments in the wider world of music, were not in touch with the grass roots of banding. Richard Smith, with his *Champion Brass Band Journal*, might have filled the need, but he seems to have concentrated on publishing short, light items rather than contest pieces. Neither does his move to London in 1878 seem to have had any immediate impact on the course of band music.

Three other Northern-based publishers of band music appeared in the 1870s. T A Haigh in Hull, J Frost & Son in Manchester and Wright & Round in Liverpool. Wright & Round is still a leading publisher of brass band music; the other two lasted for a relatively short time only, though marches published originally by Haigh still exist.

T A Haigh and J Frost & Son

Thomas Albert Haigh was born in Uppermill on 19 November 1843. Much of the following comes from a 'profile', published in *Brass Band News*.[26] Though Uppermill is in the heartland of Lancashire's brass band district, Haigh's first musical activities were in the field of vocal music; he was a member of the Saddleworth Choral Society[27] and also a singer (and later choirmaster) at Uppermill Congregational Church. Haigh became involved with bands at the age of 18 when he joined Dobcross Old Band, first playing cornet and later, baritone. He undertook a large amount of music copying for the band, and perhaps it was this which attracted him into publishing. He was also 'dabbling' in composition – the profile says that Dobcross Band played his first march in one of the now-famous Whit Friday march contests.[28] The march had the thought-provoking title, 'Be kind to thy father'.[29]

Meanwhile, Haigh progressed in his choral career, eventually becoming an examiner for the Tonic Sol-fa College. He also became a Freemason, rising to the position of Worshipful Master. In 1877 he settled in Hull, where he established his *Amateur Brass Band & Military Journal*. Though it has not been suggested previously, it is not beyond the bounds of possibility that Haigh took over some part of the business of Richard Smith, who moved his publishing business from Hull to London in 1878. The earliest Haigh publications seem to have appeared in 1879. The profile ends: 'His list of band music publications is the most extensive of any publishers in the world, containing as it does more than 2000 numbers for brass, reed, string and fife and drum bands.' Haigh's success with his band journal was reflected in an advertisement he placed in *Brass Band News* of April, 1884 which read, 'Wanted – an experienced arranger of Brass Band Music to re-arrange and re-score composers' scores ready for publication. Constant employment and good wages.' After what seems to have been a successful career in publishing, lasting some 25 years, Haigh died on 23 September 1903 in his 60th year.[30]

At around the same time that Haigh was starting his publishing business in Hull, the *Manchester Brass & Military Band Journal* was being established. In an advertisement in *Brass Band News* of July 1888 this journal claimed to be in its ninth year, indicating a founding date of 1879. The journal was published by J Frost & Son, and consisted mainly of music by either James Frost[31] himself, bandmaster of several bands in the Manchester area, or George A Frost, presumably the son. Publications seem to consist entirely of marches or dance music. From a study of advertisements appearing in *Brass Band News*, it appears that Frost published band pieces spasmodically between 1879 and 1883 and then more consistently between 1888 and 1894. The peak years, during which over 70 titles appeared, were 1889 to 1891.

Haigh had also published regularly until the turn of the century, but advertising and publishing rather more titles and producing a more varied catalogue than that of his rival. The *Manchester Journal* was based almost exclusively on titles by the two Frosts whereas, in addition to his own compositions and arrangements, Haigh also published music by other writers, including Ord Hume, William Rimmer, George Allan and Edwin Swift.

Yet the combined forces of both companies, even in addition to the music supplied by the London companies and numerous other small firms in various parts of the country, was insufficient to meet the increasing demand for music for the now rapidly-expanding brass band movement. There was, however, a larger company which specialized in the musical requirements of bands, which was closely in touch with them, which knew precisely what their requirements were and which was to influence the course of brass band music until well into the twentieth century. This was the *Liverpool Journal*, established by the firm of Wright & Round; its output of brass band music was to dwarf the efforts of other publishers for many years to come, particularly in the publication of contest pieces.

Wright & Round

Thomas H Wright and Henry Round established the *Liverpool Brass Band (& Military) Journal* in 1875, though little else is known about the company's founding. However, an 1896 catalogue which the writer discovered attached to a copy of *The Amateur Band Teacher's Guide* provided a comprehensive list of pieces published up to that time. It reveals statistics from which it appears that Wright & Round quickly became a leading publisher of music for brass band. The following table shows the number of publications during each of the first ten years of the company's existence:

Year	Publication nos	Total	Year	Publication nos	Total[32]
1875	1–24	24	1880	124–149a	27
1876	25–48	24	1881	150–174	25
1877	49–72	24	1882	175–202	28
1878	72a–97	26	1883	203–231a	30
1879	98–123	26	1884	232–261	30

With a starting point of two publications per month and a steady increase in most years, this represented a substantial contribution.

In October 1881 Wright & Round also began publishing a monthly newspaper, *Brass Band News*, devoted almost entirely to the brass band. From this point onwards there is no shortage of information since one of the paper's aims, not surprisingly, was the promotion of its sister company, the *Liverpool Journal*. During its first five years, *Brass Band News* was edited by Enoch Round – possibly Henry's father or a brother. He was succeeded in 1886 by William Seddon, who had served as bandmaster of Kettering Rifles Band. Seddon edited *Brass Band News* until his death in 1913.[33]

From the outset, the policy of the *Liverpool Journal* was to concentrate largely on pieces for brass band, but with parts for clarinets and piccolo also available, so that they could be used by brass and reed bands. The company also established journals for drum and fife bands and for string bands, but these did not become a permanent feature. Wright was the businessman (though apparently a musical one), and Round the musician. Together they created a highly successful business, publishing music not so much for leading bands as for the growing number of bands of average or less than average ability. Their publications comprised hundreds of 'lightweight' pieces suitable for performance at local functions attended by bands, and also test pieces which catered for the increasing number of brass band contests. Scott maintains that prior to the arrival of Wright & Round's mass-produced and therefore low-priced test pieces many bands did not go to contests, and that those which did had to rely mainly on manuscript arrangements, which could be quite expensive.[34] I would even argue that it was largely as a result of their output that the explosion in band contests took place.

The technique of scoring for a basic small band continued, with additional parts as 'optional extras' to bands which required them. Wright & Round adopted this idea when, in *Brass Band News* of March 1882, they published recommended instrumentations for three different sizes of band – for those with 14, those with 20 and those with 24 players. All were related to the basic 14-piece band, which was specified as follows:

Soprano, solo, repiano, 2nd and 3rd cornets
1st and 2nd horns
1st and 2nd baritones
Euphonium, B♭ and E♭ basses, bass and side drums

Bands of 20 were to use each of these, plus a solo horn, 1st and 2nd trombones (slide if possible), G bass trombone, an extra solo cornet and an extra E♭ bass. With the addition of two flugelhorns (probably playing from the same band parts as repiano and 2nd cornets), a further solo cornet and a further B♭ bass, the 24-man band began to approach the instrumentation of the present-day contesting band, though in reality it was 22 brass players plus percussion.

Through journalism, Wright & Round were helping push bands towards a standard instrumentation, and one which would exploit publications available through the *Liverpool Journal*. By 1889, in their *Amateur Band Teacher's Guide*,[35] Wright & Round were recommending an instrumentation for bands of 24 players plus percussion, the extra instruments being a flugelhorn (probably playing alongside the 3rd cornet) and another euphonium. The recommended bass section now included two E♭ basses, one medium-bore B♭ bass and one large-bore B♭ bass. The composition of the band was as follows:

Soprano   1st 2nd and 3rd horns
3 solo cornets[36]   1st and 2nd baritones
Repiano cornet   2 euphoniums
1st flugelhorn   1st, 2nd and bass trombones
2nd cornet and flugel   2 E♭ basses
3rd cornet and flugel   2 B♭ basses (one medium and one 'monstre')

With the addition of drums, this is almost identical to the formation shown in Appendix 2, and may be seen as a stepping stone from Gladney's instrumentation of 20 years earlier (see page 85).

Returning to the 1896 catalogue, during the first ten years the names of over 40 composers appeared, though some were mentioned only once. Henry Round was easily the most prolific of the writers. The second most prominent was his partner, Thomas Wright, whilst third came Frank Linter – though his first piece did not appear in the lists until 1880. Enschall was another of several late arrivals, first appearing in 1882. Both writers continued to feature in the lists for a number of years. It is very doubtful if any of the music was commissioned. Round and Wright obviously had a substantial commercial interest as composer/publishers and it is feasible that the names Linter, Enschall and others were pseudonyms used by them to create the illusion of a wider range of composers, particularly as no biographical details of them have so far been found.

The lists of pieces were headed *Wright and Round's General Catalogue*. There was no indication of instrumentation, but the first piece on the 1878 list, Round's Grand Fantasia 'The tournament' was offered for 'Full Brass Band, 5/-. No Reed or Drum parts.' Most of the items were single, though there were occasional pairs, as for example in number 95, when two glees – 'Come, bounteous May' (Spofforth) and 'Through verdant plains' (Brooks) – were offered for the 'same price as Quicksteps'. The 1880 list includes a 'Christmas Number' – with six seasonal tunes offered – 'Military, 2/6; Full Brass, 2/-; Small Do [ditto]. 1/8.' In the 1881 list there were a number of special offers. First, a triple-pack with a quadrille, a solo polka and a quickstep – all by Henry Round – was offered for military and full or small brass band. The same combinations are also offered for Wright & Round's 'First holiday number of dance music (easy)' – with four assorted dances by Round, a 'Special concert number, suitable for young bands' and a 'Second holiday number of dance music (easy)'. With these publications a new trend was set, more modest bands being well catered for with a liberal sprinkling of 'easy' music. Christmas Numbers and sets of dance music also appeared regularly in future lists.

From 1885, as the company entered its second decade, the lists became a little more informative, a short sentence about selected pieces being provided. Also the instrumentation was given – conforming to Wright & Round's standard instrumentation. It was also made clear that the instrumentation for the 'military band', in the Wright & Round catalogue, was the same as that for full brass band, but with the addition of parts for piccolo, E♭ clarinet, and 1st, 2nd and 3rd B♭ clarinets. These were, apparently, supplementary instruments, and in no way necessary for the successful performance of the pieces.

New music appeared at a rapid rate during the remaining years of the catalogue. The number of publications increased annually for several years, peaking in 1893 with 41, but dropping back to 38 by 1896. From 1886 a new group of pieces appeared each month, the double or multiple publications continuing, producing more individual items than actual published 'numbers' with, for example, as many as 57 titles in 1891.

New bands were also being formed during this period, and Wright & Round were naturally anxious that these should buy not only their latest pieces but also some of the almost 700 items which had accumulated. To stimulate this, *Brass Band News* of June 1892 announced a new package – a set of band books containing 24 pieces from their catalogue – mainly from earlier years. Called *The Enterprise Band Books*, they were described as 'a marvel of cheapness'. At 10/- (50 pence) for a set of 20 books this must have been a very attractive offer. The parts for each instrument were bound and ready for use, paged and numbered in uniform order, so that any piece could be found by the whole band at a moment's notice. Though probably intended primarily for bands which did not yet have extensive libraries, because of its convenience this package would also be attractive to those which already had some of the pieces. The publishers were very confident of the success of the idea, declaring that an edition of 100 000 copies had been printed.[37] Less than a year later – in the May *Brass Band News* of 1893 – it was announced that the first edition of *The Enterprise Band Books* had already sold out, that a second edition was selling rapidly, and that a second set containing a further 28 pieces was now available. These could be purchased for any combination at sixpence (2½ pence) for each part-book. In advertising the sixth set, in the 1896 catalogue, Wright & Round claimed, 'Having thousands of pieces to select from [a gross exaggeration] we select the best and nothing but the best for the *Enterprise*, knowing that they will be played everywhere and last forever.' Another assertion, and possibly equally exaggerated, was that '30 000 Bands in all Parts of the World play the *Enterprise*'. However, Wright & Round could justifiably say they had made an enormous contribution to the development and popularity of the brass band, and say it they did! In the 1896 catalogue under the heading, 'To our subscribers, friends and patrons', the following statement appears:

> All our rivals are at their wits' end as to what they can do to stop our progress. They do not care so much about making progress themselves, as stopping our progress. While they are eaten up with envy on account of our splendid success, and never miss a chance to sneer at us, they will never say what they have done for Amateur Bands. And for good reason – they have done nothing.

There is nothing like blowing one's own trumpet, and Wright & Round proved to be expert at it. Nevertheless, their list of successes was impressive, especially with contest music (see Appendix 8), and their stability must have been a boon to bands. '*Enterprise*' also epitomized the policy of the company. A set of *Enterprise* books was published more or less annually, until the early years of World War I. Set number 22 (containing 33 pieces) was advertised in May 1913, and the last advertisement I have found appeared in January 1915.

Unfortunately, Wright & Round did not have the vision to take bands any further than the narrow world of borrowed or eclectic music, that is, music composed in familiar idioms. By the end of the century it was becoming obvious that bands had passed their popularity peak, and inevitable that new paths would have to be trodden if they were to survive the changes which were taking place.

Other brass band publishers

The 1890s were the peak years for brass bands. Various figures have been quoted for the number of bands in existence at the time. Forty thousand, the claim made in the *Amateur Band Teacher's Guide*[38] is generally regarded as being extravagant, and though no-one has come up with an authoritative estimate, Taylor feels that 5000 would be a more realistic figure.[39] *Brass Band News* had become very popular; it was a proven vehicle for advertisements and offered a range of articles of a historical or educational nature, news items and letters. Advertisements and articles in its monthly editions give an indication of the expansion which took place in brass band publishing towards the end of the century. *Brass Band News* of April 1882 advertised the first 53 pieces in Lafleur's *Alliance Music* catalogue – 'List No 6' of overtures and grand selections, all available for military band and small or large brass band. Arrangers included Charles Godfrey and Sidney Jones. In the July edition, *Brass Band News* advertised the same publisher's quaintly-named 'Sunday Inseparables' – a collection of light pieces suitable for performance on the Sabbath.

A new pair of names appeared late in 1883, with an advertisement for a 'descriptive oriental march, La Caravanne'. The publisher was C Mahillon, of Leicester Square, London and the composer, George Asche. These names appeared with some regularity over the next few years. Advertisements during 1884 introduced several more publishers, including Alphonso Cary of Newbury and W J Willcocks & Co of London, and the December, 1886 edition of *Brass Band News* carried an advertisement for the 1887 journals of Rivière & Hawkes. There were to be two, each comprising 12 monthly issues, and as a supplement to the second, six extra pieces were offered 'gratis'. The pieces were mainly marches.

Another new company was the *London Brass Journal*, published by R de Lacy of Brixton. De Lacy himself was one of the principal contributors to this journal. By July 1888, de Lacy's advertisement was for what was now called the *London Brass & Military Band Journal*. This was advertising piece number 805 in its catalogue, though this does not necessarily mean that the firm had published that number of brass band pieces, and again, there was no indication of the date of the company's founding. The *Metzler Military & Brass Band Journal* was also established, with 26 pieces in its catalogue for brass or military band. The expansion continued, the growing numbers of publishers issuing music at an ever-increasing rate, and competition helping to keep prices down. The cost of this to bands was, in many cases, badly presented music – small print on cheap paper, and often with an abundance of mistakes.

106 *Brass Roots*

Hawkes & Son

The most significant development in the publishing of brass band music during the early and mid-1890s – outside the activities of Wright & Round – was a new journal published by Hawkes. *Brass Band News* of November 1890 carried the following advertisement: 'Messrs Hawkes & Son beg to announce that they intend to produce on January 1st 1891, an entirely new Band Journal, entitled THE ECLIPSE BAND JOURNAL.' The editor was to be Warwick Williams,[40] and between 35 and 45 publications, covering a wide variety of pieces, were to appear every year, scored for bands of 12, 16 or 20 players. At first it was not made clear for what type of band the *Eclipse Band Journal* would cater, but later advertisements indicated that parts were available for brass and reed instruments. A December 1892 advertisement claimed that the new journal's features included 'good printing on good paper, with no errors'. Ten pieces were advertised for the first quarter of 1893, with Warwick Williams, R Rimmer (probably Robert, brother of the more famous William) and James Ord Hume amongst the writers. The *Eclipse Band Journal*, like the *Enterprise* books, appeared regularly until part way through the war, still being advertised as late as February, 1916. However, this was only one part of the brass band music of Hawkes at this time, and *Brass Band News* of May 1898 carried an extensive Hawkes advertisement, with no mention of *Eclipse*. But, the music offered contained little that was new apart from some recent Sousa marches. Hawkes had also been publishing march books, perhaps as a result of the success of Wright & Rounds' *Enterprise* books, and as a stepping-stone to the *Eclipse Band Journal*.

An advertisement in *Brass Band News* of May 1899 showed Hawkes & Son breaking refreshing new ground, with arrangements of concert music from the wider world of popular music, in particular, selections from two recent musical comedies – *The Belle of New York* (by Gustave Kerker, first performed in New York in 1897 and London in 1898) and *The Geisha* (by Sidney Jones, first performed in London in 1896), along with a selection from Sullivan's *Haddon Hall* (1892), and an arrangement of Ivanovici's popular waltz, 'Donauwellen'.[41] The advertisement also stated that for this batch of arrangements, published parts would be for brass band only, with no parts for reed instruments, possibly reflecting the gradual demise of the combined brass and reed band. This type of repertoire was a significant step forward, paving the way for large quantities of the kind of music played in park bandstands for upwards of half a century. During 1900, Hawkes published more popular band music, along with patriotic marches and selections, novelty items and popular overtures – again, the stuff of which future band programmes were to be made.

The growth of Hawkes and Wright & Round made it difficult for the smaller brass band publishers to maintain their market share. Though many struggled on, selling pieces already in their catalogues, they had little capital to invest in new music. Haigh did publish a version of the march, 'The Washington Post' in 1896, at a time when it was Sousa's number one hit, but an advertisement in *Brass Band News* for Frost's *Manchester Journal* merely listed a group of reprints. By the mid-1890s there were more advertisements for second-hand instruments than for music – a sure indication that the expansion in brass band music which had been a hallmark of the Victorian era was at an end.

Amongst the numerous other short-lived publishers of brass band music were *The Australian Journal* (which had its headquarters in London) and *The Intercontinental Brass & Military Band Journal*, published in Ballarat, Victoria, Australia. From the North East of England there were advertisements in 1893 for the *Chester-le-Street Brass Band Journal*, and the *Northern Brass & Military Band Journal*, located in South Shields. Almost at the turn of the century the *Millerean Edition* of Birmingham appeared, as did some publications by John Church, in London. Another familiar name in a new disguise appeared in an advertisement in *Brass Band News* of December 1892 for the *Challenge Journal*. Offering 52 pieces per year for a guinea – post free – this was advertised under the name of J R Lafleur & Sons – probably an offshoot of the earlier Rivière–Lafleur partnership.

Some of the early publishers left the scene during the 1890s, but gradually other mainstream publishers began to incorporate brass band music in their catalogues. Boosey was still in the market of course, and was joined, in a modest way, by Francis & Day, who advertised 16 pieces in their *New Military & Brass Band Journal* of 1891,[42] and by Rudall, Carte & Co who, from the middle years of the decade, published a series of march books containing several marches by Ord Hume. Some of these books are still in use.

By the late 1890s there were some 20 publishers of brass band music. Many of them published 'journals', which generally meant that for a certain annual subscription discount rates were offered and bands received a large amount of music at a modest price. One important new publisher to appear in the 1890s was F Richardson of Sibsey, Boston in Lincolnshire. From 1894 Richardson published a series of *Brass Band Annuals*, with information about bands and band personalities, lists of contest results and, from 1896, a monthly magazine called *The Cornet*, and also a new journal of brass band music, under the same name. As an example of cheap music, *The Cornet* journal for the first quarter of 1896 consisted of 20 pieces, all of which could be bought for 22/- (£1.10p).[43] Amongst the writers were Ord Hume (probably John, brother of the more famous James Ord Hume), Jack and George Frost (of the *Manchester Journal*) and William Rimmer.

R Smith & Co

Lastly, we return to one of the oldest of the specialist publishers, R Smith & Co – established in Hull in 1857 and moving to London in 1878. Little factual information seems to have been written about Richard Smith's life or his business. He was, of course, one of the most successful of the early band trainers (see page 34). In an article in *The Illustrated News of the World* of 3 August 1861 he was described as '*The Champion Teacher of Yorkshire*' – and perhaps he was mindful of this when, four years earlier, he founded his '*Champion' Brass & Reed Band Journal*. As a cornet player he was described as 'one of the best in the kingdom, both as to tone and true musicianlike [sic] feeling'. Successful with the arrangements he scored for his bands, Smith was well qualified to enter publishing, and seems to have been the first to found a company specializing in band music. At some point he had enlisted the support of Edward Newton (see note 20, end of this chapter). A profile on Newton in *British Bandsman* of April 1889 stated that he was offered an annual retainer, plus a fee for every score produced for the *Champion Journal*. Up to this time, Newton had obliged, it was claimed, with nearly 400 pieces, including 137 marches, and many hymns and anthems. Newton was, therefore, probably the main contributor to the journal, with Smith himself adding some marches and (possibly) a few selection-type test pieces.

Richard Smith died early in March 1890 at 52 New Bond Street, London – possibly both his home and his office. His obituary, in *British Bandsman* of 15 March, revealed little about his life, but in an April issue, R Smith & Co was described as 'The leading publisher of popular brass and reed band music.' Several years later, in *British Bandsman* of February 1899, in an article headed *A Chat On Amateur Bands*, James Ord Hume implied that Smith had been connected with travelling menagerie bands prior to his involvement with brass bands.

Sam Cope (to be discussed later) became musical editor for R Smith after the founder's death, having already helped run the journal for several months, and during the latter part of 1896 the company's address was given as 'Champion House', Clapham Road, London. A few years later it moved to premises in the Strand, first at number 188 and later – and for over 70 years – at 210 Strand, London. This became one of the most famous addresses in brass band history, as it was also the address – for a similar length of time – of *British Bandsman*, the brass band's second newspaper, which appeared in 1887.

An advertisement in *Brass Band News* of March 1896 stated that the current year's pieces for the '*Champion' Brass & Reed Band Journal* were available from Derrington Street, Hull.[44] No titles were given, but with publication numbers from 946 to 971, Smith had probably been producing pieces at an average of 25 issues per year.

R Smith & Co was bought in 1898 by John Henry Iles, who was to exercise considerable influence on every aspect of brass bands. As will be seen, he established personal links with Sir Arthur Sullivan and one of the first consequences of this, as far as R Smith & Co was concerned, was their publication of a series of selections 'from Sullivan's famous operas, etc', which were commissioned as test pieces for the National Brass Band Championships, founded in 1900 by Iles. The Sullivan pieces were advertised in *Brass Band News* in August 1900, and two months later, a *'Champion Christmas Number'* was advertised, claimed as an 'absolutely new venture'. Iles was getting into his stride by November, with a large advertisement, heralding the 44th year of issue with the words:

Oldest! Cheapest!! Best!!!

Printed scores

R Smith seems to have been the first publisher regularly to print full scores; these were of the test pieces selected for the National Brass Band Championships. But there were a number of developments leading up to this which are worth recording. The first occurred in 1885, when Wright & Round published full scores for two of that year's test pieces, a selection, *The Lyric Garland* and a contest glee, *Hail! Apollo* (both by Round). Despite much publicity this was seemingly not a commercial success, as the exercise was not repeated.

Not for a decade was there apparently another move to provide full scores. *Brass Band News* of April 1895 carried an advertisement for W Williams of Alfreton, Derbyshire, who offered to copy scores for a reasonable fee. In an article in the same issue, it was claimed, 'since Christmas he [Williams] has written 57 scores of *Torquato Tasso*, 16 of *Lohengrin* and 19 of *Schubert*'. This enormous undertaking must have provided Williams with a full time job of music-copying. Not to be outdone, Wright & Round tried again, in the June issue of *Brass Band News* announcing that 'Bands contesting this season at contests where *Halevy* is test piece can have a full score loaned to them, at a very small charge, by applying to Wright & Round.'

Yet again this seems to have been an unsuccessful one-off, as there were no other such offers. It may be, however, that the assembling of full scores was becoming something of a cottage industry, as there are quite a number of very carefully prepared such scores at Besses, not in Owen's hand. Names on these scores include Thomas Valentine and TE Embury of Manchester, and B Hall of Glossop.

The British Bandsman

In September 1887 a new magazine appeared and, as Taylor points out,[45] it could not have been coincidence that this, as well as *Brass Band News*, were both launched just in time to report on a Belle Vue contest. However, the new paper took some time to establish itself as a genuine addition to the brass band press.

The new magazine was the brainchild of Sam Cope (1856–1948) – son of a West Country bandmaster, and himself a teacher, composer and conductor. As a young man he had played cornet and piccolo, and also the organ, until he lost one of his fingers in an accident. High hopes and ideals were the motivation for the paper; it would, he believed, raise the status of bands, would be technical yet friendly, and would teach and philosophize. Cope's burning ambition was to see the brass band movement develop as an amateur body, in the best sense of the word, and to see it accepted as such in other musical spheres.

The somewhat lengthy title of the early issues was *The British Bandsman. A monthly magazine for Bandmasters and Members of Military and Brass Bands*.[46] It was on sale at newsagents, railway station bookstalls and ticket agencies. During its first year the paper attracted little advertising, but was regularly sold out. Circulation figures were not published at the time, but some years later Cope wrote, 'The first issue was 1500, but I had to have a reprint. The second month ran into 2000 copies, and the third, 2500; but I was never able to exceed this, as my time was occupied very considerably in other directions.'[47]

One of Cope's early projects was to try to get rid of some of the unruliness which was rife at brass band contests. For some time there had been reports of unseemly behaviour at many events, even of the manhandling of adjudicators. In the December 1887 issue of *Brass Band News* (two months after the founding of *British Bandsman*) there was editorial comment about the excessive number of rows and grumbles during the recent season's contests. A letter in the same edition from a correspondent signing as 'Old Tyke' expressed the view that the reason for the discontent was the fact that players in certain bands were being paid – providing that they won the contest. Cope attempted to reverse the trend of bad behaviour by drawing up rules for the benefit of promoters and competitors, but the idea seems to have had little effect. He also appointed district correspondents, each of whom wrote of the activities of their local bands. Writing under pseudonyms, as Hailstone puts it,[48] 'helped them to publish and be damned!' Most of the 16 pages of the early editions were devoted to news of army bands.

In June 1888 the paper's name was changed to *The British Bandsman and Orchestral Times*. The new-style paper devoted much of its space to military band topics, along with reviews of classical concerts, and by the end of the year brass bandsmen were complaining about the balance (or lack of it) of the paper. Despite this, it survived. 1891 saw yet another title change – this time to *The Orchestral Times and Bandsman*. Cope now announced that 5000 copies were being sold, a figure increasing monthly by 100. However, the paper gradually lost its interest for brass band people as the focus shifted away from band issues. There was now no news from the district correspondents and by the end of its fifth year, to use Hailstone's words, '*The British Bandsman* had lost its identity.'[49] The trend continued as yet another title emerged – *The British Musician*, and what scant news there was about brass bands was largely derogatory. The paper also painted a bleak picture of the brass band scene, claiming that apart from the 'crack' bands 'the movement had disintegrated and lost all credibility'. All this, of course, was the view of brass banding from an office in London. However, just as the proprietors of *The British Musician* were about to abandon the brass band, there came a sudden resurgence of interest, stimulated by the nation's celebrations of Queen Victoria's Diamond Jubilee.

Whilst it is true that all was not well and that in addition to the unruliness, contests had peaked, in the North of England there was still a great deal of activity, with Belle Vue and many more contests maintaining standards and popularity. *The Brass Band Movement* reported a total of 222 contests in 1895[50] and 240 in 1896.[51] The 'Great Triumvirate' were busy improving the playing standards of many bands, the best of which were still in demand for prestigious engagements. Black Dyke, for example, were playing to massive crowds in places as diverse as Dumfries and Birmingham. During the years 1895–1897 this band attended 21 contests, winning 19 of them. Contesting, however; did not always bring satisfaction: having won the Belle Vue September contests in 1895 and 1896, both Black Dyke and their great rivals, Besses, were unplaced in 1897, in a result which seems to have caused much discontent. The two bands, as a protest, boycotted Belle Vue in 1898 – the year in which John Henry Iles found himself at the contest. Even without them, Iles was much impressed by what he heard, and decided that he must become involved. Within a year he had bought out not only *The British Musician*, but also the publishing house of R Smith & Co. From 1 January 1899 the paper reverted to the title *British Bandsman*, and in the following August a second magazine was born, coming from the same publisher. This was called *The Contest Field*, was edited by James Ord Hume, and eventually reached circulation figures of over 10 000.[52]

The Salvation Army

Another development, and one which was to have significant effects on the international brass band scene, was the formation of Salvation Army bands.

The first such 'band', which appeared in 1878, comprised four members of a family from Salisbury.[53] Reminiscent of the Distins, it comprised the father, Charles Fry, playing cornet, and his three sons, Fred, Ernest and Bert, playing another cornet, a valve trombone and a euphonium.[54] From such a small beginning the tradition of the Salvation Army band grew. It grew so rapidly that by 1886 it was claimed that there were about 400 such bands. The Army's founder, General Bramwell Booth, is said to have described the band as a 'peripatetic organ', adding that whilst the church organ had to stay in the church, his 'walking organs' were able to go out to the people.[55] However, *Brass Band News* of September 1885 reported, not without some incredulity, that General Booth had decreed that 'From this date, no [Salvation Army] band will be allowed to play from any music, excepting *The Salvation Army General Band Book*.' This was obviously not good news for Wright & Round which had, incidentally, a large number of sacred pieces in its catalogue.

By the end of the century Salvation Army bands were adopting a similar kind of instrumentation to that used by contesting bands, except that their cornet sections dispensed with the use of the repiano cornet, and many writers favoured the use of four trombones rather than the standard three of contesting bands. Not bound by contest regulations, the size of Salvation Army bands was and still is very flexible. Many pieces are scored in such a way that even a small number of players can cover all necessary parts, whilst the larger bands simply double existing parts.

Following Booth's edict of 1885, Salvation Army band music remained exclusive to its own bands. Only during the 1990s have what they call the 'outside bands' been allowed to purchase and play their music, and it is still quite rare for Salvation Army bands to play the music of other bands.

The stated aim of Salvation Army music is the spreading of the Gospel of Christ through music, and it has long been a rule that pieces written for use in Salvation Army circles must be connected with a sacred song or hymn. In the twentieth century Salvation Army band music has developed, within these limitations, on similar lines to that of original compositions for contesting bands, but it is outside the scope of this book to delve into what is undoubtedly another rich store of brass band music.

Conclusion

From this chapter it can be seen that published brass band music has quite a history, yet the names of many who contributed to that history are now completely unknown to bandsmen. Banding peaked in the 1890s and needed to find new ways in which to survive in the twentieth century. Established publishers continued to promote brass band music and were joined by other publishers such as Feldman, Bosworth, Keith Prowse and Lawrence Wright.

With the dawn of a new century the way was paved for a new era in brass band history, beginning with the founding of the National Brass Band Championships. These will be considered in the next chapter.

Notes

1. Scott, Jack L. (1970), The Evolution of the Brass Band and its Repertoire in Northern England, PhD thesis, Sheffield, p. 125, and quoting from *Musical World*, 18 March 1836.
2. MacFarlane is listed in *Catalogue of Printed Music* (Baillie and Laureen, 1981), credited with ten compositions between 1845 and 1860. He introduced the cornopean to Britain in 1833 (see Scott, *Evolution*, p. 193), and wrote a number of pieces and tutors for it. Scott describes him as a military bandmaster and credits him with having made improvements to the cornopean, the ophicleide and the lower brasses. *British Bandsman* (1 June 1899) described him as a leading English cornet player between 1835 and 1850. He was a member of the Duke of Devonshire's private band.
3. Scott, 1970, pp. 127, 129 and 200.
4. *Musical World* of 20 January 1837, quoted in Scott, 1970, p. 79. Parry was a former member of Denbigh Militia, and also music critic of the *Morning Post*.
5. Scott, 1970, pp. 126 and 194.
6. Herbert suggests that Wessell's *Brass Band Journal* did not appear until the early 1840s (*Bands*, note 120, p. 55).
7. Few of these publications are still extant, and their existence is known of mainly because of advertisements such as that quoted by Scott from *Musical World*. The journals would probably comprise the music only, and it would be virtually impossible to even guess at circulation figures.
8. Information about Boosé comes from *The New Grove* (Sadie, 1980).
9. Rudall, Rose & Carte, *Musical Directory*, 1854, quoted in Scott, 1970, p. 213.
10. This pre-dates the first English performance of the opera by some 26 years.
11. Scott, 1970, p. 138
12. Ibid., pp. 139 and 140.
13. Information from Krummel and Sadie, 1990. Rivière's name appears as arranger on a number of pieces still in the repertoire.
14. Scott, Jack L. (1970), The Evolution of the Brass Band and its Repertoire in Northern England, PhD thesis, Sheffield.
15. According the *Keighley Year Book, 1877*, this band was formed on 12 January 1845 as the Caminado Band, but later became known as Marriner's Private Brass band.
16. If this instrument really is the forerunner of the flugelhorn, the parts are surely misplaced here.
17. Who Montgomery was is uncertain, but the 'Varsovania' is a mis-spelling of 'Varsoviana', a type of slow mazurka, with characteristics of the polka – introduced to Paris in 1853 and to London shortly afterwards. Dance composers of the period wrote many such pieces, often with fanciful titles like this one.
18. The Christy Minstrels were founded by Edwin P Christy (1815–1862) who did much to promote the songs of Stephen Foster. However, the piece in the Goose Eye books may relate to the Moore and Burgess Minstrels, a rival company which appeared later.

19 Founder of Hawkes and Son.
20 Edward Newton was born in Silsden, near Keighley, in 1838. In his early years he played in a local militia band, and was a member of Craven Amateur Band (from Silsden) which won third prize at Belle Vue in 1863. For its own choice the band played a Newton arrangement, the title of which has not been preserved. On hearing this, Rivière, one of the adjudicators, is said to have predicted a successful future for the young musician. Newton wrote for a number of publishers, including Lafleur, Haigh, Wright & Round and Frost, but chiefly for R Smith (see p. 108). For further details see *The Bandsman Who Wrote a Thousand Tunes*, pages 10 and 11 in *The Yorkshire Ridings Vol. 4 Number 1, 1967*. Newton died on 27 April 1914, aged 75 (*Brass Band News*, March 1914).
21 The pieces in the Goose Eye Books seen by Scott include the following by Smith: 'Morning star polka', 'Bonnets of Blue Rock', 'Rock Villa polka', 'Lily Bell' and 'The light horseman' (listed in Herbert, 1991, *Bands*, page 39). For a fuller account of this set of books see Scott, 1970, pp. 214–216.
22 In his letter to *Brass Band News* of November 1904, Gladney stated that he first visited Belle Vue in 1867, and that none of the contests he had been to were held in the open air. Therefore, the change to indoor must have taken place between 1858 and 1867.
23 Accrington's Belle Vue record during the early years included third prizes in 1854 and 1856, and its only win – in 1858, after which it disappeared from the prize lists.
24 *The Rakeway Brass Band Year Book 1987*, p. 311.
25 The previous highest entry was in 1864, when 14 bands played.
26 October 1903.
27 Saddleworth is the collective name for the area which includes the villages of Uppermill, Delph, Diggle, Dobcross and Greenfield.
28 Whit Friday has, for over a century, been an important day for Sunday School processions, particularly in the Manchester and Oldham areas. Bands were engaged by local churches and chapels to lead their processions, and because there were so many in the area, the idea of running a contest during the evening was nurtured in a number of villages. The earliest records of such contests date from 1884, when they were held in Stalybridge and Uppermill. There are now over twenty such contests every Whit Friday evening, with more than a hundred brass bands – ranging from the very best to quite humble village and school bands – travelling around the Saddleworth area, playing in as many of these contests as possible. The evening has become known in the brass band movement as 'The Greatest Free Show on Earth'. (See Greenalgh, 1992, for a full account of the history of Whit Friday contests.)
29 This anecdote does not quite ring true. If it were, in view of information in note 28 above, Haigh would have been over 40 when he wrote this 'first' march, and at least seven years into his publishing business. The probability is that he wrote the march at an earlier age and that it was played in a contest, but not on Whit Friday.
30 Additional information about Haigh comes from *British Bandsman* of March 1889.
31 A short article about Frost in *Brass Band News* of May, 1906 states that he played soprano in the Matlock Prize Band, formed in 1860. A further comment, in *Brass Band News* of October 1910, indicates that he was by then retired and living in Radcliffe (a small town some miles north of Manchester).

32 The inclusion of extra 'a' numbers causes a slight mathematical irregularity, but the totals are as shown in the catalogue.
33 Russell and Elliot, 1936, p. 155.
34 *Stalybridge Old Band* booklet states that in 1876 the band paid its professional conductor, J Sidney Jones, the sum of £20 for an arrangement of a selection from *Le Prophète*. Jones was also on a salary of £100 *per annum* at Stalybridge; he adjudicated regularly at brass band contests.
35 Wright & Round, 1889, p. 3
36 In later years, with the disappearance of second and third flugels, most bands carried four solo cornets. As bands were allowed up to 24 players for contest purposes, they dispensed with either one of the third cornets or, more rarely, the second euphonium.
37 This would refer to parts, not to sets.
38 Wright & Round, 1889, p. 2.
39 *Brass Bands*, p. 92.
40 Warwick Williams was born in London in 1846; at the age of 10 he went to India with his father and remained there for four years, his father being in the service of the East India Company. He became a versatile musician later in life, playing the cornet, conducting, composing, and becoming (in 1893) Musical Advisor to the London County Council, with particular responsibilities for bands. He became editor of the *Eclipse Journal* and had several pieces published by Hawkes.
41 'The Danube Waves', composed for military band in 1880.
42 Francis & Day was established in 1877, publishing songs, piano music and, later, musical plays.
43 Russell and Elliott, 1936, p. 137.
44 This address may have been a temporary one during the change of premises to Clapham Road, but it suggests the company still had links with Hull, possibly storing some of the music in a warehouse.
45 *Brass Bands*, p. 78.
46 Much of the information about the early years of *British Bandsman* is taken from Hailstone, 1987.
47 Ibid., p. 259
48 Ibid., p. 14.
49 Ibid., p. 18.
50 Russell and Elliott, 1936, p. 137.
51 Ibid., p. 170.
52 Hailstone, 1987, p. 23.
53 Boon, 1978, pp. 1–5.
54 See photograph in Brand, 1979, p. 186.
55 Eric Ball's article in Brand, 1979, p. 186.

6 Into the twentieth century – the National Brass Band Championships

Changes in Music

The world of music experienced great change during the last third of the nineteenth century and the early years of the twentieth, much of which bypassed the brass band – still adhering to musical styles of the early and middle years of the 1900s. Bands appear to have made virtually no attempt to keep abreast of developments that were taking place in European art music. Even Nationalism and its expression in music seems to have gone largely unnoticed, the only acknowledgement coming in the form of a test piece for the National Championships – a selection entitled *A Souvenir of Grieg*. This was in 1908, the year following the death of the Norwegian who, along with composers such as Chopin, Glinka, Liszt, Smetana, Sibelius and others, was writing music which emphasized national characteristics.

Wagner's *Tristan und Isolde* (first performed in Munich in 1865) heralded the advent of modernism in music, though in the later *Die Meistersinger*, Wagner temporarily abandoned his experimental stance; extracts from this and from some of his earlier operas were welcomed into brass band repertoire. Though arrangements from *Tristan* and some of the later operas were occasionally performed, they seem never to have sat comfortably in brass band programmes. Likewise, the later Verdi operas found no regular place on the bandstand, whilst Wagner's musical descendants – Richard Strauss, Mahler and Bruckner[1] – were totally ignored by brass band writers of the time, their complex orchestrations and large-scale forms not appealing to the relatively miniaturist brass band writers.

Impressionism – the art of suggestion rather than statement – first found its outlet in music during the late 1880s. Debussy was to be its leading exponent but this, along with the later Expressionism – manifested in the music of Schoenberg, Webern and Berg – was completely ignored by brass bands. Those who peopled the band world had been reared on diatonic music and shared no inclination for styles designed to appeal to the intellect. Moreover, the intricacies of much new music depended on the more variable textures of the orchestra for its effect

As a result, brass band music, which during the middle years of the nineteenth century had been a reflection of international tastes of the time, had become somewhat anachronistic by the turn of the century, with its persistent pursuit of classical and romantic styles. The gulf was widened further in the 1920s with the arrival of the Neo-Classicism of Stravinsky and the highly individual idioms of Bartók, though their influences are felt in the brass band works of Edward Gregson, the first of which appeared in the late 1960s.

The English Musical Renaissance

However, on a national level some developments in British music were to find echoes in brass band repertoire. As mentioned in Chapter One, the English musical renaissance came about largely through the teachings of Parry and Stanford, and the writings of George Grove, whose first *Dictionary of Music and Musicians* appeared between 1879 and 1889. Amongst the generation of British composers which followed there were at least three of international acclaim – Edward Elgar (1857–1934), Gustav Holst (1874–1934) and Ralph Vaughan Williams (1872–1958)[2] – each of whom enhanced the musical stature of the brass band by composing for it. Four others of slightly less standing also contributed: Granville Bantock (1868–1946), John Ireland (1879–1962), the younger Herbert Howells (1892–1983) and his contemporary, Arthur Bliss (1891–1975). Bliss not only composed two brass band works but, along with Bantock, appeared as guest conductor in a number of band festivals. Frederick Delius (1862–1934), though born almost within earshot of Black Dyke Mills Band, wrote no brass band music, and was ignored by the brass band world.

Keen to re-establish a British music tradition, Parry and Stanford looked back to the music of the Tudor, Stuart and Elizabethan periods, encouraging the study of composers such as Tallis, Byrd and Purcell, whilst Cecil Sharpe was busy researching English folk-song. This branch of Nationalism came to the brass band largely through Holst's *Moorside Suite* (1928) and through transcriptions of his two Suites for Military Band (1909 and 1911). Although only the latter of these actually contains folk tunes, all convey the spirit of British folk music.

Elgar remained outside Nationalistic influences, preferring to follow in the footsteps of Brahms and Liszt. His *Enigma Variations* of 1899 have been cited as the signal that the renaissance of British music was under way, though the work owes much to the late German Romantic tradition – a trend continued in later years by several brass band composers, and present in Elgar's *Severn Suite* (1930) for brass band. This and the brass band works of the other British composers mentioned above, are dicussed in Chapter Nine.

Social changes

Extra-musical developments also had significant repercussions for bands. Trade unions had become increasingly powerful and strikes common and, as in modern times, a brass band at the head of a column of marching strikers was a familiar sight. By 1914 the working week had been reduced to between 50 and 60 hours! Yet the 'wave of prosperity' referred to on page 20 which helped improve the quality of life for many people and which also brought about a rise in musical standards was short-lived, and the financial position of most classes was being eroded by 1908. In Leeds in 1914, it was reported that a leading choir's subscription list had fallen from 1000 to 400 over the previous decade, and at around the same time the city's brass band park concert series was deprived of its annual £500 subsidy.[3] The decline in organized religion had an enormous impact on amateur music-making, particularly in vocal music; as churches and chapels lost members, so did choirs and choral societies. To quote Russell, 'The final years of pre-war England saw the beginning of a process, still continuing today, whereby the popular music society, once the pride of the whole community or at least a sizeable section of it, became a specialist organization catering for a diminishing minority.'[4]

The National Brass Band Championships

Though brass bands reached a peak during the mid-1890s, the later years of the decade and the early years of the new century provided a series of fillips, the first being Queen Victoria's Diamond Jubilee, in 1897. The celebrations marking the dawn of the new century also provided bands with numerous engagements, and was closely followed by celebrations in connection with the Proclamation and Coronation of Edward VII. Later, the end of the Boer Wars produced a further upsurge in the popularity of bands.

Despite the euphoria created by these events the most important development within the brass band world was the founding of the National Brass

Band Championships at the Crystal Palace, in 1900. These were the brainchild of John Henry Iles and were a direct consequence of his visit to the 1898 Belle Vue September contest (see page 65). Before the end of that year, Iles had acquired the publishing house of R Smith & Co and also the London-based *British Bandsman*. He immediately injected new life into the paper, attracting substantial advertising and offering free music, accessories and even instruments to those who could recruit sufficient numbers of new subscribers.[5] He also promoted band music further with his music publishing company, largely through advertising, but also through widening the scope of its publications.

The second Boer War had begun in 1899, and as the Boers claimed the first of over five and a half thousand British casualties suffered during this three-year war, Iles and *British Bandsman* became heavily involved in raising money for victims' dependants. He was able, through '*The British Bandsman* War Fund', to contribute to the *Daily Mail*'s 'Kipling Fund', set up for this purpose. One fund-raising occasion proved to be of great historical significance to the band movement as a whole, leading directly to the founding of the National Brass Band Championships. It was a massed band concert featuring ten leading bands, including Black Dyke, Besses o' th' Barn and Wyke Temperance, along with bands from the Midlands, the South, and from Scotland and Wales. Some 10 000 people were crammed in to London's Royal Albert Hall – a figure well in advance even of today's 'Last Night of the Proms', and the success of the occasion was in no small measure due to the astuteness of Iles in winning the support of Sir Arthur Sullivan (1842–1900). The son of an Irish bandmaster who became a professor at Kneller Hall, Sullivan had become an immensely influential musician. He had been knighted in 1883, and in addition to his famous operettas (mostly set to texts by W S Gilbert) he had composed incidental music to plays and ballets, church music and choral works, songs and piano pieces, orchestral works and an opera, *Ivanhoe*. He died in 1900, but during the previous year had composed a song called 'The Absent-minded Beggar' – a setting of a Kipling poem – specifically to help an appeal for funds for the relatives of war victims. The song was published by Boosey but Iles acquired the rights and asked James Ord Hume to arrange a march based on it.[6] This accomplished and the concert arranged, he needed to persuade Sullivan himself to become involved. Iles's description of how he achieved this demonstrates his persuasiveness:

> Never shall I forget that first interview. First I had to see Bendall [Sullivan's secretary], and was told that it was utterly useless. But I would not take 'No' for an answer. Eventually, he said that Sir Arthur would see me . . . I was shown into the study, and in a few minutes Sir Arthur entered, attired in his dressing-gown, and smoking the inevitable cigarette. His face was a mixture of grins and curiosity. I think he was really curious to see the persistent fellow who would not go away! . . . Within half an hour we had together laid out the whole programme of the concert and selected the artists.[7]

In the event, Sullivan conducted the 'Absent-minded Beggar March', played by the ten bands in the Albert Hall concert, which took place on 20 January 1900. He also conducted the bands plus grand organ in his hymn, 'Onward, Christian Soldiers'. The soloist in the concert was the highly acclaimed Clara Butt, already famous for her ballad recitals and as the first performer of Elgar's *Sea Pictures* (1899), and who later was to earn renown as the first to perform the song version of 'Land of Hope and Glory'.

Sullivan was moved by the concert, as Iles no doubt anticipated. Capitalizing on the impression it had made he next enlisted the great man's support to help found the National Brass Band Championships. Sullivan was a Director of the Crystal Palace Company and, apart from paving the way for Iles to organize the championships there, he helped acquire the Crystal Palace Challenge Trophy, a gold replica of the Palace. This was a relic of a nineteenth-century choral festival, found lying neglected in a vault, and valued at 1000 guineas (£1100).

The inaugural contest took place on Saturday 21 July, and was billed as part of an International Music Exhibition 'Illustrating the progress and advance of Musical Art during the Nineteenth Century.'[8] The contest was advertised in *British Bandsman* as the 'Championship of Great Britain and the Colonies'. There were three graded sections, but only a modest total of 29 bands participated. The test piece for the most advanced section was a selection, *Gems from Sullivan's Operas No 1*, specially arranged for the occasion by James Ord Hume. The adjudicators (Carl Kiefert, J O Shepherd, J W Beswisk and Dr C W Pearce) produced a somewhat controversial result: Black Dyke were awarded second prize, Besses and some other well-known bands were not even in the list of prizewinners, and the premier award was made to the relatively unknown Denton Original Band.[9] Bands in the second section – won by Kettering Town Band – played Ord Hume's selection from *The Emerald Isle*, Sullivan's last operetta, which remained incomplete on his death in November 1900. Sullivan was present at the 1900 Championships, presented the prizes, and also conducted a further performance of the march based on his 'Absent-minded Beggar'.[10] It was, in fact, Sullivan's last public appearance. Edward German completed the operetta, which received its first performance at the Savoy in 1901. This means that the Selection was arranged and played before the première and, indeed, even before the work's completion – surely a unique occurrence. The third section was won by Hucknall Huthwaite Band, playing an arrangement by John Hartmann (1830–1897) of a selection from Rossini's *William Tell*.

British Bandsman of 12 June 1901 declared that in this year there would be no second or third sections. No doubt this caused some disappointments, but in the issue of 28 September, in which the contest was described as the 'Blue Ribbon' [*sic*][11] of the brass band world, it was announced that there would also be a solo competition for cornet, euphonium and trombone players, perhaps to compensate for the loss of the lower sections.

The adjudicators for the main competition were Dr E H Turpin – Principal of Trinity College of Music, J M Rogan of the Coldstream Guards and Carl Kiefert, who had also officiated in 1900. They were given a complex marking scheme, with 20 points each for 'Ensemble', 'Style' and 'Intonation' and 10 each for the respective qualities of soprano cornet, solo cornet, the horn section, the baritones, the euphoniums and the basses. This gave a possible total of 130 points to the bands, and a likely headache to the adjudicators! Twenty-seven bands competed, the test piece was Ord Hume's arrangement, *Gems from Sullivan's Operas Number 3*, and the winner was Lee Mount Band (from Halifax) with 127 points. The up-and-coming Irwell Springs Band (from Bacup) was runner-up, whilst defending champions, Denton Original, took the third prize. There were two adjudicators for the solo contest: Walter Reynolds, a professional euphonium player, member of the Queen's Hall Orchestra and Music Director for the London County Council, and a Mr F Kettlewell. The winning instrumentalists were W Pollard of Wingates (cornet), J Jenning (euphonium) and J Locker (trombone), both of Denton.

In the massed band concert which followed the competitions, the guest conductor was Edward German, and a number of Alexander Owen arrangements of his music were featured. Denton played the *Overture – Richard* III, Besses performed the Three Dances from *Henry VIII* and the massed bands played a Coronation March, also from *Henry VIII*. Iles had shown imagination in his attempt to build bridges with other branches of the musical world.

The National Championships continued, receiving lots of publicity and, it is thought, some cash injections by the indomitable Iles. The Championships certainly had a chequered early career, and were hampered by displays of unruly behaviour by some members of the audience, especially during the announcement of awards.

Still in search of an ideal formula for the Championships, in 1902 Iles decided to organize four regional qualifying contests, hoping to encourage some less well-known bands prove that they could compete at the top level. All were cancelled due to insufficient entries, though the idea seems to have helped place the national contest itself on a firmer footing, with 89 bands playing in four sections. Twenty-one of them played in the championship section, competing for the already highly coveted Thousand-Guinea Trophy by playing excerpts from Coleridge-Taylor's *Hiawatha*.[12]

1902 was, of course, Coronation year, and in *British Bandsman* of 9 August there appeared a full-page advertisement for a 'Grand Monstre Coronation Band Festival'. A comprehensive set of rules was announced in an attempt to stamp out unfair practices such as the hiring of professional players, and of exceptionally talented players playing with more than one band.[13] On 23 August it was announced that the *Daily Telegraph*, the *Daily Express* and the *London Graphic* were each to present trophies – a good way to elicit wider publicity and at the same time enhance the prestige of the awards. Additional publicity was achieved by sending the magnificent Thousand-Guinea Trophy 'on tour', displaying it in towns which were likely to provide competitors for the Championships. The massed band concert was also given good publicity though, in retrospect, it appears to have been a less exciting affair than that of the previous year, with Iles himself and Sam Cope conducting the massed items. The hymn tune 'Sandon' was one of the items conducted by Iles, and was to become a more or less permanent feature of these events in the future. With Black Dyke playing a selection from *The Gondoliers*, Wyke playing *Beauties of England* and Kingston Mills playing 'Waft her, Angels', it was a decidedly conservative programme, although, fickle as audiences can be, it may have been a more popular success than its predecessor.

The results this year were also more in accordance with expectations, with Black Dyke heading the list of winners and Wyke in second place. Black Dyke's win completed their 'double' as, earlier in the year they had also won first prize in the Belle Vue September contest. Bands in the second section, won by Linthwaite, played *Gems from Sullivan's Operas No 3*. This established the tradition of presenting bands in this section with a test piece which had been used for the championship section in a previous year, thus encouraging them by giving them a first-class test piece. It was also good for trade, providing publishers with further opportunities to sell music already in stock. *Gems from Sullivan's Operas No 2* provided the test for the third section, won by Leicester Imperial, whilst a selection from Henry Bishop's *The Slave* was the music with which Hartlepool Boro won the fourth section. In addition to the four brass band sections there was also a class for brass and reed bands, won on this occasion by Reading Temperance Band.

The formula now established for the Nationals was the one Iles had been searching for, and the solid foundations laid in 1902 were now built on. In the following year there were five sections as well as the brass and reed contest, attracting a total of 116 bands – all competing, one must remember, on the same day and at the same venue. In this year (1903) premier honours went to Besses o' th' Barn, with a grand selection from Wagner's *Die Meistersinger*, arranged by Shipley Douglas. The win was a fortuitous one for Besses, and must have been a vital factor in Iles's decision to organize concert tours for the band, taking it, during the next few years, not only all over Britain, but also on two extended world tours.

The National Brass Band Championships were, by now, regarded by many as the most prestigious event in the brass band calendar. True, the Belle Vue contests were still going strong – both in July and in September – but these were purely band contests. The Nationals had actually become a band festival, the culmination of which was a spectacular concert featuring many of the country's leading bands, and sometimes featuring guest soloists of international repute as, for example, in 1903 and 1904, when the famous American cornet player, W Paris Chambers, thrilled the audience with his unusually large range and brilliant technique.

In 1904 yet another class was added – for boys' bands. The test piece, by Chambers, was called *Amiciaza*.[14] Out of 12 entrants, St Joseph's School, Orpington was the winner.

With the exception of the years 1914–1919 the Nationals continued to be held at the Crystal Palace annually until it was destroyed by fire in 1936. Below is a list of championship section test pieces and winners 1904–1913:

1904 Grand Selection: *Mendelssohn*	Hebburn Colliery (Angus Holden)
1905 Selection: *Roland à Ronceveaux* (Mermet)	Irwell Springs (William Rimmer)
1906 Selection: *Gems of Chopin*	Wingates Temperance (William Rimmer)
1907 Selection: *Gems of Schumann*	Wingates Temperance (William Rimmer)
1908 Selection: *Rienzi* (Wagner)	Irwell Springs (William Rimmer)
1909 Selection: *The Flying Dutchman* (Wagner)	Shaw (William Rimmer)
1910 Selection: *Gems of Schubert*	Fodens Motor Works (William Halliwell)
1911 Selection: *Les Huguenots* (Meyerbeer)	Perfection Soap Works (William Halliwell)
1912 Selection: *William Tell* (Rossini)	St Hilda Colliery (William Halliwell)
1913 Tone Poem: *Labour and Love* (Fletcher)	Irwell Springs (William Halliwell)

This list indicates that, along with a new century and the stimulation of the National Championships, new bands and two new conductors were coming to the fore. Edwin Swift was dead, John Gladney was nearing retirement and Alexander Owen, though still only in his fifties, was busy fulfilling concert tours with Besses. The conductor who first filled the gap created was William Rimmer, leading the field by conducting the winning bands at both Belle Vue and Crystal Palace in each year from 1905 to 1909, and in 1909 conducting five out of the six prize-winning bands at Belle Vue: Fodens 1st, Black Dyke 2nd, Hebden Bridge 4th, Wingates Temperance 5th and Irwell Springs 6th.

William Rimmer (1861–1936)

Described as 'The Doctor of the Brass Band World',[15] William Rimmer was born in Southport. His father, Thomas, was bandmaster of Southport Rifle Band, of which both William and his younger brother, Robert, became playing members. According to Ainscough, William joined his father's band as a drummer, at the age of 15, whilst still learning to play the cornet, but by 1882, at the age of 21, he was playing solo cornet with Southport Rifle Band under the conductorship of Henry Round, and appearing at the Belle Vue September contest.

Later the family became involved with a band in Liverpool; the programme for the Belle Vue contest of 14 July 1888[16] gives names and addresses of conductors and players in competing bands, and the 3rd Volunteers Liverpool Regiment Band is shown as being conducted by Thomas Rimmer. Robert is listed as the band's soprano cornet player and William as playing solo cornet. Later in 1888, William became the solo cornet player for Besses, but this was a short-lived appointment as he was suffering from bronchitis.[17] At around this time Rimmer made the decision (no doubt partly because of his bronchitis) to follow a career as a conductor and band trainer, working with several bands in the Southport and Wigan areas. His first significant appointment was with Wingates Temperance Band, formed in 1873 and based in the village of Wingates, near Wigan. Rimmer became the band's conductor in 1889, and during the next 20 years directed it in some 600 prize-winning performances. The most remarkable of these achievements was the 'double-double' in 1906 and 1907, that is, winning both Belle Vue and Crystal Palace contests in two consecutive years. Wingates was the first band to perform this feat, was undoubtedly one of the new names coming to the fore, and owed much of its success to the skill and musicianship of Rimmer. Another such band was Irwell Springs, formed in 1864 in the cotton-spinning town of Bacup, on the banks of the River Irwell, and within a few miles of the birthplace of Bacup Old Band, discussed on pages 44–48.[18] 'Springs', as it was known, functioned as a modest local band until the early 1890s, when it began to enjoy success in contests. In 1896 Rimmer was appointed professional conductor and the band became even more successful. In 1901 Irwell Springs Band won first prize at the Belle Vue July contest, going on to win fourth prize at its first attempt at the 'September'. Attending the Crystal Palace contest in the same year it did even better, taking second place.

Rimmer's health problems returned and he had to retire from conducting for a time. He returned to Irwell Springs in 1903, however, and the band maintained its progress, becoming double-champions in 1905, bringing Rimmer the first of his five successive 'doubles'. The band won the Crystal Palace contest again in 1908, but these successes created a heavy demand for concert engagements, and not until 1913 did it again achieve victory, by winning the last Crystal Palace contest to take place before the war, playing the first original work to be used as a test piece in the National Championships – Percy Fletcher's *Labour and Love*. This win was with the conductor who had now taken over Rimmer's mantle in the contest arena, William Halliwell.

Rimmer's other great band was Fodens, which originated during the time of the Boer War, with celebrations in connection with the famous Relief of

Mafeking. Festivities marking this event in the Cheshire village of Elworth were attended by the bands of Sandbach Volunteers and Wheelock Temperance. When, during the speeches, a local publican offered free beer to the bands, the members of the Temperance Band took umbrage, packed up their instruments and went home. The Volunteers, however, had no such misgivings and, by the time the speeches were over, its members were too drunk to rejoin the procession, which returned to Elworth music-less. This led to the formation, by the inhabitants of Elworth, of their own brass band. Its first engagement was at a memorial service following the death of Queen Victoria, in January 1901. A less sombre engagement followed in February, as the band provided music to celebrate the Proclamation of King Edward. Soon the band was in regular demand, appearing at local festivals and playing Offenbach, Gilbert and Sullivan, and Strauss waltzes.[19] However, this new band incurred the wrath of Elworth's community leaders by demanding a fee when asked to play in the village on Coronation Day (26 June 1902). The London North Western Carriage Works Band from Crewe was engaged instead, whilst the Elworth Band played in nearby Sandbach. Shortly after this the band was dissolved, but a local businessman, Edwin Foden, formed another band from its ashes. This bore the name of his company – at the time manufacturers of agricultural machinery and portable steam engines, but later renowned for its diesel wagons – and even more for its brass band.

Fodens Band had been established for a few years, having had a modest degree of success, when William Rimmer was engaged as professional conductor. On first hearing the band play he demanded a 'reconstruction', refusing to conduct it at contests with the existing membership. At first the management would not agree and Rimmer left. Subsequently those in charge realized the wisdom of his ideas, recalled him, and acceded to all his demands – good players being recruited to replace many of the virtually self-taught local musicians. The results were spectacular: the band appeared with increasing regularity in prize lists, and in 1909 won the Belle Vue September contest and gained second prize at Crystal Palace.[20, 21]

Rimmer withdrew permanently from contest conducting in 1909, following his ten championship wins within five years. These included three with Irwell Springs, four with Wingates and one each with Black Dyke, Fodens and Shaw – a band from a village near Oldham which, for a number of years, regularly appeared in the prize lists of the major contests, but whose one day of glory coincided with Rimmer's final contest. Of the others, Black Dyke is of course still going strong, as is Fodens – since 1986 under the name 'Britannia Building Society Band'. Wingates went on to win several more titles and, though not nowadays in the top flight of bands it is still an accomplished one, occasionally appearing in the prizes at major contests as well as regularly broadcasting, making commercial recordings, and enjoying a substantial round of concert engagements. After its 1913 Crystal Palace win Irwell

Springs faded into the background, but survived until 1960 when, sadly, it was disbanded. The following list shows at a glance the successes of Rimmer in his brief career as the undisputed leading conductor of contesting bands:

	Belle Vue	Crystal Palace
1905	Irwell Springs	Irwell Springs
1906	Wingates Temperance	Wingates Temperance
1907	Wingates Temperance	Wingates Temperance
1908	Black Dyke Mills	Irwell Springs
1909	Fodens Motor Works	Shaw

Rimmer, in addition to his early successes with the cornet and his great achievements with the baton, was a competent pianist and organist but, more importantly for the future of brass bands, he was also a talented arranger and, like the members of the 'Great Triumvirate', produced many pieces for his bands. Unlike them, however, he became heavily involved in music publishing and by the time of his death, probably had well over a thousand published compositions and arrangements to his credit. On retiring from conducting, he threw himself wholeheartedly into this aspect of the work, adding to his already substantial output. His compositions and arrangements will be considered in more detail in Chapter 7.

William Halliwell (1864–1946) and the St Hilda Colliery Band

Waiting to step into Rimmer's shoes was another Lancastrian, William Halliwell. Born on 11 March 1864 at Roby Mill, some five miles from Wigan, he was only three years younger than Rimmer, and followed a similar route to the podium. Having played the organ as a boy he took up the cornet when he was 16, playing with and conducting several local bands. He also played both trumpet and cornet in amateur orchestras, thus widening his musical experience and paving the way for his later success as a conductor.[22]

Shortly after Rimmer retired as professional conductor of Fodens, Halliwell was appointed as his successor and immediately justified the appointment by completing the 'double' in 1910 with Fodens, going one better than in 1909 when, under Rimmer, the band had won the Manchester contest but had come second at Crystal Palace. He went on to complete four successive personal doubles, three Belle Vue and one London wins being with Fodens. During this period his services were also secured by several other bands, one of which he was to lead to its last championship win, and another which won its first, under his baton. The former was Irwell Springs, already three-times winners of the Nationals under Rimmer, taking what was to be its last such win in 1913. A year earlier, Halliwell had led a band from the North East to the first of its five National Championship titles. This was St Hilda's Colliery Band from South Shields – only the second colliery band to win a major title, and indicative of the rise of this type of band[23] during the twentieth century. The history of St Hilda's is such that it warrants a short 'case study'.

St Hilda's was formed in 1869 by John Dennison, a member of the 3rd Durham Artillery Volunteers Band, at the request of a group of miners. None of the original members knew anything about music – several could not even read or write. Dennison became bandmaster and his 10-year old son Bob, who already played, became solo cornet player. A new set of instruments was acquired (how, is not recorded) and within a few years the band had started to enter contests. Originally designated 'The St Hilda Colliery Brass Band', it underwent various name-changes but had few successes.[24]

During 1905 a successful approach was made to the St Hilda Miners' Lodge for financial help, and the band was renamed 'St Hilda Colliery Silver Band'.[25] Shortly after this, apparently with increased resources, J A Greenwood, a promising young conductor, was appointed professional conductor. Greenwood was to become a leading figure in the brass band world and will be discussed further, both later in this chapter and again in Chapter Seven. Initially he stayed with St Hilda's for only a short time, but brought it some success. He returned in 1908, however, and helped the band consolidate its position. Achievements that year included a win in a lower section at Crystal Palace, but in the following year St Hilda's effectively announced that it was a force to be reckoned with by winning, under Greenwood, the Grand Shield section – just one section below the 'Thousand-Guinea Trophy' class.

The year 1910 brought many engagements in the wake of the band's rise in fortunes; it also saw St Hilda's first but unsuccessful attempt to win the Thousand-Guinea Trophy. The following year provided the turning point in the band's history, with the appointment of James Oliver as bandmaster, James Southern as solo trombone and even more important, through the influence of Southern, the securing of William Halliwell as professional conductor. This triple move immediately put the band into the top flight, taking second prize at Belle Vue and winning the title 'Champion Band of Great Britain and the Colonies' at Crystal Palace.

In 1913 St Hilda's managed only sixth prize at Belle Vue and second at Crystal Palace. Then, with the advent of war, fourteen members were called up for active service and the band withdrew from contesting, concentrating rather on giving concerts for various charities, and in the process raising some £13 000 – a considerable sum, possibly the equivalent today of over a million pounds.

The cessation of hostilities saw the return of most former members, and at the first post-war Crystal Palace contest, in 1920, St Hilda's – with Halliwell at the helm – were once again declared winners. During the following year the band organized a month-long tour of England. Throughout the 1920s and 1930s many works bands did this quite regularly: with unemployment and short-time working both prevalent, employers must have welcomed band tours. Furthermore, the players earned more money playing two concerts per day than they did working in the mines or factories and, no doubt, found it a far more agreeable working environment. St Hilda's crowned the year 1921 by winning at Crystal Palace for the third time. Over the next few years concert tours during the summer months escalated, so much so that the band bought its own touring bus – known in those days as a char-à-banc – equipped to carry all that the band might require whilst on tour. (In later years Fodens also had their own bus.[26])

Disaster struck in 1925 when the St Hilda colliery closed down. Every member of the band was now unemployed, and relied for survival on engagement fees and contest prize money. Following a further win at Crystal Palace in 1926, conducted by the bandmaster James Oliver, the inevitable happened: the members of St Hilda's were considered to be earning their livings as professional musicians and were therefore barred, in fairness to other competitors, from entering contests. In 1927 the band declared itself to be a professional band. The word 'colliery' had already been removed from its name and henceforth it was known simply as the 'St Hilda Band'.

For a number of years there was no shortage of engagements, and in 1931 the band went to Canada to play in an International Exhibition. Now that the band was not playing competitively the services of William Halliwell, the contest specialist, were no longer required. Subsequent conductors included Hubert Bath (the composer) and Frank Wright (a former Australian cornet champion and a powerful figure in brass bands after the 2nd World War). Alas, engagements dried up during the mid-1930s, partly due to the Depression but also, possibly, because the band was no longer in the public eye through contest successes. In December 1937 it was announced that, after ten years as a professional band, St Hilda's was to be disbanded.[27]

The events at St Hilda's, however, had little impact on the career of William Halliwell. Following his last championship success with them in 1924 in the London contest, he proceeded to a hat-trick of wins at Belle Vue with Fodens in the years 1926 to 1928, with a personal double in 1928 by virtue of also winning the Crystal Palace contest with Black Dyke, of which he had been professional conductor since 1922. He was also, for a time, professional conductor of Besses, and led them to victory at Belle Vue in 1931, following this with a further hat-trick, with another band just coming to the fore – Brighouse & Rastrick – of 'Floral Dance' fame.[28] This band had hit the headlines in 1929 by performing a different kind of 'double' – winning both the Belle Vue July and September contests in the same year, under its bandmaster, Fred Berry.[29] Over the next two years, Brighouse and Rastrick's fortunes waned as it failed to feature in the list of Belle Vue prizewinners. To remedy the situation, the band engaged Halliwell, who not only guided it through its hat-trick but who, after the band had served its penance of being barred for a year following the hat-trick,[30] brought it back to win in 1936 producing, in effect, four wins in succession for the Yorkshire Band. Meanwhile, in 1935, as Brighouse took its enforced absence from Belle Vue, Halliwell achieved another win with Black Dyke. The record of William Halliwell's winning bands in the two major contests is as follows:

	Belle Vue	Crystal Palace
1910	Fodens Motor Works	Fodens Motor Works
1911	Hebden Bridge	Perfection Soap Works
1912	Fodens Motor Works	St Hilda Colliery
1913	Fodens Motor Works	Irwell Springs
1915	Fodens Motor Works	No contest
1918	Wingates Temperance	No contest
1920		St Hilda Colliery
1921	Wingates Temperance	St Hilda Colliery
1923	Wingates Temperance	Luton Red Cross
1924		St Hilda Colliery
1926	Fodens Motor Works	
1927	Fodens Motor Works	
1928	Fodens Motor Works	Black Dyke Mills
1931	Besses o' th' Barn	
1932	Brighouse and Rastrick	
1933	Brighouse and Rastrick	
1934	Brighouse and Rastrick	
1935	Black Dyke Mills	Munn and Feltons
1936	Brighouse and Rastrick	

The Mortimer family

As we have seen, the history of brass bands has featured several families of players, often spanning generations. One of the most prominent such families was that of the Mortimers. It consisted of the father, Fred (1879–1953) and his three sons, Harry, Alex and Rex. Fred Mortimer's father had played baritone with Wyke Temperance Band and Fred (the fourth of ten children) had inherited his love of music, becoming a boy soprano and learning to play the piano. Born in Cleckheaton, he later moved to Hebden Bridge. Here he joined the local band, playing soprano cornet from 1895, and later moving to the solo cornet position. He became bandmaster in 1901, the year before the birth of Harry who, as a small boy, was taught to play the cornet by his father.[31]

In his book, *Harry Mortimer on Brass*, 'HM', as he was affectionately known, recalled being taken to hear Black Dyke rehearsing.[32] In 1908 Gladney retired and was replaced as professional conductor by William Rimmer, who was to become Harry Mortimer's idol. In fact, Rimmer was persuaded by Fred Mortimer to include Hebden Bridge Band on the list of bands of which he was professional conductor. It was obviously a reasonably accomplished band, and was to win the Belle Vue September contest in 1911, under William Halliwell, following fourth prizes in each of the two previous years. As had happened at Fodens, Halliwell succeeded Rimmer at Hebden Bridge when the latter retired from contesting. One of Halliwell's other bands at this time was the Luton Red Cross Band (no connection with the International Red Cross Society), and when a vacancy for a bandmaster occurred there, on the recommendation of Halliwell, Mortimer senior was offered the job – apparently rather more lucrative than the Hebden Bridge bandmastership. The family, at that point comprising father, mother, two boys and two girls, undertook the long journey to Luton. (The other boy was Alex, born in 1905.) Shortly after the family's arrival in Luton, Rex was born. Both Alex and Rex were to become euphonium players – Alex one of the finest of all time – whilst Harry was to build a similar reputation as a cornet and trumpet player.[33] It was Alex who was to be the prime instigator in the family's next trip, though not for some years.

After the 1914–1918 war, but still in Luton and still under maestro Halliwell, the Red Cross Band improved to such a degree that in 1922 it earned second prize in the Crystal Palace Championships, and a year later won the coveted title – the only band from the South of England ever to do so. As often happens after the first flush of success, there was disunity within the band or, more precisely, between the committee and its conductors. Both conductors wished to see the talented young Alex Mortimer playing solo euphonium, but the committee disagreed. The upshot of this was that when, some time later, one of Halliwell's other bands – Fodens – required a solo euphonium player, Alex was recommended and offered the job. As a result, the 1924 Crystal Palace contest witnessed a family with divided loyalties, one Mortimer with Fodens, and the others with Luton. As it happened, neither band was in the prizes and this may explain why an invitation soon arrived for the rest of the Mortimer family to join Alex in Sandbach, in an attempt to strengthen the Cheshire-based band.

It was not long before the move showed results. With Harry playing solo cornet, and Alex and Rex on euphonium, Fred Mortimer saw his new band, under Halliwell, achieve three successive wins at Belle Vue. This completed in 1928, Halliwell made a most unusual and selfless gesture: he recommended to the management of Fodens that from the beginning of 1929 Fred Mortimer should become the band's musical director and that in future he should conduct the band in contests. Certainly the suggestion was inspirational for Fodens, though it was obviously a personal sacrifice on Halliwell's part – he had handed over what was potentially his best band. The result was that in 1930 Fodens took the National title and then, after achieving only sixth place the following year the Mortimers and Fodens, by now Fodens Motor Works Band, made history by achieving a double hat-trick, that is, winning the Thousand-Guinea Trophy in the years 1932–1934 and again in 1936–1938. No other band has achieved this to date, either in the Nationals or at Belle

Vue. In 1935, the year in which Fodens was barred from competing, Halliwell again took the opportunity to demonstrate his skills, winning with a band from Kettering which had been in existence a mere two years. This was Munn and Felton's Works Band.[34]

Brighouse & Rastrick's 1936 win at Belle Vue saw the end of Halliwell's reign as the leading brass band conductor. In 1937 and 1938 his bands won a few of the lower-order prizes, but in the following year, at the age of 75 and with the 2nd World War raging, he retired from contesting after 20 years of highly successful work with a large number of bands. Halliwell did not compose, though he made a few fine arrangements for his bands, all of which have remained unpublished. He took part in four royal appearances before King George V and Queen Mary – two with St Hilda's and two with Fodens. The coming of the war saw the end of an era in brass band history – an era which had effectively ended in 1936, but which had lingered on for Halliwell for a few more years. He lived to the age of 82, died on 24 April 1946, and was buried in Upholland Church Cemetery, near Wigan. His legacy was to pass to Harry Mortimer.

John A Greenwood (1876–1953)

One more brass band personality from the first half of the twentieth century needs to be discussed before closing this chapter. As a conductor, John A Greenwood was destined to be overshadowed – first by Rimmer and later by Halliwell. In his arrangements and compositions also, though quite prolific, he appears to have been outshone by Rimmer, up to the death of the older man in 1936. This aspect of Greenwood's work is discussed in Chapter Seven.

J A Greenwood was born in Winsford in Cheshire. His father taught him to play the cornet and at the age of ten he joined his first band. After leaving school he played with a number of bands, and from the age of 18 played solo cornet with the then quite well-known Gossages Soap Works Band. William Rimmer was this band's professional conductor and so, as many years earlier Rimmer had come under the influence of Henry Round through playing under his baton in the Southport Rifle Band, Greenwood came under that of Rimmer.

In 1899 he was offered the position of solo cornet in the New Brighton Tower Band, a professional group which entertained its seaside audiences daily during the season. Up to this point, Greenwood had been largely self-taught, but the improvement in his income allowed him to pay for private tuition in harmony and counterpoint. According to Taylor, after the Tower went bankrupt in 1900, Greenwood conducted and played with several bands – playing under each of the then three leading conductors – Gladney, Owen and Rimmer.[35] Greenwood's work at St Hilda's has already been mentioned (page 127). Here, he led the up-and-coming band to victory in the Grand Shield section at Crystal Palace. This was a great boost for his career, though he must have been disappointed when the band appointed Rimmer to give it the final push to the top.

It has been claimed that Greenwood's failure to join the first rank of conductors was because he had to work with less able bands. This could well be true, and there is no doubt that, over the years, the most successful conductors have been those engaged by the most successful bands. This is not to say that Greenwood was unable to do good work with such material as was available to him, a fact borne out by the achievement of a rare feat in 1927 with the little-known Milnrow Public Band. By then, the May Belle Vue contest had been established (see page 57) and in this year, with Milnrow, Greenwood achieved a unique trio of awards, winning a prize at each of the three Belle Vue contests – May, July and September.

Greenwood certainly enjoyed some successes, the first of which came when he led Black Dyke to top honours at the 1914 Belle Vue September contest. He had greater success with the band of Horwich RMI (Railway Mechanics Institute), leading them into the runner-up position in 1915 and to the winning slot in each of the following two years. He tasted victory again in 1922 with Horwich at Belle Vue and then, in 1925, achieved a personal double, winning Belle Vue with Cresswell Colliery Band, and Crystal Palace with Marsden Colliery Band from County Durham – rivals of St Hilda's at that time. This was Greenwood's one and only win in the Nationals.

Greenwood outlived his two elder rivals, Rimmer and Halliwell, and continued his banding work virtually up to his death in 1953, but his post-war activities lay more in the fields of composing, arranging and adjudicating. Once again, however, fashions had changed, and after the Depression of the 1930s and the ravages of the 1939–1945 war, brass bands were fighting for survival.

So far the development of bands and their instruments have been discussed, touching upon histories of some of the more famous bands, the careers of some of the more important personalities, the development of instrumentation and scoring, and on the growth of the publishing industry so far as bands were concerned. Music played by brass bands has been shown, in general terms, in the wider context of popular and art music.

As this book is meant to focus to a large extent on the music of brass bands, the remaining chapters will be devoted largely to the work of its composers and arrangers, from about 1875 to 1936, the year which saw the death of Rimmer and the end of the Crystal Palace era.

Notes

1. In 1863 Bruckner actually composed a work, *Germanenzug*, for two cornets, four trumpets, four horns, three trombones, euphonium and tuba, with TTBB male choir. This is not, however, the instrumentation of the British-style brass band. The presence of trumpets and horns and the absence of saxhorns takes it into the realms of a brass ensemble, though the use of cornets and euphonium takes it away from standard orchestral brass ensembles.
2. The one brass band work by Vaughan Williams was his *Variations for Brass Band*. As it was not composed until 1957 it falls outside the remit of this book.
3. Russell, 1987, p. 40.
4. Ibid., p. 242.
5. Hailstone, 1987, p. 24.
6. In addition to the march version the song was also arranged as a cornet solo.
7. Quoted in Russell and Elliott, 1936, p. 174.
8. Quoted from publicity material, reproduced in Hailstone, 1987, p. 25.
9. Denton is a small town located a few miles south-east of Manchester.
10. From Sullivan's diary, quoted in Jacobs, 1991, p. 399.
11. Surely a mis-spelling of 'Blue Riband' – an award for the fastest seaborne crossing of the Atlantic.
12. *Hiawatha* is made up of three cantatas, set to the words of Longfellow's poem, and composed between 1898 and 1900, with the first performance of the complete trilogy in London in 1900. As a test piece in 1902 this was, therefore, truly contemporary.
13. The rules were printed in *British Bandsman* of 16 August 1902, and are reproduced in full in Brand, 1979, pp. 48–50.
14. This must have been transcribed from the wind band version, published by Fischer in 1901.
15. Ainscough in Littlemore, 1988, p. 24.
16. A copy of which is in the writer's collection.
17. Ainscough in Littlemore, 1988, p. 25.
18. Much of the information about Irwell Springs Band comes from the *Irwell Springs (Bacup) Band* booklet.
19. Burgess, 1977, p. 5.
20. Much of the information about Fodens comes from Burgess, 1977, published to commemorate the band's 75th anniversary. Burgess was Fodens' Secretary from 1902 to 1920. He compiled a short history of the band in 1936, and this formed the basis of the 1977 booklet.
21. The question of removing poorer players to make way for more talented ones is a perennial problem for ambitious bands. If it achieves its purpose – which it obviously did in the case of Fodens – the ill-feeling which may result is soon forgotten. Such an approach was always more likely to succeed in a works band, where the employer made the decision, than in a town or village band which relied more heavily on communal support and loyalty.
22. Much of the information about William Halliwell comes from an article by Walter Ainscough in Littlemore, 1987, pp. 33–40.
23. The colliery band which had already won a major championship was Hebburn Colliery, which took the title at the 1904 Nationals.
24. The early history of this band is recorded in a booklet, *St Hilda's Band: Premier Band of England*, published in 1936, but written by an unnamed author –

possibly James Southern, the band's long-serving secretary, manager and trombone soloist.

25 At around the turn of the century many bands were turning to the use of silver-plated instruments, and calling themselves 'silver' bands rather than 'brass' bands, though in effect they remained brass bands, still playing brass instruments. In recent times, the term 'silver' has been removed from the names of most such bands.

26 Fodens must have been one of the busiest brass bands in the 1930s. In a letter to the August *Brass Band News* in 1933 Harry Mortimer told of the band having just completed a 42-day Scottish tour and of preparing to leave again on a 35-day tour of England.

27 See article by Violet Brand in Brand, 1979, pp. 99–102, for further details about the later years of St Hilda's.

28 In 1977 Brighouse & Rastrick Band achieved greater fame than it could have done with any number of contest wins. It found itself in the pop charts, playing an arrangement by its musical director, Derek Broadbent, of Katie Moss's 'Floral Dance'. Climbing up to the number two position, the band was in demand for all kinds of unlikely engagements, including an appearance on the television programme, 'Top of the Pops'. (For further information see article by Broadbent in Littlemore, 1987, pp. 29–31.)

29 This feat was accomplished only twice in the history of the July contest (1886 to 1951), the other occasion being in 1890, when Batley Old Band won both events in the same year. Fred Berry (born Honley, 1878) had been a distinguished euphonium player before taking up the baton. He had played in Honley Band under Gladney, Linthwaite and Wyke under Swift and Besses under Owen. He played with Besses on their first World Tour, after which he resigned, due to ill-health. (Information from a 'Profile' in *Brass Band News*, December 1909, p. 4.)

30 By now the rules barred the winner of a hat-trick for one year, not two, as had been the case in the early years.

31 *Brass Band News*, October 1906.

32 Mortimer, 1981, p. 16.

33 All three Mortimer brothers later became famous conductors, but in an era not covered by this book.

34 Later, Munn and Felton's became the GUS (Footwear) Band, then the GUS Band, and now sports the rather ungainly title of the Rigid Container Group Band – so named after the company which now sponsors it.

35 *Brass Bands*, p. 119.

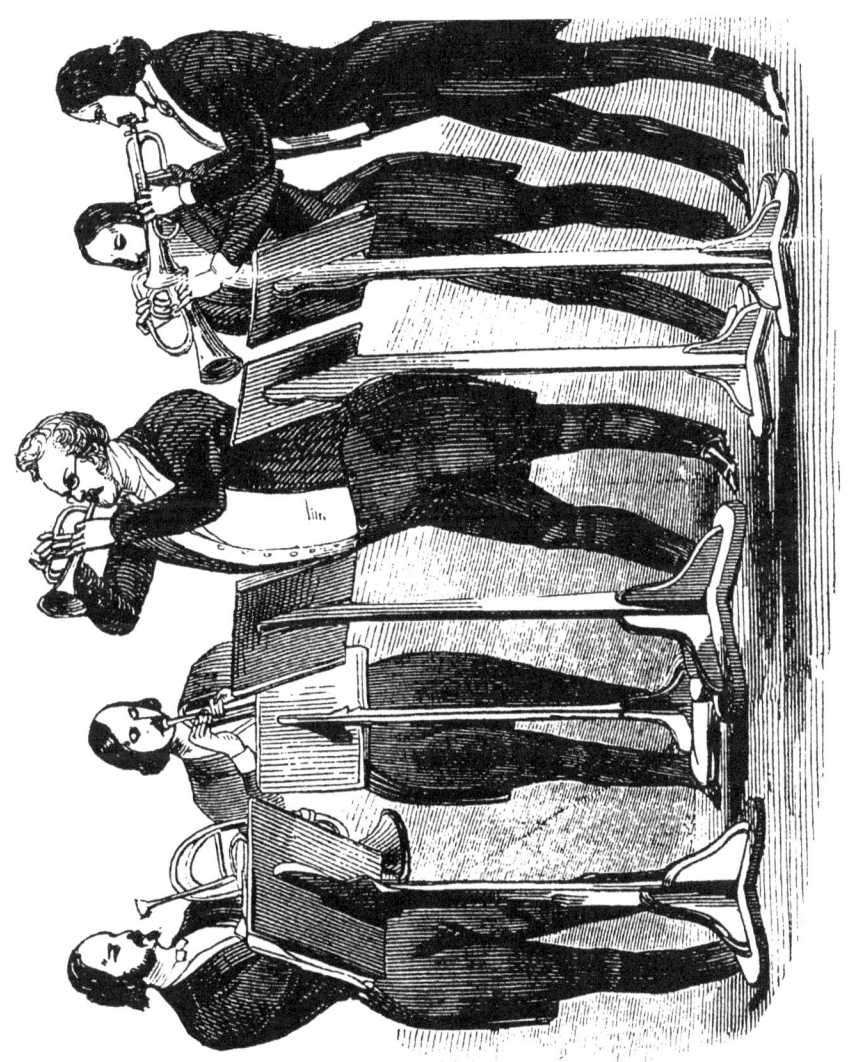
The Distin family

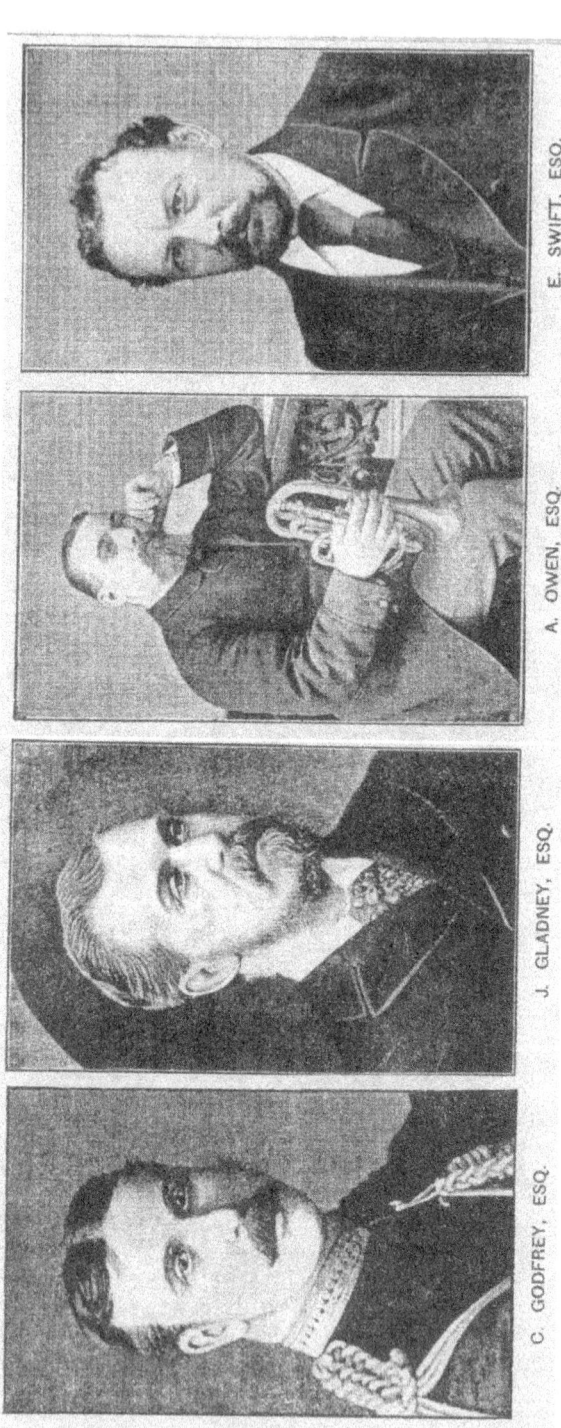

2 Four great figures from the 1880s

3 Front cover of the *Amateur Band Teacher's Guide*

THE above Hall was erected by Messrs. John Foster & Son, Ltd., in commemoration of the Jubilee in 1887 of Her late Majesty Queen Victoria, and is provided with large Concert Hall, Billiard, Reading, Lecture and Recreation Rooms. There is also a Library, Kitchen (for Instructions in Cooking), a Swimming Bath, and Public Baths for the use of the workpeople and inhabitants of the village of Queensbury.

Victoria Hall, Queensbury

SIR ARTHUR SULLIVAN'S OPINION OF THE BAND.

We may quote an opinion given by that fine musician and composer—the **late Sir Arthur Sullivan**—who, upon hearing the Black Dyke Band perform the selection from Wagner's "Tannhauser" said:—

"The performance was magnificent"—
and it is evident that the public thought so also.

Sir Arthur added:—

"I was surprised, not only at the tone and execution, but at the fire and go of the performance. In this they excelled any band I have ever heard."

SIR ALEXANDER MACKENZIE'S OPINION.

When at the Ilkley Hall Gardens, Sir A. Mackenzie making Ilkley his pleasure resort for the season, made a special visit to the gardens to listen to this famous combination. After their performance he spoke to the bandmaster, saying **That he was more than surprised at the wonderful performance of the many selections, and that it had given him the greatest pleasure in listening.**

MR. JOHN PHILIP SOUSA WRITES AS FOLLOWS:—

Elysee Palace Hotel,
Mr. H. Bower. Paris.

Dear Sir,—Allow me to congratulate you on the performance of the Black Dyke Mills Band last Sunday, at Queen's Hall, London. The band shows the effect of conscientious and persistent training, and the individual members displayed a sympathetic appreciation of the duties that rested upon them. With every wish for your continued success.

(Signed) **JOHN PHILIP SOUSA.**

LIFE AND CAREER
OF THE LATE
MR. EDWIN SWIFT,
A Self-made Musician,

Bandmaster and Adjudicator,

Trainer of many of the leading Brass Bands in the North of England.

PRICE TWOPENCE.

MILNSBRIDGE:
Fred Hawley, Printer and Publisher, Central Printing Works,
1904.

7　The One Thousand Guinea Trophy

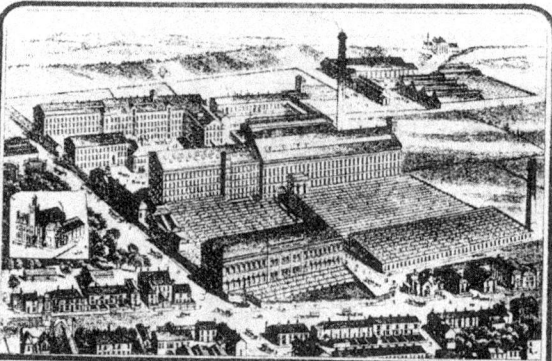

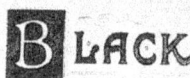

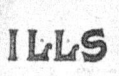

8 Black Dyke – Canada and USA tour brochure, 1906

CATALOGUE OF MUSIC.

QUICK MARCHES.

No.		Composer	No.		Composer
1.	"Stars and Stripes"	Sousa.	16.	"Amicizia"	Chambers.
2.	"El Capitan"	Sousa.	17.	"Aladdin"	Dodsworth.
3.	"Black Fury"	Rimmer.	18.	"Marmion"	Smith.
4.	"The King's Cavalier"	Rimmer.	19.	"The King's Guard"	Keith.
5.	"Punchinello"	Rimmer.	20.	"Kaiser Frederick"	Friedman.
6.	"The Cossack"	Rimmer.	21.	"The Belle of Broadway"	T. Clark.
7.	"The Southport Belle"	Rimmer.	22.	"The Distant Greeting"	Godfrey.
8.	"The Elephant"	J. Ord Hume.	23.	"Olympia"	Tom Clark.
9.	"Independentia"	R. B. Hall.	24.	"With Sword and Lance"	Starke.
10.	"Fearless"	J. A. Greenwood.	25.	"Mikasa"	J. H. Carter.
11.	"Washington City"	W. German.	26.	"Le Tournoi"	J. Gladney.
12.	"The Double Eagle"	J. F. Wagner.	27.	"Occidental"	Sousa.
13.	"Coltness Review"	E. Sutton.	28.	"Under Freedom's Flag"	Noworeski.
14.	"Battle Abbey"	Allan.	29.	"Simoon"	J. W. Allen.
15.	"Pat in America"	H. Eden.	30.	"La Reine de Saba"	Gounod.

WALTZES.

No.		Composer	No.		Composer
1.	"Casino Tanze"	Gung'l.	9.	"Tendresse"	Waldteufel.
2.	"Wendishe Weisen"	Gung'l.	10.	"The Choristers"	Phelps.
3.	"Elfein Reigen"	Gung'l.	11.	"Hochzietlieder"	Strauss.
4.	"Amorettentanze"	Gung'l.	12.	"The Blue Danube"	Strauss.
5.	"Hydropaten"	Gung'l.	13.	"Sur La Mer"	Mitchell.
6.	"Estudiantina"	Waldteufel.	14.	"Sweet Marjorie"	Aigrette.
7.	"Jeunesse Doree"	Waldteufel.	15.	"Eileen Alannah"	Bonheur.
8.	"Plui D'Or"	Waldteufel.			

OVERTURES.

No.		Composer	No.		Composer
1.	"Felensmühle"	Reissiger.	8.	"Zauberflöte"	Mozart.
2.	"Royal"	Reissiger.	9.	"Poet and Peasant"	Suppe.
3.	"Libella"	Reissiger.	10.	"Light Cavalry"	Suppe.
4.	"Olympia"	Kalliwoda.	11.	"Crown Diamonds"	Auber.
5.	"Mirella"	Gounod.	12.	"Bohemian Girl"	Balfe.
6.	"Zampa"	Herold.	13.	"La Favorita"	Donizetti.
7.	"La fille de Berger"	Adam.			

LIGHT OPERATIC SELECTIONS.

No.		Composer	No.		Composer
1.	"Princess of Kensington"	German.	12.	"The Duchess of Dantzic"	Monckton.
2.	"Madame Angôt"	Lecocq.	13.	"The Orchid"	Monckton.
3.	"San Toy"	Jones.	14.	"The Cingalee"	Monckton.
4.	"Geisha"	Jones.	15.	"The Spring Chicken"	Monckton.
5.	"The Messenger Boy"	Monckton.	16.	"Veronique"	Messager.
6.	"Esmeralda"	Thomas.	17.	"My Lady Madcap"	Reuben.
7.	"The Grand Duchess"	Offenbach.	18.	"La Poupee"	Andran.
8.	"Three Little Maids"	Reubens.	19.	"Dorothy"	Cellier.
9.	"A Country Girl"	Monckton.	20.	"Ruy Blas"	Meyer Lutz.
10.	"A Runaway Girl"	Monckton.	21.	"The Catch of the Season"	Haines.
11.	"The Girl from Kay's"	Monckton.			

SELECTIONS FROM SULLIVAN'S OPERAS.

No.		Composer	No.		Composer
1.	"Pirates of Penzance"	Sullivan.	4.	"Iolanthe"	Sullivan.
2.	"Patience"	Sullivan.	5.	"Yeomen of the Guard"	Sullivan.
3.	"Gondoliers"	Sullivan.	6.	"Haddon Hall"	Sullivan.

10 Wingates Temperance Band, 1906. (Note the 1000 guinea trophy and Crystal Palace medals)

11 Fodens Motor Works Band *circa* 1910

12　Publicity material for Besses' second world tour (1909–1911)

13 Advertisement from the 1924 Crystal Palace programme

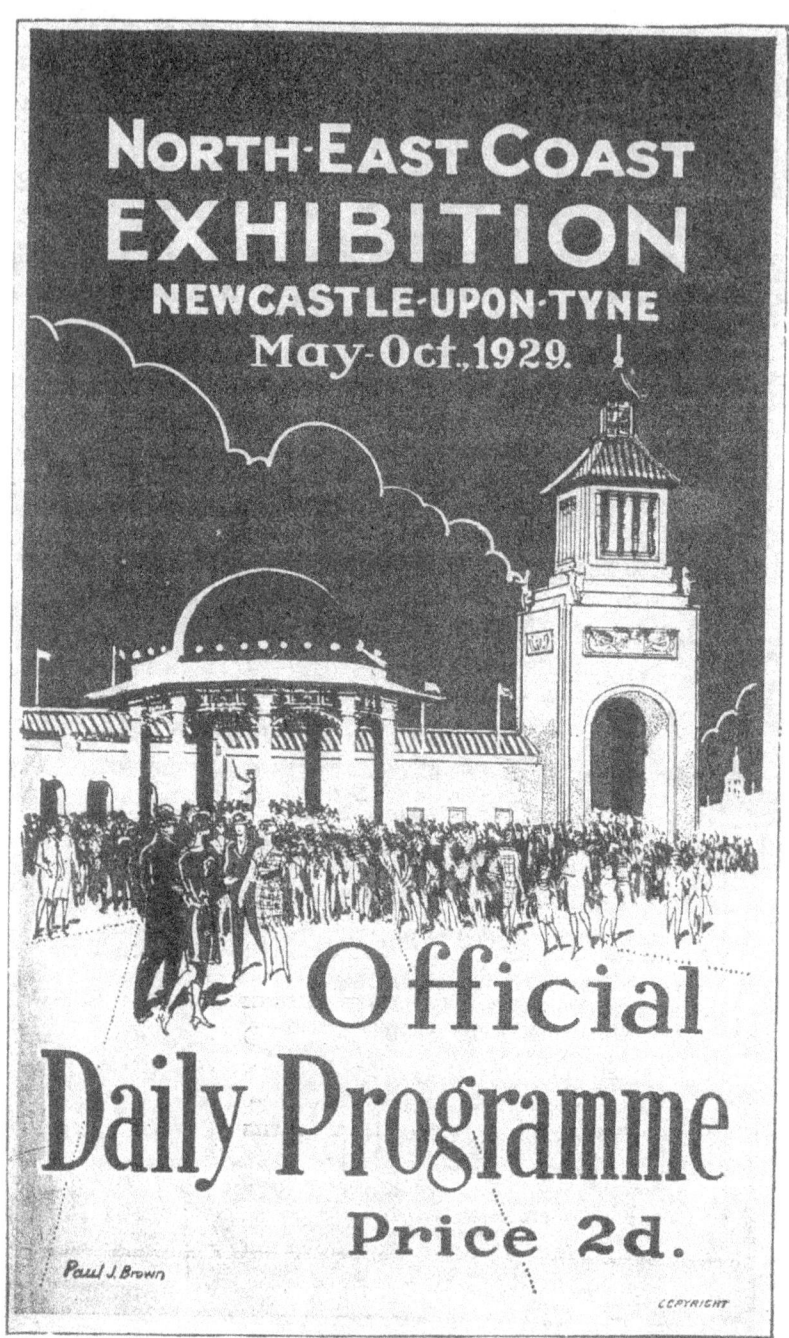

14 Front cover of a Besses programme

| Trains every few minutes | **Cheap Day Return Tickets** | Cheap Return Fares |

TO

THE CRYSTAL PALACE

by ALL TRAINS* from

LONDON BRIDGE 1/-   VICTORIA 1/-

HOLBORN VIADUCT 1/-   ST. PAULS 1/-

WATERLOO 1/1

Also from numerous S.R. Suburban Stations

Bookings also to PENGE EAST and PENGE WEST

*(Weekdays after 9.30 a.m. Sundays and Bank Holidays all day)

6D — *Quickest Way Home!* CHEAP SINGLE TICKETS TO LONDON (VICTORIA, LONDON BRIDGE and HOLBORN VIADUCT) available at Intermediate Stations — **6D**

Save Time and Money by

SOUTHERN ELECTRIC

15 Enticing the public to 'go by train' (1936)

16 Close-up of the Crystal Palace medal (photo: Studio Tristan)

7 Principal arranger/composers and their music

Introduction

Much band music up to and including the Edwardian period was original – that is, specially composed for band, not 'borrowed' from other branches of music. It was unashamedly written in well-known and popular idioms and consisted mainly of marches, dance music and solos. There were also many transcriptions of glees and other short vocal pieces.

Most music written for contests, however, was based on music from other sources, either from an opera, the music of a specific composer, or a collection of tunes with national or patriotic associations. Gladney, Owen and Swift developed this genre but they were, first and foremost, conductors. Important as their selections were to their contesting successes, these were relatively few, and incidental to their conducting. Neither the members of the 'Triumvirate' nor their contemporaries such as Grosse and Waterson would fit comfortably into this chapter.

There was, however, a substantial group of pieces specially composed for contests. Like the marches and dance tunes, they were in eclectic styles, that is to say, in musical idioms already well established, and paid little or no regard to formal musical structures. They led to the type of piece known as the 'original work', which first appeared in 1913. The First World War halted the progress of these pieces, but by 1936 they had almost totally displaced the selection in contests – especially those for the better bands. Though still eclectic, the early original works paid more regard to structure, key schemes, and to thematic development. They form an important part of modern band repertoire, have been largely responsible for what degree of acceptance of brass bands there has been in the musical world, and will be discussed in Chapter 9.

136 *Brass Roots*

Meanwhile, during the first two decades of the twentieth century, the predominance of the test piece selection was also giving way in concerts to lighter-weight selections from musical comedy or from the realms of popular music, with the emphasis on entertainment rather than on the display of technical or musical prowess. A transformation was also taking place in shorter pieces, with arrangements from the light orchestral repertoire displacing many of the dances which had previously been popular. Music in these categories will be discussed in Chapter 8. In this chapter I intend to trace developments in band music through the works of the principal arranger/composers, who have been classified according to the quantity and range of their output, bearing in mind their chronological place in band history.

The arranger/composers

The term 'arranger/composer' seems to put the work of these early writers into perspective. Their strength lay mainly in their ability to adapt music from other spheres or, having put together some melodic ideas in the rhythm of a march or of the various dances which were in vogue, or even in the guise of a fantasia, being able to harmonize and score them.

The arranger/composers who were active between 1836 and 1936 can be categorized into three broad groups. The first comprises four such musicians who stand out both in terms of the quantity and quality of their band music, as well as in the range of music written: Henry Round, William Rimmer, James Ord Hume and John A Greenwood. Of the four, Ord Hume was the most able composer, whilst through his arrangements he also helped widen the scope of band music on the lighter and more popular side of the repertoire. Round was certainly the most prolific and, as the most influential member of the early group, will be considered in most detail. As the pioneer of published music, he set a level of competence on which his successors were to build. He also established scoring techniques which exploited the capabilities of large numbers of bands, rather than making the kind of technical demands required by the Gladney, Swift and Owen unpublished arrangements. Concurrent with these four were other arranger/composers, falling into varying categories of importance.

The following table outlines the principal members of each group, although it should be noted that there were others whose contributions were too limited to warrant coverage here.

Principal	Secondary	Subsidiary
Henry Round (1838–1905)	Thomas Wright	Richard Smith
	Jules Rivière	Thomas A Haigh
	Charles Godfrey	James Frost
		George A Frost

Principal arranger/composers and their music 137

William Rimmer (1862–1936) George Allan   George Wadsworth
                             Edward Newton   Sam Cope
                             Frank Linter   Shipley Douglas
                             John Jubb   Joseph Jubb
James Ord Hume (1864–1932)   John Hartmann   Warwick Williams
                                                John Ord Hume
John A Greenwood (1876–1953) George Hawkins   Edward Sutton
                                                Harold Moss

Two more names which could be considered as part of a further group are those of Henry Geehl and Denis Wright. Wright, in particular, added considerably to the arrangement repertoire and, in fact, founded what might be called the modern school of scoring. But both also made important contributions to the 'original' brass band music repertoire and will, therefore, be considered in Chapter 9 whilst, through his lighter arrangements, Wright will also be discussed in Chapter 8.

The survey which follows is based on a collection of some 3000 titles assembled by the writer from a variety of sources, including music in band libraries and in publishers' archives, and from information contained in contemporary publicity material. Many of the early pieces seem to exist now as titles only, gleaned from advertisements, though it is likely that some of the actual music will be discovered in future research. Many more pieces exist in the form of solo cornet parts, incorporated into early editions of *British Bandsman* and, more frequently, *Brass Band News*. Others are to be found in band libraries, in various states of completeness and readability.

This book makes no attempt at a complete survey of all band music; such a project would be valuable but unwieldy. The pieces and writers discussed below do, however, paint a representative picture of brass band music published between the years 1875 and 1936. Many of the pieces do not display a publication date, and publication numbers – where given – vary when there have been reprints. Therefore dates, where quoted, are often estimates, based on advertising material, performances and/or publication numbers.

Henry Round and his contemporaries

One of the founders of the publishing house of Wright & Round, Henry Round was probably the most prolific brass band writer of the nineteenth century, if not of all time. His output included the following:

> Marches: 107 – mostly original, including many 'sacred' marches, several making use of at least one well-known tune and a few transcriptions
> Solos: 24 – mostly for cornet, but some for euphonium and trombone, including slow melodies and polkas, and mostly original
> Overtures: 14 – all original, but using musical idioms found in operatic selections

Fantasias: 24 – varying from being completely original to basically selections of existing tunes but with some degree of originality
Selections: 40 from opera, 17 composer selections, 21 based on national songs and 16 miscellaneous selections
Short test pieces: 8 – glees and quadrilles
Concert pieces: 35 – including anthems, air varies and short selections
Miscellaneous arrangements: 7 – all by known composers
Dance music: 152 – mainly quadrilles, lancers, valses, polkas and schottisches

This, even though possibly only a small proportion of his total output, represents a substantial amount of music in a variety of forms. In the archives of Besses o' th' Barn Band there are some 45 hand-written full scores of Round's test pieces. These show a growing conformity in instrumentation and methods of scoring which, apart from the apparent absence of the flugelhorn, the fact that tenor trombones are shown in tenor clef, and the placing of the euphoniums immediately below the baritones, have been maintained in the majority of scores up to the present time. Appendix 7 gives a list of these scores, illustrating the range of music and the diversity of contest venues.

In the scores the 'solo cornet' stave conveys a part for the whole solo cornet section, as in a modern score. Likewise 'repiano' at times doubles solo cornets at the unison or sub-octave, but at others joins 2nd and 3rd cornets to provide three-part harmony within the 'back row' cornets, or simply to strengthen their line. All the parts, in fact, function much the same as they do today. In most of the scores percussion parts are not shown, reflecting the tradition (which lasted until 1973) of not allowing that section to play in contests.

Most of Round's selections were tailor-made for the contest platform. They ranged from very difficult to moderately easy, catering for bands from the very highest level to modest village and junior bands. Amongst the operatic selections, those by Donizetti were the most numerous (11), but there were also selections from operas by Auber, Balfe, Gounod, Mercadante, Rossini, Verdi, Wagner, Wallace, Weber and several lesser-known composers, as well those containing music by a number of composers, such as *Opera Gems* and *Recollections of Carl Rosa*.[1] There were also selections from oratorios by Mendelssohn and Spohr. The composer selections covered some of the music of Beethoven and Schubert, but relied mainly on nineteenth-century operatic composers. *Songs of England* (still popular in the late 1940s), *Songs of Ireland* and *Songs of Scotland* all speak for themselves, but there were also titles such as *Gems of Cambria*, *Gems of Scotia* and *Gems of Erin*, as well as two Welsh medleys – *Gwalia* and *Llewellyn*. Under 'miscellaneous' could be found such colourful titles as *A Casket of Gems*, *A Cluster of Classics* and *Gems of Victorian Melody*.

By the mid-1880s there was a wide range of selections available, many arranged by Round and suitable for bands of varying abilities. Most were operatic or composer selections – collections of melodies, contrasting in style, speed, rhythm and weight, designed to test various aspects of bands' capabilities – and particularly the qualities of their soloists. The easier ones were simply called selections or, less frequently, fantasias. The more substantial ones, designed for advanced bands, were often called 'grand' selections. As Round's scores are not easily accessible, and as he was such a key figure in the establishment of commercial brass band music, it will be useful to look in detail at some of them.

Selections

The first to be considered is a selection from the oratorio, *The Last Judgement* (*Die Letzten Dinge*), by Ludwig Spohr (1784–1859), a German-born composer, violinist and conductor, who also wrote (amongst other works) 11 operas, selections from two of which found their way into brass band repertoire (*Faust* and *Jessonda*). Composed in 1825–26 and regularly performed in Victorian England, *The Last Judgement* was the first of Spohr's three oratorios. A selection from it had been used as the test piece at Belle Vue in 1879, arranged by Charles Godfrey, but it is likely that the Round arrangement was prepared for a contest in Liverpool in 1884. It is uncomplicated and based roughly on the pattern established by Gladney, whose Selection from *Elijah* was discussed on page 87. There are five extracts, simply but faithfully reproduced, and with the use of other material kept to a minimum in the linking passages.

The selection opens with part of the so-called orchestral 'Symphony' from the beginning of Part 2 of the oratorio and then proceeds to a passage from the conclusion of the opening 'Overture'. This section, an 'Allegro', is in 3/4 time and in the key of C minor.[2] In the first vocal section – an air and chorus 'Holy, Holy, Holy' – the tenor solo is given to euphonium, and the full band plays the chorus parts. Then follows an abridged version of the unfortunately-translated 'Praise His Awful Name'. In the original this is a substantial chorus, but in his selection, Round transcribed only the final 67 bars. 'Blest Are the Departed' is, for the most part, a cornet solo, though it appears as a chorus in its original setting. A two-bar modulating extension is the only passage not taken from Spohr. The oratorio's finale provides a fitting climax. It comprises the chorus, 'Great and Wonderful', a short fugal section leading to Spohr's version of an 'Hallelujah Chorus', which rounds off both oratorio and selection. The final key, C major, creates a convenient and happy relationship with the C minor opening, adding an element of unity and ending on a note of triumph. The selection, which lasts for some ten minutes, is a pleasing piece that makes few demands on even modest bands. The only solo passages are for cornet and euphonium, though as these are very slow they need skilled soloists to achieve a satisfactory style. Good breath control, a sense of phrasing and the ability to play expressively are some of the prerequisites for the successful performance of such passages.

In a selection from Wagner's *Rienzi*, dating from 1882, Round also freely abridged the chosen sections from the opera. There is no apparent key scheme, though the music stays within the range of keys in which brass band players feel most comfortable, in the order B♭, C, F, E♭, C and B♭. Closing in the 'home' key (that is, the key in which the selection opened) is not a golden rule with Round, though enough of his selections conform to this pattern to make it likely that it was done consciously.

The *Rienzi* selection consists of a mixture of vocal and instrumental passages, the instrumental parts coming from the 'Overture' and the 'War Dance' (part of the ballet). In the opera the role of Rienzi is sung by the tenor; his solos in the selection are shared by euphonium, trombone and (rather surprisingly) cornet. There is occasional simplification of accompanying figuration, but in the main, all is faithfully transcribed although, in one excerpt, Wagner's original 6/4 time is converted into 3/4, with twice the number of bars. The melody line in many of the solos follows the rhythms of the orchestral accompaniments rather than those of the solo singer, and in complex sections parts are omitted, as for example in Rienzi's 'Song to the People'; during the second half of this, trombones take over the role of the three-part male chorus and the remainder of the band plays the orchestral accompaniments, whilst the lines for tenor and soprano soloists are omitted altogether. In another part of the selection, baritones and euphoniums become effectively the 'Chorus of Senators', whilst in another, the female 'Chorus of Messengers' is played by all cornets plus solo horn. Thus, there was a conscious attempt at parity with the original.

At certain points one extract leads straight into another, whilst at others there may be an added chord, chord sequence or a cadenza. There are two cadenzas, one played by solo cornet, incorporating a modulation, and the other – non-modulating – taken by trombone. The longest section not written by Wagner is the coda which, spanning 18 bars, begins chromatically, but ends with a conventional sequence of tonic chords. Comparison with full and vocal scores of the opera suggests that the selection was arranged from the latter rather than the former and indeed, according to *Catalogue of Printed Music*,[3] a vocal score in English, German and Italian appeared in 1878. Incidentally, the first London performance was given in 1879, so Round certainly kept abreast of the times.

Another selection which calls for comment, dating from 1885, heralded Wright & Round's unsuccessful attempt to establish a market for the published full score. *The Lyric Garland*, described as a 'Grand Selection, arranged by H Round' – and mentioned on page 109 – was, in fact, a collection of melodies, some original and some borrowed. The borrowed tunes included the slow, lyrical theme from the overture *Zampa* (Hérold) and music from Act 2 of Wagner's *Lohengrin* – the part now commonly known as 'Elsa's Procession to the Minster'. Included in the score are parts for 'Drums ad lib', suggesting that the selection was designed for concert performance as well as for the contest platform. Trombones appeared above the euphonium, and the lowest stave (apart from percussion) was given to the E♭ bass – a tradition established when this was the lowest-sounding instrument, and one which took some time to work its way out of the system. It did eventually give way to the more logical one of placing the lower-sounding BB♭ bass below it. In common with other Round scores there was no special part for flugelhorn, and only a single stave for euphoniums.

Concert overtures

The concert overture had been established since the early 1830s – Mendelssohn's *Fingal's Cave* being one of the earliest examples. Often in sonata form but also adopting characteristics of the symphonic poem, these were the role models for Round's overtures, the first of which, *Knight Templar*, was written as early as 1876. The last, *Don Quixote*, seems not to have been published until 1911, six years after Round's death.

The overture *Victory* was specially composed for the 'Champion Contest' held at Blackpool on 9 July, 1887 and is described on page 58. The technical demands were not high, but to be performed successfully it required imaginative interpretation from both conductor and soloists, as there was neither an operatic plot nor words from arias or choruses to help determine the styles required. *Victory* is in four sections; the opening is the most extended and takes the form of two sets of waltzes. The first of these, in extended ternary form, displays a hint of chromaticism and some elementary motivic cross references. Nominally in B♭ major, the piece nevertheless opens in F, passing through G minor and C minor before arriving in B♭ for the first main theme (shades of Beethoven's Symphony No 1, perhaps?). This waltz ends with a reprise of the Introduction, modified and leading to the key of F (the dominant) for the second waltz. Here, a 'Tempo bolero' (possibly unique in band music of the period) proceeds to a 'bass solo' section – common in brass band marches, in which the lower brasses play a melody in octaves, whilst cornets and horns play homophonically in a style similar to a trumpet fanfare. A short, original passage leads to a 'Grandioso' and a reprise of the bolero theme, in the key of C.

A tutti coda leads to the second main section of the overture ('Andante religioso'), a sixteen-bar melody played first as a tenor horn solo, accompanied only by the other two horns and the three trombones (the most lightly-scored section). The melody is repeated, tutti, in the subdominant key, and with a florid counter-melody in baritones and euphoniums. The third section is a form of polka, the close of which takes the music into the finale, a short grand march making a suitably rousing coda. Though in no way symphonically conceived, *Victory* may be seen to follow roughly the pattern of a symphonic poem in miniature. Now long forgotten, this and other overtures by Round may be regarded as forerunners of the 'original work'.

Fantasias

The use of the term 'fantasia' in nineteenth-century brass band music is rather confusing. Quite often it was used to designate pieces which were, frankly, selections. However, the term was also applied to some pieces which were largely original but also contained some existing tunes, as well as to many which were completely original. It had no set form, and was, in essence, a selection comprising contrasting musical ideas – original and/or 'borrowed'.

An extremely popular Round piece was published in 1884, his Grand Fantasia (descriptive) – *Joan of Arc*. Its appeal may well have been the result of its programmatic nature, revealed in *Brass Band News* of June. There were, it said, six 'movements', each portraying some aspect of an event in the life of Joan:

 1st movement: 'Andante' – Vision of Joan and her resolve to take up Arms in Defence of King and Country
 2nd movement: 'Larghetto' – Farewell Visit to the Village Church, the Blessing
 3rd movement: 'Tempo di Marcia' – Army in the Distance on the march.
 'Grandioso' – Joan joins the Troops
 4th movement: Prayer Religioso
 5th movement: Attack and Victory
 6th movement: 'Allegretto' – General Rejoicings

This piece was on sale at three shillings (15p) for full brass band and two shillings and sixpence (12½p) for small brass band. It met with immediate success, and in the following August *Brass Band News* stated: 'This contest piece has proved the most successful we have ever done. Over one thousand copies have been disposed of in one month, and the second edition is now in hand.'

Why the piece proved so popular is difficult to determine. *Joan of Arc* certainly did not contain music of as high a quality as that in the better examples of the operatic or composer selections, and it had no apparent structure apart from following the moods of the six sections. The only conclusion one can draw is that perhaps there was already a desire for pieces conceived as band music. That this need was being felt is borne out by the fact that Round wrote 14 'original' overtures, though none seem to have achieved the popularity enjoyed by *Joan of Arc*.

Of the 23 Henry Round pieces labelled 'Fantasia' a particularly good example appeared in 1895. Based on Scottish songs and dances, it was used as test piece at the Kirkcaldy contest. No fewer than 16 tunes are featured, together with an original section towards the close in which, after the solo euphonium intones the words 'Weel done Cutty Sark' the band alludes, in 'The Race to the Bridge', to the Burns poem which gives its name to the fantasia – *Tam o' Shanter*. This is an imaginative score and well deserves not to be simply dubbed a selection. Two of its more unusual features are a duet cadenza for horns, and a cadenza-like passage for the three trombones. Round indulges in a piece of musical psychology by following his 'composed' section with the fantasia's finale, 'Good Night and Joy Be Wi' Ye A'', thus ensuring a meaningful and stimulating conclusion, even for listeners who may have been perplexed by the 'Cutty Sark' section but who would doubtless recognize the sequel. The duration of the work is about 14 minutes.

Biographical information about Round's early career is somewhat obscure. In addition to his writing and his activities in the publishing business, he conducted a number of bands in the Liverpool area but, according to an article reporting his death, he was never actively involved in the running of Wright & Round's. He had been editor of the *Liverpool Journal* for 30 years and died, after a long and painful illness, at the age of 67.[4] Round had dominated the brass band publishing scene, certainly for contesting bands of the time, and his place was taken by the Southport musician, William Rimmer, whose conducting career was discussed in Chapter Six, and whose arrangements and compositions will be reviewed shortly.

The second most prolific writer of band music in this early period was Round's business partner in the *Liverpool Journal*, Thomas Hargrave Wright (1836–1914). The bulk of his music is represented by his 61 marches and 83 dances, all simpler forms which imply compositional limitations. Nevertheless, his output also included a few selections, an overture, a fantasia and a cornet duet. Jules Rivière, referred to in note 17, Chapter 1, was less prolific than Wright but rather more adventurous, with six operatic selections (called fantasias) and ten concert items, as well as 37 marches and 15 dances. Most of Rivière's brass band pieces seem to have been written in a five-year period beginning in 1877, while Wright saw his first published piece in 1875 and was still writing up to the time of his death in 1914.

Round, Wright and Rivière, between them, wrote a colossal number of marches – there are over 200 titles on my lists. These would be used both for marching engagements and concerts. Dance music was also plentiful, though many of the pieces are very short – a mere 32 bars in some cases. My lists include some 250 items, made up principally of 64 valses, waltzes or valsettes, 42 polkas, 40 sets of quadrilles, 37 sets of lancers and 33 schottisches

Three further arranger/composers during this period, Richard Smith, T A Haigh and James Frost each owned their own publishing companies, which enabled them, like Round, to make their own decisions on what to write. There must have been some early pieces by Smith from his Hull days, where he founded his business in 1857 but sadly, they no longer appear extant.

Several copies of his later scores are in Besses' archive, including a grand fantasia *Honoraria* (1878), the selections *Reminiscences of Verdi* (1885) and *Reminiscences of Donizetti* (posthumously dated 1904), and two undated scores – *Gems of Wagner* and an overture by one V Delannoy, called *Leopold*. Publicity material and reports in *British Bandsman* refer to three operatic selections – *Gemma di Vergy* (Donizetti), *Patience* (Sullivan) and *Semiramide* (Rossini), a concert march and a waltz all arranged or composed by Smith. Twenty marches are on my lists, one published by T A Haigh, the remainder by R Smith & Co. Again, publication dates are uncertain, but a number of Smith's marches appeared in the Goose Eye band books (see pages 96–97), and these may be amongst his earlier pieces. It is most probable that Smith wrote many more pieces than these. Perhaps, one day, others will be discovered.

T A Haigh's known output is relatively small and was apparently all published by his own company between 1879 and 1891. Research indicates that he wrote eight marches, two operatic selections, four concert items and five dances. Even with the possibility that this is an incomplete list, his contribution to band history was more significant through his publishing (see pages 99–100) than for his compositions and arrangements. James Frost, mentioned on page 100, was joint owner (with his son) of the *Manchester Brass & Military Band Journal*. His output is varied and by no means insignificant, with 37 marches, 16 concert items, eight dances, two contest quadrilles and a solo. Between 1879 and 1894 his pieces appear both in his own lists and in those of Haigh. After this date most of them were published by Richardson. The composing career of George Frost, his son, seems to have spanned the years 1883 to 1908. In my lists there are 20 marches, 16 concert pieces, two solos and 15 dances. Most were published in the *Manchester Brass & Military Band Journal*, but some are also in Richardson's *Cornet Journal*, in the *London* and *Northern Journals*, and in Haigh's *Amateur Brass & Military Band Journal*.

The remaining arranger/composer from this group, Charles Godfrey, was at least as influential in his own way as Round, though his brass band output was much less extensive. He did not own his own publishing company but, seemingly, had his arrangements printed and sold on his behalf. As mentioned previously, Godfrey came from a family of famous military musicians and was himself bandmaster of the Royal Horse Guards from 1868 to 1904. He was, therefore, already established when he wrote his first selection for the Belle Vue contest in 1872. The selections he prepared for this and subsequent events, including those arranged for the July contests introduced in 1886 (see page 57), form the backbone of his brass band output, and he exercised a virtual monopoly on Belle Vue test pieces until his health started to fail in 1915. Of his 78 selections, 72 came from opera or oratorio and the remainder from the works of named composers. The pieces were published in limited editions and sent by the contest promoters – six weeks prior to the event – to bands which had entered. The name and address of the printer[5] appears on the parts but only in the case of copyright material is a publisher credited.

The practice of leaving it to individual conductors to write out their own full scores continued with the Godfrey arrangements, though either a short score (two-stave) or a well-cued solo cornet–conductor part was supplied. In the archives of Besses o' th' Barn Band there are hand-written full scores for several of the Godfrey selections and study of a batch written between 1890 and 1912[6] shows that the following instruments were required:

E♭ Soprano	Solo tenor	2nd euphonium
Solo cornet	2nd E♭ tenor	1st trombone
Repiano	3rd and 4th horns	2nd trombone
Flugelhorn	1st baritone	Bass trombone
2nd cornet	2nd baritone	E♭ bombardon
3rd cornet	Solo euphonium	Monstre BB♭ bass

The flugelhorn had its own separate stave, and though placed with the cornets in the score, was quite independent. The terms 'tenor' and 'horns' still remain a mystery; 'tenor' obviously implied tenor horn, and whilst the 'horn' parts would probably be played on tenor horns they may, in some bands, have been played on French horns (see page 82).

The principal soloists were undoubtedly the solo cornet and solo euphonium, and their parts called for able players with a good range and technique, a command of various operatic styles and the ability to shape cadenzas. The 1st trombone player required similar attributes, although the demands of this part were considerably less. Though occasionally visiting the upper range, the euphonium stayed in the middle and lower registers for much of the solo work, creating a bass-baritone sonority rather than the high tenor register of much of the later writing for the instrument.

Second euphonium doubled solo euphonium or basses for much of the time, though there were occasions when it played independently. In most of the scores studied, parts for euphoniums, bass trombone and E♭ bombardons were shown in bass clef, reflecting military band conventions. Tenor trombones appeared in bass clef in earlier scores and in tenor clef in later ones. The so-called 'Monstre BB♭' part was written in treble clef in all the scores. In the 1912 score – the latest in this series to be studied – solo euphonium and E♭ bass were both in treble clef, whilst 2nd euphonium was in bass.[7]

Secondary soloists – soprano cornet, flugelhorn, solo horn and 1st baritone – were employed occasionally in short solo passages, and use was often made of ensembles within the band, both accompanied and unaccompanied. The *Euryanthe* selection (1890) was the most interesting in this regard, with a trio for two cornets and trombone, followed by a quartet for soprano, baritone, euphonium and bass trombone which became a quintet with the addition of the flugelhorn. *Das Nachtlager in Granada* (1891) opened with an unaccompanied quartet of two horns, baritone and euphonium and later featured cornet, baritone and euphonium in an accompanied trio. This selection was rather more rhythmically adventurous than the others studied: a section in compound duple time contained a number of rhythmic groupings which, though commonplace today, would doubtless have deceived some of the players in the bands of 1891. The selections generally lasted about ten minutes, and there was little difference between the technical demands of the July and the September tests.

Whilst possibly not contributing significantly to the development of brass band scoring, Godfrey added a considerable amount of well-scored music to the repertoire of the better contesting bands. Through this and his adjudication work, he must be regarded as one of the leading figures in the brass band movement for over 40 years.

It is reasonable to assume that none of the music written by the arranger/composers from this early group is known to bandsmen of today. This is a pity because, even though fashions have changed, the pieces had a particular place in the development of brass band music and, in their own way, possessed qualities which deserve recognition, and which would add variety to contemporary brass band programmes.

Rimmer, Ord Hume and their contemporaries

As one would expect, the next generation of writers benefited from the experience of the earlier group, and though employing a similar musical language, had to cater for changing tastes amongst bands and their audiences. They were also probably influenced by the minor revolution caused through the arrival of John Henry Iles, though this was reflected not so much in their writing of test pieces as in the wider range of concert music which was to be a hallmark of this era.

Two arranger/composers dominated the scene from the final years of the nineteenth century until just after the end of the First World War. One, William Rimmer, continued well beyond this and was still a strong influence during the post-war years. Though he had experience in military bands and light orchestras (his father conducted the Southport Municipal Military Band and he himself was at one-time musical director of the Spa Orchestra in Harrogate) he was brought up in the amateur band movement and was essentially a brass band arranger/composer. His contemporary, James Ord Hume, was primarily a military bandsman, but later switched his allegiance to the brass band. Ord Hume and Rimmer each brought a different kind of musical experience to the brass band, and their respective contributions to its repertoire reflected these. Much of the band music of both men, as well as that by some of the other lesser figures from this group, is still played.

Even whilst active as a conductor, Rimmer saw a significant amount of his music published, and as well as developing as a conductor, was becoming quite influential in music publishing. During the earlier part of his career he had some pieces – mainly marches – published by Haigh and also by the *Northern Journal*. Amongst the marches published by Haigh (between 1880 and 1896) are two of Rimmer's most successful – 'Honest Toil' (one of his first publications – if not the very first – appearing in 1880 when he was just 18 years old) and 'Knight of the Road', dating from 1895. Another march which enjoyed considerable popularity for a time was 'Viva Petee', named after an American writer of band music who died in 1891. This was published in the *Northern Journal* in 1894.[8] There is also a handful of early Rimmer pieces, dating mainly from the 1890s, in the catalogue of Wright & Round, and a number of pieces, mostly arrangements, in the list of Hawkes & Sons, published between 1897 and 1902. Some of these were also published for military band.

During his career, Rimmer was closely associated with three music publishers, serving each as music editor. Here he was responsible for composing or arranging much of the publishers' output himself, for overseeing all publications, and generally masterminding the companies' musical policies, geared towards fulfilling the needs of bands and contest promoters. Before considering Rimmer's work for these individual publishers, here is a résumé of his total output, as it appears in my lists (see page 137):

117 marches
37 operatic selection
28 composer selections
14 national air selections
28 miscellaneous selections
8 original contest pieces – fantasias, suites and overtures
77 concert pieces – intermezzi, *air varies*, *entr'actes*, duets, etc
10 transcriptions of standard overtures
33 miscellaneous transcriptions, ranging from themes from Beethoven's 'Eroica' Symphony to the simple *Plaisir d'Amour* of Martini
30 solos, including a few transcribed 'slow melodies', but mostly original – 21 for cornet or euphonium, 5 for trombone, and others unspecified; they are mainly polkas or air varies and generally all showy
28 dance pieces – mostly waltzes and, significantly, only two sets of quadrilles and two sets of lancers – their heyday had passed by the time Rimmer had reached maturity

Turning to his work as a music editor, from 1897 to 1905 he appears to have been the first incumbent to hold this position for the *Cornet Journal*, published by F Richardson in Boston, Lincolnshire. Following this he took up a similar appointment with R Smith & Co, editing their *Champion Journal* until 1912. Finally, from 1913, he took over the musical editorship of Wright

& Round's *Liverpool Journal*, remaining there until his death in 1936. Naturally, most of Rimmer's publications found their way into the catalogues of the companies for which he was music editor.

During his eight years with Richardson at least 70 pieces were published bearing his name. The Smith years were equally productive, though for some reason, less successful – certainly in the long term. Several of his earlier *Cornet Journal* publications are still regularly played, but hardly any of the 75 or more pieces published by Smith are known even by name today. Further, his break with this company seems to have been a permanent one, whereas Richardson published many later Rimmer pieces, even during his Wright and Round years.

Whilst editing for Smith, Rimmer widened the range of his music by writing concert pieces (both original and transcribed) and a few pieces of dance music. With the exception of a concert valse 'Silver Showers' (really a cornet solo) and an air varie for band – 'Variations on a Welsh Melody', both dating from 1906 and still played occasionally, the Rimmer/Smith publications have fallen out of fashion. In fact, no band pieces by him are listed in the current catalogue.

Reference has already been made to some of Rimmer's early marches. Of 30 published by Richardson, at least nine have retained a measure of popularity:

'Old Comrades' (1895) – not to be confused with Teike's *Alte Kameraden*, composed four years later
'Viva Birkinshaw' (1896) – composed shortly after the death of the famous cornet player
La Russe (1898)
'The North Star' (1901)
'Slaidburn' (1901)
'The Cossack' (1904) – adopted by Fodens as its signature tune
'Farewell, My Comrades' (1904)
'Punchinello' (1904)
'The Australasian' (1906 or earlier) – dedicated to the bands of Australasia

Rimmer's other music for Richardson was mostly for the contest platform. None of it is to be found in the repertoire of today's bands.

There are over 130 pieces from his residency as editor for Wright & Round – a lower annual rate of production than for the other two companies. However, there is a greater proportion of substantial pieces and there is no doubt that he wrote a significant amount of music under various pseudonyms. Ainscough gives 21 of these, asserting that Rimmer composed or arranged over 800 pieces under his own name and over 300 more using other names.[9] The only pseudonym claimed by the Performing Right Society as belonging to William Rimmer is Michael Laurent. It seems certain, however, according to the present owners of Wright & Round, that E and F le Duc were Rimmer pen-names; the names W Raymond, Wilton Roche and W Royle, using the same initials are also likely candidates, and possible others include Hiram Eden and Eugene Verner. In addition to pieces written under these names it is certain that many of the contest pieces arranged anonymously were also, in fact, from Rimmer's pen – another part of his role as music editor.

Rimmer seems to have been at his best as a composer of marches during his early years. Several were published by Wright & Round in the years before he became their music editor. However, with one exception, the most popular Rimmer marches from this publishing house are from later in his career – 'The Victor's Return' (1922) and 'Royal Trophy' (1931). The origins of the exception are quite intriguing. Entitled 'Ravenswood', it remains one of the most popular of all contest marches; the earliest mention of it is in an advertisement for Haigh's *String Band Journal* in 1897, gleaned from the pages of *Brass Band News*. The brass band version is now in the catalogue of Wright & Round.

Rimmer's contest music, made up of the various types of selections and fantasias, is virtually forgotten, but some of his concert music, published by Wright & Round, has retained its popularity, including:

'Rule Britannia' (1923) – a 'Patriotic Overture', based on the famous Arne tune and on a lesser-known song, 'Come if you dare'
'Eroica' (1929) – a selection of themes from Beethoven's 3rd Symphony, scorned by many in the brass band movement because of its disregard for the structure of the original, but still played quite regularly
Lord of the Isles (1933) – described as a 'Scottish Rhapsody'
'Two Comrades' (1933) – a popular cornet duet
'The Skye Boat Song' (1934) – a setting of the well-known traditional tune, but also incorporating some original material
Hungarian Rhapsody No 2 – a transcription of the most famous of Liszt's 19 such rhapsodies, and quite a showpiece for better bands – published posthumously
Les Preludes – an abridged but successful transcription of Liszt's symphonic poem – also published posthumously

Some of Rimmer's cornet solos are still played regularly. Most have an element of variation about them, and Rimmer's own experience as a cornet soloist is evident in their technical demands. They include:

'Jenny Jones' (1899) – *air varie*
'My Old Kentucky Home' (1924) – *air varie*
'Hailstorm' (1929) – polka
'Merry-Go-Round' (1931) – a kind of caprice
'Weber's Last Waltz' (date unknown) – *air varie* (based on a theme by Reissiger)

Looking at some of the possible pseudonyms: the works written as Michael Laurent (there are nine in my lists) are of the fantasia type, though two are called overtures. These were published by Wright & Round between 1924 and 1934. They include *Alexander's Feast*, *The Ancient Mariner* and *Beautiful Britain*, titles which will be recalled by some older bandsmen. The le Duc works were also mainly easy fantasia-type pieces, used in contests by junior bands. On my list there are 11 pieces under the name E le Duc and two bearing that of F le Duc. These were also published by Wright & Round, between 1911 and 1939 (three years after Rimmer's death). Some enjoy an occasional revival, for example *O'er Hill and Dale* (1931) and *In Days of Old* (1935). Of the marches written under the so-called Hiram Eden, 'Pat in America' (1905) will be known to many bandsmen. The Eden marches on my list (three only) were published by Richardson between 1904 and 1906 and therefore belong to the group of Rimmer–Richardson marches mentioned earlier. Little, if any, of the music written under other pen names has survived, suggesting that there was a commercial disadvantage in not using Rimmer's name, as its use probably helped sell the music.

Rimmer's output and contribution were both considerable. He was the natural successor to Henry Round and even though much of his music is now forgotten, he contributed to the contest repertoire through his selections until the end of his life. Most of the operatic selections were arranged before 1914; amongst the later exceptions were two pot-pourris, *Gems from Italian Opera* and *A Souvenir of the Opera*, both published in 1928, and two from the popular operatic repertoire – *The Mastersingers* (1927) and *Carmen* (1929). His national selections also belong mainly to the earlier period, as do most of the miscellaneous ones. A few later examples of these were also useful concert items, and included *A Garland of Classics* (1926), *Sailor Songs* (1927), *Melodious Gems* (1930) and *Minstrel Memories* (1935).

Most of Rimmer's contest pieces belong to the R Smith era and were succeeded by that company's series of original compositions, beginning with *Labour and Love* in 1913. (It may, in fact, not be coincidence that this was the year in which Rimmer left the Smith dynasty; as a composer he could not compete with the likes of Percy Fletcher and Cyril Jenkins.)

Following the arrival of the original work and the virtual death of the operatic selection, Rimmer's principal contribution to the repertoire was through his composer selections, introducing bands and their audiences to music by some of the great masters, much of which they would not know. He had arranged a series of 'Memories' for Richardson around the turn of the century, ranging from *Memories of Mozart* (1898) to *Memories of Donizetti* (1905), and there was his extremely popular *Tchaikovsky*, published in 1915 but used as a second section test piece in the National Championships as late as 1962. Amongst his later composer selections was the 'Recollections' series, most of which were published in the 1930s. Other late composer selections, of a more substantial nature, included *Gounod* (1926), *Liszt* (1928), *Berlioz* (1933) and *Bizet* (1936). Through these Rimmer was able to introduce bands and their audiences to works by their composers, leading many to explore more fully the music in its original form, as well as other music by the same composers. Thus, there was an educational as well as an entertaining element in his work at this time.

Finally, Rimmer must be given credit for writing some of the earliest and finest examples of the modern contest march as well as his series of evergreen solos. His contribution to brass band repertoire is, therefore, inestimable, and his influence was to continue well beyond the time of his death in 1936.

Almost an exact contemporary, James Ord Hume was born in Edinburgh, taught himself to play a range of instruments and, in 1881, joined the Band of the Royal Scots Grays as a cornet player. Over the next ten years he established a reputation as both a performer and a composer. He left the army at the age of 25, specifically to work with brass bands as adjudicator, conductor, composer and arranger, and by the turn of the century had become a prominent figure in the banding world.[10]

From the 1890s music flowed rapidly from Ord Hume's pen, with many of his pieces published simultaneously for both brass and military band. It is claimed that he was the composer of over 1000 works, including 200 marches,[11] but though there is no reason to doubt the figures, many of the pieces were arrangements rather than original compositions. On my list of pieces (all for brass band, though many would also have been published for military band), the following are listed under 'Ord Hume, James':

83 marches
26 operatic selections
8 composer selections
12 national air selections
8 musical comedy selections
11 miscellaneous selections
34 concert pieces – all original, including overtures, intermezzi, descriptive pieces and duets
5 transcriptions of standard overtures
90 miscellaneous arrangements, including many sacred pieces, marches, operatic extracts, glees and part songs. (There is also a large number of hymn tunes, not included in this total)
4 original solos
48 solo arrangements of ballads and operatic excerpts, two-thirds of which are for cornet
17 original dance pieces
84 popular songs/dances

Haigh published the early pieces of several arranger/composers of band music, including those of Ord Hume. There are 22 titles by him on my list from this publisher – marches, concert pieces, a solo and some dance music. These were published between 1879 and 1895, indicating that Ord Hume was writing for brass band long before he terminated his military band career. There is also a handful of forgotten pieces (dating from the 1890s) in Wright & Round's catalogue, and some published by Hawkes between 1893 and 1899.

Richardson published a few Ord Hume pieces between 1896 and 1904 – marches, dance music and a selection, and certainly one of the marches from this batch has retained its popularity. Called 'Roll Away Bet', it was composed in 1903 and dedicated to the Lindley Band, which had won the Belle Vue September contest in 1900, and which appeared in the prize lists for the next few years.[12]

Between 1898 and 1906 Ord Hume wrote regularly for R Smith & Co, doubtless at the instigation of John Henry Iles, who also appointed him editor of *The Contest Field*, a sister paper to *British Bandsman* (see page 111). In 1901 Ord Hume wrote one of the most famous of all brass band marches, 'B B & C F', using the initials of the two magazines. Other well-known marches from the Ord Hume/Smith partnership include 'The Elephant' (1899), '20th Century' (1900), 'Brilliant' (1901) and 'The Victor's Return' (1905). It was also for Smith that Ord Hume, at the request of Iles, arranged the first National Championship test piece, *Gems from Sullivan's Operas No 1* (later renamed *Beauties of Sullivan*, and referred to on page 120). This was in 1900, and was followed by *Gems from Sullivan's Operas Numbers 2 and 3* – both also published by Smith and used in subsequent National Championships (see pages 121 and 122). A reference in *British Bandsman*[13] mentions a section of the third Sullivan selection being written in 5/4 time – one of the earliest examples of such writing in brass band music. None of these pieces, nor indeed any of the others in the Ord Hume/Smith range (apart from the marches) has remained in the repertoire.

By far the largest number – over 230 – of Ord Hume pieces appeared in the catalogue of Boosey. These span the years 1897 to 1930, the year in which the company amalgamated with Hawkes. The partnership continued, with a few more pieces published by Boosey & Hawkes in the remaining two years of Ord Hume's life. The best known Ord Hume march in the Boosey collection is one called 'Simplicity' (1909) – a rather misleading title, as the march is far from simple. As with other composer/arrangers, all the contest selections by Ord Hume have disappeared from the repertoire, but much of his concert music has survived – a substantial amount of it remaining popular up to the late 1950s or early 1960s, though featured less regularly in today's programmes. Much of his music in this category comes under discussion in Chapter Eight.

Ord Hume's importance as a march composer has already been discussed, but beyond this he is remembered chiefly for his transcriptions and arrangements. The overture-transcriptions, particularly of *Light Cavalry* (1894) and *Poet and Peasant* (1918) – both by Suppé, and *Raymond* (1911) by Ambroise Thomas have retained their popularity and are amongst the earliest of his arrangements to have survived. Also in this category are his versions of the two most popular 'Pomp and Circumstance' marches of Elgar (numbers 1 and 4).

As with Rimmer, it is believed that Ord Hume used a number of pen names.[14] The only one about which we can be reasonably sure he employed for his brass band compositions is that of William German. If this was an Ord

Hume pseudonym – and the style of the pieces suggests that it was – then he wrote a handful of marches for Smith which were published in 1902 and 1903. Two of these are still well known, the second particularly so; they are 'The Oriental' (1902) and 'The President' (1903).

Towards the end of his life, Ord Hume published his own music, and several titles appeared in contemporary advertisements. Here was another great contributor to brass band music. In terms of the sheer quantity of music written he is roughly comparable to Round and Rimmer, but in terms of the scope and variety of his pieces he exceeded both, helping to build substantial bridges between the brass band and other fields of popular music. In the same way that Rimmer was introducing bands to music of the masters through his selections, Ord Hume was introducing bands to music from the lighter side of the business, contributing considerably to this aspect of repertoire.

There are several other arranger/composers from this period, most of whom grew up in the brass band world, and whose music is, therefore, closer in style to that of Rimmer than that of Ord Hume. George Allan (1864–1930) was born in Shildon, County Durham, and through his marches earned for himself the title of 'March King of the North-East'. His main employment was as a wagon painter at the Shildon Railway Works, and therefore he was truly an amateur musician. In his spare time, as well as composing and arranging music, he conducted the New Shildon Saxhorn Band (now Shildon Town), and was also musical director of the local amateur operatic society.[15] Allan's brass band pieces include some 52 marches, eight concert pieces (mainly fantasias) and 18 pieces of dance music. Most were published by Haigh between 1881 (when Allan was only 17) and 1896. Richardson took his music from then until 1904, and the biography in the Durham League booklet states that he printed and published some of his own music.[16] His three best-known marches today are 'Knight Templar', 'Raby' and 'Senator',[17] though another Allan march sometimes played is 'Battle Abbey'.

Edward Newton (1838–1914 – see note 20, Chapter 6) was a quite prolific arranger/composer; amongst his output were contest selections and fantasias, and concert items – mostly arrangements, marches and dance music. A few were published by Haigh between 1883 and 1891, but the majority appeared as Smith publications, between 1887 and 1904. Some of his later music was published by Richardson between 1889 and 1909, with a small number of pieces taken by Wright & Round. There are, doubtless, several hundred Newton pieces, some of them in the Goose Eye band books (see pages 96–97), but none are played today, and his name is virtually unknown to the present generation of bandsmen. The music of Frank Linter has met with the same fate; though there are many titles under this name, to date no biographical information whatsoever has been found about him, and it is possible that Linter is a pseudonym – perhaps of Rimmer, but more likely of Wright or Round. All his pieces so far located were published by Wright & Round, appearing in print between 1880 and 1907, and comprising 45 marches, six concert pieces – mainly fantasias, and 39 pieces of dance music – mostly schottisches, polkas and valses.

Another contemporary was John Jubb (born 1852), a member of a family of band musicians prominent in the Sheffield area for many years.[18] Here is another forgotten name, though there are at least 79 published marches to his credit, together with contest and concert pieces, solos and some dance music. The *London Journal* published 35 of them, Haigh 25, and the rest were shared between the *Northern Journal*, Wright & Round and Richardson. The one march by Jubb which is remembered today, and is still a favourite with junior bands, is 'The Chieftain', published by Richardson *circa* 1895. John Jubb's son, Joseph Greaves Jubb (born 1877) composed a handful of marches, and was one of the earliest of the brass band teachers to devise a correspondence course in harmony. This is mentioned frequently in *Brass Band News*, and at one time he was referred to by the paper's correspondents as 'The Harmony Merchant'.

George Wadsworth (1855–1919), from Holmfirth, near Huddersfield, composed marches, dances and sacred pieces, many of which were published by Frost. These seem to have been published in the 1890s, whilst in the first few years of the twentieth century, Wadsworth had a number of pieces published by Richardson – many of them hymns and carols. Wadsworth's obituaries (*Huddersfield Examiner*, 25 February 1919 and *Holme Valley Express*, 1 March, 1919) state that he came from a well-known musical family, several members of which were associated with brass bands. Cornet and euphonium were his main instruments, and in addition to his work as a composer, he was a conductor and a noted adjudicator. By profession he was a monumental stonemason, and was also the sexton at a local church.

Sam Cope (1856–1947) is remembered more for his administrative work for brass bands than for his music. In 1887 he founded the *British Bandsman* (see page 110) and served as its editor from 1888 to 1895, again from 1899 to 1906, and yet again from 1930 to 1942.[19] Cope also took over the musical editorship of R Smith and Co after the death of its founder in 1890 and it was he whom John Henry Iles contacted after his historic trip to Manchester in 1898 (see pages 65). Of Cope's band pieces, older bandsmen may remember 'descriptive fantasias' such as *The Sailor's Life* and *The Mill in the Dale*. Otherwise, his music is completely unknown to the present generation of bands.

Shipley Douglas (1868–1920) was at one time a pupil of James Ord Hume's, and his arrangement of the selection from *Die Meistersinger* (Wagner) for the 1903 Crystal Palace Brass Band Championships brought him immediate fame. He wrote in a range of forms, but apart from an occasional airing of a 'humorous fantasy' based on 'Three Blind Mice', published by Richardson in 1922, he is now remembered chiefly for the splendid contest march 'Mephistopheles' (published by Smith around 1905), and to a lesser extent by another fine march, 'Peace and War' (date unknown). He wrote for various publishers, including Smith, Wright & Round, Boosey, and Richardson, as well as for other companies which were becoming involved with band music in the twentieth century – Chappell, Bosworth and Feldman.

John Hartmann (1830–1897) was the son of a peasant farmer, but joined the Prussian Army as a cornet player. He served for three years in Cologne under Henry Schallen who, in 1854, was engaged by the Crystal Palace Company to form a band. Following this appointment, August Manns, Ernest Hartmann (John's brother) and John Hartmann himself all came to England to join this band. Some time later Hartmann, already composing and arranging band music, was offered a position as bandmaster of the Tyrone Militia Band. He accepted this and, subsequently, similar posts with several other army bands. After the founding of the Royal Military School of Music at Kneller Hall in 1857, it was decreed that civilian army bandmasters such as Hartmann should enlist and pass through the School. Hartmann refused and returned to Germany. However, unable to settle back in his homeland, he soon returned to England, devoting the remainder of his life to arranging and composing for bands.[20]

A substantial portion of Hartmann's music found its way into the brass band repertoire, and there are over 60 compositions and arrangements by him. Most were published by Hawkes and consisted of marches, contest and concert music, solos and dances. Hartmann is now remembered almost entirely by his solos, some of which are still played from the original published parts. Others were arranged later, from piano versions, and published posthumously by Boosey and Wright & Round. Surviving solos include:

Arbucklenian (polka)	Rivière & Hawkes	1886
Rule Britannia (air varie)	original piano version also W & R, arr Stephens	1886,
'Lizzie' (polka)	Hawkes	1895
'Robin Adair' (*air varie* – arr Hawkins)	W & R	1911
'My pretty Jane' (*air varie*)	W & R	1922
'Facilita' (*air varie* – arr F Mortimer)	Boosey	1932
'La belle Americaine' (*air varie*)	W & R	1934
Weidekehr (*air varie*)	W & R	1935
'Gipsy's warning' (*air varie*)	Boosey	(date unknown)

Another writer, Warwick Williams (born 1846 – see note 40, Chapter 5), had over 30 brass band pieces published between 1890 and 1905, mainly by Hawkes. The majority were either concert pieces or dance music, and none are known today.

The remaining writer from this group – and one who has caused some confusion – is John Ord Hume. The confusion is due to the fact that some of his music is published under the name J Ord Hume, identical to most of that by his younger brother, James. Like James, John was a military bandmaster, though his career was less illustrious. Similarly, as a writer, he was both less prolific and less successful, though there are some 60 pieces by him, mostly marches and dance music.

Rimmer and James Ord Hume dominated this era of brass band music, and many of their pieces have survived. Of the other music from the period, marches by George Allan and Shipley Douglas are still popular as are some of the solos of Hartmann. With few exceptions no other pieces or writers from this group are known to the present generation of bandsmen. Their contribution to the development of band music was negligible and though they may have extended the catalogues of the publishers for whom they wrote, they seem to have been incapable of either innovation or bridge-building.

The final group

The remaining arranger/composers to be considered each lived beyond 1936, yet wrote music before that date to an extent which demands their inclusion. Coming close on the heels of the previous group, it is difficult to find any stylistic progress in their writings. They were, to an extent, living in the past. Certainly since the 1920s, most innovations in brass band music were taking place in London, inspired by John Henry Iles. These, to be discussed in Chapter Nine, seem to have overtaken what might be called the 'Northern School' of brass band writers and in fact, without this southern influence, despite the fact that virtually all the great bands were still located in the north, the brass band movement may well have withered and died. Nevertheless, for the sake of completeness the work of the remaining arranger/composers active in the 1930s needs to be reviewed.

By far the most prolific of the four was John A Greenwood (whose conducting career was discussed on pages 131–132). His output, also taking into account his later pieces, includes the following:

9 marches
11 overtures (original)
27 fantasias
30 operatic selections
14 composer selections
11 national selections
2 miscellaneous selections
14 concert pieces – original
5 transcriptions of standard overtures
13 miscellaneous transcriptions
22 solos – mainly original
35 dances – mostly waltzes

The marches, appearing from 1902 are, generally speaking, ordinary 'road' marches – that is, undemanding but tuneful, and suitable for playing on the march. Some are still played, but none are widely known. Some are named after famous bands – 'Irwell Springs' (1906), 'Wingates' (1907), 'Black Dyke' (1912) and 'Foden's Own' (1923), whilst a very early march called 'Winsford' (1902) – possibly Greenwood's first published piece – was named after the town of his birth. About a third of the marches were published by Richardson and the remainder, from about 1930, by Wright & Round.

Greenwood's original overtures were published between 1904 and 1922, mostly by Richardson. The fantasias, written primarily for junior bands, appeared from 1907 up to the end of his life and many of them were popular for several years after his death. These included *The Spirit of Youth* and *A Summer Day* (1932), *The Golden Age* (1933) and *Call of Youth* (1936), but are rarely performed today. The various types of selection, also appearing from 1907, published by either Wright & Round or Richardson, have had a similar fate, but of the concert pieces, the cornet duet 'Playmates' (1936) is still featured regularly, and two of the early overture arrangements, Auber's *Crown Diamonds* (1912) and Suppé's *Light Cavalry* (1925) are in the repertoire of a number of bands. The other overtures arranged by Greenwood were post-1936. Of the miscellaneous arrangements, the grand marches from Wagner's *Tannhäuser* (1924) and Gounod's *La Reine de Saba* (*circa* 1936) are still played quite regularly.

Some instrumental solos by Greenwood have retained their popularity, as have several of those composed by older generations of brass band writers. In general, marches and solos have lived on whilst other forms of band music have slipped into varying degrees of obscurity. Of the Greenwood solos which may still be heard, two are of the humorous trombone glissando type – 'The Acrobat' (1935) and 'The Jester' (1936). A cornet solo, 'Bravura' (date unknown) and the *air varie* 'My Old Kentucky Home' (1924) – for cornet or euphonium – have also retained their popularity, along with several of Greenwood's later solos. Some of the waltzes may well still be played by village bands at village functions, but none are universally known.

Of the remaining three arranger/composers the first, George Hawkins (1876–1967) was born near Nottingham. He came from a musical family, his father being an organist, choirmaster and tenor singer, and his maternal grandfather a violinist, a choirmaster and, it is claimed, a composer.[21] His early musical experiences were as a chorister and as a string player (which instrument he played is not divulged). He joined his first brass band at the age of 17 and was made bandmaster within a year.

As a conductor, Hawkins first made his mark in the North-East, moving there in 1901 to conduct Hebburn Temperance Silver Band. He next became involved with Skinningrove Miners' Band, winning the Crystal Palace Grand Shield with them in 1910. From 1913 he was professional conductor of

Harton Colliery, and in 1919 helped them to a win in the Belle Vue September contest. This was Hawkins' only major championship success, though his bands won two second prizes in the Crystal Palace Thousand Guinea competition. He was also associated with St Hilda's and Marsden Colliery bands, both located in the North-East; Parc & Dare Workmen's Band in South Wales; and Clydebank Burgh and the Scottish CWS bands in Scotland. Almost all of his music was published by Richardson, mostly between 1926 and 1936; 1936 was the peak year, some 20 of his pieces appearing. Inevitably the contest selections (over 20 of them) have disappeared from the repertoire, and I must confess to not being familiar with any of his 20 or so marches, though several of them were almost certainly popular in their time.

During the late 1920s and early 1930s, pieces designated 'descriptive' were a popular feature of bandstand programmes. Hawkins supplied a number of these, including *A Sunday Parade* (1927), *A Sunday Evening Service* and *A Soldier's Memories* (both 1929), *A Day on the Farm* (1930), *Fox and Hounds* (1931) and *A Rustic Fete* (1934). In similar vein was his earlier 'humorous fantasia' *Pop Goes the Weasel* (1924). Slightly more durable were his selections *Gems from the Overtures* (1929) and a march medley, *Famous Fragments* (1932). He also produced some cornet duets – popular in bandstand programmes, often providing an encore to the cornet solo. At least two by Hawkins enjoyed some measure of success, 'The Harlequins' (1936) and 'The Merrymakers' (date unknown).

Hawkins achieved more lasting success with his transcriptions, and it is chiefly through these that he is remembered. There are about a dozen standard overtures, and he was more adventurous in his choice of these than were his predecessors. They include two by Rossini, *The Barber of Seville* and *Semiramide* (both transcribed in 1926), and Nicolai's *The Merry Wives of Windsor* (transcribed in 1936). Selections from the operas had already been played by bands, but these were possibly the first transcriptions of the overtures. Other 'popular classics' which appeared amongst the Hawkins transcriptions included the famous Boccherini 'Minuet' (1929), Meyerbeer's 'Coronation March' (1931), Schubert's 'Marche Militaire' (1933) and a solo for trombone or euphonium, Gounod's 'Lend Me Your Aid' (1931).

The name Edward Sutton (born 1868) is known through a handful of solos which have retained their popularity. He played in the Southport Rifles Band from the age of 15, and at 20 succeeded William Rimmer as its solo cornet player. He was a Rimmer pupil but spent much of his life in Scotland, going there in 1898 to become bandmaster of Scotland's premier band of the time, Clydebank Burgh. In later years he became a respected adjudicator. There are about 30 of his pieces in my lists; undoubtedly, the most well known today are a cornet solo, 'The Paragon' (1931), composed for Harold Pinches, solo cornet player of Black Dyke at the time; and a euphonium solo, 'The Cavalier' (1932), composed for a famous euphonium player, Bert Sullivan, and originally called 'Bertini'. Another euphonium solo which enjoyed considerable success was 'The Brigadier' (1935), and in the heyday of the glissando trombone solo, several Sutton pieces became popular favourites, including 'The Jigsaw' (1932), 'The Joywheel' and 'The Parachute' (dates of publication unknown), and 'The Switchback' published by the *Scottish Band Journal* in 1905, possibly Sutton's first published piece.

One of the most popular of all cornet duets, 'Sandy and Jock' (1932) is a Sutton work, and amongst other pieces by him, popular on the bandstand, were Scottish and Irish medleys – 'Sandy's Frolic' (1930) and 'Paddy's Capers' (1936), and a patrol, 'With Kilt and Sporan' [*sic*] (1930). The 'patrol' was a popular bandstand entertainment, depicting the distant sound of a band in its quiet opening, a build-up of sound as the band came closer, and reaching a climax as the imaginary band passed by. Then, by means of a prolonged diminuendo, the sound of the band gradually faded into the distance. Bands often played this type of piece immediately before the interval and, mimicking Haydn's 'Farewell' Symphony, bandsmen would leave the bandstand one by one, with perhaps only the conductor and the drummer remaining – looking suitably surprised – to bring the patrol to a humorous conclusion.

Finally to Harold Moss (1890–1960): band people of this writer's generation well remember Moss as teacher and adjudicator. As a young man he had built a reputation as an outstanding trombonist, and joined Wingates Temperance Band in 1909. Twenty years later he was appointed musical director, remaining with Wingates until he moved to Cresswell Colliery in 1936.[22] Though he never actually won a major championship as a conductor, his bands regularly appeared in the prize lists. There are only a relatively few Harold Moss compositions – seemingly all solos, but at least three of them are still played regularly. The most popular today is his cornet solo 'The Nightingale' (published in 1929 by Richardson), reputedly written as a trombone solo and played by Moss himself, before becoming popular as a cornet piece. There are four trombone solos, each using the glissando technique, and certainly two of them are still regularly played by trombonists for lighthearted events. These are 'The Firefly' (Boosey 1927) and 'The Joker' (Hawkes, 1928). Moss also made several arrangements, a few of which were published, and several of which remain in manuscript in the library of Wingates.

Conclusion

Although other arranger/composers could have been included in this survey, it was felt that those discussed adequately represent the styles of their respective generations. All were subject to changing fashions and tastes in band music, as indeed later writers also have been. Major changes came at the turn of the century and after the First World War, with the arrival of jazz, the increase in interest in sport and ballroom dancing, the invention of radio, the cinema and the gramophone all contributing to a decline in the former popularity of the brass band.

According to Scott[23] banding was at its lowest ebb after 1918. The world had become a different place, and there were fewer bands as a result. The situation was aggravated by older bandsmen, steeped in tradition, trying to cling to the old operatic selections – music in which the younger generation was not interested. Worse was to come in the 1930s during the Depression, when many bands could not afford to continue. As band music became less fashionable there were fewer engagements, and many bandstands were closed down or even demolished. The most successful bands were able to command broadcasts, to make gramophone recordings, and continued to be popular at holiday resorts. A few accepted several week-long engagements during the summer months, but they were in a minority

It became apparent that the survival of the brass band rested on the development of a repertoire which met the changing tastes of the time. Some band writers looked to musical shows, films and dance music for their inspiration, while others broadened the appeal of 'art' music for bands by the composition of 'original works'. It is these developments to which the following two chapters will be devoted.

Notes

1. This was a collection of excerpts from the repertoire of the opera company founded, incidentally, in 1875, the same year as the founding of the *Liverpool Journal*.
2. All keys quoted are at B♭ pitch.
3. Volume 59, p. 41.
4. *Brass Band News*, October 1905.
5. The printers were F C Wood, G Cooke, Spottiswoode & Co and J W Hawker – all of London.
6. Scores studied were of the following: Donizetti: *Belisario* (July 1890) and *Linda di Chamounix* (July 1891), Weber: *Euryanthe* (September 1890), Kreutzer: *Das Nachtlager in Granada* (September 1891), Herold: *Le Pré-aux-clercs* (July 1892), Goring Thomas: *The Golden Web* (September 1894), Rossini: *Semiramide* (September 1904) and Auber: *Diamants de la Couronne* (September 1912).
7. The persistent use of bass and tenor clefs suggests that there may have been some crossover with lower brass players from the orchestra, the theatre and the military band, in all of which the use of these clefs was the normal convention. Treble clef-orientated E♭ bass players had a system of reading bass clef parts, and similarly-oriented tenor trombonists could play from a tenor clef part without very much trouble. Nevertheless, the use of these clefs, especially on euphonium parts, was something of an impediment to full and free interchange of instruments within the brass band. (It should be noted that the bass trombone is the only part now permanently in bass clef in the brass band.)

8 *Honest Toil* and *Viva Petee* were both recorded by Wingates Temperance in the early 1920s, on Regal G7532. No conductor is named on the record.
9 In an article in the *Rakeway Yearbook* 1988, p. 27.
10 Information about J Ord Hume is taken mainly from Smith, 1986, p. 314.
11 Smith, 1986, p. 314.
12 Lindley is a village on the outskirts of Huddersfield.
13 28 September 1901.
14 For examples, see Smith, 1986, p. 314.
15 Information is taken from Durham County Brass Band League's booklet, *50 Golden Years* (Evans, 1992).
16 The writer recently saw a march by Allan (Vigilant), published by *The Popular Brass Band Journal*, possibly Allan's own company.
17 These marches were probably first published by Allan himself, though they are now in the catalogue of Studio Music Company, London.
18 See *Brass Band News* of May, 1893, for details of John Jubb, and *Brass Band News* of February 1923 for information about the family – a father and four sons.
19 See *British Bandsman* of 5 September 1987 (centenary edition).
20 Information about Hartmann comes from Rehrig, 1991, Vol. 1, p. 323.
21 Information about George Hawkins comes from Cooke, 1950, pp. 85 and 86, Evans (1992), p. 37 and *Brass Band News* of March 1904.
22 Information about Harold Moss comes from Cooke, 1950, pp. 113 and 114.
23 Scott, Jack L (1970) *Evolution of the Brass Band*, pp. 104–105 and 259–260.

8 Popular band music in the twentieth century

Introduction

Much of the music discussed so far in this book fits comfortably into the category of 'popular music'. This can be defined as musical entertainment 'to please ordinary people', i.e. easy to listen to and of less intellectual content than its 'purer' art form, classical music. By implication the latter is enjoyed predominantly by the upper and middle classes, who attend opera, symphony concerts, organ recitals, chamber music and the like, whilst the working classes are deemed to prefer popular music such as operetta, musical comedy (later musicals), ballads and dance music, as well as brass band music. 'Light music', a term applied to 'those kinds of music that are a popular distillation of the traditional classical vein as distinct from the various forms of popular music that stem from folk or jazz sources',[1] is also a class of popular music, and will be discussed later in the chapter.

The term 'popular' has been applied to music since the middle of the nineteenth century,[2] and the gap between 'serious' music and that of brass bands referred to on page 117 was not an isolated phenomenon. As one commentator puts it, 'The Edwardian period was the age in which a gulf between composers and the public widened so much that communication was lost'.[3] At the beginning of the twentieth century the terms highbrow and lowbrow started to be used[4] to denote opposite cultural tastes, true 'art music', being highbrow and music for the masses (popular music), lowbrow. In reality they indicated also the type of musical function one frequented: there were many who, though they liked to be seen in places where 'highbrow' music was on offer, preferred more popular music but did not care to admit it.

Likewise, there were many in less privileged sectors of society who truly enjoyed and appreciated 'art music'.

There were many changes in the popular music scene during the early years of the twentieth century, including new influences from America and a stronger emphasis on music for young people. With the arrival of the Cake-Walk and Ragtime, sweeping through Britain from about 1912,[5] older styles were relegated. The coming of the Tango, the Foxtrot and the Slow Waltz gave ballroom dancing a completely new look, and the coming of the cinema and inventions such as the gramophone were to have dramatic effects within the 'entertainments' business.

Along with other forms of Victorian popular music, the music hall experienced a decline in the twentieth century, returning to the branch of entertainment from which, to some extent, it originated – variety. But, popular as it had been in its heyday, the music hall had little impact on brass band repertoire, with the exception of certain nostalgic medleys of songs that found favour with the mood of the post-war years, for example *Harry Lauder's Songs* and *Florrie Forde's Favourites*.

As far as brass bands were concerned, open air venues were still the foremost outlet, but there were now increasing opportunities for concert performances to supplement the decline in the number of contests which, it will be recalled, reached a peak in the mid-1890s. Music in parks was encouraged by local councils, many erecting bandstands with seated enclosures for those who wished to listen seriously, providing Saturday and Sunday concerts during the summer months. Regular band concerts were established in Leeds in 1903, soon to be followed by concerts in Sheffield.[6] In Manchester it was estimated that during 1908 some 2.6 million people attended over 500 band concerts organized by the city fathers at a cost of £3000 – recouped from local rates.[7] As mentioned earlier, some of the more skilled bands were offered week-long engagements (see pages 62–63).

Contemporary photographs suggest that audiences at brass band concerts then – as now – were predominantly middle-aged. Popular band concerts have always had most appeal for members of this age-group, programmes featuring music that would have been in vogue during their youth. Late-Edwardian bandstand programmes owed a greater debt to ballads and musical comedy than to ragtime or the 'new-fangled' dances. It was the nostalgic appeal of band music that simultaneously secured its temporary success whilst threatening its long-term failure.

With the exception of the sections on 'The dance band' and 'The brass band and popular music between the wars', this chapter concentrates on the light music element of popular music. This includes operetta, ballads and dance music – all genres touched on in Chapter One. Here they are considered in more depth, and also in the context of their use by brass bands.

Operetta, Musical Comedy and the 'Musical'

Operetta emerged towards the middle of the nineteenth century, arriving at a time when opera was becoming more complex and less to the taste of those seeking sheer entertainment rather than 'intellectual enlightenment'. In France the roots of operetta stretch back to the comic operas of composers such as Boieldieu, Auber, Hérold and Adolphe Adam, selections from some of which were played in nineteenth-century band contests. From the turn of the century the operatic overture became popular as a concert item, and amongst those favoured from the pens of these composers, the following were published and regularly played:

Adam:	*If I Were King*
Auber:	*Masaniello, The Bronze Horse, The Black Domino*
Boieldieu:	*The Caliph of Bagdad, The White Lady*
Hérold:	*Zampa*

Franz von Suppé, an Austrian composer of operetta, also provided bands with several attractive overtures with, for example, *Pique Dame, The Beautiful Galathea, The Jolly Robbers, Boccaccio* and three of the most popular of all overtures, *Morning, Noon and Night in Vienna, Light Cavalry* and *Poet and Peasant*. These overtures were, in effect, pot-pourris based on melodies from the operas. In the theatre they provided a kind of preview of some of the music which was to follow; in the concert hall or on the bandstand they were simply an attractive entertainment, enjoyable for the listener with or without knowledge of the opera itself. Much the same could be said of the musical comedy or operetta selection which, during the Edwardian period, took the place of the operatic selection in band concerts.

An operetta was literally a play set to music, with an overture, songs and dances. Jacques Offenbach (1819–1880) is regarded as the founder of French operetta. His *Orpheus in the Underworld* (1858) became popular not only in Paris but also in Vienna and London, and without doubt he influenced both Viennese operetta and British light opera. Chief sources for band music were from *Orpheus in the Underworld* and *The Tales of Hoffman*, Offenbach's only opera.

Johann Strauss (Jr) was one of the most talented operetta composers, but of his 16 works, overtures from only two found their way into brass band repertoire, *Die Fledermaus* (1874) and *The Gipsy Baron* (1885). It was his compatriot, Franz Lehár (1870–1948), actually a Hungarian-born bandmaster, who first made the transition from operetta to musical comedy in Vienna. His *Die lustige Witwe* was premièred in Vienna in December 1905 and had 483 performances in its first production. It came to London two years later as *The Merry Widow* and enjoyed even greater success, with 778 performances. It also received a warm response in New York and in Paris, where it was produced as *La veuve joyeuse*. *The Merry Widow* literally took the western world by storm. It was said to have earned £60 000 for the composer and a further £40 000 for its librettist. The 'big hits' were the song 'Vilia' and the 'Merry Widow Waltz'. Here was music which the brass band could not ignore, and selections and excerpts were to be found in many band programmes. Lehár wrote other operettas, some extremely well received, but none matching the glamour of *The Merry Widow*. Others which found their way, through selections, into band programmes, were *The Count of Luxemburg* (1909) and *Gipsy Love* (1910).

Following closely behind *The Merry Widow* came two operettas by Oscar Straus (1870–1954). *A Waltz Dream* (1907) was the more successful, although Straus's best-known song, 'My hero', came from the other operetta, *The Chocolate Soldier* (1908). Neither achieved any lasting popularity in band programmes. One more selection, often heard on the bandstand, and also originating in Vienna, was that from *Lilac Time* (arranged by Ord Hume), based on the life story of Schubert and using adaptations of his music. In its original form this was a singspiel – a play in which songs are sung, and was first performed in Vienna in 1916. It came to England in 1922 in a rather different form, more in the style of an operetta and using different Schubert excerpts.

The principal English operettas were, of course, those of Gilbert and Sullivan. The first to have any impact was *Trial by Jury* (1875), though *Cox and Box* (1867) later became a firm favourite. Unlike some of the later productions, neither seems to have penetrated brass band programmes. *HMS Pinafore* (1878), *The Pirates of Penzance* (1879), *Mikado* (1884–5) and *The Gondoliers* (1889) were quickly taken up by bands, though *Iolanthe* (1882) and *The Yeomen of the Guard* (1888) had to wait rather longer. Gilbert and Sullivan selections were almost statutory features of band programmes even as late as the 1960s, and are still quite popular.

Edward German (1862–1936 – full name, Edward German Jones) was the natural successor to Sullivan but enjoyed less popularity. He was known to brass band audiences mainly through music from his 1902 operetta *Merrie England* and to a lesser degree through *Tom Jones* (1907). Two other titles also found their way into brass band programmes – the popular dances from his incidental music to *Henry VIII* (1892) and his overture *Richard III*, both arranged by Alexander Owen for the 1901 Crystal Palace festival concert, at which German himself appeared as guest conductor (see page 121).

Operetta in America took its inspiration from *HMS Pinafore*, first seen in the States in a pirated version in Boston in November 1878, only six months after its English première. John Philip Sousa, known throughout the world as the 'March King' was one of the first American composers of operetta and in fact, his march 'El Capitan' – very popular in its brass band arrangement – comes from an operetta of the same name, dating from 1896. A more renowned writer of American operetta was Irish-born Victor Herbert

(1859–1924), and even though his operettas broke no records on this side of the Atlantic, a number of songs from them became hits, one or two appearing as brass band arrangements, including 'Kiss me again' from *Mlle Modiste* (1905) and 'Ah! sweet mystery of life', from *Naughty Marietta* (1910).

Rudolf Friml (1879–1972) came into the world of operetta and musical comedy by chance, when asked to take over the scoring of *The Firefly* (1912) from Victor Herbert, who had quarrelled with one of the singers for whom he was preparing it. Though this operetta seems not to have caught the imagination of brass band writers, two later Friml ones certainly did – *Rose Marie* (1924) and *The Vagabond King* (1925), selections from both being published within a few years of the original productions. Both shows were hugely successful, especially the former which, set in Canada and featuring the Rockies and the Canadian Mounties, was filmed three times.

The Hungarian-born American, Sigmund Romberg, was a prolific writer, but is remembered chiefly for his three Viennese-style operettas – *The Student Prince* (1924), *The Desert Song* (1926) and *New Moon* (1928). All three were made into films, and the two earlier ones became extremely popular in band programmes – especially *The Desert Song*. Frequent revivals helped maintain their popularity for many years.

Of the German school of operetta composers, only Ralph Benatzky (1884–1957) is well-known as such to brass band audiences, and that is through his 1930 'revue-operette', *White Horse Inn*, a selection from which became popular with bandstand audiences. Two minor luminaries were Paul Lincke (1866–1946) – whose 'Glow-worm idyll' comes from a 1902 operetta called *Lysistrata* – is also known for his march 'Father Rhine' and the charming 'Birthday Serenade', and Léon Jessel (1871–1942), remembered for the short concert items, 'Parade of the Tin Soldiers' (1911) and 'The Wedding of the Rose' (1922).

Derived from operetta, or light opera as it was generally called in Britain, the English 'musical comedy' is a musical entertainment with a story, spoken dialogue, songs and dances, presented in a less formal manner than in operetta. It was touched on briefly on pages 10–11, with mention of *A Gaiety Girl* and *The Geisha* (Sidney Jones), and *A Runaway Girl* (Lionel Monckton). All three were first seen in London and then exported to New York – *Gaiety Girl* and *The Runaway Girl* in 1894, and *The Geisha* two years later. Meanwhile, the German-born American, Gustav Kerker (1857–1923) was writing music for various kinds of theatrical show, and in 1897 produced his best-known work, *The Belle of New York*. Despite a run of a mere 56 performances in New York, it was highly acclaimed in London, where it opened in 1898 with no less than 697 performances, playing an important part in reversing the trend of the domination of British music in America. A selection from it remained popular in brass band programmes for many years. Sidney Jones continued writing music for the theatre, though *The Geisha* remained his most popular work, and a selection of its melodies was regularly featured by bands. Another selection which enjoyed some popularity was from his 1899 production *San Toy*. Lionel Monckton also wrote much music for the stage, and there were popular band selections from *A Country Girl* (1902), *The Arcadians* (1909) and *The Quaker Girl* (1910). Another composer of musical comedy whose name appeared in brass band programmes was Leslie Stuart (1864–1928), though he was known to band audiences mainly as the writer of music-hall songs such as 'Soldiers of the Queen' and 'Lily of Laguna'.

Two war-time musical comedy successes were *The Maid of the Mountains*, with music by Harold Fraser-Simson (1872–1944), and *Chu Chin Chow* by Frederic Norton (1896–1946). First produced in 1916, the latter had 2238 consecutive performances, with Percy Fletcher – composer of the first original work for brass band (*Labour and Love*) – as its musical director. *The Maid of the Mountains* opened in 1917 and ran for three years, with 1352 performances. Both provided popular selections for the brass band, as did a slightly later and lesser-known show, *The Lady of the Rose* (Jean Gilbert – 1922).

Musical comedy and operetta were to give way to more modern-sounding and more spectacular forms of 'Musical' – musical films and shows from Broadway and Hollywood. 1927 was an important year, with *Show Boat* on the stage and *The Jazz Singer* in the cinema. *Show Boat* brought together Jerome Kern (1885–1945) and librettist Oscar Hammerstein II (1895–1960), and after a successful run in New York, went on tour. A new production, opening at London's Drury Lane in 1928, starred the inimitable Paul Robeson singing 'Ol' man river'. *Show Boat* had numerous revivals and three film versions. Its brass band selection (arranged by the ubiquitous Ord Hume) was still popular in the 1960s. *The Jazz Singer*, featuring Al Jolson, is credited with being the first sound film.[8] Though Jolson's songs appeared in a number of brass band selections there was never, as far as the writer is aware, a selection using the actual title of the film.

Just as musical comedy lived on through revivals and through the many amateur operatic societies, so musical comedy selections were played in brass band programmes for years to come. At least three more pieces of musical theatre appeared before 1936 and led to popular selections: *Bitter Sweet* (1929) and *Cavalcade* (1931) – musical scores by Noël Coward (1899–1973), and *Glamorous Night* (1935) by Ivor Novello (1893–1951). The selections from *Bitter Sweet* and *Glamorous Night*, both in the style of Viennese operetta, enjoyed much success – at least up until the war years. *Cavalcade*, as the title almost implies, was a pageant of famous moments in British history, with incidental music using songs by various composers. It opened in 1931, but with tunes like 'The soldiers of the queen' (Leslie Stuart), 'Soldiers in the park' (Lionel Monckton), 'It's a long way to Tipperary' (Judge and Williams) and Ivor Novello's 'Keep the home fires burning', the *Cavalcade* selection retained its popularity with bands throughout the war years – and indeed for several more, by which time there was a growing list of selections from the more modern musicals.[9]

The ballad

The Victorian ballad was discussed on pages 19–20. Whilst style and sentiments changed little during the Edwardian years, its popularity was maintained. Ballad writing was actually a very good commercial proposition and fortunes were often made from a single best-seller. Many of the more popular ballads found their way into brass band programmes, mainly as cornet solos. The mellow sound and expressive qualities of the instrument were well-suited to their style, with similarities between the vocal and instrumental deliveries, both in breath control and in the use of vibrato.

This review mentions just a few of the more popular ballads. The date of publication of the band version of a ballad is often vague; in the case of early examples it may have been several decades after that of the original, but after the dawn of the twentieth century the gap seems to have been reduced to a few years with, in some cases, the brass band version appearing within a year of the original. This is perhaps an indication of the growing popularity of brass soloists, and part of the bridge-building between the brass band and other forms of popular music.

1904 was a productive year for brass solos, with the publication – for band – of Joseph Ascher's 'Alice, where art thou?', Frederic Cowen's 'The better land' and the popular ballad by Laura Lemon, 'My ain folk'. Before the end of the first decade of the twentieth century, Hermann Loehr's 'Where my caravan has rested', Henry Geehl's 'For you alone' (said to have been the first song sung in English by Caruso), and Charles Marshall's popular ballad, 'I hear you calling me' were amongst the many ballads available as cornet solos.

The '78' gramophone recording was now in vogue. Ballads were generally of an ideal length to fill one side, and as a result many were popularized through this medium. Singers such as Peter Dawson and Denis Noble recorded some, whilst the distinguished Irish tenor, John McCormack, recorded many, including 'I hear you calling me' and several with an Irish flavour, such as Ernest Ball's 'Mother Machree' and 'When Irish eyes are smiling', and Charles Glover's 'The rose of Tralee'. There was also another Hermann Loehr song, 'Little grey home in the west', Arthur Penn's 'Smilin' through', and two more extremely popular ballads – 'Macushla' by Dermot Macmurrough and 'Somewhere a voice is calling', by Arthur Tate. All these McCormack hits were popular in band programmes, again, generally as cornet solos. The almost endless list of ballad solos from the first 20 years of the century also includes 'Song of songs' (Stella Moya), 'The floral dance'

(Katie Moss – as a trombone solo) and 'The sunshine of your smile' (Lillian Raymond), all – it will be noted – written by lady ballad writers, as was the 'Kashmiri song' ('Pale hands I love') from Amy Woodforde-Finden's *Four Indian Love Lyrics*. All four of these were popular as a set, but 'Kashmiri song' was often singled out and became especially popular with cornet soloists.

Paolo Tosti, an Italian-born composer-teacher, found his way into brass band programmes through a number of songs, the most famous of which was 'Good-bye'. Tosti was appointed royal singing-master, assumed English nationality, and was knighted in 1908. Paul Rubens, heavily involved in writing musical comedy, also composed many songs, of which cornet soloists were able to play 'I love the moon'. Wilfrid Sanderson (1878–1935) was a prolific ballad writer, represented in band programmes with 'Drake goes west', 'Until' and 'Up from Somerset'. His contemporary, W H Squire (1871–1963), also wrote many ballads, and amongst those played by brass band soloists were 'In an old fashioned town' and 'When you come home dear'.

Frederic Weatherly (1828–1929), who wrote the words for around 1500 songs, also took a tune from an 1855 song collection, adding words which did much to popularize it. 'The Londonderry air', known to millions as 'Danny boy' through Weatherly's setting, was published in 1912, and within a year was being played by cornet soloists all over the country. Other solos which are difficult to exclude even from this incomplete list include May H Brahe's 'Bless this house' (still a popular cornet solo), Gordon's 'The iceberg' – arranged for euphonium by John Hartmann and therefore belonging to the earlier period, and a solo popular with trombonists during the 1930s and later, 'The trumpeter', by J Airlie Dix.

Finally, there were two composers who really belonged to the post-war period, but who were already making a name for themselves by 1920. The first was Yorkshire-born Haydn Wood who made a fortune from one of his first songs, '*Roses of Picardy*', published in 1916 and becoming a wartime hit. The second was Horatio Nicholls, a pseudonym for Lawrence Wright. He later owned a company which published orchestral music, piano music, ballads, popular songs, dance music, and music for brass and military bands. His earliest hit, as far as brass bands were concerned, was 'That old fashioned mother of mine', published in 1919 by Boosey.

As with musical comedy selections, ballads remained popular with bands at least until the end of the 1950s. They are still played quite regularly, and the older generation of players feel they represent a yardstick for brass band soloists. Lyrical playing is often demanded in all kinds of band music, yet amongst the current generation of bandsmen it is a dying art, partly due to the rarity of ballad-type solos in current band programmes.

Music in the ballroom

Changes in public taste during the early years of the twentieth century were nowhere more apparent than in the ballroom. The waltz (or valse) remained one of the principal dances and maintained its popularity until around 1910. Another popular dance of the Victorians and Edwardians, the polka seems to have fallen out of use at about the same time. The lancers were similar to the quadrilles (see pages 11–12), but they retained their popularity rather longer and, along with other 'olde tyme' dances, enjoyed a revival in the 1940s through the music of Harry Davidson, Sydney Thompson and their orchestras.

The term 'one-step' was first used about 1910. It related to a simple form of dance, with two beats in a bar, and was more suited to the amateur dancer than to the expert. 'Two-step' was a term used at first to describe any type of dance which was neither a waltz nor a set of lancers. Eventually it adopted a more specific meaning, and with the introduction of the military two-step and the Boston two-step, the six-eight march (in compound duple time) found its niche in the ballroom. The schottische had also been a popular form of dance from mid-century and was played regularly by bands; to this was added, from the late 1880s, the barn dance (though it was not played by brass bands until about 1900).

Modern ballroom dances quickly superseded those from the nineteenth century and by 1914 styles had changed completely. The modern waltz, danced at a much slower tempo than the Viennese version, was established by then, as was the foxtrot. This demanded space and skill and eventually gave way to the quickstep – in a similar rhythm and tempo, but less complex. The term quickstep,[10] however, was not used until after 1927. Meanwhile, from about 1924, the slow foxtrot emerged. In this, the tempo of the ordinary foxtrot was slowed down in the same way as had happened with the waltz a decade earlier.[11] With the arrival of the tango – via Argentina and Paris – the repertoire of the early twentieth-century dance-hall was complete. The quickstep, slow waltz, slow foxtrot and tango were to be the principal dances for the next half-century. By now, dancing was decidedly for couples rather than for groups, as it had been with quadrilles and lancers. Dancing had become far more sexually orientated, and provided convenient opportunities for boy to meet girl. This was the point at which light music and popular music began to part company.

A dance which was popular just before the end of the nineteenth century was the first of several to arrive from America. Called the 'cake-walk', this was a group dance, involving a line of men on one side and a line of ladies on the other, and its music evolved through the 'jazzing-up' of marches by black American bands. The rag followed, and the two led directly to the introduction of jazz in England, and to dances such as the Charleston, popular in the mid-1920s, and symbolic of the gaiety and turbulence of what are referred to as the 'roaring twenties'. When the famous novelist J B Priestley first heard ragtime played in his native Bradford, he imagined it 'drumming us into another kind of life in which anything might happen . . . '[12] – such was the effect of the rhythms, the verve and the energy of this new music.

The dance band

The revolution in dance music could not have taken place without the emergence of the dance band. In America its history, along with that of the concert band (or wind band) of the likes of Patrick Gilmore (1829–1892) and John Philip Sousa (1854–1932), may be traced back through the street bands of black Americans to the brass bands of the American Civil War (1861–1865). In Britain the dance band was essentially an imported concept from the States, and though in the twentieth century it developed alongside the brass band, becoming the professional wing of the band world in its wider sense, it would be quite wrong to claim that the British dance band had its roots in the British brass band. On the contrary, in its 'popular music' context, the brass band tried – not very successfully – to emulate the dance band by taking some of its music into the repertoire.

Though a significant part of the function of the British brass band had been to provide music for dancing, dance music which emerged during the twentieth century demanded a totally different style of playing from a totally different instrumentation, with saxophones instead of saxhorns, trumpets instead of cornets, and the rhythm section – piano, drum kit, guitar and bass – fulfilling a completely different role from that of basses and drums in the brass band. There was also a psychological shift. Brass bands were not normally engaged solely to play dance music; their early function was to provide musical entertainment as part of some other event – perhaps a local festival. In contrast, dance bands were engaged specifically to play dance music for the enjoyment of people who had actually paid to dance. Dance bands were, of course, known by the name of their conductors who, in turn, were called 'leaders'. Here are two interesting parallels with early village bands (see page 2).

The growth in dance bands in England was impeded by the 1914–1918 war. Following this, a number of famous names appeared: Jack Hylton formed his own band in the 1920–21 season and Debroy Somers formed the Savoy Orpheans in 1923. Other well-known dance bands which appeared during the 1920s included Maurice Winnick and Harry Roy. Apart from actual dances organized in the local dance hall or *palais de danse*, many top hotels and restaurants employed their own resident bands. As time went on more personalities appeared, including Jack Payne, Billy Cotton, Ray Noble, Geraldo, Ambrose, Oscar Rabin and Joe Loss. Several of these turned their bands into show-bands, the playing of dance music becoming just a part of their activities in the wider field of entertainment.

Radio helped popularize dance bands on both sides of the Atlantic. In Britain, the BBC not only regularly featured famous dance bands, it formed its own. Jack Payne was the first leader of the BBC Dance Orchestra, to be followed by Henry Hall, and later by Billy Ternent. Not all dance bands became show-bands; one which dedicated itself to providing music for ballroom dancing – of the strict tempo variety – was Victor Silvester's Ballroom Orchestra. By now dancing had become a popular social pastime and band leaders had become stars in their own right. Though the gap between brass bands and dance bands was becoming wider, many successful trumpet and trombone players in the dance band world had started their playing days in brass bands.[13]

Films also played an important part in the production and dissemination of popular dance music. Through the film musicals of the 1930s – such as *Gold Diggers of 1933*, *Top Hat* (1935) and *Follow the Fleet* (1936) – a major source of quality popular music appeared by Jerome Kern, Irving Berlin, George and Ira Gershwin, Richard Rodgers and others. In Britain the names Horatio Nicholls and Ivor Novello became well known as composers of such music.

The record industry had a chequered beginning. During its early days, at the turn of the century, owning a gramophone became a status symbol. Its appeal waned during the war, but with the availability of electrical recordings and lower-priced records featuring well-known artists, the 1920s witnessed a recovery. Brass bands benefited from this, and during the 1920s and 1930s made a large number of recordings, of both test pieces and more popular music.

The brass band and popular music between the wars

'Roses of Picardy' and 'Song of songs', though discussed as ballads, may equally well be described as popular songs; Lehár's 'Vilia' and 'You are my heart's delight' also, whilst clearly stemming from operetta, would also be regarded by millions as popular songs. Many tunes seen as popular songs were also frequently used for dancing, and thus Lehár's 'White dove' was commonly thought of as a waltz; 'Beyond the blue horizon', by Richard Whiting, as a foxtrot. There was even an overlap between the ballroom and the parade ground, with songs such as Colcord's 'Stein song' and Holzmann's famous march 'Blaze away' fitting comfortably into either.

Publishers recognized the multi-purpose qualities of many of these tunes and published them, almost simultaneously, for dance band, light orchestra, military and brass bands. Between 1919 and 1938 many brass band arrangements of popular tunes of the day – popular as songs or dances, or extracts from films or shows – appeared in publishers' catalogues. Boosey were amongst the first in this field when, between 1919 and 1921 they published several such pieces, arranged by James Ord Hume. Of course, they could not foresee which, if any, of the pieces in the group would be successful, but with titles such as 'Baby tank', 'The Broadway crawl' and 'Emotions', many of the early Boosey 'pops' must have been flops. One exception was their publication of Gershwin's 'Swanee', made famous in 1919 by Al Jolson and published in a band version as a one-step two years later. However, this was a line of publication not pursued by Boosey.

Three publishers with more experience in this field were Lawrence Wright, Feldman and Chappell, and between them they published an extensive range of pieces for the popular music market. The dual possibilities of many of these pieces was suggested by the use of dual designations such as 'march two-step' or 'foxtrot-march', and their suitability for bandstand or dancing platform was indicted by such tags as 'intermezzo-foxtrot' or 'intermezzo-tango'. There was also the occasional 'song-intermezzo', suitable either as a solo or as a straightforward concert item. Lawrence Wright was the composer who seemed to appear most frequently with these popular tunes for band. Amongst his better-known successes were 'Shepherd of the hills' (1927), 'Amy, wonderful Amy' (1931) and 'A bed time story' (1932). All were recorded by Jack Hylton and his Orchestra, subsequently arranged for brass band by Ord Hume, and published by the composer.

James Ord Hume was busy yet again, with over 30 publications in Feldman's catalogue between 1927 and 1932.[14] A contemporary advertisement suggested that purchasing these arrangements was 'The cheapest and best method of keeping up to date with the latest theme song successes which are issued in this famous journal'. Feldman's successes included such standard 'classics' as 'Tiptoe through the tulips' and 'Painting the clouds with sunshine' – both from a 1929 film, *Gold Diggers of Broadway*. This style of advertising was not unique to Feldman's, and slogans such as the following appeared regularly: 'Join the WRIGHT Club' (1928), 'Why not join the Chappell Band Club?' (1930) and 'Join the Boosey & Hawkes Band Club' (1931). Many of the best tunes of the period came from films, several appearing in band versions, published a year or two later than the release of the film, by which time their popularity was assured. One Ord Hume arrangement which must have been very popular was Jack Little's 'In a shanty in old shanty town'. This was first heard when it came out in the 1932 film *The Crooner*. Meanwhile, at least 15 more popular tunes were arranged by Ord Hume and published by Chappell in 1930–1931. Many were in what they called their *'Subscription' Brass & Military Journal*. Included are pieces such as 'Beyond the blue horizon', sung by Jeanette MacDonald in the 1930 film Monte Carlo and 'You are my heart's delight', popularized by Richard Tauber in Lehár's 1929 operetta *The Land of Smiles*, and published for band in 1931.

Medleys of well-known tunes were also popular in the 1930s. Feldman led the field with titles such as *Communityland, Shamrockland, Dixieland* and *Hymnland*, whilst Keith Prowse & Co published their series of *Savoy Medleys* – initially arranged by Debroy Somers and then transcribed for brass band. Not to be left out, Lawrence Wright published the very successful *Cavalcade of Martial Songs* – 'As recorded by The Band of HM Welsh Guards'. All of these appeared between 1924 and 1934.

Denis Wright (1895–1967)

Ord Hume died on 27 November 1932 and the task of arranging more of these popular tunes for Chappell fell to Denis Wright, then aged 37 and destined to become a dominant figure in the brass band world. Wright worked for Chappell as music editor of their band publications from 1931 to 1936, when he left to take up an appointment at the BBC, organizing the band section of its music department. Wright, a cultured musician, had by then become somewhat disenchanted with his work at Chappell, and looking at the titles of many of the tunes he had to arrange it is, frankly, not very surprising. Nor is it strange that, considering he was trying to establish himself as a serious composer in the brass band world (see pages 189–190), he used a *nom de plume*, writing as Frank Denham. Titles such as 'My darling', 'The captain of the fire brigade', 'Who made little boy blue', 'And the big bad wolf is dead' and 'It happened in the moonlight' make one shudder at the thought of this gifted musician hacking out such material. There were a few titles, however, which may have brought a little light into his life – Lehár's 'Vilia', from *The Merry Widow*, Irving Berlin's 'Easter parade', a waltz medley from Ivor Novello's *Glamorous Night*, Jerome Kern's 'Lovely to look at', and another Irving Berlin hit, 'A pretty girl is like a melody' – revived in the film *The Great Ziegfeld* of 1936, the year in which the band version also appeared. At least here were fine tunes and lasting successes.

All these arrangements were strictly 'commercial', that is to say, straightforward and playable at sight by many bands. They were mostly well-known tunes and therefore popular with those who frequented park bandstand concerts. In a way they formed a link between selections from operetta and musical comedy and selections from the later musicals, such as *Snow White and the Seven Dwarfs* (1938), *Oklahoma* (1943), *South Pacific* (1951), *The King and I* (1954), *The Sound of Music* (1959) and *West Side Story* (1957). These and many other selections were arranged by Denis Wright, using his real name. Wright also contributed a number of selections based on the music of a particular composer or on a particular theme. These included *Panorama* of *Famous Songs* (1932), *New Sullivan Selection* (1933), *Second New Sullivan Selection* (1934), *Sweethearts of Yesterday* (Henry Hall – 1934), *Radio Parade of 1935*, *Schubert Waltzes* (1935), *Milestones of Melody* (1935), *Viennese Memories of Lehár* (1935), *Dream of the Waltz* (1936) and *Lionel Monckton Melodies* (from an orchestral selection by Stanford Robinson, 1936).

Wright pioneered band music in many styles. He made important contributions in the area of light music, and his selections were predecessors of many more written in later years both by Wright himself and others. They bore no relationship in style to the composer-selections of earlier times or to the Feldman medleys, nor were they intended for use as test pieces, but were purely and simply for entertainment. There were no cadenzas, the different sections being linked by imaginative passages leading naturally from one tune to the next, and with any necessary modulations unobtrusively introduced.

The music described above represents only the tip of the iceberg as far as this type of arrangement is concerned. Other publishers who produced similar arrangements include Francis Day & Hunter, Campbell Connelly & Co, and Keith Prowse & Co. During the early 1930s the last-named of these promised '18 numbers a year guaranteed, along with an invitation to join our Brass & Military Band Club'. The 18 numbers were offered to brass bands for 20/- (£1) per year and to military bands for 30/- (£1.50), and must have been viewed at the time as bargains.

Light music

Early in this chapter reference was made to 'light music'. This is often associated with, for example, the palm court or the morning concerts popular in holiday resorts in times gone by. These would include excerpts from operettas and musical comedy, ballads, music from the ballroom, with probably a march and a standard overture. In fact, the recipe was quite similar to that for popular band concerts. But the actual 'light music' element would consist of pieces by such composers as Albert W Ketèlbey (1875–1959), Arthur Wood (1875–1953) and his namesake Haydn Wood (1882–1959), Eric Coates (1886–1957) and even Elgar – through his early salon pieces 'Salut d' amour', 'Chanson de matin' and 'Chanson de nuit' (the two former of which are still popular with bands). All these composers were represented in brass band programmes – especially Ketèlbey, particularly with 'In a Persian market', 'In a monastery garden', 'Sanctuary of the heart' and 'Bells across the meadow'. Other Ketèlbey pieces popular with bands included his descriptive overture *Chal Romano*, an oriental phantasy [*sic*] 'In a Chinese temple garden' and a reverie, 'The sacred hour'. These were published by Bosworth & Co Ltd, either concurrently with or shortly after their original publication, and are still played occasionally by bands.

Arthur Wood, best known for his 'Barwick green maypole' (signature tune for the radio serial *The Archers*), was musical director for a number of London theatres. At the age of 16 he was deputy to J Sidney Jones with the Harrogate Municipal Orchestra and later held a similar post under Dan Godfrey with the Bournemouth Symphony Orchestra. Wood's *Three Dale Dances* were immensely popular with bands and are still played from time to time. Rather less popular but equally effective was his *Yorkshire Moors Suite*. Haydn Wood – no relation to Arthur – was born in Slaithwaite,[15] and is best known to brass bandsmen through his ballads (see page 169).

As usual, James Ord Hume was at the forefront. Amongst his arrangements of miscellaneous concert items are such well-known pieces as 'The Turkish patrol' (Michaelis – 1902), *Rendezvous* (Allettèr – 1907), 'Poem' (Fibich), some of the Ketèlbey pieces already mentioned and some waltzes (suitable for dance or concert) – *Donau wellen* (Ivanovici – 1900), 'The choristers' (Phelps – 1904) and 'The druid's prayer' (Dawson – 1910). There were also some operatic excerpts, for example 'The soldier's chorus' (1901 – Gounod's *Faust*), 'The moon hath raised her lamp above' (1905 – Benedict's *The Lily of Killarney*) and 'O star of eve' (1907 – Wagner's Tannhäuser), the two last-mentioned being arranged as instrumental duets. Some of these retained their popularity for many years and are still heard occasionally in band concerts.[16]

The earlier music of Eric Coates, though popular with military bands, rather surprisingly almost bypassed the brass band. The only exceptions I have found are the marches 'Knightsbridge' and 'London Bridge', from his *London Suite*. The former was the signature tune for the radio programme 'In Town Tonight' and the piece which helped establish Coates as a leading composer of light music.[17] Other names which appear on many band pieces of the era include Aubrey Winter and Stanford Robinson, and names which were to become famous in brass band music of the future include Alfred Ashpole, Harold Hind, Drake Rimmer (nephew of William), Sam B Wood and Frank Wright. All of these, and many others, helped maintain the vitality of the brass band movement and enabled it to play a significant role in the field of popular music.

So far as its 'classical' repertoire is concerned, many feel that the brass band has only recently entered the twentieth century. But there can be little doubt that through its more popular repertoire it remained in close touch with contemporary developments, certainly until the mid-1930s. As in its earlier years, it reflected the styles of other forms of music – through popular music, not art music – without making any significant contribution to it. The brass band must, however, still be seen as part of the British musical culture as a whole, and not an 'isolated phenomenon' as is often suggested. The more serious side of its repertoire now needs to be examined.

Notes

1. Gammond, 1991, p. 344.
2. 'Popular music' should not be confused with 'pop music'. This term was not used until the 1950s, and therefore the music with which it is associated falls outside the scope of this book.
3. Pearsall, 1975, p. 101.
4. Ibid., p. 104. The term 'highbrow' was used first in the USA, in 1908.
5. It was in 1912 that Irving Berlin's *Alexander's ragtime band* and *Everybody's doin' it* hit Britain, the latter being used in a Revue in London that year.
6. Pearsall, 1975, p. 150.
7. Ibid.
8. Gammond, 1991, p. 295.
9. Information comes from relevant entries in Gammond, 1991.
10. Many early brass band marches were called 'quicksteps'. These should not be confused with the ballroom dance of the same name. Though the dance could be marched to and certain brass band quicksteps (those in 2/4 time) used for the dance, there is a subtle difference in the way in which they are performed: the march emphasizes the 'left, right, left' associated with marching, whereas the dance has a smoother line and is not normally of a martial nature.
11. The dates for these dances are taken from the relevant entries in Gammond, 1991.
12. Temperley, 1981, p. 88.
13. The same is true of brass players in the symphonic world.
14. Feldman advertised its *Popular Band Journal* as early as 1916 (January edition of *Brass Band News*).
15. In later life Wood composed a march especially for Slaithwaite Band. It was named after a local beauty spot, *Merrydale*.
16. Dates in this section, where given, refer to the publication of the brass band versions.
17. Some later pieces by Coates have been played by brass bands, especially his 'Dam Busters' march and 'Calling All Workers' (signature tune for the wartime broadcast series 'Music While You Work'). There are unpublished versions of two more Coates pieces, his *Three Bears Suite*, arranged by Alex Mortimer and recorded by Foden's in 1938, and the march, 'Youth of Britain' from *The Three Elizabeths*, arranged by Denis Wright and often featured by the National Youth Brass Band of Great Britain.

9 A new type of test piece – the original work

Introduction

Until 1912, music used as test pieces at major band contests consisted of selections from an opera or choral work, or from the works of a particular composer.[1] Subjects chosen had ranged from selections from long-forgotten or little-known works to those from masterworks from the eighteenth or nineteenth centuries. A glance at the list of Nationals test pieces from 1904 to 1913 (page 123) gives an indication of the diversity of choice, and takes us to the point where the present chapter begins – the arrival of the first test piece to be specially composed by a musician not primarily associated with bands.

As discussed earlier, it was John Henry Iles who became the driving force behind bands from the beginning of the twentieth century when he founded the National Brass Band Championships, though in musical matters he relied on the judgement of Herbert Whiteley, his musical adviser. It was Whiteley who, to quote Philip Maund, 'had the vision of new music for brass bands and went to great lengths to see it fulfilled'.[2] A review of the composers who wrote these new-style test pieces along with an account of some of their works, is given in this chapter.

Thirty-five original works were composed between 1913 and 1936 (see Appendix 9). Limitations of space prevents a complete survey, but during the course of this chapter, representative examples are examined in varying degrees of detail from what is a small but significant part of brass band repertoire.

Author's note: In the interests of consistency with the text throughout the book, all music examples in this chapter are shown at B♭ pitch. Readers not familiar with some of the terms used should not be discouraged. Reference to any elementary book on the subject will clarify most of the text. Ideally this section should be read alongside the relative scores.

Minor composers of original works

The first composer to write for brass band was Percy Fletcher, whose *Labour and Love* of 1913 marked the start of a transition from contest selections to later and more creative pieces. In it, the conductor was presented with a detailed synopsis, or programme, outlining the course the music would take, indicating the varying moods to be conveyed. Taking the symphonic poems of Liszt as a model, *Labour and Love* is essentially a programmatic work and, again as with Liszt, uses the device known as *thematic transformation* whereby, through changes in tempo, rhythm, scoring or dynamics, themes appear in different guises, portraying different moods or thoughts.

Percy Fletcher (1879–1932), a writer of choral and light orchestral music, was also a conductor of theatre orchestras, and it was in this role that he came to the forefront when, as musical director at Her Majesty's Theatre, London, he orchestrated *Chu Chin Chow* (Frederic Norton) and directed over 2000 performances in the show's record-breaking run, beginning in 1916 (see page 167). Prior to that, in 1909, he had entered the military band arena as a composer, winning prizes in a competition with his 'Rustic Scenes' and the march, 'Spirit of Pageantry' (also popular in a brass band version). He continued to write for military band after these successes, and also composed two works for brass band, the first of which was a turning point in the history of brass band music.

There is a popular theory that Iles commissioned Fletcher to write *Labour and Love* but, according to *British Bandsman* of 22 September 1913, Fletcher composed it first and then offered it to Iles for publication. Iles not only published the work, he chose it as the test piece for the Crystal Palace contest, also appointing Fletcher as one of the adjudicators. *Labour and Love* was to emancipate brass band contests from the domination of the selection. Described as a tone poem, the work is a musical portrayal of a scenario familiar to bandsmen, and their ability to relate to its themes helped secure its popularity. The musical argument, outlined on the first page of the score, is represented by a working man on the one hand and his wife on the other. The man, having no love for his work and finding his surroundings oppressive, sees himself as a down-trodden slave. His wife – 'the voice of love', points out that she also has her problems but that 'she meets them with a smile'. She pleads that, for the sake of herself and their children, he should try to see things differently. Her plea is heard, as 'Manfully he labours, and the Voice of Love is now to him the Sword of Might, with which his enemies – depression and despair – are vanquished'. His work now becomes a 'Labour of Love'.[3]

Ex.1

Ex.2

Ex.3

The use of thematic transformation in *Labour and Love* – albeit at a rudimentary level – may be seen in the music examples. Example 1 portrays the down-trodden slave whilst example 2 shows him engaged in his daily work. A further mood change occurs in a euphonium solo, as his soul 'cries out in an anguished lament and despair' (example 3). The other principal musical idea, the 'voice of love', is first heard as a touching cornet solo (example 4), whilst the apotheosis of the piece transforms this theme into a mood of triumph, as first the trombones and then the full band take up the theme (example 5). Being a tone poem, the construction of *Labour and Love* is quite free, nevertheless it falls comfortably into three linked sections, as follows:

Ex.4

Ex.5

Section 1: A brief, introductory 'Andante maestoso, pesante e serioso' in D minor leads into the 'down-trodden slave' theme in a solo passage shared by horn and cornet. A link makes reference to the Introduction, and leads to the 'daily work' theme.

Section 2: An 'Andante patetico' introduces the emotionally-charged euphonium solo (example 3), which culminates in a recitative-like passage. Then follows an 'Allegro drammatico', with a new theme showing the man's restless mind 'aroused into a state of rebellion' and followed by a trombone recitative portraying a mood of 'frenzied indignation'.

Section 3: The mood changes in an 'Andante e molto espressivo', as the 'voice of love' is introduced. This leads to a short duet on cornet and euphonium, symbolizing the new co-operation between man and wife. A horn solo leads to an animated cornet cadenza, paving the way for an 'Allegro marziale' and a transformation of the 'Allegro drammatico' from Section 1, a return of the 'voice of love' theme, and a conclusion in F major, the relative key of D minor, thus using a common ploy and ending a predominantly minor key piece in a major key, signifying the triumph of good over evil.

Labour and Love led bands away from the operatic selection whilst retaining a number of its characteristics – solos, recitatives and a cadenza – all in pseudo-operatic styles, the whole piece being almost a composed selection. Where it differed from the selection was in its use of the musical material, transformed in various ways, and thereby cross-referencing different sections of the piece to create a measure of unity. This was not a feature of the selection. Fletcher had helped with his composition (possibly unwittingly) to change the course of brass band contests.

Following the success of *Labour and Love*, Iles acquired another work, with the intention of using it as test piece for the 1914 Nationals. These, in fact, never took place, and neither did those of the next five years. Britain was at war with Germany, Crystal Palace had been taken over by the Admiralty, and therefore it was not until 1920 that the second original work, *Coriolanus*, came under the spotlight. Its composer was a Welshman – Cyril Jenkins (1889–1978) who, though only 25 years old when he wrote the work, had already composed several large-scale choral works. He had studied with Stanford, and amongst his considerable output of music, which included choral and symphonic works, chamber music and part-songs, there were to be four more brass band pieces.

Coriolanus moves a little closer to Liszt through its designation as a 'symphonic poem' and by its use of a literary-historical figure as its subject. Like *Labour and Love*, it has a detailed programme note, indicating that there are three sections. Again there are two sides to the musical argument – Coriolanus himself, a Roman nobleman, 'a man of rugged, bold and lofty nature, and of indomitable courage', and 'the sweet voice of the gentler affections – the love of mother and wife'. Technically a little more demanding than *Labour and Love* but musically less interesting, and without the historical advantage of being the first original work, *Coriolanus* has not enjoyed the popularity of its predecessor, though it is by no means a forgotten work.

Jenkins was also commissioned to write for the 1921 Nationals, producing an ironically-titled work which was to prove controversial. Still in Shakespearian mood, he called it *A Comedy of Errors*, but owing to the difficulty of the piece the publishers thought this an undiplomatic choice and instead, titled it *Life Divine*. This proved an inspirational decision and the piece's long-term popularity has probably been in part due to its emotive title. Elgar Howarth describes it as 'a rhetorical tone-poem in full-blown romantic style, replete with ardent sequences and Lisztian harmony'.[4] Though there is a programme note with the score, it is less descriptive than those of the earlier band pieces and begins with the words 'Certain phases of Life are common to most if not all men and the music of the Tone Poem [*Life Divine*] carries the listener through four such phases.' These, it explains, represent

> Man's outlook on life as a thing of serious dignity
> Man facing its problems with a spirit of vigorous optimism
> A reminder that times of stress and trouble are inevitable
> A portrayal of the helping and ennobling power of true love

Ex.6

Ex.7

Ex.8

This programme, rather more subjective than those of its predecessors, nevertheless helps establish the moods of the music. Though labelled 'tone poem' *Life Divine* is really a concert overture, containing definite elements of sonata form. Although the principal key is C major, the work is highly chromatic, and the opening is both striking and spectacular, beginning with a bright, spine-tingling chord, in contrast to the stark D minor openings of its predecessors. A sequential figure in the treble descends through a whole-tone scale, while the bass descends, in alternate bars, through leaps of consecutive major thirds (example 6). There is a distinct similarity here with the opening of Rimsky-Korsakov's *Sheherazade* (see example 7).[5] The whole pattern is repeated, a semitone lower, with a more decorous bass line which anticipates the first subject (example 8).

Ex.9

Ex.10

Much of the material on which the work is based appears in the Introduction, with unison trombones bringing this to a close and basses leading into the Exposition. This actually opens in G before settling in C and passing through a range of keys. A new transitional idea leads to another theme (example 9), first appearing in C before, like the others, passing through several keys. Modulating almost kaleidoscopically through a further range of keys on an ascending bass line, this part of the piece ends with a flourish of trills on cornets, as the trombones thunder out a reference to their unison theme from the Introduction. This is repeated a minor third higher, with a tremolando effect, not previously heard from a brass band (example 10). A short baritone solo brings calm and leads to the second subject, a sedate and touching cornet solo – 'Andante nobilemente' – depicting the 'ennobling power of love' (example 11).[6]

Ex.11

The Development section makes use of both old and new material and is again founded on sequence. It ends with a dramatic appearance of the opening, played even higher, with soprano cornet on its top B♭ – the highest sound so far called for in an original work. An abridged version of the Introduction leads to the Recapitulation, with a similarly shortened version of the first subject group, played *fortissimo* in the home key of C major and leading to the second subject, also played *fortissimo*. The work is rounded off with a brief Coda based on the first subject.

An examination of the technical demands of *Life Divine*, reveals an unusually wide pitch range, with not only a good deal of high-note playing but also an extended lower range. For example, there is a passage for baritones calling for a low F – a note theoretically not available on baritones of the time.[7] The fingering of some of the trills and tremolos is quite awkward, and many of the semiquaver passages are very difficult to play up to speed. *Life Divine* still remains a *tour de force* technically and, as has been pointed out, 'After the contest [in 1921] experts reckoned that the study involved in its performance had improved technique by 25 *per cent* in the case of the best bands and that of the worst by 100 *per cent*.'[8] It was a huge step forward from its predecessors, both musically and technically, indicating a total lack of inhibition on the part of the composer. The composer created the problems, and as far as he was concerned it was up to the bands to solve them!

Jenkins was to write several more band pieces, including two for the 1929 Crystal Palace contests – *Victory* for the Championship section and a long-forgotten piece called *Zamora* for the Grand Shield section. He also made a return to the scene as late as 1965, with *Saga of the North*, which was used as the test piece at the Belle Vue September contest that year. None of these had anything like the impact on brass band music of *Life Divine*, though there were one or two echoes of it in *Victory*.

Hubert Bath (1883–1945) was the next composer to write an original brass band work. He had studied at the Royal Academy of Music and his fame lay in his light orchestral music and music for a number of films. *Cornish Rhapsody* was his most successful work, and was the theme music for the

1944 film *Love Story*. *Freedom* was the name of the 1922 Nationals test piece, by Bath. Subtitled 'Brass Band Symphony No 1' it is, in reality, a three-movement suite. Its programme note adopts a similar stance to that of *Life Divine*, indicating the style and mood of each movement with a phrase philosophizing on some aspect of freedom. An interesting work, *Freedom* makes fewer technical demands than *Life Divine*. There was a slight change in the layout of its score, setting a precedent adopted in several later works. It shows the solo cornet part on the top stave and soprano on the second stave down. No-one seems to be quite sure why this was done, though the theory is that it was for the benefit of amateur bandmasters, many of whom could read only one stave at a time. That being the case, and the solo cornet line being the most important, it was easier for the untrained eye to pick it out if it was at the top of the page. The disadvantage is that to the trained eye the solo cornet part appears where the higher-pitched soprano part is expected, and vice versa. A further point worth noting is that *Freedom* has a more effective percussion part than its predecessors. Though not allowed in contests at the time, the use of percussion in concert would certainly enhance the performance, even though the only instruments called for are bass and side drums, cymbal and triangle. *Freedom* has had a number of revivals but has not maintained a regular place in the repertoire. Bath made one more contribution to the original repertoire of the brass band with his tone poem *Honour and Glory*, composed for the Crystal Palace contest of 1931.

The sequence of test pieces by London-based composers was broken by a Halifax musician, Joseph Weston Nicholl (1876–1925), who had been the professional conductor of Black Dyke between 1910 and 1912. At the age of 19, on the recommendation of the violinist Joachim, Nicholl went to study in Berlin. Later he became an organ pupil of Rheinberger in Munich, and later still of Guilmant in Paris. Over a period of many years he made transcriptions from the classical repertoire for Black Dyke, several of which are still played by the band, though they have remained in manuscript.

In 1923 a contest was organized in Halifax at the instigation of Nicholl, and it was for this that he composed his 'tone-picture', *The Viking*. Somewhat Wagnerian in style, it did not gain any lasting popularity, partly because it did not receive the coverage accorded to music written for the higher-profile London contests. The Halifax event was a great success, however, attracting a crowd of over 20 000 to the venue at Thrum Hall, home of the Halifax Rugby Club. Fodens were the winners, Black Dyke taking second place. It was intended that the contest should become an annual affair and the organizers announced that Nicholl would write a 'new dramatic symphony' for the following year. There was indeed a contest held in 1924, but the test piece was a transcription (by Nicholl) of the *Organ Sonata on Psalm 94* by Julius Reubke (1834–1858). With Nicholl's death in the following April the contest was discontinued. The North, however, now had its first home-produced original brass band composition. As a tribute to its composer, St Hilda's (the reigning National Champions) and Black Dyke combined to perform *The Viking* at a concert in Halifax a few weeks after his death, under the baton of William Halliwell.[9]

Chronologically, *The Viking* was the fourth original test piece, as the Halifax contest for which it was composed took place before the Nationals. However, the fourth composer to be called upon to write for the Nationals was Henry Geehl. He actually wrote two works in successive years – *Oliver Cromwell* for the 1923 contest and *On the Cornish Coast* for that of 1924.

Geehl (1881–1961) had studied in London and Vienna, had appeared as a piano soloist at the age of eight, and had planned to become a concert pianist. It was as a conductor and composer, however, that he forged his career, touring as a theatrical conductor and writing several orchestral works, also serving on the staff of Trinity College of Music from 1918 to 1960. Unlike the other composers so far discussed, Geehl took a lifelong interest in brass bands, writing no less than 13 test pieces, catering for bands of a wide ability range, and frequently adjudicating. In 1939 he was to help establish the Diploma of Licentiate of Trinity College London (LTCL) in Brass Band Conducting.

Ex.12

Oliver Cromwell is a concert overture in sonata form. It is highly chromatic and contains the first fugal passage in an original work. There was no programme note, but as Herbert Whiteley pointed out, the title would indicate its character.[10] Opening with a slow introduction, the overture immediately creates a sinister atmosphere, with rich harmonies, and modulations taking it through a range of keys – some quite remote from the home key of C minor. Though not supplying any major themes, reference to the Introduction is made from time to time, and the rising semitone motif which permeates the first few bars (example 12), is an important feature. The mood remains sombre with the arrival of the C minor 1st subject (example 13).

The transition takes on the proportions of a development section, and after 45 bars and further chromaticism leads to a passage derived from the Introduction which, in turn, heralds the second subject. This is a more lyrical

Ex.13

and restful theme in G (example 14), played first as a cornet solo, with supportive comments from euphonium. The short codetta introduces a distant trumpet-like theme played on muted cornets and trombones – a 'first' in an original work for the latter.

Ex.14

Ex.15

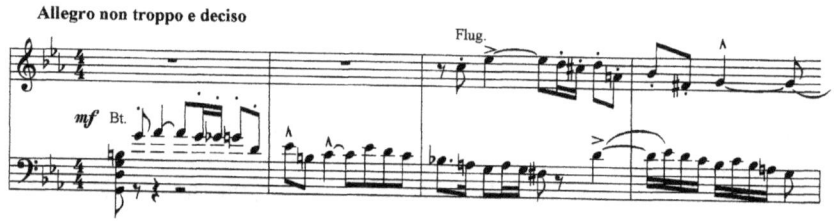

The Development begins with a fugal exposition; its subject (example 15), derived from the Introduction, is developed at some length, though never threatens to become a full fugue. Once again a reference to the Introduction leads to the Recapitulation and the return of the first subject. The abridged transition makes full use of material from the Exposition and, via a further reference to the Introduction, leads to the second subject, this time in E♭ major and more fully scored. The 'Maestoso' Coda is based on the distant trumpet motif introduced at the close of the Exposition, this time with the full glory of cornets and trombones playing *fortissimo*, and bringing the work to a triumphant end.

This undeservedly neglected overture is, both in structure and musical content, a high point amongst the early original works. In the following year (1924) Geehl composed the rhapsody *On the Cornish Coast* for the Nationals. This is less tightly-structured than *Oliver Cromwell*, but is still an interesting work. It was the first time the term 'rhapsody' had been used for a band piece, and was the first original work to introduce existing themes. There is, however, an original Introduction containing motifs to which Geehl returns from time to time. This is another work which has enjoyed occasional revivals but which has not found a regular place in the repertoire.

Though Geehl was to write regularly for brass band in the post-war years, he wrote just one further piece before the war, his overture *Robin Hood*, written for the 1936 Belle Vue September contest. It was 12 years since his previous band piece, and there were now several models with tried and tested schemes which he could employ. For this, as with *Oliver Cromwell*, Geehl wrote a classical overture, but with programmatic elements. The brief Introduction, for example, introducing what is to become the second part of the first subject group, is subtitled 'Bold Robin Hood'. In contrast, the first theme of the first subject is a dainty scherzo-like idea, portraying 'Maid Marian' and leading back to the 'Robin Hood' theme. Up to this point the music has been predominantly in F, but the transition, headed 'Friar Tuck', modulates to the dominant key (C) for the second subject, a 'Love Duet'. Here, Marian and Robin are portrayed by cornet and euphonium soloists. The Development consists of new material in the form of a pseudo-fugato, appropriately headed 'Merry making – Sherwood'. The Recapitulation veers from convention in that the order of the first subject's themes is reversed, and the transition is totally different from that in the Exposition. It leads however, as expected, to the second subject in the home key of F – played 'Grandioso' by full band and then to a short Coda based on the Introduction.

The next composer to write for brass band, Denis Wright (1895–1967), did so when he won a competition organized by Iles to find the test piece for the 1925 Crystal Palace Championships – the 25th anniversary of the festival. When Iles organized this competition his idea was to encourage established composers to write for brass band. In an advertisement which first appeared in *British Bandsman* of 28 February 1925, a prize of 100 guineas was offered for the winning entry. Similar advertisements appeared subsequently in both *The Times* and the *Telegraph*, as well as in *Musical Times* and other music magazines. An article in *British Bandsman* of 5 March appealed for composers to write for this 'woefully neglected medium'. Iles had hoped that some of the well-established composers of the day would enter the competition but this was not to be, the prize going to a 30-year-old schoolmaster who knew nothing about brass bands and had very little published music to his credit – just a few songs and a piece for piano and cello. With no prior knowledge of brass bands Wright, who taught music and modern languages, obtained scores for the two existing Geehl pieces, studied them, composed his overture *Joan of Arc*, and won the competition. He grasped the opportunity this gave him wholeheartedly, and went on to become one of the most prominent and influential personalities in the brass band world for the next 40 years, between 1925 and 1933 composing seven original works:

1925 Overture, *Joan of Arc* – winner of the competition
1926 Fantasia, *Hanover* – variations on a well-known hymn tune, chosen as test piece for a lower section in the 1928 Crystal Palace contest
1927 Symphonic Poem – *The White Rider*, composed for a lower section but actually used as the Thousand-Guinea test piece in 1927
1930 Symphonic Suite – *Tintagel*, composed as test piece for the Nationals, but turned down as being too difficult
1933 Symphonic Legend – *Princess Nada*, Belle Vue test piece, 1933; has very naïve programme
1933 Overture – *The Sea (Thalassa)*: the reason for its composition is not clear, and it seems not to have been used as a test piece during the period under review
1935 Suite – *Carnival*: a four-movement concert piece, unpublished (though one of its movements, *Valse Interlude*, was published in 1955)

However, only two of the above named works warrant further discussion. *Joan of Arc* is a concert overture in sonata form but, although well-constructed, the musical material has not stood the test of time and the piece has never commanded more than an occasional performance. *Tintagel* is by far the best of the early pieces (and this on Wright's own admission). Regrettably, it was turned down as a test piece; it would, I am sure, have been successful and, if given a warm reception, could have changed the direction which Wright took in his future compositions. Not until 1956, when Wright composed *Tam o' Shanter's Ride* for the Belle Vue September contest did he produce another work which, alongside *Tintagel*, has become standard repertoire. Nevertheless, through literally hundreds of transcriptions, his work as the BBC's first Brass and Military Band Supervisor, and through the vast amount of educational work he undertook, Wright was a key figure in brass bands from the early 1930s until his death in 1967.[11]

The year 1925, which had seen Denis Wright's introduction to brass bands, saw another and even more dramatic event in the annals of the brass band – a change of ownership at Belle Vue. The famous showground had been owned by the Jennison family since its inception in 1836; John Jennison had founded the Belle Vue September contest in 1853 (see page 33), but in 1924 a depleted Jennison family decided to sell up. From 1 January 1925 a new company was established; called Belle Vue (Manchester) Ltd, it came under the control of three people, one of whom was John Henry Iles. Before long the other two had resigned, leaving Iles in sole charge. So far, though still using selections as test pieces, the Belle Vue contests were successful and secure. As far as Iles and the Crystal Palace contest were concerned, Belle Vue had hitherto represented the opposition and there was now concern that the takeover might bring about the demise of the Crystal Palace contest, as Iles would have a conflict of interests. There was, in fact, no danger of this, Iles himself declaring that both events would 'march forward together'.[12]

The first outward sign of the new Belle Vue ownership was the introduction of original works as test pieces, the early ones being composed by Thomas Keighley (1869–1936), who was born in Stalybridge in the heartland of Lancashire bands and hometown to one of the oldest. He studied at the Royal Manchester College of Music (now the Royal Northern College of Music), and took his Doctorate at Victoria University (now Manchester University) in 1901. Not by any means a noted composer, he was more widely known as an author of musical textbooks and for his teaching pieces for piano. He did, however, compose anthems and part songs, was an organist, and also Professor of Harmony at the Royal Manchester College of Music. To him fell the distinction of writing the first original work played in the Belle Vue September contest, the first of six Keighley test pieces to be played there over the next decade. He had already adjudicated at the contest on three occasions, and had arranged test pieces for both the July and the September contests of 1924. The Keighley test pieces were as follows:

1925 Macbeth
1926 A Midsummer Night's Dream
1927 The Merry Wives of Windsor
1928 Lorenzo
1932 The Crusaders
1935 A Northern Rhapsody

The first three had no impact on the repertoire beyond serving, as *Labour and Love* and *Coriolanus* had done, to help bridge the gap between selections and the true original work. Indeed, they owed more to the fantasias and overtures of Henry Round than to the recent Crystal Palace test pieces. *Lorenzo* was both more sophisticated and more successful and, whilst never regarded as a 'classic', has retained its popularity. Designated 'tone poem', it abounds in good tunes, provides solos for all the principal players (including E♭ bass) and tests the technical capabilities of the band as a whole. It makes use of the techniques known as double- and triple-tonguing, and whilst these may not be the first examples in original works (*Freedom* called for a certain amount of triple-tonguing), they are certainly the most extensive (see examples 16 and 17). Though played without breaks, there are three main sections to *Lorenzo*:

Ex.16

Ex.17

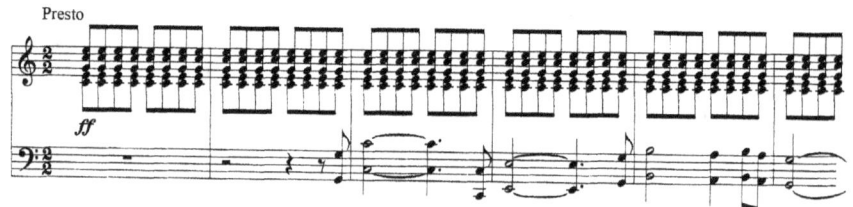

1st section:
Introduction:	C minor
Theme A:	Bass solo – cornets, horns and 1st baritone triple-tonguing; C minor (example 16)
Theme B:	Flugel and cornet solos plus tutti section; G minor
Link:	'Meno mosso, sinistramente'; chromatic, but ending on dominant of Bb
Theme C:	'Scherzando'; Bb major
Link:	Leading back to C minor and reprise of main themes
Theme A:	As before but modified close; C minor
Theme B:	Melody in horns, baritones and euphoniums; A minor
Link:	As before but a tone higher, leading to dominant of C
Theme C:	In C major, shortened and leading to mock ending

2nd section:
As the full band stops playing (often to applause from an unsuspecting audience) a horn solo emerges, in Ab major, followed by a similar solo for soprano. Then follows a short musical conversation between Eb bass, solo cornet and flugelhorn, and a full band tutti, the section ending *ppp* on a full band chord of Ab.

3rd section:
A fanfare played by all upper cornets and followed by a succession of ideas, all in festive mood and culminating in a reworking of Theme A from the 1st Section, with changed rhythm and in the major mode (see example 17).

Lorenzo was the fourth and last of the Keighley pieces with Shakespearian connotations. Whether or not there is any connection between the music and the rather minor character from *The Merchant of Venice* has not, as far as I know, been revealed, and there was no programme note. However, it remains one of the more important of relatively few original works specially composed for Belle Vue.

Keighley's next piece, *The Crusaders*, is based on Sir Walter Scott's novel, *The Talisman*. With subheadings 'Coeur de Lion', 'The Saladin', 'Edith Plantagenet', 'Kenneth the Scot', 'Blondel Sings', 'In the Camp of the Moors' and 'The Gathering and the Combat', the music is full of pomp and pageant, and a successful interpretation requires familiarity with the novel and its characters. Described as a symphonic rhapsody, the work follows roughly the pattern of the four-movement classical symphony, though there is no hint of sonata form. The brief Introduction is based on a motif which reappears, but the piece relies mainly on melodies, that depicting 'Coeur de Lion' returning a number of times. An unusual feature is a euphonium solo ('The Saladin') marked to be played *sempre senza vibrato*.

Keighley's final brass band work, dating from the year before his death, was *A Northern Rhapsody*. Like Geehl's *On the Cornish Coast*, it is based on a mixture of original and borrowed material. The score admits to 'Introducing: (a) The Hymn Tune now widely known as "On Ilkla Moor", and (b) a Morris Dance Tune frequently used fifty years ago at Mottram-in-Longendale, Cheshire, during holiday times'. Though less popular than *Lorenzo*, *A Northern Rhapsody* was a valuable addition to the repertoire, and deserves more recognition than it has had in recent times.

So far I have dealt mainly with the total output of original works by each composer in the order in which the composers themselves came to the brass band. The exception has been Percy Fletcher, whose *Labour and Love* was dealt with first. Fletcher's other test piece, *An Epic Symphony*, was composed for the Nationals of 1926 and is such a high-water mark amongst pieces by the minor composers that it warrants its own special place in this review of their original works.

Fletcher was a relatively young composer of 34 when he wrote his tone poem *Labour and Love*; when he returned to the scene 13 years later with *An Epic Symphony*, he produced a more complex work, no doubt in part because of personal maturity, but because bands also had developed and were now capable of interpreting more advanced music.

An Epic Symphony is considered by many to be the outstanding piece from the early group of composers. As with *Life Divine*, the emotive nature of the

Ex.18

title may well have contributed to the work's lasting success (especially as it appeared in the year of the General Strike), though the most important factor must be its musical content and a combination of ideas which give satisfaction to both performer and listener. All the main themes, though of widely differing character, are derived from a single idea – a more subtle form of metamorphosis (thematic transformation) than that found in *Labour and Love*. For most of the bandsmen who perform it, however, the attraction is in the challenge of the solos and the exploitation of the limited colours of the all-brass band. Listeners are often captivated by the instrumental pitfalls in the writing, and with the degree of success achieved by players in negotiating them – the classic test piece scenario.

Epic Symphony has three movements. The first, headed 'Recitare', opens with a fiery tutti (example 18), but leads to a series of recitative-like passages featuring, first of all, tenor trombones (in unison), then flugelhorn and solo cornet. After a return to the opening idea all three trombones are put to the test – individually – before the movement comes to a peaceful close, with some beautiful sonorities from the lower instruments (example 19).

Ex.19

The term 'Elegy' appears at the head of the second movement – its first use in brass band literature. Opening with a horn trio over a pizzicato-like bass (example 20), the music goes into arabesque-style virtuoso solos for cornet

Ex.20

and soprano before settling into another melody, heard first as a euphonium solo, repeated by full band, and leading to a highly emotional climax. The return of the Elegy's opening theme is more fully scored but leads to a tranquil ending, the final bar calling for just three cornets and two trombones – all muted. The finale, entitled 'Heroic March', adds purpose to the word 'Epic' in the title, is often played as a separate item, and is a masterpiece of scoring. Opening with an introduction, again featuring horns – this time with the luxury of a percussion accompaniment – the music builds up and introduces

Ex.21

Ex.22

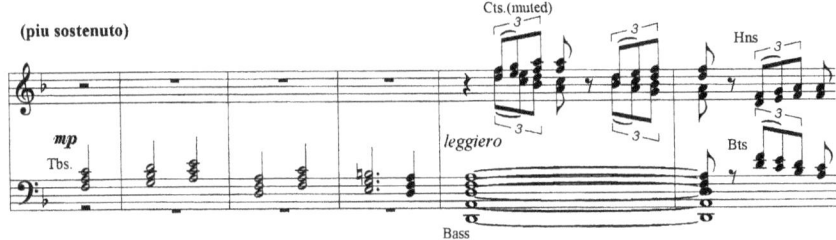

the first main theme of the March (example 21). This is developed at length before a second theme appears, played first on trombones (example 22). It is this which returns as the apotheosis of the work, with stirring full band chords and fanfare-like figures in cornets. A brief comparison of the music examples shows the relationship between the themes. *An Epic Symphony* is a fine work, and well deserves its permanent place in the repertoire.

Before turning to major composers who wrote for brass band, two more minor composers deserve a mention. The first is Haydn Morris (died 1965), who composed the suite *Springtime* for the 1931 Belle Vue contest. It has three movements – 'The Birth of Spring', 'A Love Song' and a scherzo, 'Folk Revels'. *Springtime* has enjoyed little success and I must admit to never having heard it performed. The 1935 Crystal Palace test piece was composed by a leading figure from the early days of the BBC – Kenneth A Wright (1899–1975). Wright wrote several pieces for brass and military bands, as well as a number for light orchestra. His 1935 essay, *Pride of Race*, though overshadowed by the more significant works of the 1930s, enjoyed some popularity for a number of years, but is rarely heard today. This is also a suite, its movements headed – 'The Pioneers', 'Memory', and 'March: Pride of Race'.

Major British composers of brass band music

Following the success of this 1926 test piece, Iles took a major step two years later, commissioning the first of a series of major British composers to write a test piece. 1928 was a crucial year for brass bands; there was now a repertoire of a dozen or so original test pieces but Iles, visionary that he was, wanted to bring greater credibility to brass bands by involving composers of stature.

Gustav Holst (1874–1934)

His first choice was Holst, a leading composer of his generation, who enjoyed early acclaim with *A Somerset Rhapsody* (1906–1907) and *St Paul's Suite* (1912–1913), written for the orchestra of the famous girls' school of that name in Hammersmith, of which he was director of music from 1905 until his death. However, it was his orchestral suite, *The Planets* (1914–1916) which secured his reputation and earned him international fame.

Holst had been a professional trombonist during his early career. After studies at the Royal College of Music he toured with the Carl Rosa Opera Company and then joined the Scottish Orchestra, though whilst a student he had played in a band on seaside piers during summer holidays. He composed three military band pieces – *Suite in E♭* (1909) and *Second Suite in F* (1911) and, in 1930, the Prelude and Scherzo, *Hammersmith*. Iles's approach to Holst was, therefore, one which could reasonably expect a positive response – which it did – the outcome of which was the test piece for the 1928 Crystal Palace contest, *A Moorside Suite*.

There had been a strong influence of German music in the early original works, but this was certainly not present in *A Moorside Suite*. Furthermore, it represented a conscious effort to break away from the restrictions of the major and minor key system – a move long established in orchestral music. In *A Moorside Suite* Holst made use of such devices as modal writing, canon, ostinato and, in the opening of the final movement, hinted at future idioms, with emphasis on the interval of a perfect fourth. There is no programme, though the subtitles of the movements – 'Scherzo', 'Nocturne' and 'March' indicate their respective styles. The 'Scherzo', opening in the Dorian mode,[13] is very lightly scored, with the theme announced as a cornet solo. Its first four notes permeate the movement, the climax of the first part being reached when the theme appears in canon (example 23).[14] The Trio section is based on a chorale-like theme, accompanied by an ostinato based on the opening motif of the movement (example 24).[15] The 'Nocturne' – like the 'Scherzo', the first of several such movements in brass band literature – is based on an Aeolian mode melody played on solo cornet (example 25) and leads to another chorale-like tune, played first of all *ppp* by the full band. Keighley had used this technique briefly in *Lorenzo*, but this was the first time an entire passage had been scored in this way. Here, with tutti playing as softly as possible, a totally new effect was created. After a sudden call to attention (example 26) the 'March' proceeds with a mixture of pomp, ceremony, and lighthearted dance, with more than a hint of the style of folk music.

A Moorside Suite does not display any complex musical structure (the first and third movements are quite simply ternary), yet it is a masterpiece of

Ex.23

Ex.24

Ex.25

musical economy and possibly the most innovative of all the early original works. Though composed as a test piece it is rarely used as such these days, performances being reserved for the more august brass band concerts.

J H Elliott described Holst's enthusiasm for brass bands thus: at a concert in Carlisle on 12 February 1933, Holst conducted a performance of *Moorside*, played by Carlisle St Stephen's Band, and during the course of the evening, Elliott expressed the view to Hoslt that the brass band movement 'had a great future before it'. 'It has a great present if only people could realize it', the great man retorted.[16]

Ex.26

Sir Edward Elgar (1857–1934)

Following his success with Holst, Iles was indeed looking to the future, and his next target was Elgar, England's greatest living composer and Master of the King's Music. If Holst was at the height of his career when he came to the brass band, Elgar was in his twilight as, in 1930 – at the age of 73 – he composed *Severn Suite*.

In 1920, Elgar's wife, Alice, had died, and from then until the end of his life, many of his compositions employed ideas from earlier periods. *Severn Suite* is no exception, and some of the material used comes from a group of wind quintet movements dating from 1879, the year in which Elgar had become bandmaster of a band made up of staff of the Worcestershire County Lunatic Asylum. Maund points out, however, that even in his final years, Elgar was sketching material as fast as his health would allow, as well as developing ideas which in some cases he had written many years before. Maund contends that most of the material in *Severn Suite* is original.

Elgar had two tenuous connections with brass bands during his earlier career. The first was the arrangement by Charles Godfrey of a selection from his cantata, *Caractacus* as test piece for the 1903 Belle Vue September contest. This must have been with the knowledge and blessing of the composer, though there is no evidence that he ever heard the arrangement played. Some years later, transcriptions were also made of abridged versions of both the Elgar Symphonies. They were made for Black Dyke, and the original manuscripts are still in the band's library. J A Greenwood was the arranger, and in 1919 Elgar visited Queensbury to hear the band perform them. He is said to have 'expressed his delighted approval' of the arrangements.[17] Here again was a composer with brass band links, and one who was persuaded to compose a work for the 1930 National Championships. Henry Geehl was given the job of assisting with the score. There has been much debate about how much of the scoring is Elgar's and how much Geehl's, but I do not propose to enter into that argument here. Suffice to say that the flames of the debate were fanned during 1995 by the appearance, in a sale at Sotheby's, of a manuscript claimed to be the full brass band score in Elgar's hand.[18]

A version of *Severn Suite* for orchestra appeared two years later than that for brass band. It had the same opus number (87) and was, without doubt, orchestrated by Elgar. The work is in five sections and the subtitles in the orchestral version are more colourful than in that for band:

	Band	Orchestra
I	Introduction	Worcester Cathedral
II	Toccata	Tournament
III	Fugue	The Cathedral
IV	Minuet	In the Commandery
V	Coda	Coda

The Introduction is short but in conventional sonata form, its second subject also being used as a link between movements I and II, II and III, and again at the beginning of the Coda – an abridged form of the Introduction. The Toccata has many of the characteristics of early keyboard examples, but also exploits the capabilities of brass instruments. It is in rondo form – ABABA, Elgar achieving variety by writing the B section not only in a contrasting style marked 'Grandioso', but also raising it by a semitone on its second appearance.

The Fugue is a movement of great beauty, its character well illustrated by the orchestral subtitle. The Minuet is an extended movement, again roughly in

ABABA form; the two B sections are scherzos – and quite different from each other. For further variety, the second and third versions of A take on the form of variations. The key structure of the work takes movements II and IV to the subdominant (F) and III into the tonic minor (C minor).

Severn Suite was dedicated to George Bernard Shaw. Though it has not been the overwhelming success that might have been expected, comparisons which are sometimes made with works such as *Gerontius* and the two symphonies are misleading. The very simplicity of *Severn Suite* was a virtue in the context of writing for the brass band of 1930, and it provided its own reward for those for whom it was written. That said, the scoring is not always successful, and conductors are faced with balance problems which have sometimes led to rescoring of certain passages. Also, the printed music, in the original version, is littered with mistakes – a constant source of irritation during preparation for performance. Nevertheless, *Severn Suite* remains a 'classic', and is regularly – if not frequently – performed.[19]

Sir Granville Bantock (1868–1946)

In the same year that the *Severn Suite* featured as a test piece there appeared the first of several pieces for brass band by Bantock – his *Oriental Rhapsody*. It was used as test piece at Belle Vue and therefore preceded *Severn Suite* by about a month. Bantock, a good friend of Elgar's, was highly regarded as a composer during his day, and the list of his works is quite extensive. His involvement with competitive music festivals is well documented, and he also made significant contributions to British music education. Most of his activities around the turn of the century were centred in the Midlands, and in 1908 he succeeded Elgar as Peyton Professor of Music at Birmingham University, retaining the post until 1934. Earlier, whilst earning his living primarily as a conductor with a number of theatrical companies, Bantock accepted a position as musical director at the Tower, New Brighton, conducting the military band there before converting it into an orchestra, as August Manns had done at the Crystal Palace and Dan Godfrey at Bournemouth. It must also have been during this period that J A Greenwood played in New Brighton (see page 131). A stronger connection with bands was established in 1914 when Bantock composed a *Festival March* for an Independent Labour Party Conference held in Bradford.[20]

The 1930 *Oriental Rhapsody* was based on an orchestral tone poem called *Lalla Rookh*, which dated from 1902 and which had also been used as music for a ballet in 1917. Though it has a certain amount of harmonic and melodic colour, it meanders from one idea to another in rhapsodic fashion, and the brass band version has been played only rarely since the 1930 contest. It was completely overshadowed by the later *Prometheus Unbound*, composed for the 1933 Nationals, and still regarded as a brass band classic. This, Bantock's most successful brass band composition, took its inspiration from a verse-drama of the same name, written in 1818–1819 by Shelley.[21] No previous test piece had had such a gruesome story as its inspiration, and inevitably it was in a totally different mould from any of its predecessors. Based on such a legend it is hardly surprising that some of its themes sound quite menacing as, for example, that shown in example 27 – played in octaves by the full band minus trombones on its first appearance. Another theme which grows out of it is shown in example 28; as may be seen, this subsides into a more gentle mood. *Prometheus Unbound* contains much unusual chording, and several instances of unison and two-part writing. Though less technically difficult than many other band pieces, a satisfactory performance demands a proficient band and a conductor in tune with its style. For the first time, a brass band test piece ended quietly (example 29).

Designated 'symphonic prelude', it is quite feasible that Bantock already had in mind that this was to become the opening of a more substantial work, and in 1936 he produced a version of *Prometheus Unbound* for chorus and orchestra, revising the brass band piece and using it as the Prelude.

There are several other Bantock brass band pieces, a number of which are listed in *Grove*. An overture, *King Lear*, was composed in 1932 for the now-defunct Callendar's Cable Works Band. Bantock had a particularly individual style of writing, with a strong leaning towards Oriental subjects, for example in his *Kubla Kahn*, mentioned in the text of *Grove* as a piece for men's voices, but not appearing in the list of such works. There is also a band piece with this name, but not mentioned in *Grove*. It was discussed in several editions of *British Bandsman*,[22] was published in R Smith's *Champion Journal* of 1923, and was used in a number of second section contests during April and May. Carlisle St Stephens were winners at a contest in Newcastle where it was the second section test, and there is a report that, coincidentally,[23] a Carlisle male voice choir had won a competition in Morecambe the previous week, singing *Kubla Kahn*. Reference to a choir part establishes that the band version is a transcription of the choir work, and is not, as had been assumed, original brass band music. It is based on a poem by Samuel Taylor Coleridge (1772–1834), the music faithfully following the text of the poem.

Bantock's contribution to brass band repertoire was quite extensive. He was also a keen supporter, and was the first president of the Bandsman's College of Music on its founding, in 1930.[24]

John Ireland (1879–1962)

Following the successes of Holst, Elgar and Bantock, John Ireland was the next major composer approached by Iles. It is curious that he should have

Ex.27

Ex.28

Ex.29

been singled out; there seem to be no 'brass band skeletons' in his cupboard, and his reputation as a composer was built largely on songs, piano pieces and chamber music. Whatever reasons Iles had for contacting him, he was rewarded with an excellent piece of writing.

Ex.30

Ex.31

Ireland's *A Downland Suite* (1932) has remained one of the permanent favourites in the band repertoire – largely because of the beauty and simplicity of its second movement, the 'Elegy'. Though designated suite, the work conforms to the standard four-movement layout of the classical symphony, with an extended first movement – 'Prelude', the 'Elegy' (the slow movement), a 'Minuet', and a 'Rondo' to round off the work.

The Prelude is tenary, with a number of subsidiary ideas adding variety and complexity to the basic ABA shape. The Elegy begins as shown in example 30. Its mood is one of sublime inner peace, and though a mere 36 bars long, is amongst the most profound pieces of writing in brass band literature. The 'Minuet' is also a movement of great beauty, the delicacy of its scoring rarely equalled and certainly, in the writer's view, never surpassed. The Rondo, like the Prelude, is a far more cleverly constructed movement than its title implies. As will be noted from example 31, its opening (and principal) idea is derived from the melody of the 'Elegy' which, in fact, re-appears in a glorious 'Grandioso' towards the close. It also contains occasional echoes of the 'Prelude'.

For his second test piece, written two years later, Ireland chose to write a single-movement work, the overture, *Comedy* – another piece which has stood the test of time. Again, structure and scoring are masterly. *Comedy*

Ex.32

begins with a slow Introduction, with much of its material forming the basis of ideas which follow. This may be seen as portraying the quiet, even eerie, pre-dawn streets of the Edwardian London of Ireland's youth, perhaps with a 'bobby' on his early morning rounds. The first subject is said to have come to Ireland's mind when he heard a bus conductor shouting 'Dilly, Piccadilly!' (example 32). The overture adheres to conventional sonata form, but towards the close of the Development section there is a beautiful elegiac melody. In an orchestral version (a slight reworking of the same material, called *A London Overture*) a horn obligato is superimposed on a background of woodwind and muted strings playing the main tune. This was claimed to have been inserted into the piece as a tribute to a friend, Percy Bentham, whose bizarre death in a London heatwave was caused when a poisonous substance from a straw hat entered his bloodstream.[25]

Tom Aitken, in an article headed *Mysterious 'Comedy'* in *Brass Band News* of 1 September 1984, quotes Bram Gay as saying that he regards Ireland as 'one of the few non-brass band composers to realize the true nature of the band', along with the opinion that *Comedy* and *A Downland Suite* are 'amongst our strongest pieces'.[26] Ireland had a distinctly personal style of writing and there can be no doubt that his sense of lyricism suited the band idiom admirably. Much of his melodic writing veered towards the modes, and this may be felt in both his band pieces. Ireland often associated pieces with places, and his love of the Sussex Downs and London must have been the inspiration behind these two works.

There was by now an unexpected reversal of the trend of the derivation of brass band music from other sources. Reference has already been made to Bantock using a modified version of one of his band pieces as an orchestral Prelude; this was not an isolated example. Holst's *Moorside Suite* was to find its way into the military band repertoire in a transcription by Denis Wright and into the orchestra's in one by Gordon Jacob. Elgar himself orchestrated *Severn Suite* and Henry Geehl made a transcription for military band (published in 1931), whilst a version for organ appeared as Elgar's *Organ Sonata No 2, Op 87a*, arranged by Ivor Atkins, though with major structural changes. The Ireland pieces were slightly different in that during the course of their move to the orchestra they underwent some minor structural modifications. These were made by Ireland himself, who scored a version of the

Minuet and Elegy from *A Downland Suite* for strings, and *A London Overture*, for full orchestra, based on *Comedy*.[27]

Herbert Howells (1892–1983) and Sir Arthur Bliss (1891–1975)

Howells and Bliss are the two remaining significant composers who wrote brass band music during the 1930s – Howells with *Pageantry*, composed for the Belle Vue September contest of 1934, and Bliss with *Kenilworth*, the test piece for the Nationals two years later. Both composers were relatively mature when they wrote these works (Howells was 42 and Bliss 47), but though the work of each would be known, most of the music by which they are now chiefly remembered was written after their respective first experiences of writing for the brass band.[28]

Howells, as well as being a composer, was an organist and a teacher, following Holst as director of music at St Paul's Girls School. In 1932 he had become the first John Collard Fellow of the Worshipful Company of Musicians, and this may have been one reason why Iles invited him to write a test piece. Iles himself was a member of the Company for many years, rising to the position of Grand Master, and initiating the Iles Silver Medal of the Worshipful Company of Musicians, presented annually to a distinguished member of the brass band world. Howells was, nevertheless, an unusual choice – even more surprising as he was asked to write a test piece for use at Belle Vue, Manchester, where brass band audiences were more conservative than those which gathered in London for the Nationals.

Like several other members of this group, Howells developed a highly individual style, with an unmistakably English character, and which paid tribute to earlier traditions as well as displaying the composer's love of nature.[29] The test piece he wrote for the 1934 Bell Vue September contest must have mesmerized the Northern audience, accustomed as it was to operatic selections and the music of Thomas Keighley. *Pageantry* is a three-movement suite, the movements headed 'King's Herald', 'Cortege' and 'Jousts'. It would sound very modern to those in the audience that day – it still does to the average brass band listener who has not kept pace with developments. Harmony is often modal and the score contains examples of the deliberate use of consecutive fifths – forbidden in traditional harmony, and probably sounding discordant to unsuspecting ears of the time.[30] The melodic material relies on fragments rather than phrases, and though most rhythmic aspects of the work were in no way out of the ordinary, Howells created problems for less-informed conductors of the day by employing irregular time signatures during the course of the last movement – a 5/4 bar in the middle of a section in 2/2 time, a 7/4 bar in a passage in 3/2 time, and the notorious passage shown in example 33 which would doubtless be problematical for

Ex.33

many bands in 1934. The work does not adhere to any traditional form, but relies more on the development of ideas and motifs.

Despite these modernistic ideas the music is descriptive, and it is easy to imagine a royal visit incorporating a tournament in which knights compete in tests of skill and courage. The royal presence is portrayed in 'King's Herald', and in 'Cortege' the knights process thoughtfully – perhaps in prayer, past the majesterial throne, prior to the various trials of strength and character in the finale, 'Jousts'. Probably a source of bewilderment to many in 1934, *Pageantry* is one of those pieces with which time has caught up. It has increased in popularity during the last 30 years and now sits happily beside pieces written much later – without in any way betraying its age.

In contrast, Bliss wrote a most unpretentious and accessible piece for the 1936 Nationals. It is not typical Bliss, but was immediately popular with bands, especially its finale which is often played separately. Only a handful of Bliss compositions could have been well known at the time. His *Morning Heroes* (1930), a symphony for orator, chorus and orchestra would be amongst them, while his score for the H G Wells film, *Things to Come*, written during 1934 and 1935, brought him instant widespread recognition. This could have been the reason why Iles offered him the commission for the 1936 Nationals. The work was called *Kenilworth*, and was dedicated to Kenneth A Wright, composer of the previous year's test piece and a colleague of Bliss's at the BBC.[31] The work is full of good tunes and, especially in the second movement, displays a succession of lyrical solos. It is another piece based on pageant, but in a totally different style from either *Crusaders* or *Pageantry*. The score's programme note reads as follows:

> In 1575 Queen Elizabeth paid her celebrated visit to Kenilworth Castle . . . At the Gate of the Gallery Tower, the Queen, mounted on a milk white horse, was greeted with a flourish of trumpets, and presented with the keys of the Castle. Immediately on entering the Tilt Yard, the Spirit of the Lake appeared on a floating island, blazing with torches, and welcomed her. The Queen stayed during 19 days of lively pastimes, plays, masques and pageants. The great clock stood the whole time at the hour of dining.

Ex.34

Ex.35

Ex.36

Though described as a suite, *Kenilworth* is really a single-movement work in three clear but linked sections. They are headed: 'At the Castle Gate', 'Serenade on the Lake' and 'March: Kenilworth (Homage to Queen Elizabeth)'. Pomp and ceremony are immediately evident in the opening (see example 34), which leads to a series of declamatory solos – a new style for soloists to master (see example 35). The tranquil *Serenade on the Lake* consists of a series of lyrical solos, the principal examples being for cornet and euphonium, with shorter ones for trombone, soprano and baritone; the accompaniment is sparse, requiring delicate, controlled playing. There is distinct flavour of the Dorian mode as the theme appears in canon shortly before the close (example 36). It quickly becomes apparent that the first two sections are but preludes to the main body of the work, the 'March:

Kenilworth'. Though tuneful and easy on the ear, this is a substantial movement, complex both in structure and key scheme, and based on the following:

> **Introduction:** two ideas – (i) in 2/4 time in the Aeolian mode and (ii) in 3/4 time in G major (example 37)
> **March:** Theme 'A' in G major, repeated in B major; a subsidiary theme in C and F; theme 'A' in F
> (19) Theme 'B' in Bb major; this undergoes some development and, like Theme 'A', passes through B major
> **Recapitulation** – reprise of Introduction, followed by theme 'B' in G before, at (26), themes 'A' and 'B' appear in combination (example 38)
> **Coda:** in Bb major and based mainly on the opening of the work

The movement has been very popular played by itself, and the work as a whole is still regarded as one of the treasures of the repertoire.

Ex.37

Ex.38

Conclusion

Kenilworth came at the end of an era for bands and during a time of extreme political upheaval. 'Between 1935 and 1939 the country was ruled by three kings, two prime ministers and suffered an unprecedented constitutional crisis with the abdication of King Edward VIII.'[32] Added to this, Crystal Palace was destroyed by fire on the night of 30 November 1936, and two years later John Henry Iles was declared bankrupt, having invested his wealth in the film industry and lost everything.[33]

A new type of test piece – the original work 209

Despite all, the Nationals survived – for the next two years at Alexandra Palace and then after the 1939–1945 war at the Royal Albert Hall. However, the impetus for the succession of original works had gone, as old test pieces were revived for the Nationals (*Pageantry* in 1937 and *An Epic Symphony* in 1938). There were then to be no more London contests until 1945, and though the Belle Vue contest soldiered on, bands were badly hit by the war, losing their younger players to the armed forces, whilst older ones were involved in many hours of overtime on behalf of the war effort. Nevertheless there was, by 1936, a repertoire of specially-composed test pieces. Remarkably, one-third of these are still played with some regularity, with others receiving occasional performances. More importantly, they form the base on which a substantial repertoire of original brass band music has since been built and which, perhaps, will one day provide the material to take this study forward through further developments, particularly during the post-1950s.

Notes

1 Even beyond this date it was only the National Championships which used original works. The first such work to be used at Belle Vue did not appear until 1925.
2 Quoted from a letter to the author. Maund works in music publishing and has contributed a number of articles to *British Bandsman*. He has made several suggestions regarding the content of Chapter Nine.
3 Quoted from the score.
4 Howarth, 1988, p. 109.
5 This was pointed out to me by Dr Derek Scott.
6 The second subject here appears in the subdominant key, an unusual though not unique variation from its normal place in the dominant.
7 A fourth valve, operated by the player's left hand, is a normal part of the modern baritone and extends the range of the instrument's lower register. It was, however, rare in 1921.
8 Bainbridge, 1980, p. 67.
9 Information from *Brass Band News* of August 1923, August 1924, July 1925, and Gammond, 1980, pp. 84 and 85.
10 *British Bandsman*, 4 August 1923.
11 For further information about Denis Wright the reader is referred to the present author's book, *Doctor Denis* (Egon, 1995).
12 Information about changes at Belle Vue comes from Hailstone, 1987, p. 166 and Nicholls, 1989, pp. 17, 32 and 33.
13 Modes were scales which dominated European music until around 1600, when they were superseded by major and minor scales. Many twentieth century composers have used them in their compositions; two found in *Moorside* are Dorian and Aeolian. The charm of the modes is that each has its own pattern of tones and semitones. The Dorian mode may be found by playing all the white keys on the piano for one octave, beginning on the note D. By doing the same, but starting on A, the notes of the Aeolian mode will be found.

14 Canon is another ancient device often used by modern composers, in which a melodic strand appears against itself in one or more other parts, at a later time and at a different pitch.
15 An ostinato is a short figure repeated persistently.
16 Russell & Elliott, 1936, p. 186.
17 Maurice Johnstone in *Sounding Brass*, Spring, 1972, p. 9.
18 See *British Bandsman* of 20 May 1995. The score, expected to fetch between £25 000 and £30 000 failed to reach the reserve price, and was withdrawn.
19 Some years ago Geoffrey Brand prepared a new edition of the *Severn Suite*, based on the assumption that much of the scoring had been done by Henry Geehl and that, had Elgar himself scored the work, it would have been closer to the orchestral version. Current research suggests that Elgar did, in fact, do most of the scoring himself, but Bram Gay has produced what he calls a 'performing edition' – like that of Brand, in the same key as the orchestral version. This takes into account Elgar's personal comments on the original scoring. For the 1996 British Open Championships (the former Belle Vue September contest) this version of *Severn Suite* appeared as the test piece. In addition to the change of key, it incorporates modifications taken from Elgar's orchestral version and removes some of the anomalies found in the original score. The new version has had a mixed reception, some commentators welcoming it but others feeling that the original version was the more successful of the two.
20 Russell and Elliott, 1936, p. 181.
21 Prometheus was a character from Greek mythology who was – gruesomely – chained to a rock, and visited daily by an eagle which devoured his liver. Each night the liver grew again, only to be snatched by the eagle on its next visit. This went on for some thousands of years before Prometheus was rescued by Heracles.
22 4 November 1922, p. 3, 18 November 1922, p. 4, 1 February 1923 and 17 February 1923, p. 3.
23 *British Bandsman*, 2 June 1923, p. 3; two later Bantock works have found favour with brass bands; a transcription by Frank Wright, in 1952, of the orchestral overture *The Frogs of Aristophanes* (1936) and a less well-known overture based on another Greek mythological figure, *Orion*, introduced into the repertoire as a test piece in 1956 – ten years after the composer's death.
24 This college has no particular base, nor does it train or educate. Its sole purpose is to examine brass band instrumentalists and, more particularly, brass band conductors.
25 See Tom Aitken article in *Brass Band News*, September, 1984, p. 7.
26 Bram Gay is one of the 'elder statesmen' of the brass band world. He was a protégé of the late Harry Mortimer, at the age of 14 succeeding him as principal cornet player of Fodens. He went on to become a professional trumpet player – playing principal trumpet with the Hallé orchestra, musical editor of the brass band music of Novello and, until his retirement in 1996, orchestra director at the Royal Opera House, Covent Garden.
27 In more recent times, Geoffrey Bush transcribed the first and last movements of *Downland Suite* for strings, so that the full suite is now available in that form, and Philip Sparke transcribed *Comedy Overture* for wind band.
28 Each wrote one more band piece – Howells composing *Three Figures* for the 1960 National Championships, and Bliss *Belmont Variations* for those of 1963.
29 *Groves*, 5th edition, Volume 4, p. 389.

30 This idiom was also used in Fletcher's *Epic Symphony* – see examples 21 and 22.
31 It would appear that the structure of *Kenilworth* was influenced by the 1935 Kenneth Wright work
32 Hailstone, 1987, p. 202.
33 Ibid., p. 212.

10 Retrospect

In this volume I have tried to cover the principal developments in music played by bands during the period, and also suggested its likely roots, together with the effects of musical style from both popular and 'classical' genres. I have also attempted to annotate as many as possible of the more significant bands which have played their part in these trends. Several of them still perform, continuing to contribute to their own histories and that of the brass band movement as a whole. Yet to attempt to cover a hundred years of any branch of music in depth is a formidable undertaking, especially in an area in which relatively little research has so far been carried out, and many gaps will be found. There is much still to be written about the early histories of some of the bands, especially those of Black Dyke and Besses o' th' Barn, about the professionalism of these and other bands such as Fodens and St Hilda's, especially as manifested in their touring activities – both at home and abroad.

Besses is the most travelled of them all, having undertaken two world tours, each lasting almost a year and a half. On the first, during 1906 and 1907, they visited America, Canada, Hawaii, Fiji, New Zealand and Australia, and on the second, lasting from November 1910 to February 1912, touring South Africa, New Zealand and Australia. There were also a number of reciprocal visits by bands from Australia. Black Dyke toured America and Canada for six months during 1906, at about the same time as the early part of Besses' first tour, and Besses returned to Canada in 1932, playing at the Canadian National Exhibition in Toronto. Fodens spent five weeks in South Africa in 1936, during which time Crystal Palace was burned down. Perhaps here is a worthwhile topic for future research.

Overseas tours have continued, but in a completely different form. Because of working constraints bands can rarely be away from home for more than two weeks at a time. On the other hand, air travel, along with vast improvements in roads and railways, has reduced travelling time. This, to some extent, has cancelled out the problems created by more pressing work demands. From about the time of the end of World War II bands have made regular trips to Europe; the earliest such visits were undertaken by Fodens and the relatively young Fairey Aviation Works Band when, as part of ENSA (Entertainments National Service Association – an organization formed to entertain the troops), they gave concerts in Holland. Since then – particularly from the late 1950s – short European tours or visits have been undertaken by literally hundreds of bands, great and small. Several bands have also visited North America, Russia and Japan, and a few have visited Australia. Salvation Army bands, taking advantage of their organization's international network, have had many successful exchanges. In 1996 Salford University's brass band broke new ground by visiting Brazil – the first such band to play there. Together with the influence of radio, gramophone recordings and the growing market for CDs, these tours have helped stimulate the spread of the phenomenon of the British brass band. However, the only successful series of international brass band contests has been the European Brass Band Championships, in which leading bands from a range of European countries have competed annually since 1978 for the title 'European Brass Band Champions'.

Australia and New Zealand have each had substantial brass band movements for over a century, and each holds its annual National Championships – along with smaller regional events. The founders of the movements in these two countries were the immigrants who settled there during the latter part of the nineteenth century. Canada also had the makings of a brass band movement, but American influence seems to have stifled this until relatively recently. Interest in brass bands is enjoying a revival across the Atlantic, and there is now a North American Brass Band Association (NABBA) which, counting a handful of bands from north of its border with Canada, has a membership of around 100 bands. NABBA holds an annual National Championships, and has done so since 1983. Japan now boasts some 20 adult brass bands. There are also many of them in junior high schools, but so far they have held no contests. Inevitably the possibility of a world brass band competition is discussed from time to time, but the cost of world-wide travel for large groups of amateur musicians has so far thwarted any such contest. The most serious attempt took place in Brisbane, Australia in 1988 when, as part of the country's bicentennial celebrations, a so-called World Brass Band Championship was organized. No top British band was present, and the winning band was Göteborg Brass from Sweden.

In Britain the National Brass Band Championships have survived. They take the form of a series of regional knock-out competitions, with the two highest-placed bands in each region joining the previous year's champion and runner-up in the finals in the Royal Albert Hall, London. This event attracts world-wide interest, and a sizeable proportion of the audience is made up of foreign visitors. Bands in lower sections are also catered for by the Nationals, with a series of regional contests run in conjunction with those for championship section bands, but with the finals held in various locations throughout the country.

The Belle Vue showground is no more, though the remnants of its brass band contests have survived in two other events. The September contest has, for some years, been known as the British Open Brass Band Championships; it is an invitation contest featuring what are currently regarded as the top 20 or so bands. The event was held for many years in Manchester's Free Trade Hall, but following its closure, moved to the Bridgewater Hall for the 1996 event. In 1997 it is to be held in Birmingham, in Symphony Hall. The other event, known as the Grand Shield contest (the same shield as was formerly used at Crystal Palace), is held in May as a qualifying contest for the September event, with bands taking the top two places each receiving an invitation to take part in the 'Open'. Though taking the place of the great Spring Festivals held at Belle Vue, it actually assumes the form of the original July contest (see page 57).

Over the past 50 years in Britain, bands have come and gone, their arrival or departure often reflecting the nation's economic booms and slumps. Sponsorship has shifted substantially from industry to commerce, many former works or colliery bands now being subsidized by building societies, insurance companies, breweries, Co-operative Societies and so on. The music played has continued to change and develop in both its popular and serious modes. Though bands survived the Depression, history was to repeat itself after World War II, when the lack of popularity was due largely to the fact that bands relied on much pre-1939 music for their programmes, much of which was regarded by the population at large as old-fashioned. Still, bands struggled on. In the 1960s a key change took place, with a swing from predominantly outdoor concerts to a significant number of indoor events. This was an advantageous move for bands, but it militated further against older music by stimulating a new generation of writers to exploit the new performance conditions. When bands had played almost entirely in the open air, projecting to often very large crowds was the first priority; therefore the doubling, trebling and even quadrupling of parts was standard scoring practice. This also helped smaller bands, because even if not all the parts were being played, it was almost certain that the resultant sound would give a feeling of completeness. The cost of this was, of course, lack of variety of tone-colour, in a type of ensemble which inherently already had a restricted colour range.

Since the early 1960s brass band scoring has been revolutionized. Playing indoors has allowed bands to cultivate their more subdued playing; composers and arrangers have been able to use lighter and more varied textures, have called for the use of a variety of mutes, and extended the range of percussion instruments. Not only have timpani and glockenspiel become standard equipment along with the bass and side drums, cymbals and triangles used almost from the beginning; but also the use of xylophone, vibraphone and tubular bells, bongos, claves, bell trees and a whole range of small instruments has become quite normal. The modern composer or arranger is, therefore, writing for a more sophisticated ensemble than did his predecessors, even though the basic size and playing personnel of the band itself has changed little. Quite apart from shifting tastes, therefore, much of the lack of popularity of music from earlier times is due to developments in scoring, and it is not surprising that only a limited number of pieces have retained their popularity.

According to Scott, Erik Leidzen[1] once described the brass band as the 'Third National Sport', the other two being football and cricket. Scott himself goes on, however, 'But the spirit of banding goes much deeper than winning prizes. It has become a way of life for thousands of working men and their families. And so, hopefully, it shall always be.'[2]

It has, in fact, gone even further. With the encouragement of music in schools, the introduction of brass bands to music festivals, and through their performance of music by leading international contemporary composers as well as more traditional programmes, brass bands have become important for the musical lay person, amateur instrumentalist and professional musician alike.

Vast changes have taken place within the brass band movement since 1936, but the century leading up to that year will surely be seen as the period in which the roots of band music were firmly established – roots from which the modern brass band has flourished to become a musical force throughout the civilized world.

Notes

1 Leidzen (born 1894), was a Swedish composer who settled in the United States, and who was closely associated with Salvation Army music.
2 *Evolution of the Brass Band*, 1970, p. 268.

Appendix 1 – Opera

A summary of the most popular operas from which selections were used in brass band contests in the nineteenth century.

British   Balfe: *The Siege of Rochelle* (London 1835)
The Bohemian Girl (London 1843)
The Bondsman (London 1846)
Satanella (London 1858)
Il Talismano (London 1874, four years after Balfe's death)

Benedict: *The Lily of Killarney* (London 1862)
Goring Thomas: *The Golden Web* (Liverpool 1893)
Macfarren: *Robin Hood* (London 1863)
Wallace: *Maritana* (London 1845)
Lurline (London 1860)
The Amber Witch (London 1861)
Sullivan: *Ivanhoe* (London 1891)

French

Grand opéra:
Auber: *Muette de Portici ('Masaniello')* (Paris 1828, London 1829)
Méhul: *Joseph und seine Brüder* (Paris 1807)
Meyerbeer: *Robert le Diable* (Paris 1831, London 1832)
Les Huguenots (Paris 1836, London 1842)
Le Prophète (Paris 1849, London 1849)
L'Etoile du Nord (Paris 1854)
L'Africaine (Paris 1865, London 1865)

Opéra-comique:
Adam: *La Dame Blanche* (Paris 1825, London 1826)

	Auber:	*Si j'étais roi* (Paris 1852)
		Fra Diavolo (Paris 1830, London 1831)
		The Bronze Horse (Paris 1835)
		Le Domino Noir (Paris 1837)
		The Crown Diamonds (Paris 1841)
	Bizet:	*Carmen* (Paris 1875, London 1878)
	Boieldieu:	*The Caliph of Bagdad* (Paris 1800)
	Gounod:	*La Reine de Saba* (Paris 1862)
		Faust (Paris 1859, London 1863)
		Mirella (Paris 1864, London 1864)
		Roméo et Juliette (Paris 1867, London 1867)
		Cinq-Mars (Paris 1877)
	Hérold:	*Zampa* (Paris 1831)
		Le Pré aux Clercs (Paris 1832)
	Meyerbeer:	*Dinorah* (Paris 1859, London 1859)
	Offenbach:	*Orpheus in the Underworld* (Paris 1858, London 1865)
		The Tales of Hoffmann (Paris 1881, London 1907)
	Thomas:	*Mignon* (Paris 1866, London 1870)
German	Flotow:	*Alessandro Stradella* (Hamburg 1844)
		Martha (Vienna 1847)
	Humperdinck:	*Hänsel und Gretel* (Weimer 1893, London 1894
	Kreutzer:	*Das Nachtlager von Granada* (Vienna 1834)
	Lortzing:	*Zar und Zimmerman* (Leipzig 1837, London 1871)
		Der Wildschütz (Leipzig 1842, London 1895)
		Undine (Magdeburg 1845)
	Nicolai:	*Merry Wives of Windsor* (Berlin 1849, London 1864)
	Spohr:	*Faust* (Prague 1813, London 1852)
		Jessonda (Kassels 1823)
	Wagner:	*Rienzi* (Dresden 1842, London 1879)
		The Flying Dutchman (Dresden 1843, London 1870)
		Tannhäuser (Dresden 1845, London 1876)
		Lohengrin (Weimar 1850, London 1875)
		Tristan and Isolde (Munich 1865, London 1882)
		The Mastersingers (Munich 1868, London 1882)

	Weber:	*The Valkyrie* (Bayreuth 1876, London 1882) *Preciosa* (Berlin, 1821) *Der Freischütz* (Berlin 1821, London 1824) *Euryanthe* (Vienna 1823, London 1833) *Oberon* (London 1826 – English text)
Italian	Bellini:	*Il Pirata* (1827) *La Sonnambula* (Milan 1831, London 1831) *Norma* (Milan 1831, London 1833) *Beatrice di Tenda* (Venice 1833) *I Puritani* (Paris 1835, London 1835)
	Cherubini:	*The Water Carrier* (Paris, 1800)
	Donizetti:	*Anna Bolena* (Milan 1830) *L'Elisir d'Amore* (Milan 1832, London 1836) *Torquato Tasso* (Rome 1833) *Lucrezia Borgia* (Milan 1833, London 1839) *Gemma di Vergy* (Milan 1834) *Lucia di Lammermoor* (Naples 1835, London 1838) *La Fille du Régiment* (Paris 1840, London 1847) *La Favorita* (Paris 1840, London 1843) *Linda di Chamounix* (Vienna 1842, London 1843) *Poliuto* (Naples 1848)
	Mercadante:	*Il Giuramento* (Milan 1837)
	Ricci:	*Crispino e la Comare* (Venice 1850)
	Ponchielli:	*La Gioconda* (Milan 1876)
	Rossini:	*The Italian Girl in Algiers* (Milan 1808, London 1819) *Tancredi* (Venice 1813) *The Barber of Seville* (Rome 1816, London 1818) *La Gazza Ladra* (Milan 1817) *Cinderella (La Cenerentola)* (Rome 1817, London 1820) *Moses in Egypt* (Naples 1818) *Semiramide* (Venice 1823, London 1824) *William Tell* (Paris 1829, London 1830)
	Vaccai:	*Giulietta e Romeo* (Milan 1825)
	Verdi:	*Nabucco* (Milan 1842, London 1846) *I Lombardi* (Milan 1843) *Ernani* (Venice 1844, London 1845)

Attila (Venice 1846)
Luisa Miller (Naples 1849, London 1858)
Stiffelio (Trieste 1850)
Rigoletto (Venice 1851, London 1853)
Il Trovatore (Rome 1853, London 1855)
La Traviata (Venice 1853, London 1856)
Sicilian Vespers (Paris 1855, London 1859)
Aroldo (Rimini 1857)
Un Ballo in Maschera (Rome 1859, London 1861)
La Forza del Destino (St Petersburg 1862, London 1867)
Aida (Cairo 1871, London 1876)

Russian Glinka: *A Life for the Tsar* (St Petersburg 1836)
Russlan and Ludmilla (St Petersburg 1842)
Tchaikovsky: *Eugene Onegin* (Moscow 1879)

Appendix 2 – Band formation (pre-1920 to post-1936)

Soprano cornet (E♭)	1	Tenor trombones (B♭)	2
Cornets (B♭)	8 or 9	Bass trombone (G)	1
Flugelhorn (B♭)	1	EE♭ basses	2
Tenor horns (E♭)	3	BB♭ basses	2
Baritones (B♭)	2	Drums	1 or 2
Euphoniums (B♭)*	1 or 2		

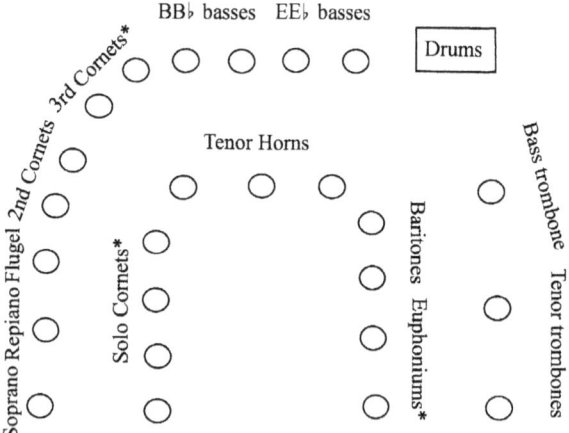

* For contesting purposes bands were restricted to a maximum of 24 players. Most bands carried two euphoniums and one 3rd cornet, but others dispensed with the 2nd euphonium in favour of two 3rd cornets. Some bands carried two of each, dispensing with one of the four solo cornets.

Appendix 3 – Black Dyke part-books

Existing books
Clarinet (D♭ or E♭)
Solo Cornet (A♭ or B♭)
Cornet Secondo (A♭ or B♭)
Fugle Horn [sic] (E♭ or D♭)
Alto Sax Horn (A♭ or B♭)
Tenor Trombone (tenor clef, concert pitch)
Ophicleide (bass clef, concert pitch)
Bass Drum

1	Quick March	
2	Cavatina	
3	Waltz	
4	Polka	
5	Hallelujah Chorus	Handel
6	Aria: Anna Bolena	Donizetti
7	Quadrille: Como	
8	Polka	
9	Cavatina: La Sonnambula	Bellini
10	Death of Nelson	Braham
11	Cavatina: Attila	Verdi
12	Quadrille	
13	Cavatina: Lucrezia Borgia	Donizetti
14	Cavatina: Torquato Tasso	Donizetti
15	Missing	
16	Trio and Coro	
17	Yorkshire Waltz	Enderby Jackson
18	The Heavens Are Telling	Haydn
19	Waltz	
20	Overture	
21	Polka	
22	Gruss an Homburg Waltzes	

23	Overture: Tancredi	Rossini
24	Quadrille: Bonnie Dundee	arr. F Galloway
25	Grand Selection: Norma	Bellini
26	Waltz: Fair Star	
27	Let Their Celestial Concerts	
28	Quadrille	
29	Polka: The Echoes of Mont Blanc	Jullien
30	Grand March	
31	Galop	
32	Quadrille	
33	Grand Selection: Attila	Verdi
34	Waltz	
35	Overture: Magic Flute	Mozart
36	Grand Selection: Linda	Donizetti
37	Grand Scena: Il Trovatore	Verdi
38	Waltz: Mountain Daisy	
39	The Soldier's Polka	
40	Grand Selection: La Traviata	Verdi
41	The Wedding March	Mendelssohn
42	Overture: Caliph of Bagdad	Boieldieu
43	Quadrille: Horton	Jullien

Appendix 4 – Music from Crystal Palace 1860–1863

Full scores

'Volunteer Artillery & Rifle Corps March' composed and arranged Enderby Jackson	26 July 1862
'Hallelujah Chorus' arranged by J Smyth, Bandmaster Royal Artillery, Woolwich	17 July 1862
Grand Waltz, 'Das Musikfest' composed and arranged by Enderby Jackson	14 May 1862
'General Jackson's Schottische' by J W Tidswell[1]	(undated)
'God Save the Queen'	(no date and no arranger named, but probably made for the 1860 event by Jackson)
Grand Selection from '*La Forza del Destino*' Verdi, arranged J Smyth, Bandmaster RA, Woolwich	20 June 1863

Parts

Mendelssohn's 'Wedding March' arranged by Mr Enderby Jackson of Hull	(undated)
'Rule Britannia' arranged by Mr Enderby Jackson of Hull	(undated)
Chorus 'Heavens Are Telling' arranged by Mr Tidswell	(undated)

223

'God Save the Queen' (the parts match the score – see above)

Scores

'Grand Coronation March' by Meyerbeer, arranged by J Smyth, Royal Artillery	(undated)
'Grand Prize Quadrille', 'Crystal Palace Contest, composed and arranged by Enderby Jackson, 21 Prospect St, Hull'	(undated, but instrumentation identical to that of God Save the Queen)
Selection '*Le Prophète*' Meyerbeer, arranged J Smith [*sic*] RA	1862
Selection '*Robert le Diable*' Meyerbeer, arranged for the National Brass Band contest for 1862 by James Smythe [*sic*] RA	(Enderby Jackson 14 August 1862)

Note: The dates, where given, are probably those on which copies of the scores were made. They are all in the same hand – probably Jackson's.

Note

1 According to Taylor (p. 43), a Mr Tidewell 'of the Belle Vue Brass Band, late of Wombwell's Circus band' conducted a massed band of 240 performers following the 1855 Belle Vue contest, and both *Brass Band News* of December 1881 and the *Stalybridge Centenary Booklet* refer to a Mr Tideswell, the former describing him as 'a veteran bandmaster'. In view of the general laxity of name-spelling in band publications of the time, these could all be one and the same person (see note 13, Chapter 4).

Appendix 5 - John Gladney's arrangements

Selections

			Cadenzas	Clefs
1869	Attila	Verdi	1	bass
1869	Lucrezia Borgia	Donizetti	1	treble
1870	Il Flauto Magico	Mozart	0	bass (2 sopranos)
1874	Stiffelio	Verdi	0	tenor/bass
1876	William Tell	Rossini	0	bass
1876	Elijah	Mendelssohn	0	treble
1882	Weber's Works			
1887 (?)	Beethoven (Fantasia) (played by Kingston Mills as 'show piece' after winning at Belle Vue in 1887)		3	treble
Undated	Faust	Gounod	0	treble
Undated	Mendelssohn (Fantasia)		0	tenor/bass
Undated	Meyerbeer's Works			
Undated	Prophète, Le	Meyerbeer	5	modern copy
Undated	Spohr		3	tenor/bass
Undated	Tannhäuser	Wagner	0	bass

Transcriptions

Overture	Egmont	Beethoven
Overture	Son & Stranger (incomplete, and written on R Cocks & Co ms paper)	Mendelssohn
Overture	Libella	Reisiger
Inflamatus	Stabat Mater	Rossini

Aria　　　Il Flauto Magico　　Mozart
(bass trombone solo, accompanied by horns, baritones, euphoniums and basses)

Appendix 6 – Alexander Owen's arrangements and compositions

		Publisher	Date
MARCHES			
Killarney		T A Haigh	1879
Prosper the Art (Masonic March)		W&R	1884
Around the World		Ms	1906
Pelorous Jack		Ms	1910
CONTEST MUSIC			
Operatic selections (etc.)			
Faust	Berlioz	Ms	1888
Faust (Grand Contest Sel No 1)	Berlioz	J Frost	1888
Faust (Grand Contest Sel No 2)	Berlioz	J Frost	1888
William Tell	Rossini	Ms	1895/6
Oberon	Weber	Ms	1898
Walküre, Die	Wagner	Ms	1898
Bohemian Girl, The	Balfe	Musical Mail	1909
Flying Dutchman, The	Wagner	Musical Mail	1909
Huguenots	Meyerbeer	Boosey	1912
Elijah	Mendelssohn	Ms	Undated
Profeta, Il	Meyerbeer	Ms	Undated
St Paul	Mendelssohn	Ms	Undated

228 Appendix 6

Tristan und Isolde	Wagner	Ms	Undated

Composer selections

Auber's Works (Grand Selection)		T A Haigh	1879
Rossini (Reminiscences of/Rossini's Works)		Ms	1882
Heroic (Fantasie)	Weber	Ms	1884
Beethoven's Works		Ms	1887
Weber		Ms	1890
Rossini (Grand Selection)		R Smith	1896

CONCERT MUSIC

Coronation March from Henry VIII	German	R Smith	1901
Judex – solo & chorus	Gounod	R Smith	1901
Richard III (Overture)	German	R Smith	1901
Coronation March	Frederick Bridge	R Smith	1902
Coronation (Grand March)	Percy Godfrey	R Smith	1902
Rosamunde (Overture)	Schubert	R Smith	1902
O Come Let Us Worship	Mendelssohn	Ms	Undated
O Sing Unto the Lord	Bach	Ms	Undated
We Never Bow Down (Chorus)	Handel	Ms	Undated

SOLOS

Grosvenor, The (Polka)	Cornet	W&R	1885
Frascati, Clad With Beauty (Van Bree)	Cornet	R Smith	1902
Hide Thou Thy Hated Beams, and Wafther, Angels - Jephtha (Handel)	Trombone	R Smith	1902
Goodbye Sweetheart (*Air varie*)	Cornet	W&R	Piano – 1912
Mermaid's Song, The (*Air varie*)	Cornet	W&R	Piano – 1912 (arr Hazelgrove)
Angels Guard Thee (Godard)	Trombone	Ms	Undated

Appendix 7 – Henry Round scores at Besses

		Venue	Date
Grand Selection: Rigoletto	Verdi		1881
Grand Selection: Rienzi	Wagner	Trawden	1882
Selection: Un Ballo in Maschera	Verdi	Trawden	1883
Grand Selection: Crispino	Ricci	Manchester	1884
Selection: The Last Judgement	Spohr	Holywell	1884
Grand Selection: Wagner		Colne	1886
Selection: Weber		Edinburgh	1890
Grand Selection: Rossini		Leeds	1891
Selection: Il Giuramento	Mercadante	Portobello	1891
Grand Selection: Mozart			1892
Selection: Marino Faliero	Donizetti	Rothwell	1882
Selection: L'Elisir d'Amore	Donizetti		1894
Grand Selection: Verdi			1892
Grand Selection: Bellini		Blackpool	1894
Selection: Gems of Scotia		Kirkcaldy	1893
Grand Selection: Schubert		Heanor	1895
Selection: William Tell	Rossini		1894
Grand Selection: Halevy		Colne	1896
Selection: Lucrezia Borgia	Donizetti	Southport	1895
Selection: Gems of Victorian Melody			1897
Selection: Lucia di Lammermoor (copied by Thos Valentine)	Donizetti		1899
Selection: Oberon	Weber	Manchester	1900
Selection: Betly	Donizetti		1900
Selection: Belisario	Donizetti	Manchester	1901

Selection: Gems of British Song		Kirkcaldy	1902
Selection: Songs of Ireland		Kirkcaldy	1903
Selection: Anna Bolena	Donizetti	Manchester	1903
Selection: A Casket of Gems		Manchester	1903
Selection: Lortzing			1904
Selection: A Night in Granada	Kreutzer	Manchester	1905
Selection: Gemma di Vergy	Donizetti		1905
Selection: Satanella	Balfe		1906
Selection: A Cluster of Classics		West Australia	1906
Selection: Songs of Sentiment			1913
Selection: Recollections of Carl Rosa		Truro	1900 (or 1914)
Fantasia: Romeo & Juliet	Bellini		1889
Fantasia: Luisa Miller	Verdi		1886
Fantasia: Tam o' Shanter		Kirkcaldy	1895
Fantasia: Eureka		Edinburgh	1896
Fantasia: Rob Roy		Kirkcaldy	1904
Overture: Victory	Round	Blackpool	1887
Overture: Excelsior	Round		1888
Overture: Nil Desperandum	Round	Leicester	1890
Glee: The Forest Queen	Round	Rochdale	1882
Behold & See/Lift Up Your Heads	Handel	Rochdale	1884

Appendix 8 – Wright & Round successful test pieces

The 1896 catalogue showed some of Wright & Round's most popular test pieces, with the number of times each had been chosen. The list is headed:

BRASS BAND CLASSICS

Joan of Arc	56
Maritana	49
Nil Desperandum	45
Excelsior	44
Mario Faliero	41
Victory	39
Pride of Wales	39
Linda di Chamouni [sic]	39
Weber	37
Hours of Beauty	35
Il Guiramento	32
Romeo and Juliet	31
Bohemian Girl	26
Lyric Garland	22
Pride of Ireland	21

Shorter pieces on the list include the following:

Forest Queen	48
Diana	28
Medusa	26
Galatea	25

Pandora	24
The Heavens Are Telling	23

Note: The list is more extensive than this, going down in some cases to single figures. However, the above gives an indication of the success of some of the test pieces published in the *Liverpool Journal*.

Appendix 9 – Original works 1913–1936

Year	Title	Composer	Publisher	Venue
1913	Labour and Love	Percy Fletcher	R S & Co	Crystal Palace
1914	Coriolanus	Cyril Jenkins	R S & Co	Crystal Palace (1920)
1921	Life Divine	Cyril Jenkins	R S & Co	Crystal Palace
1922	Freedom	Hubert Bath	R S & Co	Crystal Palace
1923	Oliver Cromwell	Henry Geehl	R S & Co	Crystal Palace
1923	The Viking	J Weston Nicholl		Halifax
1924	On the Cornish Coast	Henry Geehl	R S & Co	Crystal Palace
1925	Joan of Arc	Denis Wright	R S & Co	Crystal Palace
1925	Macbeth	Thomas Keighley	R S & Co	Belle Vue
1926	An Epic Symphony	Percy Fletcher	R S & Co	Crystal Palace
1926	A Midsummer Night's Dream	Thomas Keighley	R S & Co	Belle Vue
1926	Hanover	Denis Wright	R S & Co	Crystal Palace 1928, Junior Cup
1927	The White Rider	Denis Wright	R S & Co	Crystal Palace
1927	The Merry Wives of Windsor	Thomas Keighley	R S & Co	Belle Vue
1928	A Moorside Suite	Gustav Holst	R S & Co	Crystal Palace
1928	Lorenzo	Thomas Keighley	R S & Co	Belle Vue
1929	Victory	Cyril Jenkins	R S & Co	Crystal Palace

Year	Title	Composer	Publisher	Venue
1929	Zamora	Cyril Jenkins	R S & Co	Crystal Palace 1929, Grand Shield
1930	Severn Suite	Edward Elgar	R S & Co	Crystal Palace
1930	Oriental Rhapsody	Granville Bantock	R S & Co	Belle Vue
1930	Tintagel	Denis Wright	Hawkes	
1931	Honour and Glory	Hubert Bath	R S & Co	Crystal Palace
1931	Springtime	Haydn Morris	R S & Co	Belle Vue
1932	A Downland Suite	John Ireland	R S & Co	Crystal Palace
1932	The Crusaders	Thomas Keighley	R S & Co	Belle Vue
1933	Prometheus Unbound	Granville Bantock	R S & Co	Crystal Palace
1933	Princess Nada	Denis Wright	R S & Co	Belle Vue
1933	Thalassa (The Sea)	Denis Wright	B & H	
1934	Pageantry	Herbert Howells	R S & Co	Belle Vue
1934	Comedy Overture	John Ireland	R S & Co	Crystal Palace
1935	Pride of Race	Kenneth Wright	R S & Co	Crystal Palace
1935	A Northern Rhapsody	Thomas Keighley	R S & Co	Belle Vue
1936	Kenilworth	Arthur Bliss	R S & Co	Crystal Palace
1936	Robin Hood	Henry Geehl	R S & Co	Belle Vue

Glossary of terms

Air varie – a type of solo popular with brass band and other instrumentalists. Basically, it is an air or melody – generally a well-known song or ballad – which appears first in its original form and is then subjected to variations of increasing complexity. Often it has an original introductory section with one or more cadenzas, and is used as a vehicle to display the technical skills of the performer.

Bass horn – not a horn at all but a form of serpent made of brass or copper, but with a 'V'-shaped form and upright bell.

Bombardon – the bass tuba of brass and military bands, generally known today as the 'E♭ bass'.

Cornet à pistons – the French name for cornet, sometimes also used in Britain during the nineteenth century.

Cornett – a Renaissance wind instrument with a brass mouthpiece but calling for the use of woodwind fingering techniques. It should not be confused with the modern cornet.

Cornopean – the name by which the early cornet was known in Britain up to the middle of the nineteenth century.

Crook – a detachable coil of tube which could be inserted into a brass instrument, especially the natural horn, in order to add to its tubular length and hence make a different set of notes available. Crooks were succeeded by valves, though in the nineteenth century they were often used in conjunction with valves.

Descriptive – a name used in connection with a piece of music which describes an event or a scene, for example, *A Military Church Parade* or *The Forge in the Forest*. It may be used by itself or in conjunction with some other musical name, for example, 'descriptive overture'. Popular in the 1920s and 1930s, it often called for 'effects' such as a bird-whistle, a cuckoo or the sound of an anvil. It was usually the percussionist's job to produce these sound effects.

Divisi – when a band part or orchestral part intended for a group of players splits temporarily into two lines, the players themselves dividing into two groups to perform them.

Double- and triple-tonguing – the techniques of tonguing rapidly, which allows a more rapid performance of passages or of repeated notes. When the notes are grouped in twos or fours the syllables *tu-ku-tu-ku* are enunciated, producing 'double-tonguing'; 'triple-tonguing' is used when notes are grouped in threes, in which case the player uses the syllables *tu-tu-ku-tu-tu-ku*.

Euphonium – often described as the 'cello of the brass band', this instrument contributes considerably to the characteristic band sound and ranks second in importance only to the cornet (the 'violin of the brass band'). It succeeded the bass saxhorn though differed little from it, and was developed by Sommer in 1843.

Glissando – the technique of gliding from one note to another. The only instrument in the brass band capable of performing a natural glissando is the trombone. It is achieved by moving the slide, making the tube gradually longer or gradually shorter and thereby lowering or raising the sound of the note through an infinite number of pitches, rather than producing conventional tones and semitones. Players of valve instruments have developed a kind of glissando technique known as 'half-valving'. In this, the valves are pressed only part-way down and the player forces sound out of the instrument, producing a similar effect. Eddie Calvert made this technique famous with his recording of *Cherry Pink and Apple Blossom White*, in the 1950s. (Calvert, as a boy, was a member of Preston Town Silver Band.)

Harmonic series – the series of frequencies of the spectral components of the sound produced when a single note (the 'fundamental') is played. For a cornet, trumpet or flugelhorn, these notes would be as shown in the example, but sounding a tone lower.

The harmonic series

The term is commonly (though incorrectly) applied to the series of notes playable on a bugle, or on any other brass instrument, without changing the length of its tube by means of a valve or a slide.

Hautboy – the English form of the French word *Hautbois*, a name applied to the higher-pitched shawms, and early forms of oboe.

Key bugle – the instrument is also known as the **Kent Bugle** in honour of the Duke of Kent, under whose patronage it was introduced into British military bands.

Keyed bugle – a treble instrument of the ophicleide type, with keys similar to but larger than those used on a clarinet. It was invented by Joseph Halliday, an Irish Bandmaster, originally with five keys, and patented in 1810. More keys were added later.

Massed band – the term applied when two or more bands play together.

Nationalism – a conscious expression of national feeling and a nineteenth-century musical trend marked by the inclusion of such elements as folk song, folk dance or traditional rhythms of a particular country, or musical subjects based on national lifestyles or historical figures.

Ophicleide – the bass member of the keyed bugle family, invented by Halari in Paris in 1817. It had a conical bore and used keys to open or close its quite large tone-holes.

Pedal notes – the fundamentals, or the lowest notes playable with a given tube length. They are not generally considered to be within the normal range of the instrument (except in the case of the ophicleide). The lowest pedal note is, in fact, an octave lower than the lowest note in the example shown under 'Harmonic series'. Trombonists and euphonium players have often used Pedal notes in their solos, and modern composers are increasingly calling for their use.

Quadrille (or Quadrilles) – a short dance, in five 'movements', each with its own quite elaborate steps, danced by four couples in square formation. It was brought to England from Paris circa 1816, and though popular for many years, was eventually superseded by the **Lancers**. Sets of both *Quadrilles* and *Lancers* were often based on popular tunes of the day, or melodies from opera. Each dance was in simple or compound duple time, with regular 4- or 8-bar phrases.

Schottische – a round dance which came to England from Europe in about 1848. Probably not of Scottish descent, it has a strong dotted-quaver-semiquaver rhythm, with four beats to the bar.

Serpent – a wooden instrument with leather binding and with a mouthpiece similar in size to that of the euphonium. It was about eight feet long and acquired its name because of its serpentine shape. Its notes are produced by finger holes along its length – sometimes with keys attached. Its natural scale is B♭.

Triple-tonguing – see 'double- and triple-tonguing'.

Vibrato – an undulation of the pitch of a sound which adds warmth and expression. It is commonly used by singers, string players and oboists, and more rarely by other wind instrumentalists in the symphony orchestra. Many brass band players of the past used the technique indiscriminately and acquired a bad reputation for its misuse. The modern-day brass band player is, however, able to control the vibrato, to play with or without it, and uses it with discretion.

Viol – a family of bowed string instruments, developed in the Renaissance period and superseded by the violin family.

Waits – originally the watchmen who sounded their horns (and other instruments) within walled towns on the hour during the night to let the townspeople know that all was well. From the sixteenth century they began forming themselves into groups – the forerunners of the town band. Amongst the earliest of such groups were those in Bristol, Chester, Norwich and York. The Waits often wore a highly colourful livery or uniform (a further link with bands). Their demise began following the Napoleonic wars and was more or less completed with the advent of the Municipal Reform Act of 1835.

Bibliography

Books

Baines, Anthony (1976), *Brass Instruments*, London: Faber & Faber.
Baillie and Laureen (ed.) (1981), *Catalogue of Printed Music*, Vol. 59, London: British Museum.
Bainbridge, Cyril (1980), *Brass Triumphant*, London: Muller.
Bevan, Clifford (1978), *The Tuba Family*, London: Faber & Faber.
Blom, Eric (ed.) (1954), *Groves Dictionary of Music & Musicians*, 5th ed., London and New York: Macmillan.
Boon, Brindley (1978), *Play the Music Play!*, 2nd ed., London: Salvationist Publishing & Supplies Ltd.
Brand, Violet and Geoffrey (ed.) (1979), *Brass Bands in the 20th Century*, Letchworth: Egon.
Bridges, Glenn D. (1972), *Pioneers in Brass* (special edition), Detroit: Sherwood Publications.
Brown and Stratton (1897), *British Musical Biography*, Birmingham: Stratton.
Burgess, F.D. (1977), *By Royal Command, The Story of Fodens Motor Works Band*, Webberley: Stoke.
Carse, Adam (1951), *The Life of Jullien*, Cambridge: W Heffer & Sons.
Cooke, Kenneth (1950), *The Bandsman's Everything Within*, London: Hinrichsen.
Dudgeon, Ralph T. (1993), *The Keyed Bugle*, Metuchen, NJ and London: The Scarecrow Press.
Evans, V. (compiled) (1992), *Durham County Brass Band League, Golden Jubilee*, Co Durham Books.
Farmer, Henry (1912), *The Rise and Development of Military Music*, London: Reeves.

Gammond and Horricks (ed.) (1980), *Music on Record 1 – Brass Bands*, Cambridge: Stephens.

Gammond, Peter (1991), *The Oxford Companion to Popular Music*, New York: OUP.

Gardiner, William (1838), *Music and Friends Volume 2*, London: Longman Brown and Longman.

Goldman, Richard Franko (1946), *The Concert Band*, New York: Rinehart.

Greenhalgh, Alec (1992), *Hail Smiling Morn*, Oldham Leisure Services.

Hailstone, Alf (1987), *The British Bandsman Centenary Book*, Baldock: Egon.

Hampson, Joseph N. (1893), *Origin, History and Achievements of the Besses o' th' Barn Band*, Northampton: Rogers.

Hardy, Thomas (1993 ed.), *Far from the Madding Crowd*, Ware: Wordsworth Editions Limited.

Herbert, Trevor (1990), *The Repertory of a Victorian Provincial Brass Band*, Popular Music, Volume 9/1.

Herbert, Trevor (ed.) (1991), *Bands – the Brass Band Movement in the 19th & 20th Centuries*, Buckingham: Open University Press.

Hesling White, J.E. (ed. Sowrey, B.G.) (1906), *A Short History of the Bramley Band*, Bramley: Witts.

Horwood, Wally (1980), *Adolphe Sax 1814–1894, His Life and Legacy*, Bramley, Hants: Bramley Books.

Howarth, E. & P. (1988), *What a Performance!*, London: Robson Books.

Jackson, Enderby (undated typescript in author's collection), *Autobiography of Enderby Jackson* (unpublished).

Jacobs, Arthur (1992), *Arthur Sullivan – A Victorian Musician*, 2nd ed., Aldershot: Scolar Press.

Krummel and Sadie (ed.) (1990), *Music Printing and Publishing*, New York: Norton.

Lea, Sidney (ed.) (1912), *Dictionary of National Biography*, London: Smith, Elder & Co.

Leach, Isaac (compiled) (1908), *History of the Bacup Old Band*, Bacup: LJ Priestley (based on 'Reminiscences' which appeared in *Bacup Times* during 1893).

Littlemore, Allan (ed.) (1987), *The Rakeway Brass Band Year Book 1987*, Hollington: Rakeway.

Littlemore, Allan (ed.) (1988), *The Rakeway Brass Band Year Book 1988*, Hollington: Rakeway.

Massey, Ron (1996), *Meltham and Meltham Mills Band 1846–1996*, Meltham: Burnhouse.

Mortimer, Harry (with Alan Lynton) (1981), *Harry Mortimer on Brass*, Sherborne: Alphabooks.

Millington, William (1884), *Sketches of Local Musicians*, Pendlebury.
Newcomb, S.P. (1980), *Challenging Brass*, Takapuna, New Zealand: Powerbrass Music Co.
Newsome, Roy (1995), *Doctor Denis*, Baldock: Egon.
Nicholls, Robert (1989), *Looking Back at Belle Vue, Manchester*, Altrincham: Willow Publishing.
Pearsall, Ronald (1973), *Victorian Popular Music*, Newton Abbot: David & Charles.
Pearsall, Ronald (1975), *Edwardian Popular Music*, Vermont and Vancouver: David & Charles.
Perrins, Barrie (1984), *Brass Band Digest*, Baldock: Egon.
Raistrick, Arthur (1938), *Two Centuries of Industrial Welfare*, London: Friends' Historical Society.
Rehrig, William H. (1991), *The Heritage Encyclopedia of Band Music (Vols 1 & 2)*, Westerville, Ohio: Integrity Press.
Rose, Algernon (c.1895), *Talks With Bandsmen*, London.
Russell, Dave (1987), *Popular Music in England 1840–1914*, Manchester: Manchester University Press.
Russell, J.F. and Elliott, J.H. (1936), *The Brass Band Movement*, London: Dent.
Sadie, Stanley (ed.) (1980), *The New Grove*, London: Macmillan.
Schwarz, H.W. (1957), *Bands of America*, New York: Da Capo Press.
Scott, Jack L. (1970), *The Evolution of the Brass Band and its Repertoire in Northern England*, PhD thesis, Sheffield.
Smith, Norman E. (1986), *March Music Notes*, Louisiana: Program Note Press.
Taylor, Arthur R. (1979), *Brass Bands*, London: Granada Publishing Ltd.
Temperley, Nicholas (ed.) (1981), *The Romantic Age 1800–1914*, London: Athlone Press.
Zealey, A.E. and Ord Hume, J. (ed.) (1926), *Famous Bands of the British Empire*, London: J P Hull.

Booklets (un-named authors)

Amateur Band Teacher's Guide (c. 1889), Liverpool: Wright & Round.
Irwell Springs (Bacup) Band (1914).
Life and Career of the late Mr Edwin Swift (1904), Milnsbridge.
Sketches of Famous Bands (1896), Sibsey: F Richardson.
Stalybridge Old Band 1814–1914, Stalybridge.
St Hilda's Band, Premier Band of England (1935).

Brass band scores

Bantock, Granville (1933), *Prometheus Unbound*, London: R Smith.
Bliss, Arthur (1936), *Kenilworth*, London: R Smith.
Fletcher, Percy (1926), *An Epic Symphony*, London: R Smith.
Geehl, Henry (1923), *Oliver Cromwell*, London: R Smith.
Holst, Gustav (1928), *A Moorside Suite*, London: R Smith
Howells, Herbert (1934), *Pageantry*, London: R Smith.
Ireland, John (1932), *A Downland Suite*, London: R Smith.
Ireland, John (1934), *Comedy*, London: R Smith.
Jenkins, Cyril (1913), *Labour and Love*, London: R Smith.
Jenkins, Cyril (1921), *Life Divine*, London: R Smith.
Keighley, Thomas (1928), *Lorenzo*, London: R Smith.

Other sources

Advertising material in the Ainscoe Collection
Bacup Public Library (census lists)
Belle Vue prizewinners' lists
Besses o' th' Barn Band library
Black Dyke Mills Band library
Brass Band News, from October 1881 to August 1933 (Salford)
Brass Band News, September 1984
British Bandsman, from September 1887 to December 1929 (Beaconsfield)
British Bandsman, 5 September 1987 (Centenary edition)
British Bandsman, 20 May 1995
Crystal Palace contest programmes (Ainscoe Collection)
Crystal Palace entry form 1860 (Black Dike)
Harmonicon, Vol. 1 (1833) (in Henry Watson Library)
Holme Valley Express, 1 March 1919 (in Huddersfield Local Studies Library)
Huddersfield Examiner, 25 February 1919 (in Huddersfield Local Studies Library)
Illustrated News of the World, 3 August 1861 (copy of extracts in author's collection)
Keighley Year Book, 1977 (Keighley Herald – in Keighley Local Studies Library)
Manchester Guardian, The, August and September 1887 (in Manchester Central Library)
Meltham & Meltham Mills Band library
Musical Opinion & Musical Trade Review, 1 July 1896 and 1 September 1896 (in Henry Watson Library)

Musical World, 3 November 1855; 14 July 1860 (in Henry Watson Library)
Sounding Brass, Spring 1972, London: Novello
Times, The, 11 & 12 July 1860 (copy of extract in author's collection)
The Yorkshire Riding, Vol. 4, No. 1, 1967 (in Keighley Local Studies Library)

Index of names and subjects

3rd Liverpool Volunteers, 124
4th Lancashire Rifle Volunteers, 44, 46–7, 71
Accrington Band, 44, 47, 98, 114
Accrington contest, 46, 87
Adam, Adolphe, 164
Adams, Stephen, 20
Agricultural Revolution, 2, 37
Ainscoe collection, 76, 78
Air varie, 19, 235
Allan, George, 100, 137, 153, 156
Alliance Musicale, 95, 105
Almaine, D', 94
Alphonso Carey, 105
Althorn, 96
Alto tuba 95 (see also flugelhorn)
Amateur Brass & Military Band Journal (see T A Haigh)
Amateur Band Teacher's Guide, 101–2, 105
Arban, Jean Batiste, 14
Arditi, Luigi, 16
Artney, D', 75
Auber, 7, 138, 164
Australian Journal, 107

B♭ bass (see basses)
Bacup, 44, 46, 66 note 16, 124
Bacup contest, 50
Bacup Old Band, 44–5, 47–8, 50, 52, 124
Balfe, 8, 16, 138
Ballad, 19, 163, 168–9, 172, 175–6
Ballroom, 163, 170, 175

Bandmaster, 30, 48, 52, 71, 98, 130
Bandstands, 12, 160, 163, 174
Bantock, 10, 117, 201–2, 203
Baritone, 26, 66, 78, 82, 86, 95, 102
Baritone tuba, 95 (see also baritone)
Barn dance, 19, 170
Barnoldswick contest, 55
Bartók, 117
Bary (see baritone)
Bass clarinet, 26
Bass horn, 235
Bass tuba 95 (see also euphonium)
Basses, 25, 52, 85, 91, 95
Bath, Hubert, 128, 185–6
Batley Old Band, 32, 34, 51, 60
Bayreuth, 68 note 39
BBC, 174, 190, 207
BBC Dance Orchestra, 172
Bean Brothers, 5, 29
Beethoven, 7, 13, 65, 76, 138
Belle Vue, 190, 200, 214
Belle Vue contest (July), 43, 57, 122, 124, 128, 132, 134 note 29, 144, 214
Belle Vue contest (May), 57, 132
Belle Vue contest (September), 28, 31–3, 38, 42–5, 47, 49–51, 53–9, 65–6, 67 note 25, 83–4, 86, 96, 98, 110–11, 119, 122–32, 139, 144, 152, 158, 185, 189, 193, 196, 199, 201, 206, 210
Bellini, 7, 17
Benedict, 16
Berg, 117

Berlin, Irving, 172
Berlioz, 26
Berry, Fred, 128, 134 note 29
Besses o' th' Barn Band, 2, 5 note 4, 13, 30, 53, 54, 57, 60–1, 64, 66, 79–80, 87–8, 109, 111, 119–22, 124, 128–9, 138, 144–5, 212
Besson & Co, 48, 60
Beswick, J W, 120
Birkinshaw, Fred, 51, 60
Birmingham, 52, 64
Birmingham contest, 35
Birmingham Daily Post, 64
Bishop, Henry, 8
Bizet, 8
Black Dyke (Dike), 2, 3, 30, 33–4, 39, 44–5, 47, 50–4, 57, 62–3, 65, 67–8, 72–3, 75, 79–80, 83, 85–7, 89–90, 111, 119–20, 122–3, 125–6, 128–9, 132
Blackpool contest, 58–9, 141
Blaina Band, 5
Bliss, 117, 205–7
Boarshurst Band, 62
Boer War, 118–9, 124
Boieldieu, 7, 164
Bombardon, 25, 83, 235
Boosé's Journal, 94, 152, 154, 173
Boosé, Carl, 41, 94
Boosey & Hawkes, 12, 28, 93, 95–6, 152, 173
Boosey's Journals, 40, 68, 94, 169
Boosey, Thomas, 95
Booth, Bramwell, 112
Border Rifles Band, 40
Boston contest, 35
Bosworth & Co, 112, 155, 175
Bournemouth, 200
Bournemouth Symphony Orchestra, 12, 176
Bower family (Black Dyke), 52
Bowley, Mr, 41
Bradford contest, 58
Brahms, 7, 118
Bramley Old/Temperance Band, 4, 40–1, 64
Brass & reed band, 31, 95, 101, 106, 108, 122
Brass band, 5, 12, 15, 20–1, 24, 27–30, 32, 43, 62, 75, 80, 83, 103, 106, 132, 172, 200

Brass Band Annual, 107
Brass Band News, 9, 105, 110, 137
Brass quartet, 20
Bridlington, 64
Brighouse and Rastrick Band, 128–9, 131
Bristol contest, 35
Britannia Building Society 125, (see also Fodens)
British Bandsman, 9, 65, 110, 119, 137, 152
British Bandsman & Orchestral Times, 154, 189, 201
British Musician, The, 111
British Open Championships, 31, 214
Broadclough Band, 44
Brocklesby Yeomanry Band, 28
Brook, Jonas and Brothers, 49
Bruckner, 116
Bugle (see Keyed bugle)
Burnley Band, 98
Burnley Volunteers Band, 49
Burton Constable, 12, 28–30, 35
Buslingthorpe Band, 34
Butt, Clara, 20, 120

Cadenzas, 78, 85–6, 140, 143, 145, 175
Cake-walk, 170
Callender's Cable Works Band, 201
Calverley Band, 64
Campbell Connelly & Co, 175
Carlisle St Stephen's Band, 198, 201
Carr, George, 84
Cavatina, 73
Cerveny, 25
Challenge Journal (see J R Lafleur & Sons)
Chambers, W Paris, 123
Champion Brass Band Contest, 61
Champion Brass Band Journal (see R Smith & Co)
Chappell, 12, 84, 93
Chappell Brass Band Journal, 95, 155, 173–4
Charleston, 170
Cherubini, 7
Chester-le-Street Journal, 107
Chesterfield Band, 39, 46
Chopin, 7, 116
Choral societies, 20–21
Christy Minstrels, 113 note 18
Church Band, 47

Church bands, 18
Church, John, 107
Clay Cross Band, 46
Clayton-le-Moors Band, 47, 54
Clefs, 72, 77, 82–3, 85–6, 138, 145, 160 note 7
Clegg family, 3
Clegg's Reed Band, 2, 13–14
Clydebank Burgh Band, 158
Coates, Eric, 176, 177 note 17
Cocks, R & Co, 93–4
Colne Band, 47
Colne contest, 58
Comettant, Oscar, 27
Constable, Sir Clifford, 28
Contest Field, The, 111, 152
Contrabass(o) (see basses)
Cooke, T S, 91 note 30
Cope, Sam, 9, 108, 110, 122, 137, 154
Cornet, 23, 80, 94
Cornet Journal (see F Richardson)
Cornet, The, 52
Cornet-à-pistons, 13, 24, 235
Cornholme Band, 53
Corni (see French horn)
Cornopean, 6, 235
Courtois Union Band, 84, 91 note 27
Coxlodge & Hazelrigg Band, 3
Crawshay, Robert, 31, 75
Cremorne Gardens contest, 40, 41
Cresswell Colliery Band, 132, 159
Crooks, 23, 235
Crooner, The
Crotch, William, 8
Crowe, A G, 46
Crystal Palace, 8, 17, 51, 57, 97, 119–20, 123, 155, 165, 182, 200, 208
Crystal Palace Band, 155
Crystal Palace contest, 31, 38, 40–2, 44, 53, 59, 65–6, 75–6, 79, 81, 84, 94–6, 124, 126–30, 132, 154, 158, 185–6, 189, 191, 196 (see also National Brass Band Championships)
Curwen, John, 18
Cyfarthfa Band, 31, 38–9, 75–6

Daily Express, 122
Daily Gazette, 64
Daily Mail, 119
Daily Mail (Birmingham), 64
Daily Telegraph, 60, 122
Dalton, James, 29

Dance band, 172
Darlington Band, 39
Darlington contest, 35
Debussy, 117
Delius, 117
Denham, Frank, 174
Dennison, John, 127
Denton Original Band, 120–1
Depression, 128, 132, 160, 214
Dewsbury Band, 32, 39
Distin family, 14, 27–8, 112
Distin's Brass Band Journal, 95
Distin, Henry, 27–8, 78, 94
Distin, John, 27
Dobcross Band, 99
Doncaster contest, 35
Donizetti, 7, 17, 43, 88, 138
Double championship, 122, 124, 126, 128
Double-tonguing, 74, 191, 236
Douglas, Shipley, 122, 137, 154, 156
Dowlingate, Mr, 32
Droylsden Reed Band, 43
Drum & fife band, 104
Drums, 83, 86, 140, 186, 215
Duc E & F le, 148–50
Durham contest, 53

E♭ bass (see basses)
Eclipse Journal, 106, 115
Eden, Hiram, 149–50
Edinburgh Exhibition, 62
Elgar, 117–18, 198–201, 203
Ellis, George, 44, 47, 71
Ellwood, John, 32
Elworth Band, 125
Embach, 5
Embury, T E, 109
Enschall, 102–3
Enterprise Band Books, 103–4, 106
Euphonium, 25, 82, 86, 88, 95, 236
European Brass Band Championships, 213

Fairey Aviation Works Band, 213
Fantasia, 139, 142–3, 149, 157, 191
Farmer, Henry, 41
Fawcett, Joseph, 54
Feldman, 112, 155, 173–5
Fletcher, Percy E, 150, 167, 179
Floral Dance, 128, 134 note 28
Flotow, 7

Flugelhorn, ix, 24, 80–1, 85–8, 95, 138
Foden, Edwin, 125
Fodens (Motor Works) Band, 123–6, 128–31, 186, 212
'Follow the Fleet', 172
Foster, John, 30, 31, 75
Foxtrot, 170
Francis, Day (& Hunter), 107, 175
French horn, 6, 81–2, 84
Friml, Rudolph, 165
Frost, G A, 100, 107, 136, 144
Frost, J & Son, 99–100, 107, 144, 154
Frost, James, 100, 107, 114 note 31, 136, 143–4
Fry family, 112

Galashiels Band, 61
Galloway, Frank/James/John, 30, 73, 90 note 7
Galop, 11
Geehl, Henry, 137, 187, 199
German, Edward, 120–1, 165
German, Thomas, 57
German, William, 152
Gershwin, George/Ira, 172
Gilbert and Sullivan, 10, 16, 18, 63–4, 76, 125, 165
Gilbert, W S, 17, 119
Gilmore, Patrick, 35 note 2, 42, 64
Gladney, John, 15, 48–55, 57, 60, 63, 65, 67 note 25, 81, 83–9, 98, 123, 129, 131, 135–6, 139
Gladney, John (Sr), 46
Glasgow Exhibition, 61
Glee, 20
Glinka, 7, 116
Glossop Volunteers Band, 57
Gluck, 17
Godfrey, Charles (Jr), 15, 21 note 27, 41, 43–4, 56, 62, 76, 98, 105, 136, 39, 144–6, 199
Godfrey, Charles (Sr), 21 note 7, 41, 76
Godfrey, Dan, 21 note 7, 176, 200
Godfrey, Dan (Jr), 12, 16, 22 note 7, 176, 201
Godfrey, Fred, 21 note 7
Gold Diggers of 1933, 172
Gold Diggers of Broadway, 173
Goose Eye & Newsholme Band, 96–7
Goose Eye band books, 96–7, 114 note 21, 144, 153
Gossages Soap Works Band, 131

Göteborg Brass, 213
Gounod, Charles, 7, 18, 43, 138
Grand opera, 18
Grand selection, 139–40
Grantham contest, 35
Gray, Frank, 40–1, 66 note 5, 78
Great Industrial Exhibition, 14, 31
Great Triumvirate, 48, 50, 52–4, 67 note 25, 111
Greenwood, John A, 127, 131–2, 136–7, 156–7, 199, 200
Gregson, Edward, 117
Grieg, 8, 116
Groenings, Franz, 61, 68 note 53
Grosse, Herr, 43, 83, 85, 98, 135
Grove, George, 8, 117
Gungl, Josef, 11
GUS (see Munn & Feltons)

Haigh, T A, 99–100, 107, 136, 143–4, 147, 149, 151, 153–4
Haliday, Joseph, 4, 6 note 13
Halifax contest, 186
Hall, B, 109
Hall, Henry, 172
Hall, Richard, 29
Hallé Orchestra, 43, 49, 57
Halliwell, William, 123–4, 126–32, 187
Hampson, Joseph N, 89
Handel, 8
Hanley Mission Band, 58
Hardman, Daniel, 5
Harmonic series, 23–4, 236
Hartlepool Borough Band, 122
Hartmann, Ernest, 155
Hartmann, John, 76, 120, 137, 155–6
Harton Colliery Band, 158
Hat-trick, 47, 51, 54, 67, 128, 130
Hawes contest, 8
Hawkes & Son, 95, 106, 147, 151–2, 155
Hawkes, Oliver, 95
Hawkes, W H, 95–6
Hawkins, George, 137, 157–8
Haydn, 76
Hebburn Colliery Band, 157
Hebden Bridge Band, 123, 129–30
Helicon, 26
Her Majesty's Private Band, 59
Herbert, Victor, 165–6
Hérold, 164
Hesling, William, 34

Index of names and subjects   249

Heywood Rifles Band, 57
Holden, Angus, 123
Holmes Hull Tannery Band, 28–9
Holst, 117, 197–8, 201, 205
Horn (see French horn)
Horwich RMI Band, 132
Howells, 117, 205–6
Hucknall Huthwaite Band, 120
Hughes, Samuel, 4, 6 note 15, 84
Hull contest, 33, 37 note 35, 73–4
Hull Flax and Cotton Mills Band, 29
Hullah, John Pyke, 18
Hyde British Legion Band, 67 note 34
Hyde contest, 55

Iles, John Henry, 51, 65–6, 109, 111, 119–20, 146, 152, 154, 156, 178, 182, 189–190, 196, 201, 205, 208
Illustrated News of the World, 108
Illustrated Sporting & Dramatic News, 60
Impressionism, 117
Industrial Revolution, 2
Intercontinental Brass & Military Band Journal, 107
Ipswich contest, 35
Ireland, John, 117, 203–5
Irish Exhibition contest, 59
Irwell Springs Band, 121, 123–6, 129

Jackson, B D, 60
Jackson, Ceres, 51
Jackson, Enderby, 13, 15, 29–31, 33–5, 38, 41–2, 65, 66 note 10, 70–1, 77
James Bagnall's Iron Works Band, 39
Jazz, 160, 170
Jazz Singer, The, 167
Jeffery, Charles, 63–4
Jenkins, Cyril, 150, 182, 185
Jennison, John/James, 33, 56, 85, 190
Jolson, Al, 167, 173
Jones, J Sidney, 21 note 4, 96, 115 note 34, 176
Jones, Sidney, 10, 21 note 4, 105
Jubb, John/Joseph, 137, 154
Jubilee Contest, 58
Jullien, 13–15, 28, 30, 43, 49, 76

Kappey, J A, 68 note 49
Keighley, 62, 96
Keighley contest, 53
Keighley, Thomas, 55, 68 note 46, 191, 205

Keith Prowse & Co, 112, 173, 175
Kendall, Ned, 35 note 2
Kent bugle (see keyed bugle)
Kerker, Gustav, 166
Kern, Jerome, 172
Kettering Rifles Band, 101
Kettlewell, F, 121
Keyed bugle, 23–4, 27, 94, 237
Keyed trumpet, 23
Kidsgrove contest, 53
Kiefert, Carl, 120–1
Kingston Mills Band, 51, 55, 61, 67 note 34, 122
Kipling Fund, 119
Kirkcaldy contest, 142
Koenig, Adolphe, 41
Koenig, Hermann, 13–15

Lacy, R de (see *London Brass Journal*)
Lafleur, J R & Sons, 107
Lafleur, René, 95
Lancers, 170
Lanner, Joseph, 11
Laurent, Michael, 148
Leader, 30, 40, 44, 48, 50, 80
Lee Mount Band, 121
Leeds contest, 35, 58
Leeds Forge Band, 60–1, 63
Leeds Joppa Band, 34
Leeds Railway Foundry Band, 34
Leeds Smith's Band, 34
Leeds Temperance Band, 71
Lehár, 164–5
Leicester contest, 35
Leicester Imperial Band, 122
Leng, George, 41
Levy, Jules, 76, 90 note 10
Limerick National Band, 60
Lincoln contest, 35
Lindley Band, 51, 152
Linter, Frank, 102–3, 137, 153
Linthwaite Band, 52–3, 62–3, 87–8, 122
Liszt, 116, 118, 179–82
Liverpool, 63
Liverpool contest, 35, 44, 58, 139
Liverpool Journal (see Wright & Round)
Livesy, Mr, 39
Loftus contest, 58
London & Home Counties Band Association, 65
London Brass Journal, 105, 144, 154
London Graphic, 122

Index of names and subjects

London Lead Company, 3
London N W Carriage Works Band, 125
Longbottom, Samuel, 31, 34, 39, 79, 91 note 17
Lord family (Bacup), 45, 47
Lortzing, 7, 17, 43
Luddites, 2
Luton Red Cross Band, 129–30

MacFarlane, George, 93, 113 note 2
Macfarren, George, 16
Mahillon, C, 105
Mahler, 116
Manchester Brass & Military Band Journal (see J Frost & Son)
Manchester Exhibition, 62–3, 68 notes 56 and 58
Manns, August, 155, 201
March, 105, 151, 156, 170, 175
Marriner's Band, 64, 96, 113 note 15
Marsden Colliery Band, 132, 158
Massed bands, 119, 122, 237
Matlock Band, 46
Maybrick, Michael (see Stephen Adams)
Melling, James A, 31, 138
Meltham & Meltham Mills Band, 84
Meltham Mills Band, 39, 49–51, 53–4, 67, 80, 86–8, 98
Mendelssohn, 7
Mercadante, 43, 138
Merthyr Tydfil, 31, 75–6
Metzler Military & Brass Band Journal, 105
Meyerbeer, 7, 18, 26–7, 42–3
Middleton contest, 58
Milerean Edition, 107
Military bands, 2, 12, 25, 35 note 3, 82, 179, 201
Millars, Haydn, 41
Milnrow Public Band, 132
Modes, 197, 206, 208, 210 note 13
Monckton, Lionel, 167
Monstre double B, 83, 91, 102
Montgomery, 113 note 17
Moritz, Wilhelm, 25
Mortimer family, 129–31
Moss, Harold, 137, 159
Mossley Band, 53, 55, 68
Mossley Temperance Band, 28, 31–2
Mozart, 17, 43, 76
Munn and Feltons Works Band, 129, 131, 134 note 34

Musard, Philippe, 12–14
Musical, 167–8, 174
Musical comedy, 10–11, 62, 136, 163, 166–7, 169, 174–5
Musical Progress, The, 95
Musical Times, 9, 96, 189
Mussorgsky, 8

National Brass Band Championships, 17, 51, 80, 109, 113, 118–9, 120–4, 126, 130, 150, 152, 178, 186–7, 189, 193, 199–200, 209, 213–14 (see also Crystal Palace contest)
National Brass Band Contest, 33
Nationalism, 116–7, 237
Nelson contest, 46, 53, 58
Nenthead, 3
Neo-classicism, 117
New Brighton contest, 58
New Brighton Tower Band, 131, 200
New Mills Old Band, 3
New Shildon Saxhorn Band, 153
New York, 15
New Zealand, 42, 66 note 11
Newcastle contest, 201
Newcastle Exhibition, 62–3
Newton, Edward, 97, 108, 114 note 20, 137, 153
Nicholls, Horatio, 169, 172
Nicolai, 7
Norland contest, 55
North American Brass Band Association, 213
Northampton contest, 35
Northern Journal, 107, 144, 147, 154
Norwich contest, 35
Novello, 9, 12, 93
Novello, Ivor, 172

Offenbach, 7, 125, 164
Oldham Rifles Band, 55, 60–1, 63
Oliver, James, 127–8
One-step, 170
Opera, 43
Opéra-comique, 18
Operetta, 164–7, 172, 174–5
Ophicleide, 13, 83, 237
Orchestral Times and Bandsman, 111
Ord Hume, James, 71, 100, 106–8, 111, 119–21, 136–7, 146, 151, 153, 156, 173–4, 176
Ord Hume, John, 107, 137, 155–6

Original work, 135, 150, 160
Overture, 141–2, 149, 157, 164, 175, 183, 187, 189, 191
Owen, Alexander, 48–50, 53–7, 60, 65, 67 note 25, 80–1, 84, 88–9, 121, 123, 131, 135–6, 165

Paley, John, 51, 63–4
Pamer, Michael, 11
Parc and Dare Workmen's Band, 158
Parry J (Denbigh), 94
Parry, Hubert, 9, 117
Parry, Joseph, 76
Patrington Band, 29
Payne, Jack, 172
Pearce, C W, 120
Peel, J, 39
Pemberton Old Band, 51
Percussion (see drums)
Perfection Soap Works Band, 123, 129
Périnet, Etienne F, 24
Perry, George, 39, 66 note 3
Peterborough contest, 35
Peterloo Massacre, 2
Phasey, Alfred J, 4, 6 note 15, 25, 46
Phaseyophone, 25
Piccolo cornet, 95 (see also soprano cornet)
Piddletown (Puddletown) Brass Band, 3
Pinches, Harold, 158
Piston 83–4 (see also cornet)
Polka, 11, 141, 170
Posthorn, 24
Professional conductor, 48, 54, 124, 127–9, 131, 157
Promenade concerts, 12–14, 28
Purcell, Henry, 8, 117

Quadrille band, 11, 30
Quadrille(s), 11–12, 170, 237
Queensbury, 30, 199
Queensbury contest, 55
Queenshead, 30, 75
Queenshead Band, 31
Quickstep, 170, 177 note 10

Ragtime, 163, 171
Raine, George, 88
Ramsbottom Rifles Band, 47
Raymond, W, 148
Reading Temperance Band, 122
Repiano cornet, 80, 138

Reynolds, W, 121
Richardson, F & Co, 9, 93, 107, 144, 147–8, 150–1, 153–5, 157–8
Rigid Containers Group Band (see Munn & Feltons)
Rimmer, Robert, 106, 123–4
Rimmer, Thomas, 123–4
Rimmer, William, 107, 123–6, 129–32, 136–7, 143, 146–51, 153, 156, 158
Rimsky-Korsakov, 8
Rivière & Hawkes, 16, 76, 95, 105
Rivière & Lafleur, 95, 107
Rivière, Jules, 22 note 17, 95, 113, 136, 143
Robinson, Stanford, 176
Rochdale contest, 58, 62
Roche, W, 148
Rodgers, Richard, 172
Rogan, J M, 121
Romberg, Sigmund, 166
Rossini, 7, 17, 43, 138
Round, Enoch, 9, 101
Round, Henry, 101–3, 124, 131, 136–40, 142–4, 150, 153, 191
Royal Academy of Music, 9, 185
Royal Albert Hall, 16, 119–20, 209, 213
Royle, W, 148
Rubens, Paul, 169
Rudall, Carte & Co, 107
Rudall, Rose & Carte, 28
Rumigny, Lt-Gen, 26
Rushden Temperance Band, 60

Saddleworth, 114 note 27
Salisbury, 112
Salt, Titus, 31
Saltaire Band, 31, 39, 64
Saltaire Exhibition, 62–3
Salvation Army, 111
Salvation Army bands, 112, 213
Salvation Army General Band Book, 112
Sandbach Volunteers Band, 125
Sanderson, Wilfrid, 169
Sax, Adolphe, 26–8, 95
Sax, Charles, 26
Saxhorn, 14, 26, 28, 72, 82, 95
Saxhorn – alto/baritone/soprano, 26
Saxhorn – bass, 25–6, 29, 83, 85
Saxhorn – tenor, 25–6, 29, 81
Saxophone, 26
Scarborough, 71
Scarborough Spa Band, 49

Schoenberg, 117
Schottische, 78, 170, 237
Schubert, 7, 138
Schumann, 7
Scotch contest, 61
Scottish Band Journal, 159
Scottish CWS Band, 158
Seddon, William, 101
Selection, 39, 42, 44, 73, 94, 135–6, 138–40, 142–3, 145–6, 150, 157–8, 164–9, 174, 191
Serpent, 82, 237
Shaw Band, 123, 126–6
Sheffield contest, 58, 63–4
Shepherd, J O, 120
Short, William, 59, 68 note 50
Sibelius, 116
Silver bands, 127, 134 note 25
Silvester, Victor, 172
Skinningrove Miners' Band, 157
Skipton contest, 45–6
Slide trumpet, 23
Slow foxtrot, 170
Smetana, 116
Smith's (Leeds) Band (see Leeds Smith's)
Smith, R & Co, 34, 65, 71, 86, 93, 95, 97, 99, 108–9, 111, 119, 144, 148, 150, 154, 201
Smith, Richard, 34, 39, 71, 82, 95, 97, 99–100, 108, 136, 143–4, 152–3
Smyth, James, 14, 76–8, 90 note 11
Sommer, 25
Soprano cornet, 24, 26, 79–80, 86, 95
Sousa, 165
Southern, James, 127
Southport Rifles Band, 123–4, 131, 158
Spohr, 7, 43, 65, 138–9
Squire, W H, 169
St Hilda (Colliery) Band, 123, 126, 127–30, 132, 158, 187, 212
St Joseph's School Orpington, 123
Stalybridge Borough Band, 54, 60
Stalybridge Old Band, 3, 30, 48, 54, 79
Stanford, C V, 9, 117
Stead, Edwin, 50–1, 67 note 32
Stead, James/Wright, 50
Stead, Richard, 50, 67 note 32, 68, 98
Stonewall Jackson, 78
Strauss, Johann (Jr), 7, 11, 76, 125, 164
Strauss, Johann (Sr), 7, 11, 13–14
Strauss, Richard, 116

Stravinsky, 117
Strutt, George & Joseph, 3
Stuart, Leslie, 167
Sullivan, Arthur, 8, 16–17, 65, 109, 119–20
Suppé, 164
Sutton, Edward, 137, 158–9
Swift, Edwin, 48, 52, 53, 55, 57, 60, 67 note 25, 84, 87–9, 100, 123, 135–6
Swift, Fred/Lawrence, 53
Symphonic poem, 141–2, 179, 182

Tango, 170
Tchaikovsky, 8
Tenor horn, 26, 77, 81, 86–7, 95
Ternent, Billy, 172
Thematic transformation, 179
Tidswell/Tideswell/Tidewell, 91 note 13, 97
Timpani (Tymp), 88
Todmorden contest, 46
Tone poem, 179, 183, 191
Tonic Sol-fa, 18
Top Hat, 172
Tosti, Paula, 169
Tours, 122, 127–8, 212–3
Trawden Band, 45
Trawden contest, 58
Trimnell, Thomas Tallis, 31
Triple-tonguing, 11, 74, 191, 236
Trombone, 4, 6 note 14, 25, 52, 67 note 18, 82
Trombone – alto, 25, 78
Trombone – bass, 25, 78, 82, 84, 86, 91 note 21
Trombone – tenor, 25, 78, 82, 86, 138
Trombone – valved, 25, 36 note 5, 82
Trumpet, 35
Tuba 25 (see also bombardon and basses)
Turpin, H, 121
Two-step, 170

University of Aberystwith, 76

Vaccai (Vaccaj), 34, 37 note 36
Valentine, Thomas, 109
Valse, (see waltz)
Valsette (see waltz)
Valve, 5, 24, 26, 50
Varsoviana, 113 note 17
Vaughan Williams, 117

Index of names and subjects   253

Verdi, 7, 17, 42–3, 73, 116, 138
Verner, Eugene, 149
Victorian Era contest, 59
Volunteers, 47, 54

Wadsworth, George, 137, 154
Wagner, Richard, 7, 16–7, 53, 65, 73, 88, 138
Waits, 238
Waldteufel, Emil, 11
Walker, James, 5, 29
Wallace, John, 76, 138
Wallace, Vincent, 8, 16
Waltz, 11, 141, 157, 170, 172
Waterson, James, 43, 84–5, 91, 98, 135
Weatherbury Band, 3
Weatherly, Frederic E, 20, 22 note 22, 169
Weber, 7, 17, 43, 88, 138
Webern, 117
Wembley Park contest, 59
Wessel & Co, 94, 113 note 6
Weston Nicholl, J, 186
Wharton's Reed Band, 2, 3, 30
Wheelock Temperance Band, 125
Whit Friday, 99, 114 note 28
Whiteley, Herbert, 178, 187
Wieprecht, Wilhelm, 26
Willcocks, W J & Co, 105
Williams, W (Alfreton), 109

Williams, Warwick, 46, 106, 115 note 40, 137, 155
Wingates Temperance Band, 121, 124–6, 129, 159
Winterbottom St Martin Band, 3
Winterbottom, John, 15, 22 note 13
Winterbottom, William, 15, 22 note 13, 43–4, 46, 98
Wold Brass, 92
Wombwell's Band, 44, 71
Wombwell, George, 66 note 13
Wood, Arthur, 176
Wood, Haydn, 169, 176
Wood, Henry J, 13, 16,
World Brass Band Championships, 213
Wright & Round, 9, 93, 99–104, 106, 109, 112, 137, 143, 147–51, 153–5, 157
Wright, Denis, 137, 189, 209 note 11
Wright, Frank, 128, 176
Wright, Kenneth A, 206
Wright, Lawrence, 111, 169, 173
Wright, Thomas H, 101–2, 136, 143, 153
Wyke Old Band, 60–1
Wyke Temperance Band, 53–4, 60–1, 63, 87, 119, 122, 129

Yeadon Old Band, 40
York Waits, 5

Index of titles of music referred to in text

(NB: titles often occur in different languages. Here they are shown in the one most commonly used in the book.)

Adam, Adolphe
  If I were King, 164
Adams, Stephen
  Holy City, The, 20
  Star of Bethlehem, The, 20
Allan, George
  Battle Abbey, 153
  Knight Templar, 153
  Raby, 153
  Senator, 153
Allettèr
  Rendez vous, 176
Ancliffe, Charles
  Nights of Gladness, 11
Appoloni
  L'Ebreo, 51
Asche
  Caravanne, La, 105
Ascher, Joseph
  Alice where art thou? 168
Auber, Daniel
  Bronze Horse, The, 164
  Crown Diamonds, The, 157
  Domino Noir, Le, 164
  Masaniello, 96, 164
  Muette de Portici, 43, 44
  Niege, La, 47
  Reminiscences of Auber, 42–3, 45

Balfe, Michael W
  Bohemian Girl, The, 8, 16
  Bondsman, The, 39
  Killarney, 19
  Satanella, 43
  Talismano, Il, 43, 51
Ball, Ernest
  Mother Machree, 168
  When Irish eyes are smiling, 168
Bantock, Sir Granville
  Festival March, 200
  Lalla Rookh, 200
  King Lear, 200
  Kubla Khan, 200
  Oriental Rhapsody, 200
  Prometheus Unbound, 200–1, 211
    note 21
Bath, Hubert
  Cornish Rhapsody, 185
  Freedom, 186, 191
  Honour and Glory, 186
Baynes, Sydney
  Destiny, 11
Beethoven, Ludwig van
  Beethoven (arr Gladney), 87
  Beethoven's Works (arr Owen), 55, 88
  C minor Symphony, 64
  Egmont, 87

Beethoven *cont.*
　Eroica (arr Rimmer), 149
　Fidelio, 17
　Hallelujah to the Father, 47
　Pastoral Symphony, 14
Bellini, Vincenzo
　Norma, 13, 73
　Pirata, Il, 34
　Puritani, I, 14
　Sonnambula, La, 73
　Suona la Tromba, 14
Bemberg
　Elaine, 42, 51
Benedict, Julius
　Lily of Killarney, The, 16
　Moon Hath Raised Her Lamp, The, 176
Berlin, Irving
　Easter Parade, 174
　Pretty girl is like a melody, A, 174
Berlioz, Hector
　Berlioz (arr Rimmer), 150
　Faust, 53, 54, 88
Benatzky, Ralph
　White Horse Inn, The, 166
Bernstein, Leonard
　West Side Story, 174
Bishop, Sir Henry
　Home Sweet Home, 19
　My Pretty Jane, 19
　Selection of Sir Henry Bishop's Works, 20
　Slave, The, 122
Bizet, Georges
　Bizet (arr Rimmer), 150
　Carmen, 150
Bliss, Sir Arthur
　Belmont Variations, 210 note 28
　Kenilworth, 205, 206–9, 211 note 31
　Morning Heroes, 206
　Things to Come, 206
Boccherini, Luigi
　Minuet, 158
Boieldieu, François
　Caliph of Bagdad, The, 73, 164
　Dame Blanche, La, 164
Brahe, May H
　Bless this House, 169
Brooks
　Through Verdant Plains, 103

Bruckner, Anton
　Germanenzug, 133 note 1

Chambers, W Paris
　Amiciaza, 123
Chopin, Fryderyk
　Gems of Chopin, 123
Churchill, Frank
　Snow White and the Seven Dwarfs, 174
Clay, Frederic
　I'll sing Thee Songs of Araby, 19
Coates, Eric
　Knightsbridge, 176
　London Bridge, 176
Colcord
　Stein Song, 172
Coleridge Taylor
　Hiawatha, 121, 133 note 12
Cooke
　Seasons, The (Glee), 87
Cope, Sam
　Mill in the Dale, The, 154
　Sailor's Life, A, 154
Coward, Noel
　Bitter Suite, 167
　Cavalcade, 167
Cowen, Frederic
　The Better Land, 168
Crotch, Dr William
　Palestine, 8

Danks, Hart P
　Silver Threads Amongst the Gold, 20
Dawson
　Druid's Prayer, The, 176
Delannoy
　Leopold (arr R Smith) 144
Dix, J Airlie
　Trumpeter, The, 169
Donizetti, Gaetano
　Anna Bolena, 73
　Elisir d'Amore, L', 94
　Favorite, La, 47, 51, 67 note 22
　Gemma di Vergy, 144
　Linda di Chamounix, 73
　Lucia di Lammermoor, 34
　Lucrezia Borgia, 39, 50, 73, 85–7, 96
　Memories of Donizetti (arr Rimmer), 150

Index of music titles

Donizetti *cont.*
  Reminiscences of Donizetti (arr R Smith), 144
  Torquato Tasso, 73, 109
Douglas, Shipley
  Mephistopheles, 155
  Peace and War, 155
  Three Blind Mice, 154
Duc, E le
  In Days of Old, 150
  O'er Hill and Dale, 150

Eden, Hiram
  Pat in America, 150
Elgar, Sir Edward
  Caractacus, 51, 199
  Chanson de matin, 175
  Chanson de nuit, 175
  Enigma Variations, 118
  Gerontius, 200
  Organ Sonata No 2, 204
  Pomp & Circumstance Nos 1 & 4, 152
  Salut d'amour, 175
  Severn Suite, 118, 198–200, 204, 210 note 19
  Symphonies, 199

Farmer, Henry
  Rifle Galop, 78
Fibich, Zdenko
  Poem, 176
Fletcher, Percy E
  Epic Symphony, An, 193–6, 209
  Labour & Love, 123–4, 150, 167, 178–82, 193–4, 211 note 30
  Rustic Scenes, 179
  Spirit of Pageantry, The, 179
Flotow, Friedrich von
  Martha, 96
  Stradella, 32
Fraser-Simson
  Maid of the Mountains, The, 167
Friml, Rudolph
  Firefly, The, 166
  Rose Marie, 166
  Vagabond King, The, 166

Geehl, Henry
  For You Alone, 168
  Oliver Cromwell, 187–89
  On the Cornish Coast, 187, 189, 193
  Robin Hood, 189

German, Edward
  Henry VIII (March and Dances), 121, 165
  Merrie England, 165
  Richard III (Overture), 121, 165
  Tom Jones, 165
German, William
  Oriental, The, 153
  President, The, 153
Gershwin, George
  Swanee, 173
Gilbert and Sullivan (see Sullivan)
Gilbert, Jean
  Lady of the Rose, The, 167
Glinka, Mikhail
  Life for the Czar, A, 7
  Russlan & Ludmilla, 7
Glover, Charles
  Rose of Tralee, The, 168
Gordon
  Iceberg, The, 169
Goring Thomas
  Golden Webb, 43
Gounod, Charles
  Faust, 44–5, 176
  Gounod (arr Rimmer), 150
  Lend me your aid, 158
  Mirella, 51
  Reine de Saba, La (Grand March), 157
  Romeo e Giulietta, 51
  Soldiers' Chorus, The (Faust), 176
Greenwood, J A
  Acrobat, The, 157
  Black Dyke, 157
  Bravura, 157
  Call of Youth, 157
  Foden's Own, 157
  Golden Age, The, 157
  Irwell Springs, 157
  Jester, The, 157
  My Old Kentucky Home, 157
  Playmates, 157
  Spirit of Youth, The, 157
  Summer Day, A, 157
  Wingates, 157
  Winsford, 157
Grieg, Edvard
  Souvenir of Grieg, A, 116

Haigh, T A
  Be Kind to thy Father, 99

Halevy
  Halevy, (selection), 109
Handel, George F
  Dead March in Saul, 45
  Hallelujah Chorus, 29, 39, 74, 77
  Messiah (choruses), 46, 47
  See, the Conquering Hero Comes, 45
Hartmann, John
  Arbucklenian, 155
  Belle Americaine, La, 155
  Facilita, 155
  Gipsy's Warning, 155
  Lizzie, 155
  My Pretty Jane, 155
  Niege, La, 63
  Robin Adair, 155
  Rule Britannia, 155
  Weidekehr, 155
Harwood, Edward
  Vital Spark, 45
Hawkins, George
  Day on the Farm, A, 158
  Famous Fragments (arr), 158
  Fox and Hounds, 158
  Gems from the Overtures (arr), 158
  Harlequins, The, 158
  Merrymakers, The, 158
  Pop Goes the Weasel, 158
  Rustic Fete, A, 158
  Soldier's Memories, A, 158
  Sunday Evening Service, A, 158
  Sunday Parade, A, 158
Haydn, Franz Joseph
  Creation, The, 14, 32, 34, 98
  Farewell Symphony, 159
  Heavens are Telling, The, 39, 74, 77
  Mass No 2, 39
  Trumpet Concerto, 23
Herbert, Victor
  Mlle Modiste, 166
  Naughty Marietta, 166
Hérold
  Zampa, 42, 63, 140, 164
Holst, Gustav
  Hammersmith, 196
  Moorside Suite, 117, 196-8, 204
  Planets, The, 196
  Second Suite in F, 117, 196
  Somerset Rhapsody, 196
  St Paul's Suite, 196
  Suite in E♭, 117, 196

Holzmann
  Blaze Away, 172
Howells, Herbert
  Pageantry, 205-7, 209
  Three Figures, 210 note 28
Humperdinck
  Hansel & Gretel, 43, 51
Ireland, John
  Comedy, 203-5
  Downland Suite, A, 203-5, 211 note 27
  London Overture, A, 204-5
Ivanovici
  Donauwellen, 106, 176
Jackson, Enderby
  General Jackson's Schottische, 77
  Grand Prize Quadrille, 78
  Londesborough Galop, 34, 78
  Musikfest Waltz, Das, 77
  Venetian Waltz, 34-5, 78
  Volunteer and Rifle Corps March, 78
  Yorkshire Waltzes, 33, 73-4, 78
Jeffery, Charles
  Evening Star, 63
Jenkins, Cyril
  Coriolanus, 182
  Life Divine, 182-6, 194
  Saga of the North, 185
  Victory, 185
  Zamora, 185
Jessel, Leon
  Parade of the Tin Soldiers, 166
  Wedding of the Rose, The, 166
Jones, Sidney
  Gaiety Girl, A, 10, 166
  Geisha, The, 10, 106, 166
  San Toy, 167
Joyce, A
  Songe d'Automne, 11
Jubb, John
  Chieftain, The, 154
Jullien
  Echoes of Mont Blanc, 74
  Great Exhibition Quadrille, 14
  Horton, 74
  Hymn of Universal Harmony, 15
  Pietro il Grande, 14
Keighley, Thomas
  Crusaders, The, 191, 193, 206
  Lorenzo, 191-3, 197

258   Index of music titles

Keighley *cont.*
  Macbeth, 191
  Merry Wives of Windsor, The, 191
  Midsummer Night's Dream, A, 191
  Northern Rhapsody, A, 191, 193
Kerker, Gustav
  Belle of New York, The, 106, 166
Kern, Jerome
  Lovely to Look At, 174
  Show Boat, 167
Ketèlbey, Albert W
  Bells Across the Meadow, 175
  Chal Romano, 175
  In a Chinese Temple Garden, 175
  In a Monastery Garden, 175
  In a Persian Market, 175
  Sacred Hour, The, 175
  Sanctuary of the Heart, 175
Koenig, Hermann
  Post horn galop, 14–15
Kreutzer
  Nachtlager von Granada, 51, 146

Laurent, Michael
  Alexander's Feast, 149
  Ancient Marriner, The, 149
  Beautiful Britain, 149
Lehár, Franz
  Count of Luxemberg, The, 165
  Gipsy Love, 165
  Merry Widow, The, 165
  Viennese Memories of Lehár, 175
  Vilia, 172, 174
  White Dove, 172
  You are my Heart's Delight, 172, 174
Lemon, Laura
  My Ain Folk, 168
Levy, Jules
  Whirlwind Polka, 76
Liddle, Samuel
  Abide with me, 20
Lincke, Paul
  Birthday Serenade, 166
  Father Rhine, 166
  Glow Worm Idyll, 166
Liszt, Ferencz
  Liszt (arr Rimmer), 150
  Preludes, Les (arr Rimmer), 149
  Hungarian Rhapsody No 2 (arr Rimmer), 149
Little, Jack
  In a Shanty in Old Shanty Town, 173

Loehr, Hermonn
  Little Grey Home in the West, 169
  Where my Caravan has Rested, 169

Macfarren, Sir George
  Robin Hood, 44–5
Macmurrough, Dermot
  Macushla, 169
Marshall, Charles
  I Hear You Calling Me, 169
Maybrich, Michael (see Stephen Adams)
Melling
  Orynthia, 32, 34
Mendelssohn, Felix
  Elijah, 53, 64, 87, 139
  Fingal's Cave, 141
  Grand Fantasia on the Works of Mendelssohn, 42
  Mendelssohn – Grand Selection, 123
  O great are the depths, 47
  Wedding March, 39, 74, 77
Mermet
  Roland à Roncevaux, 123
Meyerbeer, Giacomo
  Africaine, L', 42–3, 63, 83, 98
  Coronation March, 78, 158
  Dinorah, 51
  Etoile du Nord, L', 51, 53, 88
  Hugenots, Les, 96, 123
  Prophet, Le, 34, 76, 78, 88, 115 note 34
  Robert le Diable, 43, 50, 76, 78, 84, 98
Michaelis
  Turkish Patrol, The, 176
Molloy, James
  Love's Old Sweet Song, 20
Monckton, Lionel
  Arcadians, The, 167
  Country Girl, A, 167
  Lionel Monckton Melodies, 175
  Quaker Girl, A, 167
  Runaway Girl, A, 11, 166
  Soldiers in the Park, 11
Montgomery
  Fair Lady, The, 96
  Golden Stream, 96
  Whisper of Love, 96
Moore, Thomas
  Believe me if all those Endearing Young Charms, 19

Index of music titles 259

Moore *cont.*
  Last Rose of Summer, The, 19
Morris, Haydn
  Springtime, 196
Moss, Harold
  Firefly, The, 159
  Joker, The, 159
  Nightingale, The, 159
Moss, Katie
  Floral Dance, The, 168–9
Moya, Stella
  Song of Songs, 168, 173
Mozart, Wolfgang A
  12th Mass (Kyrie & Gloria), 28, 39, 47, 73
  Magic Flute, The, 45, 73, 86
  Memories of Mozart (arr Rimmer), 150
  O Isis and Osiris, 86
  Souvenir de Mozart, 43

Nevin, E
  Rosary, The, 20
Nicholls, Horatio
  Amy, Wonderful Amy, 173
  Bedtime Story, A, 173
  Cavalcade of Martial Songs (arr), 174
  Shepherd of the Hills, 173
  That Old Fashioned Mother of Mine, 169
Nicolai, Otto
  Merry Wives of Windsor, The, 158
Norton, F
  Chu Chin Chow, 166
Novello, Ivor
  Glamorous Night, 174

Offenbach, Jacques
  Orpheus in the Underworld, 164
  Tales of Hoffman, The, 164
Ord Hume, James
  20th Century, 152
  B B & C F, 152
  Brilliant, 152
  Elephant, The, 152
  Roll Away Bet, 151
  Simplicity, 152
  Victor's Return, 152

Parry, Sir Joseph
  Aberystwyth, 76
  Tydfyl Overture, 76

Paxton, Stephen
  Mass, 34
Penn, Arthur
  Smilin' Through, 168
Perry
  Intro (Scena) & Polacca, 34, 39
Phelps
  Choristers, The, 176
Pizzi
  Gabrieli, 42, 51
Ponchielli, Amilcare
  Gioconda, La, 51
Purcell, Edward
  Passing By, 20

Raymond, Lillian
  Sunshine of Your Smile, The, 169
Reubke, Julius
  Organ Sonata on Psalm 94, 186
Rimmer, William
  Australasian, The, 148
  Cossack, The, 148
  Farewell My Comrades, 148
  Garland of Classics, A (arr), 150
  Hailstorm, 149
  Honest Toil, 147
  Gems from Italian Opera (arr), 150
  Jenny Jones, 149
  Knight of the Road, 147
  Lord of the Isles, 149
  Melodious Gems (arr), 150
  Merry-go-Round, 149
  Minstrel Memories (arr), 150
  My Old Kentucky Home, 149
  North Star, The, 148
  Old Comrades, 148
  Punchinello, 148
  Ravenswood, 149
  Royal Trophy, 149
  Rule Britannia, 149
  Russe, La, 148
  Sailor Songs (arr), 150
  Silver Showers, 148
  Skye Boat Song, 149
  Slaidburn, 148
  Souvenir of the Opera (arr), 150
  Two Comrades, 149
  Variations on a Welsh Melody, 148
  Victor's Return, 149
  Viva Birkinshaw, 148
  Viva Petee, 147
  Weber's Last Waltz, 149

260　*Index of music titles*

Rimsky-Korsakov
　Scheherezade, 183
Rodgers, Richard
　King and I, The, 174
　Oklahoma, 174
　Sound of Music, The, 174
　South Pacific, 174
Romberg, Sigmund
　Desert Song, The, 166
　New Moon, 166
　Student Prince, The, 166
Rossini, Giachino, A
　Barber of Seville, 29, 43, 158
　Gazza Ladra, La, 51
　Rossini's Works (arr Owen), 54, 88, 91 note 31
　Semiramide, 45, 51, 88, 144, 158
　Stabat Mater (Inflamatus), 14, 87
　Tancredi, 73
　William Tell, 7, 39, 47, 53, 63, 76, 88, 120, 123
Round, Henry
　Casket of Gems, A, (arr) 138
　Cluster of Classics, (arr) 138
　Don Quixote, 141
　Gems of Cambria, (arr) 138
　Gems of Erin, (arr) 138
　Gems of Scotia, 138
　Gems of Victorian Melody, (arr) 138
　Gwalia, (arr) 138
　Hail! Apollo (glee), 109
　Joan of Arc, 142
　Knight Templar, 141
　Llewellyn, 138
　Lyric Garland, The, 109, 140
　Opera Gems, 138
　Recollections of Carl Rosa, (arr) 138
　Songs of England, (arr) 138
　Songs of Ireland, (arr) 138
　Songs of Scotland, (arr) 138
　Tam o' Shanter, 143
　Tournament, The (fantasia), 103
　Victory, 58, 141
Rubens, Paul
　I Love the Moon, 169

Sanderson, Wilfrid
　Drake Goes West, 20, 169
　Until, 169
　Up from Somerset, 169

Schubert, Franz
　Gems of Schubert, 123
　(adapted) Lilac Time, 165
　Marche Militaire, 158
　Schubert, 109
　Schubert Waltzes, 175
Schumann, Robert
　Gems of Schumann, 123
Smith, Richard
　Amazon, The, 97
　Bonnets of Blue Rock, 114 note 21
　Christy's Gem, 97
　Darling Josie, 97
　Dear Old Days, 97
　Glory to the New Born King (arr), 97
　Hark the Glad Sound (arr), 97
　Honoraria (fantasia), 144
　Light Horseman, The, 114 note 21
　Lily Bell, 114 note 21
　Morning Star Polka, 114 note 21
　Mother Kissed Me in My Dreams, 97
　Rock Villa Polka, 114 note 21
　Sing Unto the Lord (arr), 97
　Starry Night, The, 97
　Trinity (arr), 97
Somers, Debroy
　Savoy Medleys, 174
Sousa
　El Capitan, 165
　Washington Post, The, 107
Spofforth
　Come, Bounteous May, 103
　Hail Smiling Morn, 20, 29, 46, 96
Spohr, Ludwig
　Faust, 139
　Jessonda, 51, 139
　Last Judgement, The, 42, 139
Squire, W H
　In an Old Fashioned Town, 169
　When you come Home Dear, 169
Straus, Oscar
　Chocolate Soldier, The, 165
　Waltz Dream, A, 164
Strauss, J (Jr)
　Blue Danube, The, 11
　Fledermaus, Die, 164
　Gipsy Baron, The, 164
Strauss, J (Sr)
　Radetsky march, 7

Index of music titles 261

Stuart, Leslie
  Lily of Laguna, 167
  Soldiers of the Queen, 167
Sullivan, Sir Arthur
  Absent-Minded Beggar, The, 119, 120
  Beauties of Sullivan, 152
  Cox and Box, 165
  Emerald Isle, The, 120
  Gems from Sullivan's Operas No 1, 17, 120, 152
  Gems from Sullivan's Operas No 2, 17, 122, 152
  Gems from Sullivan's Operas No 3, 17, 53, 121–2, 152
  Gondoliers, The, 18, 122, 165
  Haddon Hall, 106
  HMS Pinafore, 18, 165
  Iolanthe, 165
  Ivanhoe, 119
  Lost Chord, The, 17, 19
  Martyr of Antioch, 53
  Mikado, The, 18, 165
  New Sullivan Selection, 175
  Onward Christian Soldiers, 17, 120
  Patience, 63, 144
  Pirates of Penzance, The, 18, 63, 165
  Second New Sullivan Selection, 175
  Trial by Jury, 165
  Yeomen of the Guard, The, 165
Suppé, Franz von
  Beautiful Galathea, The, 164
  Boccaccia, 164
  Jolly Robbers, The, 164
  Light Cavalry, 152, 157, 164
  Morning, Noon and Night in Vienna, 164
  Pique Dame, 164
  Poet and Peasant, 152, 164
Sutton, Edward
  Brigadier, The, 159
  Cavalier, The, 158
  Jigsaw, the, 159
  Joywheel, The, 159
  Paddy's Capers, 159
  Parachute, The, 159
  Paragon, The, 158
  Sandy and Jock, 159
  Sandy's Frolic, 159
  Switchback, The, 159
  With Kilt and Sporan, 159

Tate, Arthur
  Somewhere a Voice is Calling, 168
Tchaikovsky, Peter I
  Tchaikovsky (arr Rimmer), 150
Thomas
  Raymond, 152
Tosti, Paula
  Good-bye, 169

Vaccaj (Vaccai)
  Giulietta e Romeo, 34
Vaughan Williams
  Variations for Brass Band, 133 note 2
Verdi, Giuseppe
  Aida, 51, 86
  Aroldo, 51
  Attila, 34, 47, 73
  Ballo in Maschero, Un, 45
  Ernani, 34, 39, 43, 94
  Forza del Destino, La, 76, 78
  Nabucco, 7, 34, 39, 51
  Reminiscences of Verdi (arr R Smith), 144
  Traviata, La, 73
  Trovatore, Il, 16, 32, 39, 42, 73

Wagner
  Bayreuth (arr Swift), 53, 88
  Flying Dutchman, The, 7, 16, 123
  Gems of Wagner (arr R Smith), 144
  Lohengrin, 7, 16, 109, 140
  Meistersinger, Die, 116, 122, 150, 154
  O Star of Eve, 176
  Rienzi, 7, 94, 123, 140
  Souvenir of Wagner (arr Kappey), 59
  Tannhäuser, 7, 16, 53, 76
  Tannhäuser (Grand March), 157
  Tristan und Isolde, 88, 116
  Wagner (arr Round), 61
  Valkyrie, The, 55, 88
Wallace
  Amber Witch, The, 46
  Lurline, 8, 44
  Maritana, 8, 46
Weber
  Euryanthe, 51, 145
  Freischütz, Der, 14, 29, 43, 46
  Heroic (arr Owen), 88
  Oberon, 46, 88
  Preciosa, 39
  Weber (arr Owen), 88

262 *Index of music titles*

Wegel
  Swiss Family, The, 34
Weston-Nicholl, J
  Viking, The, 186–7
Whiting, Richard
  Beyond the Blue Horizon, 172
Wood, Arthur
  Three Dale Dances, 176
  Yorkshire Moors Suite, 176
Wood, Haydn
  Roses of Picardy, 169, 172
Woodford-Finden, Amy
  Four Indian Love Lyrics, 169
Wright, Denis
  Carnival, 190
  Dream of the Waltz (arr), 175
  Hanover (Variations), 190
  Joan of Arc, 190
  Milestones of Melody (arr), 175
  Panorama of Famous Songs (arr), 175
  Princess Nada, 190
  Radio Parade of 1935 (arr), 175
  Sea, The (Thalassa), 190
  Sweethears of Yesterday (arr), 175
  Tam o' Shanter's Ride, 190
  Tintagel, 190
  Valse Interlude, 190
  White Rider, The, 190
Wright Kenneth A
  Pride of Race, 196

Wright, Lawrence (see Horatio Nicholls)

Miscellaneous pieces
  Auld Lang Syne, 61
  Bonnie Dundee 74
  Beauties of England (selection), 122
  Communityland (medley), 174
  Christy's minstrels' songs, 96
  Confidence, 97
  Danny Boy (see Londonderry Air)
  Dashing White Sergeant, The, 46
  Dixieland (Medley), 174
  Florrie Forde's Favourites, 163
  German Waltz, 97
  God save the Queen, 32, 39, 77
  Harry Lauder's Songs, 163
  Hymnland (medley), 174
  John Brown's Body, 45
  Londonderry Air , 169
  Moss Rose Waltz, 97
  Pot-Pourri of country airs, 29
  Rule Britannia, 38, 60, 77
  Sandon, 122
  Shamrockland (medley), 174
  Silsden Quick Step, 97
  Soldier's Polka, 74
  Tourni, Le (arr Gladney), 87
  Waft her, Angels, 122

For Product Safety Concerns and Information please contact our EU representative GPSR@taylorandfrancis.com
Taylor & Francis Verlag GmbH, Kaufingerstraße 24, 80331 München, Germany

www.ingramcontent.com/pod-product-compliance
Lightning Source LLC
Chambersburg PA
CBHW052031300426
44116CB00024B/1257